(ch 1, 2, ...)

donald.frase@dla.mil

CYBER STRATEGY

Cyber Strategy

THE EVOLVING CHARACTER OF
POWER AND COERCION

Brandon Valeriano, Benjamin Jensen,
and Ryan C. Maness

OXFORD
UNIVERSITY PRESS

OXFORD
UNIVERSITY PRESS

Oxford University Press is a department of the University of Oxford. It furthers
the University's objective of excellence in research, scholarship, and education
by publishing worldwide. Oxford is a registered trade mark of Oxford University
Press in the UK and certain other countries.

Published in the United States of America by Oxford University Press
198 Madison Avenue, New York, NY 10016, United States of America.

CIP data is on file at the Library of Congress
ISBN 978–0–19–061809–4

9 8 7 6 5 4 3
Printed by Sheridan Books, Inc., United States of America

Contents

Preface

THIS BOOK COMES at a critical time. From the uncomfortable realization that Russia is using the digital domain to create dissent in Western societies to the proliferation of ransomware linked to North Korea, we are witnessing a new era of rivalry in cyberspace. Intrigue and covert action are back in vogue as preferred foreign policy options. While they might make for great spy thrillers on the silver screen, these age-old dark arts run the risk of creating conflict traps as nuclear powers probe adversary resolve.

To understand competition in the digital domain, this book uses theory and evidence to map cyber strategies rival states use to achieve a position of relative advantage. We seek an empirically grounded foundation from which to ask the central question of 21st-century competition: how will emergent technologies shape world politics, and through it, foreign policy and military strategy?

We find that there is less to fear than the cyber doom headlines suggest. States find cyber operations difficult to leverage for effect; they are not game-changing methods in the conduct of warfare that guarantee victory at the speed of light. Instead, cyber strategies represent a further step in the evolution of conflict toward precision and restraint reflective of the overall decline of interstate war between advanced adversaries. The battlefield has evolved to a series of covert actions in the shadows and more diffuse efforts to mobilize dissent in a targeted state's population. The 2016 US election illustrates this shifting character of competition, with Russian operatives purchasing Facebook and Twitter ads to amplify its propaganda portrayal of America as a democracy in decline. You should fear your social media feed, and the state-backed botnets lurking behind it, more than you do cyber bombs seeking to paralyze critical infrastructure.

This new world is prone to political warfare, undermining adversaries from within, not decisive battles over key terrain. Wars will continue, but they will be scarce compared to the constant struggle in the shadows between rivals in cyberspace. To understand this emerging competition, scholars owe policy makers rigorous, evidence-based examinations that help states minimize risks. While scholars and pundits alike find offering revolutionary, game-changing perspectives on cyber conflict exciting, this process is fraught with error and overextends projections based on few pieces of evidence. In the worst case, these exaggerations contribute to threat inflation, leaving states misallocating resources for cyber first strikes without seeking to counteract the war over opinion in the shadows.

Countering the resurrection of political warfare in our digital lives requires policy derived from data analysis, not speculation based on limited case studies. We started this analytical journey in our prior book, *Cyber War versus Cyber Realities*, by scoping the cyber domain and continue the project here by evaluating the efficacy of cyber strategies. Of course, there is much more to be done and we hope others will test us, challenge us, and push us (and others) forward.

Brandon Valeriano
Benjamin Jensen
Ryan C. Maness
September 2017

Acknowledgments

THIS WORK IS an equal collaboration among three authors inspired by a larger, supportive community. While sometimes difficult, the project could not have been completed without each of us pulling our weight and bringing unique abilities to the table. We have many people to thank for helping us complete this project. We first note those whom we as a team thank, then acknowledge personal support received by each of us.

Because we are a team, there are too many people to thank, and it is our error if we forgot to mention you. Everyone we have come across has been critical in helping develop this research. In particular, we thank and are deeply indebted to Angela Chnapko at Oxford University Press for shepherding this project along.

We thank everyone that has hosted us for a workshop or talk during the generation of this project, including James Anderson, Tim Stevens, Jackie Kerr, Herb Lin, Scott Shackelford, Kathy Powers, Kristin Gleditsch, Jacek Kluger, Damien Van Puyvelde, Steve Coulthart, Kyle Beardsley, Peter Feaver, Sean Lawson, Steve Lobell, Roy Allison, Ursula Daxecker, Audrey Cronin, Chris Whyte, Joseph Nye, George Lawson, Dick Betts, Jason Healey, John Arquilla, Hy Rothstein, Doug Borer, BJ Strawser, and Sarah Bliss.

We thank the following institutions and organizations for hosting us: Stanford University, the Marine Corps University, Naval Postgraduate School, Livermore Labs, Indiana University, Claremont McKenna University, University of New

Mexico, Essex University, King's College, NATO CCDCOE, the Norwegian Institute for Defence Studies, Claremont Graduate University, Hull University, University of Texas at El Paso, Duke University, Virginia Military Institute, University of Utah, University of Oxford, University of Amsterdam, George Mason University, Harvard Belfer Center, the London School of Economics, Bard College, Georgetown University, Columbia University, St. Andrews University, and the Peace Research Institute of Oslo.

We held a book workshop in May of 2017 at American University with funds generously provided by the Marine Corps University Foundation, led by Lieutenant General Richard Mills (Ret.), and Colonel (Ret.) Jon Sachrison. We are deeply indebted to each of the participants, who were:

Nadya Kostyuk, University of Michigan
Michael Horowitz, University of Pennsylvania
Evan Perkoski, University of Connecticut and Denver University
Sean Lawson, University of Utah
Erica Borghard, United States Military Academy West Point
Shawn Lonegran, United States Military Academy West Point
Miguel Gomez, ETZ Zurich
Matt Fay, George Mason University
Chris Whyte, George Mason University

Brandon Valeriano:
I remain grateful to the University of Glasgow, Cardiff University, and the Marine Corps University for providing institutional homes during the construction of this project. In particular, I am indebted to Donald Bren for the award of the Donald Bren Chair in Armed Politics, which was critical in providing the time and space needed to complete this behemoth of a project.

Personally, I thank new friends and old for their advice and support. My family has been important as always, including my parents and sister Sienna plus her husband, Steve Mejia, and my new nephew, Anthony. Going back to my undergraduate years at Whittier College, I thank my mentor, Fred Bergerson; the recently passed on Les Howard; and the vigorous as ever Mike McBride. John A. Vasquez has been a critical mentor and lifelong friend. His guidance and influence is the heart of this project. I also thank some of the more senior people in the field who have been instrumental in my career, Patrick James in particular, and also Nazli Choucri, Joseph Nye, J. David Singer, William Thompson, and James Lee Ray.

I thank many of my peers and friends in the field and those that came before me, in particular Steven Saideman, Laura Sjoberg, Allison Pytlak, Cullen

Hendrix, Michael Horowitz, Sean Lawson, Melissa Michelson, Victor Marin (and Jaime), Tad Kluger, Emily Kluger, Joe Young, Sara Mitchell, Doug Gibler, Dennis Foster, Sam Whitt, Tom Scotto, Dan Nexon, Tony Craig, W. K. Winecroft, Scott Wolford, and Paul Hensel. I also thank my colleagues at Glasgow and Cardiff including Cian O'Driscoll, Georgios Karyotis, Philip and Sara Habel, Adrian Florea, Richard Johnson, Shaina Western, Zac Greene, Hollie Greene, Victoria Basham, Chris Carmen, Christian Bueger, Ann Harrington, Peter Sutch, Andrea Calderaro, Simone Tholens, Campbell Craig, Alena Drieschova, Sergey Radchenko, and Claudia Hildabrand. Finally, the Niskanen Center provided a DC home for me to start the long process of understanding the policy world. In particular, I thank Matt Fay, Ryan Hagemann, Joey Coon, Jerry Taylor, Louisa Tavlas, and Josh Hampson.

There are many in the community of cyber security research scholars whom I thank, including: Derek Reveron, Jason Healey, Nina Kollars, Jackie Kerr, Michael Sulmeyer, Miguel Gomez, Jon Lindsay, Erik Gartzke, Josh Rovner, Heather Roff, Chris Demchak, Herb Lin, J. D. Work, Tim Stevens, Chris Whyte, and Rob Knake.

And of course, Ben Franklin, who once said, "Either write something worth reading or do something worth writing."

Brandon Valeriano,
Donald Bren Chair of Armed Politics, Marine Corps University
Alexandria, VA
September 2017

Benjamin Jensen:
Books take a family. They start in the conversations you have with mentors, such as the wise counsel I received from giants like John Richardson, Abdul Aziz Said, Charles Tilly, and James Goldgeier. They require a nurturing scholarly environment. I found that ecosystem in the American University, School of International Service, in the halls of the Marine Corps University, at the Atlantic Council, and through generous support I received from Steve Weber and Betsy Cooper at the Center for Long-Term Cyber Security and the Hewlett Foundation. Most of all, books require patience and sacrifice. Thank you, Yana, Max, Oksana, and my parents for being supportive of my Don Quixotesque adventure to craft policy-relevant scholarship.

Benjamin Jensen, PhD
Associate Professor, Marine Corps University
Scholar-in-Residence, American University

Senior Non-Resident Fellow, Atlantic Council
Burke, VA
September 2017

Ryan C. Maness:
My gratitude is especially extended to the faculty and staff of the Defense Analysis Department at the Naval Postgraduate School. You have been welcoming and appreciative of the work I have been doing and will do in the future. It is an honor and a privilege to call all of you peers. I hope to continue my career in professional military education and researching on behalf of and for the US Navy. Special thanks to John Arquilla, Dorothy Denning, Hy Rothstein, Doug Borer, and B. J. Strawser for making this opportunity happen for me. Thanks also go out to Northeastern University, Buffalo State, and the University of Illinois at Chicago.

I also thank those who helped me get to this point in my career, especially my mentor, friend, and coauthor Brandon Valeriano. Derek Reveron and Mitchell Orenstein served as invaluable mentors as well. Great professional advice has been given to me by Jason Healey, Erik Gartzke, and Joseph Nye.

I always dedicate any project to my late parents, Karen and Ted, for whom I strive to be the best scholar and also human being. I also dedicate this book to my siblings, Adam and Ashley, my Aunt Beverly and Uncle Tony, and my cousins, Mike, Kerrie, Jeff, and Misty. And of course, Scratch and Ruby, who have been laying at my feet throughout the years when I write.

Ryan C. Maness
Assistant Professor
Defense Analysis Department
Naval Postgraduate School
Monterey, CA
September 2017

CYBER STRATEGY

1

INTRODUCTION

Are Cyber Strategies Coercive?

The Effects of Cyber Conflict Strategies

During the 2016 US presidential elections, Russian hackers unleashed a "new form of political sabotage" (Lipton, Sanger, and Shane 2016). Lines of code replaced the secret White House tapes of Watergate fame as Russian hackers passed stolen e-mails from Democratic Party political operatives to WikiLeaks in an attempt to undermine the US election. At the same time, Russian information warfare operatives seeded social media networks with stories about racial unrest to propel an image of America in decline. According to the *New York Times*, it was "the perfect weapon"; designed to undermine the American electoral institutions and, through them, confidence in the next elected government of the United States (Lipton et al. 2016).

The Russian data breaches and disinformation campaigns represent a 21st-century form of political warfare (Kennan 1948). Cyber strategy has come of age and often can have a coercive impact. In this new age, coercion, the exploitation of potential force short of war (Schelling 1960: 9), combines with disruption, cyber espionage, overt propaganda manipulation, and covert psychological warfare in an effort to shape the behavior of rival groups (Valeriano, Maness, and Jensen 2017a). These campaigns are likely here to stay.

Major powers now employ cyber strategies to gain a position of advantage relative to their rivals. Small states and nonstate actors attempt to use cyber operations to punch above their weight to maximize their political goals. States have begun to attack their enemies' credibility through cyber operations as well as propaganda spread in comment fields, social media, and cable news broadcasts. These operations seek to achieve effects without using conventional displays of force. Major powers use precision cyber strikes to sabotage their enemies and cyber espionage to steal sensitive information, while lacing the target with intrusions to prepare for future crises. However, few have uncovered how to measure and understand the effects of cyber conflict and its coercive potential. The efficacy of the cyber instrument of power to pressure target opposition states, shape their behavior, and manage escalation between rivals remains an open question in need of investigation. As an academic and policy community, we have not yet assessed the range and impact of cyber strategies in this age of competition. This book is a step in that direction.

Similar to covert action, cyber operations and other coercive diplomatic instruments short of war have a long history of use internationally. Covert action is "the effort of one government to influence politics, opinions, and events in another state through means [that] are not attributable to the sponsoring state" (Anderson 1998: 423). From Sun Tzu and Kautilya to Thomas Schelling and Alexander George, covert action and coercion are major themes in strategic and military theory. Rival states seek to compel one another and manage escalation risks through a variety of instruments. However, we are often drawn to the frame of outright war in describing these cyber interactions. What we witness in cyberspace is not war and mainly falls in the domain of limited coercive operations and actions designed to alter the balance of information as well as manage escalation risks in long-term competitive interactions.

Our entry into this topic is to theorize and evaluate the efficacy of modern cyber strategies and how states influence rivals in the digital domain. We argue that these campaigns are neither as revolutionary nor as novel as they seem when evaluated with evidence. Through an examination of cyber strategies employed by nation-states, we argue through empirically based evidence that cyber strategies produce limited coercive and signaling effects. Examining cyber strategy in its varying forms, we find that cyber disruptions, short-term and long-term espionage, and degradation operations all have their own distinct logic. Disruptions, from website defacements to limited-duration denial of service attacks, are low-cost, low-risk ways of signaling escalation risk and displeasure between rival states in an era of connected states. Just like spy craft of old, cyber espionage allows rivals to steal information and alter the balance of information to enhance their bargaining position while gaining access for future actions. However, it is cyber degradations that are the primary coercive instrument in this new era, using even partial destruction to signal resolve.

The coercive effects of these cyber strategies are limited. First, neither disruptions nor espionage compel in the traditional sense. States use them to shape future interactions and limit escalation more than they do to seek concession in the present. When states do compel a rival through cyber degradation, which is measured as a change in behavior in the target that is strategically advantageous to the initiator, the cyber operation tends to occur alongside more traditional coercive instruments such as diplomatic pressure, economic sanctions, and military threats and displays. Cyber operations complement rather than replace traditional statecraft. We find that cyber means serve as an additive foreign policy tool in modern strategic competition.

Our treatment of cyber coercion and the effects of cyber conflict builds on earlier investigations, often organized as case studies (Lindsay 2013; Healey and Grindal 2016) or macro historical treatments (Healey 2013). Here, we seek to expand the literature by inductively developing a typology of cyber strategies and testing derived hypotheses empirically. To that end, we extend the Dyadic Cyber Incidents and Dispute (DCID) Dataset, version 1.1 (Maness, Valeriano, and Jensen 2017), to investigate the strategic logic of cyber operations by coding escalation dynamics and concessions from 2000 to 2014. This is an empirical portrait of how rival states use cyber strategies to achieve a position of relative advantage in long-term competition.

This study comes at a critical time as we confront the utility, and also the fears, created by cyber conflict. High-profile cyber incidents appear each day, and seem to suggest a new disorder in modern conflict. In the summer of 2017, a cyber operation launched by the United Arab Emirates (UAE) led to a diplomatic and economic crisis with Gulf states isolating Qatar and ejecting them from the Gulf Cooperation Council (Valeriano, Maness, and Jensen 2017b). The ongoing Ukraine conflict represents more than just a digital testing ground for Russian cyber action. The use of cyber intrusions alongside conventional and unconventional operations is a demonstration of the power to destroy the confidence in a government's ability to protect the population (Greenberg 2017a). The hype and hysteria around the WannaCry (BBC News 2017) ransomware attack launched by North Korea in the summer of 2017 shows how simple malicious code can alter perceptions of safety and protection in the digital age. However, before we develop suggestions for sound foreign policy responses to state-backed cyber intrusions or craft international frameworks that constrain the proliferation of politically motivated malware, we should theoretically and empirically investigate cyber strategies and their efficacy. This book hopes to offer academics, students, and policy makers a forum along these lines to think through the logic of competition in the digital domain.

Debating Effects: Is Cyberspace Revolutionary or Evolutionary?

To date, the academic literature on cyber conflict can be divided into two main perspectives: revolutionary and evolutionary. The revolutionaries see lines of malicious code the same way sailors of old gazed at dreadnoughts and airpower acolytes dreamed of strategic bombing: a revolutionary break that would transform strategy and the very power of nations. The evolutionary perspective, on the other hand, suggests a dynamic process of competition and learning between rival states. Cyber strategies are not a radical departure from past practice nor a pathway to dramatic new effects. The new capability simply amplifies traditional forms of coercive diplomacy as states seek to shape their rivals' strategic decisions.

Seen from a revolutionary perspective, cyber war creates a new reality (Farwell and Rohozinski 2011, 2012). The declassified portions of the 2006 US *National Military Strategy for Cyberspace Operations* (Rumsfeld 2006: 4) promises bold changes, stating, "Cyberspace affords commanders the opportunity to make decisions rapidly, conduct operations, and deliver effects at speeds that were previously incomprehensible." For Clarke and Knake (2010: 303), the speed and global nature of cyberspace conflicts suggests an "ongoing nature of cyber war, the blurring of peace and war, adds a dangerous new dimension of instability." Klimburg (2017: 2) takes it furthest, stating, "the activities of states are making cyberspace a domain of conflict, and therefore increasingly threatening overall stability and security not only of the Internet but also of our very societies."

Cyber revolutionaries argue the new domain reflects a revolution in military affairs arising from asymmetric capabilities that give offense the upper hand and erode traditional deterrence models.[1] The traditional state system will give way to a new international system where digital walls will be constructed (Demchak and Dombrowski 2011). Vulnerabilities on the digital front make us weak and increase the probability for catastrophe (Demchak 2011). Cyber revolutionists see lines of code as "potent cyber weapons" that create "strategic instability" (Kello 2013: 8).

Cyber capabilities could provide adversaries a means of holding populations and critical infrastructure at risk (Koppel 2015). They also offer a means of rendering a military command and control network inoperable at decisive moments. As Mazanec (2015: 4) notes, "cyber warfare capabilities are leading to a new [revolution in military affairs] RMA, wherein cyber capabilities will play an increasingly desirable role in military conflicts and become deeply integrated into state doctrine and military capabilities." Powerful, connected states then become vulnerable. Along these lines, People's Liberation Army (PLA) officers envision future wars in which Chinese hackers, operating alongside military units, disrupt stock markets and take down power grids in the United States (Liang and Xiangsui 1999).

In other accounts, cyber capabilities transform the struggle inside the state. Young protesters rely on social media to mobilize their fellow citizens and challenge corrupt regimes (Diamond 2010). Cyber methods could even offer new coercive vectors and lead to dangerous security dilemmas. As witnessed with the North Korea attacks on Sony Pictures, cyber operations can impose costs and destabilize leadership to achieve a concession (Sharp 2017). The ease of successful espionage operations in cyberspace amplifies the security dilemma (Buchanan 2016). Seen from the revolutionary perspective, cyber strategies will be central to future rival campaigns designed to coerce or destroy the opposition.

Yet, there is no guarantee that innovation translates into a military revolution. Intelligence estimates on new capabilities are often uncertain (Mahnken 2003). Even powerful states can face bureaucratic challenges (Horowitz 2010) or cultural dynamics (Adamsky 2010) when attempting to translate new capabilities into coercive power. In the end, evolutionary rather than revolutionary change is more likely (Murray and Millet 1998), as new technologies enter the military and political front slowly.

Cyber conflict is no different. Cyber operations offer new vectors of attack that can be used to probe an enemies' resolve, manipulate information, or degrade adversary networks, but they do not change the game of great power politics or hierarchies inherent in regional rivalry systems. Entrenched political realities still triumph in the digital age, making revolutionary change difficult from a strategic perspective.

From the evolutionary perspective, the road to decisive victory is neither certain nor short.[2] Gartzke (2013: 43) writes, the "internet poses no revolution in military affairs." According to Gartzke and Lindsay (2017a), cyber threats are often exaggerated. There are inherent difficulties associated with cyber coercion. Cyber operations against infrastructure or military targets that only temporarily harass a state are unlikely to generate enough harm to be coercive.

Furthermore, even successful attacks, once identified, have fleeting effects. There is a patch problem in cyberspace. According to Nye (2017: 48), "as states contemplate CNA [computer network attacks], they must confront the complexity of networks and possibility of unintended consequences. Since targeted vulnerabilities may be patched and because some networks are more resilient than others, attackers cannot be certain of the timing, persistence, or scope of the effects of their cyberattacks." This dynamic introduces an important element of caution into the decision-making process. States do not know whether their cyber operations will work, and even if they do, which ones will blow back on the attacker.

The evolutionary perspective proceeds with caution and questions many of the more extreme claims of revolutionaries. Rid (2013) suggests cyber sabotage will be unlikely because it does not achieve effects. Gartzke and Lindsay (2015) argue deception will be a key method of cyber action, but by no means decisive. Others (Borghard and Lonergan 2017; Gartzke 2013) have proposed a combined arms approach to cyber, suggesting these digital intrusions will not be used in isolation. Rid (2013) advances the idea that violence in the context of cyber operations has not happened and is unlikely. Moore and Rid (2016) go even further to note the dubious utility of using the Internet to recruit extremists through the Dark Web. Valeriano and Maness (2015) articulate a position of cyber restraint, where adversaries on the digital front are constrained in their options and are unlikely to engage in cyber conflict because of the normative restrictions, the ease of proliferation of cyber weapons, and risk inherent with untested options. In a data investigation, Valeriano and Maness (2014, 2015) find that while cyber conflicts are proliferating, they are mainly low-level conflicts that do not escalate to what might be called cyber war. Instead, cyber conflict becomes a new way to show force and extract concessions among rival states fighting in regional competitions.

There is also the question of uncertainty with respect to battle damage assessments. In traditional military operations, battle damage assessment helps an attacker determine whether or not a target has been destroyed. It is not uncommon for attackers to waste additional ordinance on an already destroyed target, due to the complexity of assessing whether or not something was destroyed and ensuring higher confidence of an effect. This dilemma is compounded in cyber conflict. There is a "residual uncertainty" in the attackers' minds about their effectiveness (Nye 2017: 48). This uncertainty is key to understanding just how revolutionary cyber strategies might be; given the risks, uncertainty, and norms against the application of cyber tools, will they really be transformational on the military and diplomatic battlefield?

According to the former US deputy secretary of defense William Lynn (2010: 99), "whereas a missile comes with a return address, a computer virus generally does not. The forensic work necessary to identify an attacker may take months, if identification is possible at all." Acts of cyber coercion can be attributed (Lindsay 2015a), yet there is still the question of its origins and direction, introducing the responsibility problem. According to Rid and Buchanan (2015: 25), cyber operations targeting critical infrastructure like a power plant resulting in a "minor power outage could be a warning shot, a failed attempt at a major strategic network breach, or an inadvertent result of reconnaissance." Lines of command and control in cyberspace are uncertain. Some states rely on proxies and criminal networks to do their bidding. Other states have internal actors itching to 'hack back' and return to the days of privateers where private citizens can international policy (Keeney 2017).

Though problems of attribution can be overcome, cyber operations inject sufficient ambiguity to limit a strategic response. According to Nye, attribution limits the utility of deterrence by threat of punishment. For Nye (2017: 55), "retaliatory

threats of punishment are less likely to be effective in cyberspace, whe
of the attacker is uncertain; there are many unknown adversaries; and I
assets can be held at risk and for how long is uncertain." For us, the is
tribution but responsibility. Given sufficient time, cyber forensics tenc ⌐ ⌐ identify
who launched an attack. The complication for analysts arises in understanding the
decision-making process within the aggressor state.

Cyber capabilities operate more in the ambiguous world of spies and saboteurs
than they do the open battlefield. Historically, there are certain forms of manipulation, coercion, and influence that benefit from remaining concealed. For Gartzke
(2013: 47), "espionage, covert operations, and certain kinds of political theft or
murder function most effectively when the perpetrators are unknown or indeed
when the operations themselves remained undisclosed." There are similar advantages
to certain forms of cyber operations and there is a utility to responding to cyber
provocations with covert signals (Carson 2017). Yet, "most forms of political conflict, however, encourage disclosing an initiator's identity. Coercion requires attribution. . . . this credibility problem likely mirrors the attribution problem and is
perhaps equally likely to make internet aggression problematic for initiators as for
possible targets" (Gartzke 2013: 47).

Put another way, if the strength of ambiguity is accessing, infiltrating, and
undermining an opponent from within while limiting their ability to retaliate, the
downside is a sufficiently clear signal. If a cyber coercive campaign is ambiguous
enough, the action is, in theory, less likely to result in a concession. Cyber strategies
might therefore be considered a form of covert action (Carson and Yarhi-Milo
2017; Brantly 2016) and signaling. The initiator might leave just enough clues to
attribute the attack and send a signal short of a significant retaliation threshold in
the conventional domain. They will only partially claim credit to ensure compliance.
Furthermore, subtle signals and indirect denial can be a form of tacit bargaining
that enables actors to manage escalation risk in the context of repeated conflict
(Carson 2016).

Our Contribution: Cyber Strategies

Our view builds on the evolutionary perspectives surveyed in the previous section.
We treat cyber operations as a modern form of covert signaling and coercion with
limited effects. Rival states develop cyber strategies, using these operations to amplify rather than replace other instruments and power in long-term competition.
Furthermore, only higher-cost and complex cyber degradation attacks, designed
to undermine adversary networks, tend to produce coercive concessions. There are

few decisive victories in the digital domain. Rather, cyber operations act as ambiguous signals of resolve that rivals use to manage escalation risks and shape enemy decisions. Table 1.1 lists the three hypotheses and subarguments that guide our analyses throughout this volume.

WHAT IS CYBER STRATEGY?

At its core, strategy is a dialectic of opposing wills (Beaufre 1963: 22).[3] Strategy denotes a "set of ideas" about how to "employ instruments of power" to impose your will and achieve objectives at a higher level than individual battles or crisis standoffs (CJCS 2017: I-13). Rival groups, in our treatment powerful states, seek to use a variety of instruments to achieve a position of relative advantage in wartime and

TABLE 1.1

Hypotheses of cyber strategy: Coercion, signaling, campaigns

Cyber Coercion

H1. Cyber operations produce limited concessions

H1a. Cyber degradation produces limited concessions

H1b. Differences in latent cyber capacity do not increase the probability of a concession

H1c. The number of past cyber incidents by the initiator does not increase the probability of a concession

Cyber Signaling

H2. Cyber strategies produce limited escalation

H2a. Differences in latent cyber capacity do not increase the probability of crisis escalation

H2b. Changes in cyber latent capacity do not increase the probability of crisis escalation in noncyber domains

Cyber Campaigns

H3. There are unique combinations of cyber operations and traditional instruments of power that increase rival concessions

H3a. The more coercive diplomacy inducements used in addition to cyber, the more likely a concession

H3b. Cyber operations are more likely to achieve a concession when combined with positive inducements

H3c. Targeting civilian networks is less likely to produce a concession peacetime. This competition involves interdependent decisions and expectations about rival behavior (Schelling 1960: 3). Strategy is as much about gaining leverage in the future as in the present.

Rival states engage in constant competition across all domains (i.e., land, air, sea, space, cyber) and using instruments as varied as economic sanctions and diplomatic demarches to displays of military force and covert action. Therefore, strategy is "an inherent element of statecraft at all times" (Earle 1943: viii). For French Admiral Raoul Castex, strategy guides campaigns in both peacetime and wartime and extends to instruments of power and influence as varied as battleships and diplomatic conferences (Castex 1937: 9–17). For Robert Osgood, strategy "must be understood as nothing less than all plans for utilizing the capacity for armed coercion—in conjunction with the economic, diplomatic, and psychological instruments of power—to support foreign policy most effectively by overt, covert, and tacit means (1962: 5).

Strategy then is a theory, a set of assumptions about how to influence rivals. In this sense, strategy is the "art of creating power" (Freedman 2008: 31), a bridge that directs all resources of the security community to a political end (Gray 2011). Like the Clausewitzean view of war, this art of power has an enduring nature and a changing character. The enduring nature concerns the directing of resources toward a political end. The changing character resides in the ways and means available to rivals in a given context. Interconnected material and social factors—from new technology, political institutions, and the distribution of strategic resources to emergent norms—shape strategy (Heuser 2010: 19–24). It follows then that the growing range of human activity in the digital domain should produce new strategies that connect cyber operations to a larger set of political objectives.

While modern cyber strategy, like defense strategy, involves long-term investment in infrastructure, training, and capabilities development for offense, defense, and intelligence activities, this book focuses on how rival states use cyber operations as part of crisis bargaining strategies. Rivals, by definition, are always on the cusp of a crisis or already engaged in many on multiple fronts (Diehl and Goertz 2001). They are constantly seeking a position of relative advantage through the means available, including cyber instruments and new ways to combine them with traditional forms of power.

Cyber strategy, therefore, can be thought of as a modern variant of coercive diplomacy,[4] *It is much, much more; it is an information/culture war tool* a political-diplomatic strategy that aims to influence a [rival's] will or incentive structure. It is a strategy that combines threats of force, and if necessary, the limited and selective use of force in discrete and controlled increments, in a bargaining strategy . . . the aim is to induce an adversary to comply with one's demands, or to negotiate the most favorable compromise possible, while simultaneously managing the crisis to prevent unwanted military escalation. (Levy 2008: 539)

Unlike traditional perspectives on coercion, coercive diplomacy can involve positive inducements and is not singularly focused on producing concessions (compellence) or stopping an action before it occurs (deterrence). Cyber strategies, like coercive diplomacy, are much broader than traditional perspectives on coercion. While rival states can and, as we show, do use cyber operations to compel, they more often than not use the digital domain to signal and steal as a means of shaping long-term competition.

To understand long-term competition and coercion more broadly, we look to scholars who have blazed a path theorizing how new technological developments shape strategic interactions. Byman and Waxman's (2002) *Dynamics of Coercion* was written in the run-up to the war in Iraq (2003) and after the Kosovo War (1999), confronting the dominance of strategic air power and precision strike technologies. Pape's (1996) *Bombing to Win* was written after the first Persian Gulf war in 1991 and the celebrated advances of the strategic bombing campaign on Iraq (1992–1993). Perhaps most critically, Schelling (1960, 1966) wrote his master works after the Korean War and in the midst of the nuclear revolution. These works investigate how advances in the power to hurt shape the character of international politics and the types of decisions national leaders confront when facing rival states.

Our work builds on this tradition to investigate the "the power to hurt online" (Gartzke and Lindsay 2017a: 5). Much like these earlier studies, we find that new technological means, in the form of cyber operations, confront decision makers with a shifting strategic calculus. Cyber action represents, but is not limited to, a new domain of coercion that sits on an escalation ladder between economic coercion and the use of physical force short of nuclear exchange (Libicki 2009, 26).

Our work comes after the Russian attempts to use a combination of cyber operations and propaganda to undermine the democratic process in the Ukraine (2014), the United States (2016), France (2017), and Germany (2017). China has shifted the age-old art of espionage online and staged a complex series of data breaches, characterized by journalists as the "greatest brain robbery" of all time (Stahl 2016). The United States and Israel used binary code to replace the saboteurs of old in the Stuxnet (2010) operation, and, in the process, amplified the larger coercive diplomacy campaign targeting Iranian nuclear proliferation.

Cyber operations signal rivals and shape how they manage crises. Through intrusions, logic bombs, website defacements, viruses, and distributed denial of service (DDoS) operations, an actor can compel an adversary short of physical attack or signal the risks of further escalation. For Nye (2017: 45), the mechanisms such as threats of punishment, denial, entanglement, create a deterrent effect in cyber. Consistent with the coercive turn a dissuasion logic in cyberspace more akin to crime than deterring Similarly, in our treatment, cyber strategy is broader than traditional understandings of coercion and involves a more varied set of instruments rival states use to achieve a position of relative advantage in long-term, predominantly peacetime, competition.

The coercive effects of cyber operations appear to be limited at best. The temporary impact on network operations, responsibility issues, lack of credibility, and ambiguity inherent in cyberspace operations all limit the coercive potential of cyber methods. Once identified, the "target can patch or otherwise neutralize the threat. Therefore, if attackers rely on the difficulty of attribution to protect themselves, then they cannot make coercive demands that would reveal their identity" (Gartzke and Lindsay 2017a: 17). It is difficult to achieve coercion when the effects of cyber operations can either be easily reversed or the damage minimized through limiting the effectiveness of the next attack by closing the access points used the first time. Therefore, we must broaden our gaze beyond coercion to understand how rival states employ cyber strategies.

FORMS OF CYBER STRATEGY: DISRUPTION, ESPIONAGE, AND DEGRADATION

If strategy is a concept concerning how to influence rivals in pursuit of political objectives, then what forms of interaction help states create the power to do so in the digital domain? This book introduces three distinct strategic logics in cyberspace: disruption, espionage, and degradation. These logics build on earlier work on coercive diplomacy (George, Hall, and Simons 1971; George 1991) and coercion (Schelling 1960, 1966; Kydd and Walter 2006) as well as recent explorations of cyber coercion (Gartzke and Lindsay 2017a, Borghard and Lonergan 2017), but with an important caveat. Cyber strategy need not seek a direct concession and tends to occur predominantly in covert, as opposed to overt, space. Rival states use indirect cyber instruments to shape long-term competition more than to seek immediate concessions.

Based on empirical investigation, we posit three forms of cyber strategies employed by rival states for the years 2000–2014: disruption, espionage, and degradation. Cyber disruptions are a low-cost, low-payoff form of cyber strategy designed to shape the larger bargaining context. These cheap signals likely do not achieve sufficient leverage to compel a target.[5] Rather, they seek to probe an adversary: testing their resolve, signaling escalation risk, and supporting larger propaganda efforts. These website defacements and DDoS incidents are a form of tacit bargaining. According to George Downs and David Rocke, "tacit bargaining takes place whenever a state attempts to influence the policy choices of another state through behavior, rather than by relying on formal or informal diplomatic exchanges [alone]" (1990: 3). Low-cost cyber disruptions pressure a rival, through either signaling the risk of crisis escalation or, in combination with propaganda efforts, undermining public confidence in existing policy preferences. Website defacements often echo particular narratives designed to limit policy options for a rival, portraying the opposition as extreme versions of evil, for example, the way website defacements characterize the Ukrainian government as fascists or Nazis.

As a strategy, cyber espionage focuses on altering the balance of information to achieve a position of advantage. Activities can range from simple network penetration to retrieve information to manipulating data to corrupt a rival's confidence in their own systems. These actions are not coercive in the traditional sense. Rather, they concern long-term competition and how rival states seek to exploit information asymmetries. Espionage represents efforts to steal critical information or manipulate information asymmetries in a manner that produces bargaining benefits between rival states engaged in long-term competition.

Yet, just because you steal or manipulate does not mean you gain a position of advantage. All information has a time value, and hacked data often expires rapidly. Information stolen in the past must be relevant in the future. Stealing information through infiltrating networks does not mean you steal the right information at the right time. Furthermore, just because you steal something does not mean you know what is valuable as opposed to what is just noise. Furthermore, large troves of information are difficult to process and rarely lead to innovation (Gilli and Gilli 2016). China frequently encounters this challenge in its massive cyber espionage campaigns, including the OPM hack that stole personal information of over 20 million people with ties to the US government (Lindsay 2015b). Espionage is a strategy of influence and positioning that seeks to manipulate the balance of information in order to achieve a position of advantage. New pathways of information bring new opportunities for espionage. Yet, strategically, cyber espionage can be of limited value due to the constraints of harvesting and sharing data, much less converting the proverbial needle in haystack into political, military, or economic advantage over the long term.

Cyber degradation—coercive operations designed to sabotage the enemy target's networks, operations, or systems—is more likely to have a compellent effect than disruptions or espionage. Yet, this effect is rare because many times the target is hardened or too complex to be knocked out for extended periods as a result of malicious cyber actions. This form of cyber strategy resembles denial coercion used in airpower (Pape 1996) and tends to exhibit sunk costs due to its complexity and tailored design (optimized for a specific system and to achieve destructive effects). This high-cost, high-payoff dynamic makes degradation a costlier signal (Fearon 1997) and thus more likely to achieve effects, but the results are complicated when examined carefully.[6] The Stuxnet operation launched against Iran, similar unsuccessful "left-of-launch" actions directed toward North Korea to prevent them from advancing their missile program, or even actions against Russia in response to the election hacks of 2016 are all examples of cyber degradation.

AMBIGUOUS SIGNALS: DEMONSTRATING RESOLVE AND MANAGING ESCALATION

If cyber operations, contrary to much of the headlines and hype, do not produce political concessions between rival states, what is their purpose in the great game of international politics? We find that the utility of cyber strategy is as a form of political warfare optimized for the 21st century that relies on tacit bargaining and ambiguous signaling to help rival states achieve a position of relative advantage in long-term competition. Ambiguous signals are covert attempts to demonstrate resolve that rely on sinking costs and raising risks to shape rival behavior. In a crisis, states can also face problems clearly communicating their intent through signals. This challenge is amplified in cyberspace, where "the linkages between intent, effect, and perception are loose" (Libicki 2012: xvi). This dynamic creates a condition in which signals "can be as or more ambiguous when they take place or refer to events in cyberspace than they are when limited to the physical world" (Libicki 2012: xv). There are also unique signaling challenges associated with cyber coercion that limit its power to hurt. According to Borghard and Lonergan (2017: 7), "signaling in cyber space is the problematic of all domains (land, sea, air, space and cyber) because the signal may go unrealized. In other words, in cyberspace only the initiator may perceive the engagement." Similarly, for Gartzke and Lindsay (2017a: 26), "The biggest obstacle to cyber coercion is the difficulty of credibly signaling about potential harm that depends on secrecy to be harmful. . . . Sacrifice of anonymity on which offensive deception depends exposes the cyber attacker to retaliation. Coercive cyber threats thus tend to be more generalized, which undercuts their effectiveness in targeted or crisis situations."

This ambiguity decreases the certainty of the message, but not necessarily the utility of the signal to shape rival behavior. Rivals use cyber methods, as they do other forms of covert action in peacetime, to gain a position of advantage while signaling resolve and the risks of further escalation. In this manner, cyber strategies, even coercive degradation efforts, can be stabilizing, providing rivals a means of engaging in competition short of war.

Rather than herald a revolutionary break in the history of warfare, the employment of cyber operations between rivals can create strategic stability and reinforce traditional power dynamics. For Gartzke and Lindsay (2017a), there is a distinct stability-instability paradox in cyberspace. The open architecture of the Internet creates a unique vulnerability. If the target of coercion disconnects, they are no longer as vulnerable. Therefore, the aggressor has to operate either covertly or beneath a threshold to avoid retaliation. Furthermore, the aggressor knows that if it crosses that threshold they risk a cross-domain response. A state could respond with economic sanctions, as seen in the Russian hack of US elections, or outright military force.

Since most forms of cyber strategy investigated here are optimized for covert action, they reflect a desire to signal resolve while keeping conflicts limited. Like covert action, cyber options work in the shadows and can help rivals engage in tacit cooperation "to steer dangerous encounters to the backstage as a way to safeguard the external impression of their encounter as a limited conflict" (Carson 2016: 105). Plausible deniability in cases where attribution is fairly obvious (e.g., Russian incursions into Ukraine in 2014–2015 or attacking the US election in 2016) works not necessarily to hide the identity of the attacker but rather to provide justification for the defender to moderate their response.

This signaling dynamic leaves us with the question of how you compel a rival state if they do not know they have been breached in the first place. That is, how can covert action compel rivals? In 2016, the Obama administration planted "cyber bombs" in Russian networks as a retaliation for the election hack (Carson 2016). Yet, if you do not signal the opposition that you have this deadly tripwire installed, how can you expect to affect their behavior and compel them to back down in their efforts to attack the American democratic process? Furthermore, if you send too explicit a signal, you give the target the opportunity to patch their network, reducing your coercive leverage.

Despite the promise of quick wins in the digital domain, there are complex signaling dynamics in cyberspace that make producing concessions difficult. For example, consider North Korea. There have been frequent disputes between the United States and North Korea over the Korean state's attempts to develop ballistic missiles capable of delivering nuclear warheads. One way to stop this coming conflict is to acquire what has been called "left of launch" attack abilities. As Broad and Sanger (2017) put it, "the idea is to strike an enemy missile before liftoff or during the first seconds of flight."

While seemingly novel, left of launch approaches depend on using cyber methods to prevent the adversary from acquiring the technological prowess to launch missiles in the first place or give up due to repeated development failures. To sustain its sabotage effect, the cyber intrusion must remain secret. The target must continue to believe they are having difficulty fielding functioning military hardware. Therefore, there is the dilemma inherent in cyber coercion: how can you coerce the opposition to change their behavior when the method of coercion must be concealed to reach its maximum effect?

In fact, the idea of secret cyber operations is often overstated. A cyber action, by definition, can be witnessed and observed by any capable adversary. These actions are covert in that they are deniable (Carson and Yarhi-Milo 2017: 128). States leverage cyber tools because they can avoid responsibility for their actions and generally avoid attributing their operations for days, if not years, after the event. Covert actions can be coercive, but to be effective, a covert operation needs to be intelligible and credible (Carson and Yarhi-Milo 2017). In other words, even though the initial intrusion was covert, states must suspect their rival conducted the attack and, in doing so, demonstrated a degree of resolve.

The advantage of using cyber tools lies not in their often-reported speed, global reach, cheapness, or ease of use, but rather in the ability, like other forms of covert action, to deny responsibility. The problem is that credibility is a critical factor in convincing an adversary that their actions will have consequences. The break in the link between responsibility and credibility can mean that cyber actions may not be backed by any notions of capability and resolve of the attacking country, but rather through some sort of mystical process of cyber escalation that will theoretically compel the opposition to give in because of future consequences.

This problem is manifest in Stuxnet and the Olympic Games campaign, perhaps the most famous series of cyber incidents, where the United States and Israel breached the nuclear networks of Iran. At first, Iranian leadership were not sure what caused their centrifuge systems to run over capacity. Officials initially thought basic human error, rather than an aggressive cyber operations, produced the damage (Sanger 2012). The case highlights the intelligibility problem of covert coercive signals. When seeking to change behavior of the defender through secret means, the attacker must establish the consequences of further misbehavior while retaining sufficient deniability (Carson and Yarhi-Milo 2017).

The path to influence through cyber action is murky at this point, and we know little about how cyber actions can influence and change behavior. Brantly (2016) makes the clear point that cyber actions are the result of rational actor expected utility calculations, but we have yet to test the proposition that capabilities are critical in coercion, and we know little about the specific constraints or opportunities decision makers perceive. Furthermore, Whyte (2016) theorizes that cyber coercion will be limited due to sociopolitical constraints rather than technological limitations.

While theoretically "game-changing" as Syring's (2016) US Senate testimony notes, "left of launch" programs that rely on cyber actions are ambiguous signals that are not about simply making a concession as much as they are about signaling escalation risks and generating coercive options short of war. Ambiguous signals are the hallmarks of coercive campaigns and instead leave the attacker and the defender alike with too many unknowns to have confidence that aggressive action will change behavior.

The key challenge is in interpreting signals. As Sanger and Broad (2017) note in their exposé on the use of cyber tools against North Korea, many analysts are skeptical because one can also blame setbacks on insider error, manufacturing problems, or basic mistakes rather than cyber offensive action. Yet, rival states persist in using cyber operations, despite their limited effect, due to a lack of better options. Better to temporarily erode North Korea's missile program through malware than risk war on the Korean peninsula if precision missiles destroy key facilities.

THE RIVALRY CONTEXT

In this work we focus on rivalry—long-standing historical animosity between two parties with a high degree of competitiveness, the existence of repeated conflict, and a series of reciprocated engagements over a long period of time (Diehl and Goertz 2001).[7] This context is critical because if one were to expect an effect from cyber actions, it would most likely be displayed in the context of a rivalry (Valeriano and Maness 2012). In short, rivalry cases serve as critical tests of strategic competition and conflict between digitally capable powers.

Rivalry also serves as a key case-selection device, making our empirical examination manageable. To date, most cyber security scholars have avoided empirical research beyond single case studies outside of a few exceptions.[8] When evaluating theories, we must leverage the known cases we have in order to understand the system and interactions as they stand. Any other move would be irresponsible and consist of speculation rather than rigorous research. Cyber security issues are critical for the national security discourse, and as such, we should examine them empirically as opposed to relying on our imagination.

We have demonstrated in the past that cyber interactions between rival states can be coded and examined empirically (Valeriano and Maness 2014; Maness and Valeriano 2016), and our next step is to investigate the effects of coercion on rival states. There are 126 active pairs of rival states as of the last version of the data (Klein, Diehl, and Goertz 2006). We extend these actively engaged enemies and examine their behavior in cyberspace to understand just how coercion works in the modern battle-space when used between commitment adversaries.

A key limitation of this book is that it only investigates cyber coercive effects among the rival population. While we do not investigate the entire universe of state action, we are convinced that we capture a critical sample of state-based cyber conflict. We would miss engagements between states such as China and Costa Rica or Russia and the Philippines, but these states rarely engage in coercive cyber conflict. We also fail to investigate coercive cyber activities between nonstate initiators and states as targets. While this might be problematic overall, we are also convinced that interactions between states as targets and nonstates as initiators would need an entirely different theoretical lens by which to examine effects. The issues at stake are often related to governance and identity as opposed to strategic competition between large powers seeking regional, if not global, hegemony. There is also the issue that the majority of cyber interactions between nonstate initiators and state targets are either criminal in nature or involve ongoing antiterrorism operations that remain classified at the time of writing.

We also might see a much different use of cyber strategies and methods of harm in the future (Clarke and Knake 2010), thus biasing our results based on the limited use of cyber operations in the present. Yet, we are bound by the past and question the extent to which we can predict the future course of cyber exchanges between rivals. To promise more would be problematic, as would be limiting our analysis to only a few cases that might represent ransacking history to produce the results we intend.

MAJOR FINDINGS

We find that cyber operations produce *only limited concessions*. Examining 192 episodes of cyber exchanges between rivals, we find that only 5.7% achieve compellent success and lead to an observable concession. In our treatment, we expect only cyber degradation to produce a sufficiently costly signal to alter rival behavior. The other forms of cyber strategy, disruption and espionage, have a different logic. They are not coercion in the traditional sense. Seen in this light, cyber degradations tend to achieve concessions at rates consistent with broader studies of coercion examined in the next chapter. Revisiting the cyber escalation ladder (Libicki 2012), the rarity of cyber concessions makes cyber degradations less effective instruments of coercion compared with economic warfare or the limited use of military force. Despite the limited effects of cyber coercion, there is a unique strategic logic in the new domain.

Yet, even this finding is limited. Coercive outcomes associated with cyber degradation are also skewed by traditional measures of power. Military and economic power appear to be better explanatory factors of rival concessions than cyber operations.

However, we do have evidence that past cyber incidents are associated with limited escalation. Parsing out our findings, we notice that this usually means a small move up the escalation ladder but not significant horizontal or vertical escalation (Smoke 1977).

Furthermore, the overwhelming majority of the degradation events evoking concessions involve the United States (89%). In other words, objective success in cyber coercive exchanges between rivals may be a function of US strategy or mastery in cyberspace. Pundits who claim the United States is lagging in the digital domain are wrong (Johnson 2017 Shinkman 2016, Chalfant 2017). There is a clear actor without peer competitors and it is the United States.

Figure 1.1 breaks down each type of coercive method initiated by rival states from the years 2000 to 2014.[9] Overall, there has been a rise in cyber incidents since the turn of the century, with various peaks and valleys. While cyber incidents are increasing, this increase appears to be directly correlated with espionage and disruption campaigns, not the more malicious degradation activities that many fear in the discourse. In short, there appears to be a stable system of cyber norms where the worst events are avoided and instead the majority of what we see are traditional forms of statecraft enabled now by digital methods of attack.

Last, there are unique escalation dynamics in cyberspace. Even when cyber exchanges between rivals escalate, they remain limited in scope outside of ongoing military conflict (Russia–Georgia 2008, Russia–Ukraine 2014). That is, rivals may use cyber operations to probe the enemy, test their resolve, and signal the risks of significant escalation. These findings are explored in chapter 3, which presents the empirical analysis of the utility of cyber coercive methods.

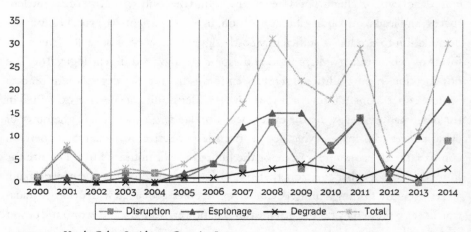

FIGURE 1.1 Yearly Cyber Incidents, Coercive Intent: 2000–2014

Our second set of findings concerns the efficacy of cyber strategy, which is the subject of chapter 4. There appear to be unique forms of coercion more likely to achieve objective success in the digital domain, albeit in combination with other instruments of power. Consistent with key findings from earlier coercion theory (Byman and Waxman 2002), combinations and synergies matter. Almost all instances of cyber degradation identified in the database occurred alongside cyber espionage incidents preceding the degradation, as well as broader diplomatic, economic, and military efforts to compel a rival. Stuxnet illustrates this combined logic. Despite the United States and Israel's success infiltrating Iranian networks, Tehran likely conceded due to diplomatic isolation, domestic changes and elections, assassinations of key personnel, and economic sanctions, not to mention the looming threat of military intervention. Cyber coercion adds another vector for pressuring an adversary to change their behavior, but it must be evaluated in its proper geopolitical context. What we find is that only certain combinations will work in terms of producing concessions from rival states, and this includes the use of positive diplomatic and military inducements as opposed to strictly negative actions that include threats, displays of force, and even military actions.

Similarly, consistent with key findings from earlier coercion theory (Pape 1996), the target matters. There is no strategic benefit to brutalizing civilians. In fact, using cyber capabilities to target noncombatants may be considered a war crime, according to the editor of the *Tallinn Manual* (Schmitt and Biller 2017). Rivals seeking to compel rivals through cyber operations targeting civilian networks do not succeed in achieving a compellent concession. Similar to the findings that study the efficacy of airpower campaigns (Pape 1996) and terrorism (Abrahms 2006), targeting civilian networks is less likely to produce coercive concessions. Civilian vulnerability does not appear to affect coercion (Horowitz and Reiter 2001).

After our macro empirical analysis of cyber strategies, we then turn to three case study chapters that cover the most active states in the international cyber landscape: Russia, China, and the United States. We find that each country produces a different strategy that is conducive to its strategic goals, national interests, and position in the hierarchy of the international system. Russia is a declining power that has a corrupt political system and a flailing economy that limits military spending. Its cyber strategy of disruption and disinformation is a cheaper way to seek its political goals in the international system. China is the rising power that is attempting to bridge the gap economically, militarily, and technologically with its status quo competitor, the United States. Chinese leaders employ a strategy of digital espionage to steal technological secrets of the more advanced Western powers as well as Japan in an attempt to hasten their goal of replacing the current superpower as the world's most powerful country. The United States has technological superiority over both Russia and China and will use its cyber capabilities sparingly so as not to give its adversaries access to these superior capabilities. In fact, we see US cyber actions often used as counterespionage against China and Russia. Chapters 5, 6, and 7 unpack these cyber great powers' actions in more detail.

Why Studying Cyber Strategy Matters

The term "cyber war" is becoming near ubiquitous. Many analysts assume it will happen, it is happening, and, more critically for this book, it is an effective means of compelling adversaries. The notion that cyber tools offer a cheap but powerful advantage to states animates the cyber security discourse. The resulting fear of cyber operations creates unrealistic expectations and contributes to threat inflation. We are left with a false promise of impact absent a strategic logic.

Yet, analyzing the efficacy of cyber strategies is an empirical question that requires theory and evidence to support policy. Assuming these methods can work with little dissection of how, when, or in what context they might be effective is problematic, if not dangerous. With every innovation in technology, futurists promise dramatic changes that skew how decision makers calculate cost and benefit. For these revolutionaries, lured by the false promise of technology, new toys bring new joys, while others question the utility of any innovation absent evidence.

Do cyberattacks really achieve the goals of the attacker? Do they compel the adversary to change their behavior through either demonstrated attacks or the fear of future attack? The current discourse seems to assume that cyber methods are cheap, easy, and effective ways of weak states to achieve their ends and catch up with competitors. The problem is that we need more than hunches and inclinations to move forward. We need empirical research to understand the process of cyber conflict and behavior inherent in cyber interactions between rivals.

We move beyond the streetlamp effect (Hendrix 2017) in research design. Rather than being attracted by dramatic events, our assessment of cyber strategy is driven by what we can actually observe in interactions of rival states. Having context and perspective is critical to understanding these exchanges.

Our understanding of cyber strategy and its coercive potential is much more complicated than the discourse evident in scholarship. Moving away from dramatic cyber effects brings us to the more realistic position that the effects of cyber operations might be marginal based on cost and effort as well more oriented toward tacit bargaining between rival states engaged in long-term competition. That is, they are low-cost efforts, at least relative to large-scale conventional efforts, and have correspondingly minimal impacts on the target. The other perspective we offer here is that the combining cyber operations with either positive or negative conventional inducements is the more accurate way to discuss the implications of cyber maneuvers, but these actions are costly, complicated, and require massive amounts of coordinated energy to achieve a reaction in the target. The more we study the impact of cyber actions, the more we find that those actions that do achieve a desired change in behavior in the target are rare, marginal in comparative impact, and costly in terms of giving up techniques to the adversary. These findings have important implications for policy makers. We now turn to the theory that guides the empirical inferences of this book, chapter 2, which unpacks our cyber strategy typology.

2

HOW RIVAL STATES EMPLOY CYBER STRATEGY

Disruption, Espionage, and Degradation

OUR CENTRAL QUESTION is: *how do states use cyber strategies to influence their rivals?* This chapter introduces three types of cyber strategies: disruption, espionage, and degradation. Examining the viability of these approaches and their objectives guides our empirical investigation. We advance the position that serious cyber degradation operations will be the most effective coercive strategies in terms of producing concessions, but despite the promise of a cyber revolution the overall rate of success is not higher than traditional forms of coercion such as diplomatic threats or limited economic sanctions. Degradation strategies reflect costly options often paired with other conventional coercive measures. These less frequent cyber actions can achieve success but risk unintended consequences.

Empirically, cyber operations seeking to degrade the opposition are not the norm. Instead, simple disruption and espionage actions, especially short-term espionage, dominate rival cyber exchanges and offer a form of signaling that helps states engage in a process of competitive learning while seeking a position of relative advantage in long-term competitive relationships. The importance of signaling strategies in cyber relations has gone relatively unexamined in the field, and this is the advance we offer in this project.

As a form of hostile covert action (Brantly 2016: 18; Carson and Yarhi-Milo 2017), cyber strategies can represent ambiguous signals designed to probe adversary intentions and manage escalation risk. These simpler attacks are the least a state can do to achieve effects, and they fail more often than not in this context. The reality is that cyber intrusions do not produce concessions in targets in isolation. Rather, they often act as additive measures that amplify existing signals. When cyber options do seem to induce change, these incidents tend to be part of larger campaigns that combine other instruments of power and positive inducements. In examining the targets and impact, similar to more traditional forms of overt coercion like limited airpower strikes (Pape 1996), it appears targeting civilians through cyber means does not work.

In this chapter, we dissect the core strategic logic of cyber operations that seek to influence rival behavior and enhance a state's bargaining position. We do not focus on network defense or resilience, though these activities do alter long-term competition. Rather, we examine disruption, espionage, and degradation as ways of exerting pressure and gaining leverage. This focus necessitates a close look at the literature on coercion. After defining coercion and establishing the expected threshold of concessions based on surveying multiple studies, we then highlight debates about power and resolve in the traditional coercion literature to extract important considerations for our empirical investigation. The inherent ambiguity, primacy of signaling, and temporary effects in cyber operations distort power and resolve in the digital domain. Cyber operations tend to have limited coercive potential due to the nature of the strategies, their goals, and the restraint used when launching cyber operations. While cyber strategies tend not to produce concessions, they appear to help rivals contain escalation and affect the long-term decision-making calculus through espionage. We propose that there are unique strategies that do increase the efficacy of cyber coercion, while the more commonly used methods tend to fail to achieve their goals.

Coercion as Strategy

Coercion is the use of threats, punishment, or escalation of costs during a crisis or conflict to alter the foreign policy behavior of the target.[1] The application of force is more potential than actual, taking minimal actions to alter the cost-benefit calculation of an adversary short of using "brute" force that results in escalation to a major military campaign (Schelling 1966). Escalation is to be avoided at all costs, since the goal is to attain objectives without having to resort to the application of conventional force to achieve these ends. It also possible to use coercion during war to threaten escalation, expansion, or the entry of new weapons to drive the opposition away from the battlefield. The central task of any coercive strategy, either in war or peacetime, is "to create in the opponent the expectation of costs of sufficient magnitude to erode his motivation to continue what he is doing" (George 2009: 77).

Coercion is but one logic of cyber strategy, specifically degradation. In studying cyber operations, we focus on a particular form of coercion: *compellence*. For Schelling (1966: 69), there are important differences between "a threat intended to make an adversary do something and a threat intended to keep an adversary from doing something." Threats designed to maintain the status quo are deterrent in nature. Threats designed to initiate a behavior change are compellent. Our choice to focus on compellence is driven by the need to examine the efficacy of operations that seek to achieve demonstrable effects. Compellence is about changing behavior, while deterrence is about preventing behaviors, the latter being difficult to observe empirically. The other key issue is that cyber actions are common, at least at the lower levels of severity (Valeriano and Maness 2014). Therefore, our desire to understand the effectiveness of these already ongoing and proliferating actions drives our study.

In its traditional form, compellence is discussed as offensive measures connected to threats rather than positive inducements. In this respect, compellence is often differentiated from coercive diplomacy (George 1991: 5), but this is not our goal. We are interested in how cyber operations are integrated with positive and negative diplomatic, economic, and military inducements in order understand the complete range of inducements necessary to change the behavior of the adversary. A true assessment of the utility of cyber operations includes both compellence operations and coercive diplomacy efforts that include positive inducements.

In theory, compellence is more difficult than deterrence (Schelling 1966: 75; Art 1980: 8). By definition, when states seek to change the status quo the act provokes resistance (Snyder and Diesing 1977: 24–25; Jervis 1979). Attempts at military coercion in particular tend to invoke a defiant response in the target (Leng 1993: 13). Active manipulation and outlining acceptable ranges of behavior often provoke the opposition to behave in a manner opposite of the desired course. Compellence is difficult, complicated, and costly; but it is also empirically observable, making it a situation ripe for examination.

The meaning of success is often uncertain in compellence (Byman and Waxman 2002: 33). Observing success is a subjective process, as is observing victory. States often have multiple goals, some of which rely on the cooperation and revolve around "things that cannot be physically seized: policy changes, apologies, elections or plebiscites, and reparation payments" (Sescher and Fuhrman 2017: 25). To get past this complication, we assess observable changes in rival behavior that we characterize as concessions. The reality of cyber operations is that, more often than not, the target will behave in a manner unexpected to the attacker.

Studies of Coercion

The long history of coercion as a form of diplomatic practice provides a guide through which to view cyber operations in our current era. Coercion is common, but prone to failure. According to Lebow (2007), Thucydides documented 10 coercive campaigns in the Peloponnesian War that tended to fail, leading to provocation and escalation. Chandragupta (340–297 BCE) and his adviser Kautilya used coercive threats to build the Mauryan Empire (Modelski 1964). After the rise of Augustus, the Romans drew on what strategists today call forward-deployed forces as a coercive instrument and signaling mechanism to threaten rivals (Campbell 2001).

In researching coercion in the modern era, Cable (1981, 2016) outlines the practice of gunboat diplomacy and using displays of naval power as a threat in diplomatic crises. Lebow (1984) maps 20 pre–World War II crises, each of which involved multiple coercive signals, showing the contingent nature of crises. After the Berlin Airlift and Cuban Missile crises, debates about the use of coercive threats and strategic bargaining in the nuclear age shaped Cold War deterrent strategies (George and Smoke 1974; Jervis 1979; Huth and Russett 1990).

Post–Cold War research on coercion substantiate the view that modern states, especially great powers, find achieving concessions through threats an elusive task. The use of airpower to compel rogue states (1995 Operations Deliberate Force, 1998 Operation Desert Fox, 1999 Operation Allied Force) renewed academic and policy interest in the efficacy of coercion. Scholars studying these campaigns, and the utility of military force in general, find that conventional airpower campaigns, especially if countervalue (i.e., targeting civilians or civilian infrastructure), appear to produce limited results (Pape 1996; Byman and Waxman 2000).

New studies on the history of coercion find that material advantages and military capability gaps between strong and weak states do not appear to translate into concessions at the expected levels (Sechser 2010; Haun 2015). Nuclear weapons do not produce significant increases in coercive outcomes (Sechser and Fuhrmann 2017). Other studies demonstrate that coercive campaigns by actors such as the United States against smaller nuclear states like North Korea incur a significant escalation risk (Lieber and Press 2013).

The interest in coercion extends to the study of political violence and terrorism after the attacks on September 11, 2001, and the escalation of an already global counterterror campaign by a US-led coalition against Al Qaeda. In an effort to ground the strategic logic of terrorism, multiple studies analyze the extent to which terrorism, as a strategic signal optimized for extracting policy concessions from democracies, achieves success.[2] These studies demonstrate a similar limited utility of coercion when used by actors willing to leverage terrorism as a strategy. For example,

Abrahms (2006) finds that only 7% of coercive terrorist campaigns achieved even a partial concession from the target. He challenges an earlier study on terrorism (Pape 2003), which found coercive success rates greater than 50%. Specifically, more maximalist coercive objectives, such as regime change or changing identity, narrow the bargaining range while targeting civilians tend to deepen resolve and limit concessions (Abrahms 2006).

Lastly, studies on coercion can extend to civil unrest and peaceful protests (Chenoweth and Stephan 2011). Coercion is not restricted to negative inducements, such as sanctions, threats of force, displays of military force, or limited strikes. The ability of a challenger to generate mass participation and create mobilization to sustain protests is more likely to achieve concessions than the use of force. In fact, coercive success, though often elusive, often relies on positive inducements. This finding echoes earlier work on coercive diplomacy that similarly highlights the importance of positive inducements, but relates them to interstate competition (George 1991; Art and Cronin 2003).

As seen in Table 2.1, previous studies on the effectiveness of coercive campaigns suggest that they successfully compel an adversary between 7% and 57% of the time.[3] Overall, the average rate of successful coercion across these studies is 33.38%. In other words, if cyber operations produce concessions, a third of the time they are not a particularly effective compellent form of statecraft.

We argue that temporary effects and ambiguity in cyberspace reduce the compellent threat. As Libicki (2016: 190) states, "the effects of almost all cyberattacks are temporary and the impact of such cyberattacks depletes over time." If an effect of an attack is minimized through time, this adds the key consideration of temporality (Stevens 2015) into estimations of cyber effects. Another key point is that once revealed, cyber intrusions can be patched and the avenue of attack is then closed.

Ambiguity is critical, since cyber actions function similarly to covert actions. Concealed attacks limit the ability to make overt coercive demands (Carson and Yarhi-Milo 2017). Additionally, there are incentives to conceal capabilities in cyberspace, where revealing network access tends to shut off future attack vectors and limit espionage. If you use it, you lose it in cyberspace. In short, cyber options cannot be used repeatedly against a prepared adversary, so the utility of coercive attacks is short-lived.

FORMS OF COERCION

There is a variety of coercive forms relevant for this study. Each form has a distinct logic that implies different levels of force and targets. The relative threat of force,

TABLE 2.1

Assessing Concession Rates in Coercive Campaigns

Author(s)	Sample (N)	Dependent Variable	Success Rate[a]
Blechman and Kaplan (1978)	US 1946–1976 (37)	Long-term positive outcomes linked to US compellence	19%
Hufbauer, Schott, and Elliot (1990)	State economic sanctions campaigns 1914–1990 (115)	Sanctions success	34%
George and Simon (1994)	US coercive diplomatic campaign 1942–1991 (7)	Success rate of US coercive diplomacy to induce a policy change	29%
Pape (1996)	US coercive air campaigns 1942–1991 (7)	Strategic, Operational or Decapitation[b]	57%
Pape (1997)	State economic sanctions campaigns 1914–1990 (115)	Sanctions success	4%
Art and Cronin (2003)	US coercive diplomatic campaign 1990–2001 (7)	Success rate of US coercive diplomacy to induce a policy change	31%
Pape (2003)	Suicide terror campaigns 1980–2001 (11)	Target policy change	55%
Abrahms (2006)	Coercive terror campaigns[c] (42)	Partial policy change	7%
Secsher (2011)	All state efforts at compellence 1918–2001 (210)	Successful compellent threat	41%
Haun (2015)	US coercive efforts in asymmetric interstate crises, 1950–2011 (23)	Successful coercion outcome	52%

[a] Average based on 52, 19, 34, 29, 57, 4, 31, and 41. Implies a standard deviation of 16.04 (so cyber coercion should be between 17.37 and 49.41).

[b] Pape codes multiple outcomes by category; success rate reflects success in at least one category.

[c] Abrahms analyzes groups as opposed to acts over time.

Source: The table is adapted and updated from Sechser (2007).

applied through pressure points over the course of a crisis, tends to determine the coercive potential. Over time, the coercer can target the power base, create unrest, decapitate the regime, debilitate the country's critical infrastructure, or deny rival states their preferred course of action by using multiple instruments of coercion, creating a synergistic effect.

George (1991) finds that there are multiple forms of coercion. Blackmail is the use of threats to force an adversary to "give up something of value without putting up resistance" (George 1991: 5). Coercive diplomacy uses a mix of diplomatic and military instruments to signal the costs of a continued, hostile course of action while showing positive benefits of an alternative policy. Blackmail and punishment are some options, but the reduction of sanctions, new trade agreements, and outright tribute are possible avenues. This push and pull between positive and negative coercive endeavors is critical for our work.

The coercer can seek to punish an actor by inflicting pain (i.e., raise the costs of action) or by denying an adversary from achieving an objective (i.e., lower the perceived benefits of a particular course of action).[4] States apply punishment either directly or in a gradual manner (e.g., risk strategy) against countervalue, mainly civilian, targets (Pape 1996). In Douhet's (1921) original characterization of the power of strategic bombing, air attacks against civilian centers would force citizens to demand an end to war. Cyber actions targeting civilians would be a clear form of punishment seeking to alter behavior in the target state.

There are variants of punishment. Coercion can take the form of eroding the elite's power base, weakening the adversary, and generating unrest. Power base erosion entails "threatening a regime's relationship with its core supporters" (Byman and Waxman 2002: 50). Coercion by weakening implies "debilitating the country as a whole" (Byman and Waxman 2002: 50). Generating unrest as a coercive mechanism entails "creating popular dissatisfaction with a regime" (Byman and Waxman 2002: 50). Chenoweth and Stephan's (2011: 10) study of nonviolent resistance movements illustrates how mobilization and "higher levels of participation contribute to a number of mechanisms necessary for success, including enhanced resilience, higher probabilities of tactical innovation, expanded civic disruption (thereby raising the costs to the regime of maintaining the status quo), and loyalty shifts involving the opponent's erstwhile supporters, including members of the security forces."

Denial takes the form of either targeting military units directly or separating elites from their source of power. According to Pape (1996: 19), "denial strategies target the opponent's military ability to achieve its territorial or other political objectives, thereby compelling concessions in order to avoid futile expenditures of further resources . . . denial strategies make no special effort to cause suffering to the opponent's society, only to deny the opponent the hope of achieving the disputed territorial objectives. Thus, denial campaigns focus on the target state's military strategy." According to Byman and Waxman (2002: 78), "denial works when adversary leaders recognize that they cannot gain benefits and will continue to pay costs if they do not concede."

This focus explains why denial forms of coercion tend to be more successful. For Pape (1996: 20), punishment strategies will rarely succeed, risk strategies will fail, and denial strategies will achieve a concession more often as long as they target a state's military strategy. Specifically, he argues that punishment, and their weaker form risk strategies, rely on inflicting pain beyond the reach of conventional military forces (Pape 1996: 20). Under this logic, for cyber operations to produce concessions through punishment, the strategies would have to produce more pain than conventional military force application, a phenomenon we simply have not yet seen. Horowitz and Reiter (2001) similarly find that targeting civilians tends to be unsuccessful in producing concessions. Therefore, the successful coercive strategy should hold military targets of value at risk. If these denial strategies are more successful, this logic should translate to cyber coercion.

Pape (1996) suggests that an alternative to punishment, risk, and denial is decapitation. In this reading, the use of airpower for decapitating enemy leadership and command structures emerged as a targeting strategy during the air campaign in the Gulf War. According to Pape (1996: 78), "regardless of the strength of a state's field forces or military-industrial capacity, if the leadership is knocked out, the whole house of cards comes down. These counter-leadership raids also cause little collateral damage if intelligence about the targets is right."

Scholars extend this decapitation strategy to counterterrorism and counterinsurgency.[5] Most scholarship finds that decapitating (i.e., killing or capturing) militant leaders increases the probability of an insurgency ending and reduces the number and intensity of attacks. Alternatively, Phillips (2011b) demonstrates that decapitation strategies fail when leveraged against drug cartels in Mexico. Since cyber operations have yet to "kill" rival state leaders, we do not incorporate this coercive form into our study.

The literature on terrorism highlights coercive strategies linked to costly signaling (Kydd and Walter 2006; Abrahms 2006). Terrorist groups are seen as too weak to impose their will through direct confrontation and thus seek to persuade a target audience through demonstrating their commitment to the cause (Kydd and Walter 2006: 50). They must find a way to convert otherwise cheap talk into costly signals sufficient to evoke a concession. However, there are limits to these costly signals. Abrahms (2006: 41) finds that terrorism as a form of coercion tends to only work when the attacker retains limited objectives and does not target civilians.

Kydd and Walter (2006: 51) identify five coercive strategies used by terrorist groups: attrition, intimidation, provocation, spoiling, and outbidding. Attrition seeks to persuade the target that the terrorist group is strong enough to impose large costs—a strategy that could be applied to cyber interactions. Intimidation seeks to persuade the target that the terrorist group has the power and resolve to punish disobedience as a form of behavior modification. Provocation entails baiting a target into acting in a manner that alienates the population. Spoiling and outbidding are ways of internally changing the support for a terrorist group among the opposition. Spoiling seeks to decrease support for more moderate opponents. The goal of outbidding is to demonstrate that terrorists have greater resolve than other opposition groups. Each of the logics outlined here helps us draw out the explicit coercive strategies engaged by cyber adversaries.

FORMS OF CYBER COERCION

Rattray (1999: 3) notes, "[early cyber security] studies, however, pay little heed to the relationship between ends sought and the utility of information warfare as a means of achieving those ends." His work (Rattray 1999: 4) suggests that there are four enabling conditions for strategic warfare in cyberspace: (1) offensive freedom of action, (2) significant vulnerability to attack, (3) minimal prospects for escalation, and (4) the ability to target an adversary's center of gravity. All of these conditions propose dramatic and revolutionary effects for cyber strategies. To understand fully the impact of cyber operations we have to connect these strategies to strategic processes.

Existing work on cyber coercion argues that many of the strategies used in conventional coercion are evident in digital interactions. In studying cyber deterrence, Nye (2017) identifies four strategies: punishment, denial, entanglement, and norms. Entanglement and norms are restraining factors, while punishment and denial are traditional coercive options where costs are imposed. As Wolford (2014) demonstrates, resolve is easy to signal in coalitions that go up against strong powers but difficult against weak powers because the risks of escalation are higher and resolve is harder to achieve when the coalition might disintegrate. Entangling factors can then discourage resolute signals and restrain actors from escalation if misperceptions are avoided.

Sharp (2017) sees two successful forms of cyber coercion in examining the Sony Hack: destabilizing leadership and cost imposition. As the costs escalate, the target will have to alter its decision calculus. In this case, Sony capitulated quickly but then reserved its decision to not distribute the movie *The Interview* when the US Government and President Obama came down hard in favor of not giving in to an aggressor. Eventually Sony distributed the movie both by traditional means and through Netflix. While the behavior of the target changed, the outcome was not what North Korea intended. Yet, they did issue a signal about the consequences of satire directed at North Korea, and we have yet to see similar forms of ridicule since the event. While this event was not compellent, since the leadership did not change behavior, it was an effective use of cyber tools to signal to the adversary the potential consequences of ridiculing the leader of North Korea.

Borghard and Lonergan (2017) distill the coercive literature into six distinct cyber strategies: attrition, denial, decapitation, intimidation, punishment, and risk. Four of these strategies build on Pape's (1996) original work on airpower (denial, decapitation, punishment, and risk), while attrition and intimidation parallel insights from the terrorism literature. Drawing from the terrorism literature and its emphasis on how actors produce costly signals, Borghard and Lonergan (2017: 4) integrate Schelling's (1960, 1966) work to argue, "the essence of successful coercion is communication." For Schelling, the target of coercion must understand not only who is coercing them but also what behavior must change for the threats to stop. Libicki (2016: 190) makes the point that understanding the object of coercion is difficult in cyber operations. Most critical networks are not controlled by government actors, which makes understanding the decision-making calculus a critical element of successful coercion.

The importance of clarity collides with the benefits of ambiguity and cognitive limitations in cyber practice. According to Borghard and Lonergan (2017: 5), "in the vast majority of international crisis, political leaders default to ambiguity, rather than clarity, or threats; leaders often prefer to retain flexibility to escape from costly or imprudent commitments or be adaptive in their responses to an adversary's behavior."[6] The structure of the system produces incentives for bluffing that complicates bargaining (Fearon 1995). Cognitive limitations, misperception, and inaccurate frames could cause even clear signals to break down (Jervis 1976).

Cyberspace compounds the dilemmas inherent in coercion. Unless the attempt at cyber coercion is detected, only the initiator may know of its existence. The target does not know what to do if it is unaware of the attempt, leaving them less clear on the intent of the use of power or the resolve of the initiator. Furthermore, "even if a target state realizes it has been attacked, it is difficult to infer the intent" (Borghard and Lonergan 2017: 7). Coercion tends to need clear attribution to send a credible threat. There are benefits to masking intrusions in cyberspace that parallel covert action (Gartkze 2013; Carson and Yarhi-Milo 2017), but the covert is more likely to be overt, though deniable, in the context of a rivalry. When there is a clear enemy, persistence of conflict, and a steady stream of disputes, it is generally clear where attacks are coming from.

States seek coercive concessions by demonstrating their power to hurt digitally and by imposing costs. Actors default to latent signaling of their cyber power because revealing information about capabilities is costly to the attacker in cyberspace. Credibility emerges not just from past actions but also from the potential for future action.

Scholars debate the efficacy of offense and defense in cyberspace. Rattray (1999) argues that offense is easy in cyberspace, giving attackers the advantage. Alternatively, Bryant (2016: 68) argues that defense has the advantage. Specifically, he contends, "a defender will gain local cyberspace superiority by successfully blocking the enemy from achieving his offensive objectives, and protecting friendly access to cyberspace systems." In this conception, denial is critical but maintaining access for the attacking force is paramount.[7]

There is little evidence that the attacker has the advantage in coercive operations. Understanding the type of cyber operation employed is critical in order to understand how costs are increased by the signal, which would then lead to compellent success. In our typology, there are low-cost, low-payoff disruptions and high-cost, high-payoff degrade attacks against critical infrastructure targets. Borghard and Lonergan (2017: 16–17) posit, "disruptive attacks . . . seek to operationally diminish a system to the point that a user lacks confidence in its ability to perform some function . . . governments may find cheap, fast, and easy cyber operations appealing even when they are less effective for the purposes of coercion. Put simply, governments may hit what they can, rather than the optimal target to coerce another state." Neuman and Poznansky (2016) suggest swaggering attacks demonstrate the ability to access networks and cause further harm.

Alternatively, degrade attacks "take two forms: the rare cyber-attacks that generate an effect felt in the physical world, and the more common destruction of digital information, which can be almost as dire as physical attack for many pieces of infrastructure" (Borghard and Lonergan 2017: 16). Seen in this light, the most effective cyber coercive actions, as costly signals, are complex actions that hit well-defended networks seeking to degrade, destroy, or delete information from the target.

Yet, the literature also suggests the utility of espionage as coercive events (Carson and Yahri-Milo 2017). Revealing information, seeking advances in technology and innovation through digital extraction, or altering data are all critical costs that the attacker can impose on the defender when leveraging espionage methods. Deception is a critical factor that is drawn out through cyber methods (Gartzke and Lindsay 2015), and these methods can often be coercive. The key caveat is that not all cyber espionage operations are coercive, some simply seek to keep tabs on an adversary or prepare the landscape for future aggression during a pause in hostilities, but other espionage actions are outright compellent in intent.

Cyber coercion is the power to hurt through digital means and finding ways to produce both costly and cheap signals that alter a larger bargaining situation between, at a minimum, two adversaries. Cyber coercion strategies therefore seek ways of demonstrating power and resolve consistent with altering the behavior of the target. Table 2.2 catalogs the range of strategies referenced as having compellent potential.

The Strategy Turn

We take a broader view and see cyber operations as exerting pressure and influence beyond the realm of traditional coercion. In our study, states use cyber operations to seek a position of advantage relative to their rivals. The focus tends to be on long-term competition, short of total war, that extends beyond coercion by punishment

TABLE 2.2

Cyber Coercive Strategy

Author(s)	Coercive Form	Description	Assessed Effectiveness (*Degree*)	Cyber Strategy
Lindsay and Gartzke (2017)	Disruption	Low-cost cyber operations such as website defacement designed	Low	Cyber Disruption
Borghard and Lonergan (2017)	Intimidation	to harass and limit escalation	Moderate	
Neuman and Poznansky (2016)	Swaggering	Demonstrating capabilities and resolve through burning vulnerabilities and revealing network access	Moderate	
Lindsay (2017)	Espionage	The use of cyber operations to steal information, deceive, influence through propaganda, or conduct covert action like sabotage and counterintelligence	Moderate	Cyber Espionage
Gartzke and Lindsay (2015)	Deception	The manipulation of information for offensive or defensive advantage in cyberspace	Moderate	
Poznansky and Perkoski (2016)	Blackmail	Leveraging stolen assets for coercive gain	Moderate	

(*Continued*)

TABLE 2.2 Continued

Author(s)	Coercive Form	Description	Assessed Effectiveness (*Degree*)	Cyber Strategy
Libicki (2016), Borghard and Lonergan (2017)	Denial [d]	Attack the plan; increase the cost of achieving military objective through destroying or disabling command networks or critical capabilities	High	Cyber Degradation
Borghard and Lonergan (2017)	Attrition	Erode adversary capability and lower probability they can retaliate through cyber raiding and exhaustion tactics attacking networks that enhance military capability	High	
Sharp (2017)	Cost Imposition	Cyber operations impose costs through forcing the target to patch vulnerabilities and lowering their reputation	High	
Borghard and Lonergan (2017)	Decapitation [b,c]	Target C4ISR networks to achieve strategic paralysis or destabilize leadership reputation and standing in domestic coalitions.	High	
Nye (2017) [a]	Punishment [b]	Cyber operations attacking civilian infrastructure and networks	Low	Assessed by Target Type [e]
Borghard and Lonergan (2017)	Risk	Ratcheting up punishment through targeting civilian infrastructure and civilian networks	Low	

TABLE 2.2 Continued

Author(s)	Coercive Form	Description	Assessed Effectiveness (*Degree*)	Cyber Strategy
Gartzke and Lindsay (2017)	Control [d]	Active defense measures that increase costs of coercion and defend use of friendly networks	Low	*Not assessed*

[a] Nye focuses on deterrence not compellence. We infer this coercive form, unlike entanglement and norms, would have a compellent corollary.

[b] Also in Stephen Walt. 2010. "Is the Cyber Threat Overblown?" *Foreign Policy*, March 30.

[c] Also in Sharp (2017) as destabilizing leadership.

[d] Nye (2017) discusses deterrence by denial, but the logic is similar to control.

[e] Punishment and risk are analyzed later with respect to target type.

and denial to signaling as a form of escalation management, propaganda, and manipulating the long-term balance of information.[8]

First, rival states use cyberspace to signal to their adversaries and advance their interests beneath a threshold likely to generate a deadly retaliation. These cyber disruptions reflect "low-cost, low-payoff irritants widely available" (Gartzke and Lindsay 2017: 3–4). These moves represent ambiguous signals that lack clear illumination of costs imposed beyond what the imagination can create or perceive.

Intimidation and swaggering, though treated as coercive in the physical domain, are forms of disruption in the digital domain. For Borghard and Lonergan (2017: 37–38), "in cyberspace, intimidation typically takes the form of website defacement and e-mail spamming campaigns. While these operations are technically easy to conduct because they involve fewer resources and a lower skill set compared to other types of operations, their impact on the recipient can vary dramatically. The effect these attacks produce is typically perceived as an annoyance, rather than a strategic message, because these types of attacks are fairly common and easy to recover from." While this interpretation of effect is technologically unambiguous, the perceptive and psychological impact of such tactics can vastly outweigh their technical impact. The 2007 attack on Estonia is a dramatic example of a low-cost effort that achieved dramatic effect, yet there was no concession.

Swaggering as a form of disruption involves similar low-cost, low-risk signaling. For Neuman and Poznansky (2016), an actor can "burn vulnerabilities," that is, reveal a low-level network intrusion, as a means of signaling capability and resolve. The logic is similar to terrorism as a coercive form of intimidation designed to signal power and resolve (Kydd and Walter 2006: 66). As a form of intimidation, cyber swaggering involves selectively revealing capabilities in order to influence a bargaining episode. These low-level incidents reduce uncertainty about otherwise secret cyber capabilities, and represent a form of sunk costs signaling resolve and communicating issue salience. That said, they tend to be so low-cost their logic is less to compel than it is to pressure and influence. They are indirect as opposed to direct.

Building on these approaches, we define cyber disruption as *low-cost, low-pain initiatives that harass a target to influence their decision calculus*. Examples of cyber disruptions include distributed denial of service (DDoS) attacks or defacements of high-profile government webpages, or escalating risk by hacking financial services networks via malware. Cyber disruptions are typically short in duration. Initiators do not invest extensive resources in these quick attacks. These ambiguous signals are easy to employ, but more importantly, they are easy to misinterpret and overreact to.

Cyber disruptions seek to upset some aspect of the target's presence and posture in cyberspace as a means of signaling. Specifically, they can be thought of as bargaining efforts designed to demonstrate that a particular course of action is undesirable to the initiator. In this respect, the attack signals the ability to inflict future pain and costs, makes the target question their network security and behavior, and casts a shadow of the future. The target, knowing it will interact with the initiator in the future, may alter its decision calculus and change its behavior.

Cyber disruptions meet their objective if they successfully disrupt some aspect of the target's network. For example, during the 2008 Russian invasion of the Georgian separatist region of South Ossetia, widespread defacements plagued the Georgian government's websites for a time in order to sow confusion in the government and larger populace. The damage is usually not severe enough to cause long-term impacts. Given that cyber disruptions are low-cost and low-pain, the probability of witnessing these events is high but the probability of successfully changing the behavior of the target is low and will be rarely witnessed. Rather, the logic is to shape the competition as opposed to produce an immediate outcome.

While it is tempting to treat cyber disruption as a form of coercion by punishment, such a move would be flawed. First, the danger with disruption operations may be in categorizing them as violence. Kilovaty (2017) argues, "disruption . . . is something an information society cannot tolerate, particularly when directed against civilians and civilian objects. That could be just as violent as destruction, if not more." This discourse is typical from those who believe we have missed the onset of cyber war and cyber "Pearl Harbor" (Lawson and Middleton 2016). Cyber disruptions send signals to probe a rival state's capabilities and intentions. They do not kill people. Furthermore, they inflict short-term damage often easily repaired and tend, in the case of website defacements, to use symbols that amplify larger political warfare campaigns that use propaganda to influence targeted populations.

Where cyber disruptions shape and signal rival states short of producing concessions, cyber espionage has a more complex logic. Espionage is an undertheorized area in international relations. Its reach can extend from the realm of spies seeking to identify capabilities and intentions to more diffuse practices such as deception, planting false information, and stealing trade secrets to advance economic interests. In our treatment, cyber espionage is a broad category capturing intrusions that steal information, conducting digital deception operations, blackmail, false flags, or other forms of subversion and manipulation aided by digital means. This broad range of activities, variously labeled strategic services, special activities, and covert action is an enduring form of statecraft. Kautilya, a fourth-century-BCE political advisor, detailed multiple forms of subversion, blackmail, and treachery required to advance power and influence in the Mauryan Empire (Watson 1992: 58–63; Modelski 1964). Lindsay (2017) notes, when speaking of cyber espionage, "the dark arts of surveillance and subversion find new expression in cyberspace, and most cyber operations rely on deception to collect intelligence or steal intellectual property, exert influence through propaganda or sabotage, or defend against these activities." Cyber espionage is about altering the balance of information to produce a bargaining position of advantage. For Lindsay (2017), "stolen data can be used not only to improve decision making by policymakers and commanders, but also to influence foreign opinion through blackmail or propaganda."

The most elusive, but arguably most important, attribute of cyber espionage is the ability to manipulate information for coercive effect. Lindsay (2017) posits, "cyber operations are most useful on the lower end of [a spectrum of covert action] to manipulate information and opinion." Consider the United States election in 2016 and how Russia used cyber espionage alongside propaganda to undermine Hillary Clinton's candidacy. Russian operatives leveraged stolen e-mails as a means of influencing public opinion through bot networks and the traditional media (ODNI Report 2017).

Espionage integrates the art of the ruse and baiting an adversary into a serious misstep. For Gartzke and Lindsay (2017a: 21), "deception is an underappreciated strategy that is particularly promising for network protection. . . . deception can confuse, delay, misdirect, or even harm the attacker, for instance by enabling the exfiltration of harmful malware to infect the attacker's home network." Manipulation can cause an adversary to make a suboptimal decision, giving their rival an enduring position of advantage. In other words, espionage is not just about stealing information but also it helps rival states shape long-term competition.

The most destructive form of cyber espionage may be the manipulation of information. This would entail either gaining access to information or altering it. As Rattray (1999: 10) highlights, "vicious—but bloodless—information wars in which corporate databases are savagely raided, manipulated, or destroyed for advantage in the global marketplace are held up as the wave of the future." This proposed future cyber hellscape has not materialized, but it is the most devastating implication of espionage activities.

Building on these approaches, we define cyber espionage as efforts to alter the balance of information or manipulate perceptions by digital means in a manner that produces bargaining benefits. These benefits may be long-term material components of military power, such as stealing the plans for the F-35, or intellectual property that helps long-term economic growth. We also distinguish between long-term and short-term cyber espionage operations. Short-term cyber espionage gains access that enables a state to leverage critical information for an immediate advantage. Long-term cyber espionage seeks to manipulate the decision-calculus of the opposition far into the future through leveraging information gathered during cyber operations to enhance credibility and capability. This access may even involve setting honeypots to disrupt an attacker or manipulating public opinion through releasing sensitive information. The outcome of espionage is not compellence but a position of advantage that helps a rival state manage long-term competition.

⌈Consistent with bargaining theory (Schelling 1962), by deceit or bluff you can create information asymmetries that increase the costs of resistance and increase the probability that you can coerce the target. Cyber espionage operations are often low cost and low risk in that escalation tends to be contained to the espionage domain, but increasingly states are employing the information they use to coerce the opposition. Cyber espionage operations can include activities ranging from Trojans, viruses, worms, and keystroke logs to achieve their objective by infiltrating the opposition, collecting or altering information, and leaving the scene without being noticed at the time.⌋

Information is the equalizer for many states. In theory, increased information allows a rising power to catch up, leaping technology by generations through stealing intellectual property or military plans. Digital means of intelligence gathering can serve as the great equalizer, allowing a state to gather up vast amounts of information to bolster a stuck or failing industry. Altering information is the more insidious form of cyber manipulation.

Similarly, manipulating public opinion can alter the balance of power and resolve in a dispute. Manipulation of the information environment means more than just altering the bargaining situation, but also changing the beliefs, prior knowledge, and expectations of the target state by altering key sources of data. For China, this means developing means of acquiring research not otherwise achievable by normal means. For Russia, manipulation of information is not a new method, but, aided by digital processes, the strategy becomes more powerful, unbound by time and space, and pernicious in altering the behavior of targeted populations through large-scale distribution.

The problem with cyber espionage arises in digesting and reproducing technological advances. There are large, often underappreciated transaction costs associated with filtering through stolen information (Lindsay 2015). Shifting through millions of files and source documents can be a time-consuming task that consumes massive amounts of computing power. Even if the information is digested, it is not a sure path to innovation and replication. Gilli and Gilli (2017) argue that diffusion of drone technology has so far been difficult, since organizational capacity and knowledge about the process of production might be lacking, even if the specific technology is not. We likely would see the same process in the context of cyber espionage.

Furthermore, as the 2016 Russian cyber and disinformation campaign during the US election demonstrates, stolen data designed to manipulate public opinion may not have the desired effect. We can locate no evidence of a direct link between Wikileaks revelations and changing the mind of the average voter (Valeriano, Maness, and Jensen 2017a). Instead, it likely reinforced preconceived negative views of Hillary Clinton, rather than altering views.

Whereas cyber disruption and espionage focus on long-term competition and shaping rival behavior, degradation is a more direct, blunter instrument of coercion. Cyber degradation is a category that captures denial, attrition, decapitation, and cost-imposing strategies. These variants all share a common goal: to change the cost-benefit calculation of an adversary through disabling a critical system or capability, commonly through sabotage. It is thought that by degrading the target's capabilities, the attacker can invoke a change in behavior in the defender.

Our concept of cyber degradation builds on a concept of attrition and denial. Borghard and Lonergan (2017: 34) suggest that cyber attrition can

> erode the adversary's military capability such that the target can no longer resist . . . in particular, cyber raiding—targeting an enemy in its weakest areas—is the common tactic of attrition . . . it is difficult, if not impossible, to destroy a state's military capabilities through the exercise of cyber power alone. However, it is theoretically possible to force a gradual erosion of its capabilities—especially of its confidence in them—as vulnerable targets are attacked and as governments are forced to divert considerable resources to investigating and repairing them until the cost of continued resistance becomes unbearable.

Nye (2017: 56) finds that cyber denial strategies undermines the target's resources and changes the cost-benefit calculation at the heart of coercion. Building on Pape's (1996: 13) original formulation, Borghard and Lonergan (2017: 35) argue, "a denial strategy involves increasing the costs to an adversary such that achieving its military objectives—such as taking a piece of territory—becomes prohibitive or impossible."

Assuming leadership or critical command and control networks are a center of gravity, decapitation has a similar logic. Following Pape (1996: 79), Borghard and Lonergan (2017: 36) argue, "decapitation strategies seek to achieve strategic paralysis by targeting command and control centers, leadership, critical economic nodes, and key weapons systems." For Sharp (2017: 13–15), decapitation is a form of destabilizing the leadership. Cyber operations can achieve coercive effects from blackmail, degrading, coalitions, or denying open communication. As previously discussed, our approach does not examine decapitation. We focus on coercion between rivals, which tends to occur predominately during peacetime competition, during the years 2000–2014. Cyber decapitation likely has more utility as a coercive approach in wartime.

Last, cyber degradation could involve cost-imposition strategies.[9] Sharp (2017: 14) declares, "cyber operations are well suited to impose costs. The interconnectedness of modern information technology means that the consequences or a cyber operation will extend beyond the targeted system [leading to] other costs including its international and domestic political reputation." Beyond reputational costs, cyber degradation, by disabling a key system, can increase the cost-benefit calculation at the core of coercion, forcing a change in behavior because of the possible effects.

Building on these approaches, we define cyber degradation as high-cost, high-pain efforts that seek to degrade or destroy critical capabilities through computer networks. These operations destabilize the target, highlighting critical vulnerabilities and pushing the target onto a defensive footing that limits their ability to respond to a crisis. By raising the costs or risks associated with responses, cyber degradation as a form of coercion increases the probability of concession. They are costly signals, where disruption and espionage are weak inducements that shape long-term competition.

Degrade operations tend to involve more sophisticated viruses, worms, and logic bombs. The actions are costly and complicated, requiring cooperation among many different bureaucratic units and sometimes different countries. The Stuxnet operation cost over 300 million dollars and involved multiple agencies in the United States and Israel (Sanger 2012b). The operation was a large, complex project beyond the reach of most states. For this reason, these operations are rare, even though the likelihood of success is higher than other forms of cyber coercion. Cyber degradation is more likely to evoke concessions due to the resources, collaboration, and effort required to launch such operations. These insights lead to our first hypothesis:

H1: Cyber degradations are more likely to produce concessions

THE LOGIC OF COERCION

Two mechanisms could explain whether cyber degradation produces coercive outcomes: power or resolve. Coercive exchanges between historic antagonists constitute a form of bargaining. In these exchanges, "exploitation of potential force" helps states gain concessions in "variable-sum games," where outcomes for each side are dependent on the choices of the other side (Schelling 1960: 5). Furthermore, these interactions produce a "powerful common interest in reaching an outcome that is not enormously destructive of values to both sides" (Schelling 1960: 6). Coercion only works if it does not result in significant escalation. If a state accurately assesses its rival's power and resolve, it can determine how much to concede to avoid a conflict spiral. The problem is that it is difficult to assess power and resolve. Therefore, cyber coercion is a particularly limited form of coercion that will fail to achieve concessions most of the time.

Relative power has the potential to affect coercion. Military might should, in theory, produce concessions (Art 1980; Snyder and Diesing 1977). The larger the power imbalance, the more painful it is to resist. For Press (2005: 24), "decisionmakers are not interested in abstract measures of national power; when they confront threats during real crises they ask themselves: can the adversary do what he threatens to do and achieve his objective at a reasonable cost?" This assessment tends to preface offensive military capabilities in the air and naval domain as well as economic instruments.

Uncertainty about relative power and intentions shapes how states form their foreign policies to influence adversaries and allies. This logic extends to coercion. In realism, the subject of uncertainty is rooted in the structure of the international system.[10] While in theory it may be easier to approximate the military capabilities of great powers (Wagner 2007), there is still a question of how those capabilities combine with domestic structures (Lobell, Ripsman, and Taliaferro 2009), cognitive bias (Jervis 1976), organizational interests (Snyder 1984), and/or prevailing strategic preferences (Johnston 1998). Soft power and perception then become critical factors in understanding how power is observed and how states respond to coercive events (Nye 2004).

From a bargaining perspective, private information can cloud judgments about an adversary's capabilities (Fearon 1995).[11] States can bluff and overstate their capabilities in an effort to produce a concession. In retrospect, the Iraqi government in 2003 appears to have exaggerated its possession of weapons of mass destruction. Alternatively, states may overestimate their own capabilities relative to those of an adversary (Blainey 1973: 122; Sescher 2007: 29).

Recent research challenges the traditional view that, according to Thucydides, the strong do what they will and weak suffer what they must. Sescher (2010) argues powerful actors often find coercive diplomatic campaigns less effective because assessments of military power interfere with the ability to estimate resolve, leading to suboptimal crisis outcomes. Powerful actors overestimate their own capabilities and discount the ability of weaker actors to endure pain. Furthermore, Haun (2015) argues that the desire for simple survival on the part of weaker actors creates incentives to resist more powerful actors. Specifically, Haun (2015: 40) contends, "domestic and international survival concerns place an upper limit on the demands to which a weak state is willing to concede." This process is evident in the interactions between the United States and Iraq, where Baghdad had been reluctant to concede due to internal and external challenges that would be exacerbated by concessions to American demands.

Power matters less than resolve, demonstrated willingness to act, and credibility. Rather, bargaining power between rivals should arise from each side's perceptions of the other's "comparative resolve" (Snyder and Diesing 1977). Rather than signal strength through latent capacity, rivals can signal resolve through limited escalation, what Schelling (1960: 9) calls the "exploitation of potential force."[12]

This logic should extend to the cyber domain. The latent cyber capacity of a state conducting a degradation operation, measured as its connectivity and the knowledge capital required to hack rivals, does not increase the probability of a concession. Cyber power is less important than demonstrated resolve. Furthermore, differences in latent cyber capacity should have less of an effect on the rate of concession than the conventional military balance (Gartzke 2013: 63). Cyber operations are additive. They complement rather than replace traditional forms of coercion. Rival states still care about the location of aircraft carrier battlegroups and bomber wings.

The question then is what produces resolve in the context of cyber exchanges between rivals. Past actions and the situational context of a crisis both build a reputation for resolve. In a rivalry with repeated crises, past actions are a critical factor in predicting behavior. If a state in a rivalry experiences multiple and repeated past conflict interaction, this serves as a signal for both credibility and resolve independent of the intention of a cyber operation.

In addition to a reputation for resolve, credibility can emerge from issue salience. The value of a particular issue varies by type (Hensel 2001; Press 2005). Different issues produce different "reputation stakes" (Press 2005: 25). For example, a state's territorial integrity tends to have higher salience than a peripheral dispute. The survival interests of the weaker party in a crisis can also alter rational crisis bargaining (Haun 2015).

We must also consider multiple intervening and antecedent conditions affecting efforts to coerce an adversary. Regime type can create audience costs or domestic blowback from backing down in a crisis (Schultz 2001; Weeks 2008). Actor motivation (including fear, honor, and issue salience) can influence the efficacy of coercion. Lebow (2007: 170) finds that almost all episodes of compellence reviewed in the works of Thucydides end in failure, highlighting two important aspects of coercion: "the widespread belief that others can be dissuaded or persuaded by credible threats based on superior military capability; and the propensity of people who are the targets of threats to downplay risks and costs when it is contrary to their desires or needs." Similarly, other studies find that five seminal cases of compellent threats by Sparta all failed despite the military imbalance, due to the target's ideological motivation and willingness to pay short-term costs in blood and treasure to preserve long-term strategic advantages (Missiou-Ladi 1987).

The fact that most cyber coercion is anonymous creates a "credibility problem" (Gartzke 2013: 47). For Press (2005: 11), "a country's credibility is affected by its record for keeping or breaking past commitments . . . a history of breaking commitments reduces credibility, while a history of keeping commitments increases it." Credibility is critical for success in coercive operations. Holding true to commitments will enhance a state's ability to coerce the opposition.

The ambiguity of cyberspace complicates signaling. States must know whom to concede to, and in cyber operations it is often not clear that the leadership of the aggressive state actually ordered the attacks. Borghard and Lonergan (2017: 20) declare that attribution issues and the benefits of concealing cyber operations make it difficult to demonstrate credibility. There are also reassurance dilemmas in cyberspace. The target needs to know that if it complies with the threat it will not be subject to punishment.[13] These parallel issues highlight the inherent issues with ambiguous signals in cyberspace. While the attribution problem is clearly overstated, in the context of cyber actions the ambiguity issue exacerbates credibility problems.

The number of past cyber incidents should not alter the probability of a concession. Cyber degradation works as a costly signal not as a reminder of the past interactions. Just as latent cyber capacity should not influence compellence, past actions should not alter the rate of concessions in rival interaction in cyberspace.

Cyber Strategy: Signaling and Escalation

The logic of cyber strategy is not just about coercion. In fact, only cyber degradation should produce near-term concessions in the digital domain. Rather, the utility of cyber operations rests as much in their use to signal rivals engaged in long-term competition, often centered on managing escalation risk.

How and why crises escalate is a major area of study in international relations (Leng 2004).[14] Crises tend to be form of competitive risk-taking. These competitive situations are "disputes over measurement" (Blainey 1988: 122), as each side seeks information about their adversary. Each party assumes risk by taking escalatory moves such as military displays or economic threats to illuminate the other side's degree of interest and mobilizable capabilities.[15] Escalation allows actors to test resolve. Snyder and Diesing (1977) portray crisis escalation as a means of determining the balance in capability and resolve short of war. Minimal escalation moves, including covert action, assume risk to test a rival state's resolve. This process can create a "tit-for-tat" cycle of reciprocal behavior until the parties find the level at which the crisis stabilizes or one of the actors concedes. In other words, what can appear as a conflict spiral, each side escalating, can actually stabilize a crisis by communicating information about resolve and capabilities.[16]

This concept of escalation as a learning process finds support in the crisis literature. Bueno de Mesquita, Morrow, and Zorick (1997) argue that crises allow states to gain information about capabilities and, as a result, moderate escalation dynamics. Jones, Bremer, and Singer (1996: 201) contend that the longer a dispute continues, the higher probability of settlement. Brecher and Wilkenfeld (2000: 843) find that states tend to match behavior. Similarly, Gochman and Leng (1983) posit that states tend to escalate to higher levels of hostility only if the crisis is triggered by a physical threat. The vast majority of crises tend to involve small moves to test the opponent. Leng (1993: 86) argues that only 15% of crises match the expectations of conflict-spiral models of escalation.

Yet, rivalry has the potential to alter this competitive learning process. Colaresi and Thompson (2002) find that rivalry increases the likelihood of escalation. Rivalry amplifies uncertainty and worst-case bias assumptions. States in a rivalry are more likely to use force or take advantage of their opponent's vulnerability to gain a position of advantage (Blainey 1973), a phenomenon Colaresi and Thompson (2002: 272) refer to as the "death watch hypothesis." Furthermore, rivalry can trump conflict-constraining factors such as regime type (Rasler and Thompson 2001).

Do cyber operations produce escalatory commitment issues or offer a form of ambiguous signaling that limits escalations? In the bargaining literature, commitment issues refer to incentives not to trust the other party. This propensity to mistrust shapes rational decision-making, producing suboptimal outcomes.[17] Mistrust is clearly high in the cyber security field, as sharing of information on vulnerabilities and capabilities is limited to nonexistent, even in domestic contexts.

Seen from a bargaining perspective, the prisoner's dilemma, security dilemma, spiral model of arms races, offense-defense balance, coups, and democratic transitions are all examples of commitment issues.[18] Commitment issues produce a general inefficiency condition that can lead to bargaining failures, an escalation as opposed to some degree of concession, based on assessments about power (Powell 2006: 181). Uncertainty produces suboptimal outcomes.

Shifts in relative power and offensive advantages can create incentives for preemptive first-strikes and preventive military action designed to ward off concessions likely as the balance of power shifts (Powell 1999, 2006). Offensive advantages or shifting power should create more unstable crises.[19] If there were a large expected change in future cyber power, commitment issues could produce incentives to escalate.

Uncertainty about intentions and the threat of an actor reneging on their commitments is a dynamic at the heart of the prisoner's dilemma. These commitment issues create incentives for "defecting" and securing inefficient short-term gains. In the classic prisoner's dilemma, an actor faces a choice between either "cooperating" or "defecting." Applied to coercion, states confront a choice between conceding or escalating.

Given that cyber operations are a relatively new phenomenon, one would also expect these disputes to generate additional uncertainty about capabilities. This uncertainty can be tied to Blainey's (1973: 122) classic explanation for the causes of war, "wars usually result when the fighting states disagree about relative strength." The literature argues that new technologies of coercion shift relative power and can create incentives for preemptive action (Powell 1999, 2006). Given the initially covert nature of cyber intrusions, they exacerbate information asymmetries about the state's intentions (Powell 1999). While collecting information on capabilities is possible, it is also difficult and prone to inaccuracy, given the hidden nature of cyber budgets (Craig and Valeriano 2016). The difficulty of identifying cyber capabilities creates further challenges for rivals seeking to estimate relative capabilities in a crisis.

Commitment issues have implications for escalation dynamics in cyberspace. In the offense-defense balance, changes in factors ranging from geography and alliance dynamics to military technology can create offensive advantages.[20] As they represent a unique "technology of coercion" (Powell 1999: 14), there are reasons to expect new capabilities like cyber methods to amplify offensive biases. The perception that defense is difficult often colors the strategic planning inherent in cyber conflict. Second, changes in relative national power create distributional effects that motivate rising states to challenge rivals (Powell 1999: 20, 2004). Seen in this light, it is tempting to believe that a change in cyber power should be associated with higher crisis hostility levels.

Alternatively, cyber strategies can be viewed as ambiguous signals that limit escalation. There is no evidence that offensive dominance makes it more likely powerful states will intervene to protect the status quo. More often than not, when a strong state escalates against a weaker power, that state is not gaining strength, but rather seeking to upset regional norms against the acquisition of nuclear power, such as in the case of the Stuxnet attack, and similar cyber degradation attempts directed against North Korea's ballistic missile program. Escalation in cyberspace is likely a function of norms, past behavior, and resolve rather than capability leveling.

In the coercion literature, actorss send signals that change the perceived costs of action. The costlier the signal, the more likely a state is to concede. Costly signals are threats designed to achieve a concession short of war (Fearon 1992, 1997). Actors engaged in competitive interactions tend to exaggerate their capabilities or project resolve to push the competition into conflict (Fearon 1995). Most actors seek to get the maximum concession short of assuming the risk of conflict or using precision resources. Talk is cheap, and because of this dynamic, actors have incentives to speak loudly and not back up threats with actual action. Therefore, there is a need to ensure the signal is seen as being backed up by force, the stick, if the first attempt does not invoke a behavior change.

There are usually two ways to make a coercive signal more credible: mobilizing enough military forces to back up the rhetoric, known as sunk costs, or making commitments to domestic audiences that can hold leaders accountable, known as audience costs.[21] The costlier the signal to the coercer, the more likely it is they will carry out the threat.

How do actors produce a costly signal, given the inherent ambiguity and attribution limitations surrounding cyber capabilities? Neuman and Poznansky (2016) propose costly signals can emerge from "burning vulnerabilities," revealing a successful intrusion in an adversary's network. This allows the aggressor to send a signal about credibility and intention. The question then is why would a state waste a zero-day vulnerability against a target? According to Neuman and Poznansky (2016), "the burned vulnerability does not inflict pain itself, but works by revealing the sophistication of these latent weapons." Yet, these burned vulnerabilities are often of limited value and likely have short lifespans. For example, why keep a vulnerability secret if it applies to Windows XP or 7, when these systems are rarely used? This idea fits in with Libiciki's (2007) contention that cyber actions deplete through time.

We argue that low-level cyber actions are signaling mechanisms designed to limit future escalation and establish credibility. If vulnerabilities are burned, it is not a demonstration of capability but rather a demonstration of credibility. The target will then wonder what other vulnerabilities that the attacker has at their disposal, as the initiator has already been successful in invoking a breach and is apparently willing to disclose credible efforts to breach networks. The capacity to achieve successful intrusions into targeted networks invokes the shadow of the future for successive cyber actions. If a state is able to breach a system once, it is likely they will do it again in the future. However, this signal is limited and temporary. The ability of the defender to respond to initial breaches is quite standard in the cyber security field, and, barring continued negligence, targets are harder to penetrate a second time.

The use of cyber strategies offers a new forum for tacit bargaining and signaling between rivals designed to probe intentions and manage escalation. Traditional measures of resolve link to credibility, as the actors assume the costlier the signal, the more credible. Though the ambiguity of cyberspace limits coercive potential, it offers a means of probing rivals and testing resolve while limiting rival response. We refer to this dynamic as ambiguous signaling, and see its manifestation in the cyber realm as extending the logic of covert action to a new domain. This process limits dramatic escalation; low-level breaches and disruptions represent the process of communication in this battlespace rather than standard escalation to violence. In this context, we must rethink what escalation means in cyberspace.

In peacetime, rival states expect covert activities short of war (Carson 2016: 114). While a state does not want an individual act revealed initially, they expect its effect will signal to an adversary that the initiating state has sufficient capability and resolve to escalate a crisis. Libicki (2016: 281) suggests, "the decision to escalate via cyberspace may signal a disinclination to escalate via kinetic attack." Along these lines, covert cyber action forms a particular form of tacit collusion between rivals interested in avoiding uncontrolled escalation (Carson 2016: 114).

Rivals are less interested in using cyber coercion to force a humiliating, short-term concession than they are in avoiding escalation and simply signaling displeasure. The ambiguity of cyberspace, like earlier covert action and political warfare, may "minimize reputational stakes and preserve freedom of action" (Carson 2016: 104). Cyber coercion, like covert action, can be a tool of escalation management

As an ambiguous signal, the intent of cyber operations is to limit escalation and probe rival intentions. Not all coercion is about producing immediate concessions. Schelling (1960: 5) sees competitive interactions between states as bargaining situations where "the ability of one participant to gain his ends is dependent to an important degree on the choices or decisions that the other participant will make. The bargaining may be explicit, as when one offers a concession; or it may be by tacit maneuver." Fearon (1995: 401) finds that because of information asymmetries, bargaining and coercion involve a "risky process of discovery." For Powell (2004), uncertainty about the costs of fighting or the distribution of power itself creates incentives for probing an adversary and "learning while fighting." States can use small, coercive acts short of costly promises to domestic constituents or mobilizing their military to screen their opponents (Powell 2006: 345).

Schelling (1960: 87) theorizes, "the mixture of conflict and mutual dependence that epitomizes bargaining situations" puts a premium on communicating intentions, either directly or tacitly through action, and gaining intelligence about the other side's next move. In bargaining situations, "the best choice for either [actor] depends on what he expects the other to do, knowing that the other is similarly guided, so that each is aware that each must try to guess what the second guesses the first will guess the second to guess and so on, in the familiar spiral of reciprocal expectations" (Schelling 1960: 87). There is an established literature in economics looking at tacit collusion in noncooperative business competition (Vasconcelos 2005). Similarly, Carson (2016) has examined covert action as a form of tacit collusion by states seeking to avoid unintended escalation.

Furthermore, rivals engaged in long-term competition make coercive decisions under the "shadow of the future" (Axelrod 1984). The definition of "rivalry" assumes a series of repeated interactions. For Sescher (2010: 18), multiple-round coercive exchanges produce a situation in which the coercer uses the initial rounds to identify their opponents' resolve and capabilities, using a separating equilibrium to differentiate among weak targets, with low resolve and/or low power, and tough targets, with high resolve and/or high power. Rivals may use low-level or covert incidents, such as cheap talk, to retaliate and establish a tit-for-tat (Axelrod 1984) process to manage escalation.

These dynamics, which include probing an adversary's power and resolve as well as seeking to reduce escalation risk, should extend to cyber coercion. Cyber operations as low-cost, lower-risk ambiguous signaling mechanisms enable states to signal resolve and avoid escalation. Despite their revolutionary appeal, cyber methods do not necessarily produce escalation risks. They are a form of signaling that help states gain a position of advantage while still communicating the risks of escalation. Disruptions are a cheap means of accessing networks and harassing rivals. Even espionage, if outed, signals risks, producing signaling benefits even when access is lost. This insight leads to our second hypothesis.

H2: Cyber operations produce limited escalation

Past interactions will likely be associated with limited escalation, but this is part of the process of rivalry tit-for-tat bargaining. In the context of rivalry, the ability to coerce can be enhanced thought multiple interactions where the initiating state gets a measure of the target state's ability to withstand demands. Yet, this process is dependent on a certain number of interactions. Leng (1983) finds that states that conceded more than three times in the past are more likely to escalate to war after this cut point because the reputation costs for backing down are extreme for domestic political audiences.

Coercive Strategies

Whereas cyber disruptions and espionage signal and alter the balance of information to help states gain a position of advantage in long-term competition, degradation is coercive. Coercion changes behavior by manipulating the costs and benefits of action (Pape 1996: 80). These signals rely on a threat or even the limited application of some form of influence, such as economic sanctions, limited airstrikes, or blockades, to alter an adversary's decision-making calculus (Byman and Waxman 2002: 3). Understanding the form and elements of coercive attempts, their variation, and specific classification is a key task in estimating the effectiveness of compellence operations. We need to understand how degradation works, ideally as a campaign that combines other cyber capabilities with other instruments of power.

Earlier studies of international crises find that how rival states apply coercive strategies and pressure as part of long-term competition is a better predictor of outcomes than comparative capabilities (Levy 1988: 507, 1993: 122–123, Leng 2004). Status quo powers tend to use "reciprocating strategies" (Leng 1993) that maximize aspects of the tit-for-tat logic (Axelrod 1984), often leveraging nonmilitary instruments or limiting the use of military power to threats and displays. Rival states open with a demonstration of resolve that combines sticks and carrots, or negative and positive coercive inducements, and seek more cooperative moves in the next interaction (Leng 1993, 2004). States use a variety of actions to demonstrate resolve and seek leverage short of war.

The combination of instruments matters. The cumulative effects and broader diplomatic context can affect whether or not states gain a position of relative advantage in a rivalry. Synergies and combinations are more likely to produce concessions (Byman and Waxman 2002: 31). For Byman and Waxman (2002: 20), "coercers seldom rely exclusively on one instrument at a time." They apply pressure over time, incrementally changing the relative threat of force, by combining activities ranging from low-cost, low-liability air strikes and support to insurgency to political isolation and economic sanctions. This leads us to our third hypothesis:

H3: There are unique combinations of cyber operations and instruments of power that increase rival concessions.

First, the means matter in cyber strategy. How rival states combine instruments of power should produce a position of advantage, if not be associated with clear concessions. Coercion, like propaganda and espionage efforts, exists not in an isolated moment but usually as part of a larger campaign creating pressure (Byman and Waxman 2002: 33). These campaigns tend to integrate multiple instruments and power and produce a cumulative effect.

The combination of instruments should produce additive effects. For Biddle (2004: 3), military power derives from the "modern system" of force employment, "a tightly interrelated complex of cover, concealment, dispersion, suppression, small-unit independent maneuver, and combined arms . . . [that] reduce vulnerability to even twenty-first century weapons and sensors." The combination of fire and maneuver, often highlighted as blitzkrieg, produces not just battlefield outcomes but also coercive effects (Mearsheimer 1985). Gartkze (2013: 63) argues, "for cyber aggression to have lasting effects, a virtual attack must be combined with physical intervention . . . if cyberwar functions not as independent domain but as part of a broader coordinated military action, then the conventional military balance is the best indicator of where the most important threats exist in cyberspace." As Brantly (2016: 96) notes, cyber actions can be a force multiplier and enhance action in other domains.

This additive effect of combining instruments of power should extend beyond military force or threats of cyber degradation. Most bargaining literature tends to disproportionately focus on military power. At one level, this emphasis makes sense. The power to hurt in its most manifest form as punishment takes the form of physical destruction. However, strategy is the realm of multiple instruments of power and not limited to military force. States can punish along multiple vectors. The power to hurt is not limited to physical attack.

Second, the ways, concepts for achieving relative advantage, matter in cyber strategy. Consistent with the concept of coercive diplomacy, the combination of positive and negative inducements should produce strategic advantage, if not observable concessions. Positive inducements can also be offered in a crisis. In US joint military manuals, planners should think across a DIME construct of diplomatic, information, military, and economic instruments of power. The literature on coercive diplomacy similarly captures this logic of practice and how strategists seek to combine multiple instruments of power alongside positive inducements to seek concessions. For example, one could argue the combination of economic sanctions and diplomatic pressure against a background threat of military action altered the Iranian elite's perceived costs and benefits of continuing to pursue a nuclear program. Observations of cyber coercion demonstrate this logic: the inclusion of positive inducements should make a concession more likely.

Third, the ends, political objectives, matter. Rival states that target civilian infrastructure should produce fewer concessions than those that target critical military and intelligence systems. For Pape (1996), punishment and risk strategies tend to break down because they target civilians. The question is whether this strategic logic extends to the cyber domain. Specifically, does targeting civilian networks as opposed to government networks have an impact on the probability of concession?

Early airpower theory holds a different view. Holding cities hostage forces regimes to capitulate to adversary coercive demands (Douhet 1921). According to Clark and Levin (2009), cyber options represent a means of targeting populations. Civilians will be subject to network-born disruptions targeting critical infrastructure vital to the economy and governance. Chinese officers have openly imagined broad-based targeting of civilian networks, from stock exchanges to power grids, in the opening stages of a conflict with the United States (Liang and Xiangsui 2002).

In determining whether or not to concede in cyberspace, the target of coercion calculates "whether it can absorb the cost and, if so, whether the coercer can ratchet up the cost to the target while avoiding too much cost itself" (Borghard and Lonergan 2017: 13). This calculation depends on the target of cyber coercion. Critical infrastructure (i.e., energy plants and distribution, sewage, hospitals, etc.) and military command and control systems are likely more costly than commercial networks or firms, and hence carry more coercive potential. In this respect, civilian targets have limited utility in cyber rivalry. According to Gartzke (2013: 57), "shutting down power grids, closing airports, or derailing communication could be tremendously costly, but most damage of this type will be fixed quickly and at comparatively modest investment of tangible resources. Regardless, damage of this type is sunk. Losses expected over a given interval cannot be recovered whatever one's reactions and so should not have much direct impact on subsequent policy behavior."

Conclusion

The introduction of cyber operations to the strategy playbook rival states use in long-term competition simply adds a new vector for statecraft and diplomacy. Reading across the coercion literature and new perspectives on cyber operations provides an outline for a theory of how cyber strategy enables states to seek a position of relative advantage and core propositions on the issues of ambiguity, resolve, salience, credibility, and repeated interactions. This theory is limited to rival states.[22]

Cyber operations offer a limited form of coercion. They are not likely to produce concessions when compared to other instruments of power such as economic sanctions or military threats. As ambiguous signals, cyber operations offer a form of tacit bargaining better thought of as covert action than military threats or displays. Cyber operations provide a means of probing rival resolve while seeking a position of advantage and limiting their ability to respond. They provide a mechanism for gaining a position of advantage. Cyber signaling, espionage, and coercion can be stabilizing and evoke a process of normative assurance (Nye 2017).

Cyber operations that focus on degrading adversary critical capabilities and target military and intelligence networks are more likely to produce concessions. Even when cyber operations do compel rivals, we expect to find evidence of higher-order combined approaches that integrate multiple instruments of power and include positive inducements.

Here we predict that cyber coercion will be limited. The factors of credibility, resolve, and capability are all clouded in cyberspace. Understanding this process, though, requires us to empirically examine outcomes in the recent history of cyber interactions. A logically consistent theory built on the literature and sound insights is empty without empirical confirmation. The remainder of the book tests these propositions through a mix of empirical examinations and case studies in order to fully understand the process of cyber coercion.

3

THE CORRELATES OF CYBER STRATEGY

Introduction

This chapter explores the effects of cyber strategies through an empirical lens. We chart an emergent logic of practice that illustrates how rival states compete for influence in the digital domain. While many scholars and pundits have speculated on the theory and nature of cyber operations, there is a lack of empirically grounded work on how states use cyber mechanisms to achieve a position of relative advantage. This step is critical. Much of the cyber security field speculates on the possible without examining the probable. To date, scholars prefer theory generation based on high-profile case studies rather than systematic data collection to study how states employ cyber operations and what these techniques, in the aggregate, imply about cyber power and strategy.

In this chapter, we address this empirical gap and conduct a series of quantitative tests to answer the following questions based on data we have collected covering the years 2000–2014:

1. Do cyber operations compel rival states to alter their behavior?
2. Are there unique escalation dynamics in cyberspace?

The results of the data analyses suggest that cyber operations rarely produce concessions. Despite its promise, the digital domain demonstrates minimal coercive utility to date. Furthermore, a state's latent cyber capacity, as a proxy measure of a state's potential cyber power, is not a significant predictor of coercive potential. The analysis demonstrates that more traditional arbiters of strategic competition such as military or economic power are likely better predictors for explaining rival behavior. National security advisers and political leaders are often driven more by the location of aircraft carriers and the inherent economic costs of crises than they are hordes of hackers writing malicious code. Great power politics appear to be the enduring forms of statecraft that manifest in militarized disputes, economic coercion, and diplomatic threats with cyber security efforts playing a backseat role in determining outcomes.

The strategic logic of cyber strategies appears to lie less in compelling a rival than it does in offering an ambiguous signaling mechanism. Ambiguous signals demonstrate resolve through sunk costs associated with covert action and raising escalation risks. These weak signals seek to shape rival behavior as opposed to producing an immediate concession. Cyber operations appear to be a form of covert action that allows rivals to signal resolve and manage escalation risks (Carson 2016; Carson and Yarhi-Milo 2017). Cyber strategies create limited escalatory dynamics in cyberspace and tend to result in more "tit-for-tat" cross-domain responses in the diplomatic, economic, and military realms. The results likely reflect how rivals use cyber intrusions as a tacit maneuver to test resolve and signal the risks of future escalation rather than actions that result in escalation to war. Much like prior research on rival behavior (Valeriano 2013), we find that rivals have learned to manage relations and the added dimension of cyber activities is only a new form of communication between historic antagonists.

The focus of this chapter is on the discussion and interpretation of the results of the data analyses based on hypotheses testing originating from the theoretical arguments of the previous chapter. The remainder of the chapter proceeds as follows. First, we review and examine cyber strategy in its international context by analyzing a sample of all state-initiated cyber compellent acts with the Dyadic Cyber Incident and Dispute Dataset (DCID), Version 1.1 (Maness, Valeriano, and Jensen 2017). Based on this analysis, cyber operations appear best suited for limited harassment and manipulation objectives through digital espionage and disruption, yet are relatively more successful via cyber degradations acts. In line with earlier coercion studies, there is no single-domain decisive "victory" through compellence if the goal is to alter the behavior of the target state. Second, we refine this analysis through examining differences in power between rivals or demonstrated willingness to launch cyber operations, such as reputation and credibility as aspects of resolve, as efforts to affect political behavior. Finally, we evaluate whether or not cyberspace produces escalatory dynamics between state rivals.

The Dyadic Cyber Incident and Dispute Dataset

To evaluate cyber strategies, we examine publicly attributed cyber incidents between rival states between 2000 and 2014 in the Dyadic Cyber Incident and Dispute Dataset (DCID), Version 1.1 (Maness, Valeriano, and Jensen 2017). While there is always some uncertainty about cataloging conflict events of any sort, this problem is multiplied in the cyber domain, where many actions, namely espionage, are initially covert. Yet, there is reason to believe that publicly documented incidents are a reasonable sample of the entire population of cyber coercive events.

There are limits to secrecy and a certain bargaining power in ambiguity. Most cyber operations do not remain secret after their effect becomes apparent. Intense media interest, cyber security firms rushing to show their prowess and secure contracts, and even government leaks, if not outright reporting by the initiator, help close the awareness gap for cataloging cyber actions. To that end, the study builds on earlier cyber rivalry research (Valeriano and Maness 2014, 2015) to use coding criteria for identifying cyber incidents between rivals.[1]

While any examination may miss cases and sources, this data snapshot represents a focused, reliable, and verified method of examining part of the universe of cyber operations.[2] Rival states (Klein, Diehl, and Goertz 2006) are used because this subsample of states is the most conflict prone, is the most likely to use cyber tactics, and represents an achievable data collection strategy (Valeriano and Maness 2012). Limitations on the data collected are the fact that we can only report and code what is publicly available in the unclassified setting. To this end, we stop our coding process at 2014, as it can take years for many state-initiated cyber events to be made public and attribution is a process that can take experts years to report accurately. However, we move forward with the confidence that we have a reliable snapshot of cyber strategic events to make theoretical justifications, empirical inferences, and policy judgments based on the findings of this chapter and the ones that follow.

Furthermore, focusing on rivals makes data collection achievable because coding all states and nonstate actors would be a prohibitively arduous and time-consuming research process and, while important, is beyond the scope of the current study. Rivals are the most disputatious and war-prone group in the international system (Diehl and Goertz 2001). After years of review, presentations, and evaluation by both classified and unclassified audiences, we argue that our sample is as comprehensive as possible for the universe of cases that are of interest.

The data utilized here represents a clear advance on the DCID version 1.0 in that we expand the coding to include outcomes, strategies, and new actors (Valeriano and Maness 2014, 2015). While the focus remains on rival states given our general inability to code all state actions, we also include conceptions of critical national security targets that are not specifically agents of the states. More importantly for this analysis, version 1.1 of the data includes the coding of interactions from 2000 to 2014 with the specific intent of considering goals of operations, the achievement of objectives, and whether targets were compelled to change their behavior as a result (see Appendix 1). We seek not just to identify incidents but also to catalog associated variables and effects.

The DCID version 1.1 uses 126 rival state pairs extracted from the Klein, Diehl, and Goertz (2006) enduring rival dataset and Thompson's (2001) strategic rival dataset. We identify 192 incidents within multiple disputes extracted from these rival dyads.[3] The initiation must come from the government or there must be evidence that an incident was government sanctioned. For the target state, the target must be a government entity, either military or nonmilitary or a private entity that is part of the target state's national security apparatus (power grids, defense contractors, and security companies), or an important multinational corporation. Nonstate actors or entities can be targets but not initiators as long as they are critical to state-based systems.

We eschew the term "cyberattack" throughout because there are thousands, if not millions of daily "cyberattacks." Our research design assesses cyber operations often made up of multiple intrusions and specifies method, objective, and other attributes that allow us to meaningfully analyze coercion. The coding method specifically follows the Correlates of War (COW) procedures in examining sources throughout history, in the media, and, new for cyber conflict, from government or critical cyber security firm reports (Singer and Small 1994). Most incidents and disputes must be verified and attributed using more detailed sources such as cyber security company reports, long-form investigative reporting, and government policy reports. We have established objective standards for coding cyber incidents and disputes.

Another limitation is that we use subjective evidence to code a change of behavior. We seek to overcome bias and subjectivity by opening our coding process to external review and collaboration by other cyber professionals. In an effort to reinforce replication, we are able to specify our coding procedures and have external sources collaborate our coding choices.

We are also depending on publicly available information on cyber actions, a complicated process that we negotiated in prior studies (Valeriano and Maness 2015). We contend that there are sufficient amounts of information available to the public to assess the efficacy of cyber strategies, particularly coercive degradation attempts.

There are incentives for covert events to become public. Cyber security firms search for malware to justify business models and acquire new clients. There is similarly intense interest in the news media given the novel nature of the technology. Finally, governments need to justify their decision to invest resources.

Appendix 1 goes into more detail as to the specifics of these descriptions of the variables coded. The specific variables and other pertinent information listed in the DCID dataset are as follows:

- the dyad (states involved), with only two states recorded per incident[4]
- the start and presumed end date of interaction
- the method of the incident
- the type of interaction
- the type of target
- the initiator of the interaction (COW country code)
- the specific political objective of the cyber incident
- whether or not the incident successfully achieved its objective
- whether or not the political objective evoked a concessionary change in behavior of the target state
- whether or not a third party was involved in the initiation
- whether or not a third party was a target of the interaction
- whether or not an official government statement was issued by the initiator
- severity level on a 0–10 scale
- damage type

To be counted as an incident, an event requires the manipulation of code or hardware for malicious purposes.[5] The means have to be digital but the target may be physical or digital. For the purposes of this study, we code goals and intent based on the political objectives for each cyber incident initiated by states. Chapter 2 details our definitions for each of the major objective types: cyber disruption (e.g., website defacements, limited Distributed Denial of Servier or DDoS), cyber espionage (e.g., short-term network access and deception, stealing intellectual property), and cyber degradation (e.g., malware sabotaging networks and temporarily eroding capability). These forms of coercion are potentially compellent in that they seek to alter the behavior of a target in the present.[6]

It should be remembered that here we are concerned with political, diplomatic, or military impact and concessions as they relate to independent cyber actions.[7] This conceptualization is very technical as it does not focus on net warfare, the idea of being able to completely destroy an enemy in cyberspace. Rather, we focus how cyber rivals manipulate information to advance political interests. Our conceptualization also goes beyond technical impact. While Stuxnet was an effective technological operation in terms of implementation and delivery, taking a step back and exploring the political and diplomatic impact of the operation when combined with other coercive instruments is the task we are faced with here.

Cyber Coercion Propositions
HYPOTHESIS 1

H1. Cyber degradation is more likely to achieve a concession.

Degradation strategies signal resolve through sunk costs. They require that the specific target in question be disabled or destroyed for extended periods of time so that the government capitulates to the demands of the initiating state. Therefore, degradation strategies should be stealthy and sophisticated, and should require elaborate planning before the incident is launched. These complex operations may have a lower probability of infiltrating the target, but if they do, they will have a higher probability of changing the behavior of a target state. The efficacy of cyber degradation can be evaluated by comparing its concession generation rate with other forms of coercion and with other cyber strategies.

Cyber espionage focuses more on altering the balance of information over the long term or gaining system access in the short term. This dynamic makes concessions significantly less likely. In the short term, cyber espionage, consistent with covert action, either gains access or merely sends an ambiguous signal of resolve altering short-term strategic calculus. Therefore, the efficacy of cyber espionage should be reduced when compared to cyber degrade incidents. There is a different strategic logic at play.

Cyber disruption—as a low-cost instrument—is less likely to compel, since it typically is a harassment technique. Website defacements and DDoS attacks disrupt the daily lives of civilians or punish the military through harassment in a manner that signals resolve and escalation risk, but is insufficient to compel a rival state.[8] There are elements of denial strategies in these operations, but the effects tend to be short-lived with a declining utility over time. When compared to cyber degradation efforts, we should witness less efficacy in terms of compellent behavioral changes for cyber disruption operations.

The efficacy of coercive cyber degradations can be compared to other coercive instruments through analyzing the observed concessions relative to other studies. As outlined in the previous chapter, cyber coercion should work equal to or less than other forms of conventional coercion given the ambiguous character of cyber signals and credibility issues. As Table 2.1 reports in chapter 2, the average rate of coercion activities that evoke a behavioral change for conventional activities based on averaging prior studies is 33.38%. Hence, even though cyber degradation should produce more concessions than cyber espionage and disruption, which have different strategic logic and objectives, we would expect to find a lower rate than this in cyber actions.

In addition, we can further test the coercive potential of cyber degradation through comparing observed concessions to controls associated with power. The coercion literature revolves around the central question of what produces concessions: power, which would be manifest and latent capabilities, or resolve, which would be demonstrations of intent. This query stands at the core of intelligence analysis as well, where analysts are often trained to catalog the adversary's order of battle (capability and capacity) to try to infer their intent and estimate their resolve. Most of the contemporary coercion scholarship, reviewed in previous chapter, hypothesizes that resolve and credibility, or expectations that the initiator will follow through on their threats, matter more than power (Haun 2015). Resolving this debate in the context of the rivalry population is our challenge when moving beyond the description of how the process of cyber coercion works. The next question clearly is, why do some methods work while others do not?

We assess the relationship between changes in cyber power and rates of coercive concessions by determining whether power differentials have an impact on concessions being witnessed in the data. Cyber power is an important dimension of modern statecraft, but it may not be as revolutionary or decisive as pundits claim and may only be suitable for limited objectives. As Gartzke (2013: 63) states, "if cyberwar functions not as an independent domain but as part of a broader coordinated military action, then the conventional military balance is the best indicator of where the most important threats exist in cyberspace." The real relationship between cyber action and concessions may lie with traditional power dynamics, such as economic or military power, a subject we explore in chapter 4.

To analyze the relationship between power and coercive outcomes in cyberspace, we constructed a latent cyber capacity index expanding on our efforts in Valeriano and Maness (2015: 26). This index captures two forms of cyber power: infrastructure and knowledge capital. Infrastructure includes variables such as broadband subscriptions per 1,000 people and other usage variables that reflect the degree to which there is sufficient connectivity to sustain cyber operations.[9] For infrastructure, we used World Bank variables including the number of broadband subscriptions per 1,000 people, the number of secure Internet servers per 1 million people, and the percentage of high technology exports out of total manufacturing exports for each country for each of the years under analysis. Knowledge capital seeks to capture whether the state has a high enough level of science, technology, engineering, and math (STEM) education and personnel who, all things being equal, are more likely to have an aptitude for computer program manipulation or hacking. Regarding knowledge capital, variables include the number of Internet users per 1,000 people, the absolute number of scientific and technical journal articles published in a country, and the number of residents from each country who have applied for patent applications for each year (World Bank Data 2017). We integrate these two components of cyber power into a single variable: latent cyber capacity.[10]

The variable allows us to look at state's inherent connectivity in a manner that separates it from other measures of power. The use of per 1,000 measures means that the variable tends to overestimate small, highly connected societies while missing isolated countries that invest in covert cyber capabilities. For example, take South Korea and North Korea. South Korea is highly connected but to date engages in few documented cyber operations despite its high broadband penetration and internet usage. North Korea on the other hand is intentionally cut off from the world and lacks sufficient power generation to enable broad-based connectivity. Yet, North Korea is active in the cyber realm, using cyber operations to threaten rival states and signal its resolve.

The latent cyber capacity variable allows us to test whether or not cyber capacity, as a proxy for a state's connectivity that could be converted into strategic instruments, is associated with observed concessions. We can also compare whether or not cyber power or more traditional forms of state power affect concessions. Given our approach to cyber strategies as an ambiguous signaling mechanism, we argue that power matters less than resolve because even though there are sunk costs, these costs are not dramatic outside of a few examples such as Stuxnet.

Latent cyber capacity will not necessarily translate into concessions. As Slayton (2017: 82) notes, "the costs of cyber operations will not depend on the features of technology alone, but instead on the skills and competence of the actors and organizations that continually create, use, and modify information technology." This suggests that conventional measure of capability will have little bearing of the efficacy of cyber actions. The key factors are talent, the functional ability of organizations to innovate, and how these skills are translated into actionable cyber tools.

We argue that higher levels of latent cyber power should be a useful proxy for cyber capabilities in the absence of a cyber capabilities dataset, which will take years to construct and may not even really be possible (Craig and Valeriano 2016). Cyber power, though important, likely is not associated with concessions, because there are other factors such as resolve, weakness of the defender, and ease of target that are more likely to influence success when it comes to cyber conflict. Furthermore, cyber power should demonstrate a weaker relationship than traditional forms of power such as military strength and economic might. This is because cyber likely complements rather than replaces traditional tools of the influence in rivalry.[11] To assess this relationship, we compare latent cyber capacity and traditional measures of state power.

To control for past interactions relative to power consideration, we test whether past cyber behavior influences the odds of concession. Specifically, we measure credibility by proxy through looking at the effect of past cyber incidents on the expected rate of concession. This variable is measured by the number of past cyber incidents that preceded the one being measured for each event. Consistent with the current calculus school of strategic decisions, national security advisers and leaders will focus more on the crisis at hand than on past actions (Press 2005). Applied to cyber strategies, past cyber incidents should not alter the expected rate of concessions but could be a factor for the expectation of escalation in the rivalry context.[12] The observed rate of concession can also be compared with controls for economic power, military power, cyber capacity, and regime type. Given that these attributes would be, at least partially, observable by decision makers, they should produce more of an impact on concessions than previous cyber episodes.

METHODS AND MEASUREMENT

Where the analysis undertaken involves independent and dependent variables that are both categorical, cross-tabulation and chi-squared tests are appropriate. Cross-tabulations assume normal distributions and produce null hypotheses based on expected values that are normally distributed. If the data in the sample deviate from the norm at the 95% confidence level, that is, if there is a significant difference between the expected and observed values, then these null hypotheses are rejected. Chi-squared tests measure the "goodness of fit" of an observed sample of variables and also assume normality.[13]

When interval independent variables or a mix of interval and categorical independent variables are measured against binary dependent variables, we use the binary logistic regression method with directed dyads. Directed dyads allow us to enhance our robustness of the central limit theorem's premises and include a directional assumption of who is the initiator and who is the target for each cyber incident in the DCID. This method will allow us to predict which independent variables are the best predictors for concessions from a target as a result of a cyber incident, along with measures of latent cyber capacity and binary variables of past cyber incidents and regime type, which are explained in detail later.

Chapter 2 notes that combining existing studies on coercion shows an average success rate of 33.38%. That is, coercion tends to work only one-third of the time. These studies reflected a wide range of coercive instruments including economic sanctions, terrorism, limited air power campaigns, and coercive diplomatic episodes combining multiple instruments of power as well as positive inducements. Due to their diverse subject matter and methodological orientation, these studies had a wide effectiveness range, varying from 7% to 57% success rates. Given that the application of cyber power is a relatively new phenomenon in rival state relationships, this variation helps us situate its relative effectiveness. For cyber coercion to be successful it should change the political behavior of the target more than 17%–37% of the time.[14]

It is of note that there are two outcome variables in this analysis but we primarily depend on change of behavior, or concession, as the main unit of interest. The first variable measures whether the objectives of the initiating states are met. This is defined as the accomplishment of the basic goals of operation. For example, if the operation was an intelligence operation, were the plans stolen? If the incident was a disruptive effort, such as a DDoS attack, were the target networks shut down? Was the target compromised? Did the degradation-style attack breach the network and destroy files or industrial control systems beyond repair? If the operation was thwarted, who stopped it and how? These were the questions that were asked during the coding of these variables. If there was a successful breach of the target network, we code this outcome variable as "1," a "0" is coded if the effort was blocked or thwarted by the target state.

The second dependent variable measures concession: a change of behavior in the target state. For a concession to be coded, a state must achieve a political or military objective. For example, if Russia's goal in the Estonian hacks in 2007 was to alter Estonian behavior leading to respect for ethnic Russians, did the hack achieve this?[15] An outcome for this variable is coded as "1" if it there was an observable concessionary behavioral change, "0" if there was not.

The use of binary, conditional codes is an established, if oversimplified, practice in studying coercion (Huth, Gelpi, and Bennett 1993; Sescher 2011). Critics note that binary approaches that code a compellent case "success" or "failure" may not capture "the complex and often subtle effects of coercive threats" or the ways in which coercion can backfire (Byman and Waxman 2000: 13–14).[16] Yet, in order to measure the efficacy of cyber power, each episode must be coded with respect to its inferred strategy and whether or not that coercive approach met its desired objective and had a concessionary effect on its target. This question of intent is compounded in cyberspace, where the attacker often masks their effort. To overcome these challenges, the study relied on three independent coders and the results were reviewed by military practitioners who either had joint operational planning experience or worked at one point with cyber capabilities.[17]

Control variables include measures of economic and military power for each country year spanning the 2000–2014 period. Economic power is extracted from the World Bank and is measure in gross domestic product (GDP) in constant 2010 US dollars (World Bank 2017). Military power is measured as total defense expenditures by each country in constant 2015 US dollars and is extracted from the Stockholm International Peace Research Institute (SIPRI) dataset (SIPRI 2017).

We also measure power with the Composite Index of National Capability (CINC) scores, which capture annual values regarding total population, urban population, iron and steel production, energy consumption, military personnel, and military expenditures in order to measure the capacity to project power in the cyber domain (Singer, Bremer, and Stuckey 1972). These scores lie between 0 and 1 and are in decimal form, and make up the total percentage share of power in the international system. States with higher percentages, such as China and the United States, will have higher percentage CINC scores than smaller states such as Pakistan or South Korea.

Our final control variable captures whether or not the initiating state is a democracy, according to the Polity IV measures of freedom for all states in the international system (Marshall, Jaggers, and Gurr 2011). We reduce regime type to a binary variable, autocracy or democracy. This simplification allows us to integrate the score into risk models and determine odds ratios. Regime type is an important factor in the coercion literature tied to audience costs (Fearon 1994). Even when the coercive signal is covert, as is the case with cyber operations, democracies signal a willingness to escalate and incur the costs of being publicly outed (Carson and Kari-Milo 2017, 135).

Cyber Signaling Propositions

What is the relationship between cyber coercion and escalation? The introduction of new cyber capabilities into a rivalry could trigger crisis escalation. Two perspectives emerge. First, the ambiguity inherent in cyber coercion "has the potential to trigger unintended escalation because it is difficult to distinguish between hostile and benign intentions when an outside actor is perceived to have accessed a critical system" (Borghard and Lonergan 2017).[18] Lin similarly finds an increased risk of escalation in cyberspace, where "attempts to send signals to an adversary through limited and constrained military actions—problematic even in kinetic warfare—are likely to be even more problematic when cyber-attacks are involved" (Lin 2012: 57). New capabilities have the potential to produce inadvertent escalation, because states have little experience in how to tackle new forms of conflict (Posen 1996). While the security dilemma is an enduring concept, it has the potential to be especially acute in intelligence operations and cyberspace (Buchanan 2017).

Alternatively, by burning a vulnerability and revealing the ability to access target networks, cyber incidents, as a form of covert action, should produce a costly signal that limits future escalation. There may even be a stability-instability paradox in cyberspace in which states are subject to low-level intrusions but restrained in conducting larger, escalatory cyber operations attacking vital economic networks or destroying critical infrastructure (Lindsay and Gartzke 2016). That is, the goal of cyber operations may be to signal and manage escalation risks as opposed to produce decisive concessions. This logic produces our second hypothesis.

HYPOTHESIS 2

H2. Cyber operations produce limited escalation.

We evaluate how cyber operations enable ambiguous signaling and escalation management by testing whether cyber incidents between rivals produced increased retaliation in the cyber, diplomatic, economic, and/or military domains. First, we determine whether cyber is escalatory in its own domain. We would expect to find limited escalation or no responses, given the dynamics of cyber strategies.

Second, we look at whether or not cyber produces escalation in other domains (diplomatic, economic, military). Pundits often speak of cyber methods as existing in an isolated ecosystem, when the process is more complicated than this. Responses to cyber actions need not always come in the digital space, but more likely might be exhibited through traditional forms of responses like diplomatic communication, economic threats, or simple retaliation like seizing assets and compounds.

Third, we determine whether cyber latent capacity, as a proxy for cyber power, alters escalation dynamics. We expect the cyber domain to produce limited escalation. Cyber operations, as a modern form of covert action producing an ambiguous signal of resolve, produces a tit-for-tat type response, limiting escalation. The rival checks the adversary, and shifts the risk of escalation to them. We now turn to the next section on methods and measurement of uncovering the escalation dynamics as a result of cyber coercive action.

METHODS AND MEASUREMENT

To evaluate escalation dynamics associated with cyber incidents, we use a Cox survival regression, also known as a proportional hazards model (Hjort and Claeskens 2006), with directed dyads. Cox survival regressions use the time to event as the dependent variable, and this is measured as the number of days from the start date of the cyber incident by the initiator or, for covert espionage campaigns, the start date that the cyber incident was publicly exposed, and the escalatory response in either the cyber, diplomatic, economic, or military domains by the target. We expect a cyber operation's relative noncoercive attributes to produce limited escalation.

The dependent variables used to evaluate escalation consisted of two types: cyber escalation and noncyber escalation. To code cyber escalatory responses, we use the updated severity data from the DCID 1.1 (Maness, Valeriano, and Jensen 2017). Specifically, we code whether or not there was a response to the incident within 3 months. This variable is binary, and is coded as "1" if the cyber response from the target state is higher in severity than the original cyber incident from the initiating state. The severity scale ranges from 1 to 10 and is detailed in Appendix 1.

To code noncyber responses, we used the Integrated Crisis Early Warning System (ICEWS) dataset, which is an events dataset that collects data for the years 1995–2015; it includes events ranging from diplomatic threats to military action, and includes initiations and targets from both state and nonstate actors (Boschee et al. 2015). Variables are coded as either negative or positive, based on whether they are a positive inducing and friendly foreign policy action or a negative, more threatening and unfriendly one. Coded variables are measured on interval intensity scores and can include diplomatic negotiations, which include high-level meetings between state diplomats as well as telephone conversations between leaders; economic reduction of trade, where bilateral deals are altered or terminated; and military usage, which includes all use of conventional military force by one state against another. This variety and the differing severity of foreign policy actions make the ICEWS data the most-suited and encompassing collection of noncyber variables for the purposes of this analysis.[19]

However, as we are trying to capture escalation in testing these hypotheses, we focus on coding only the negative foreign policy actions as responses to a cyber incident, which are listed in Table 3.1. Positive inducements are used in chapter 4. Only diplomatic threats, economic embargoes/sanctions and trade reductions, or military usage, displays, or threats are considered as escalatory actions from the target state, and only these are coded within a 3-month period from the start date of the cyber incident launched by the initiator in the rival dyad. For espionage incidents, which much of the time remain secret for a period, we code the foreign policy response within 3 months of the date of public revelation of the incident.

The choice of a 3-month cut-line is based on empirical analysis of major crises datasets and the time needed to coordinate modern national security bureaucracies. From an empirical standpoint, the average length of crises in the International Crisis Behavior (ICB) dataset is as follows: 1918–2013: 4.95 months (Brecher et al.

TABLE 3.1

Conventional foreign policy actions: ICEWS dataset

Diplomatic	Economic	Military
Threaten: Threaten to break-up or withdraw from discussion, negotiation, or meeting	**Embargo/Sanction**: Stop or restrict commercial or other material exchange as a form of protest or punishment	**Usage**: All uses of conventional force and acts of war typically by organized armed groups not otherwise specified
	Reduce trade: Decrease or terminate provision of economic aid and/or trade with a country	**Display**: All military or police moves that fall short of the actual use of force, not otherwise specified

2016). Zooming into recent crises, the average for 2000–2013 is 5.87 months. Yet, when one breaks out crises, the majority falls into the 1- to 3-month timeframe (18), compared with other time ranges (4–6 months: 10, 7–12 months: 5, over 12 months: 6). In addition, using 3 months provides enough time for a coordinated response across all of the instruments of coercive diplomacy. The hack of the US Office of Personnel Management (OPM) became public in June 2015. By the end of July 2015, the United States was developing a noncyber retaliation in the form of targeted sanctions (Sanger 2015). All models use similar control variables to the cyber coercion propositions. Specifically, we use regime type, power measures, and the presence or absence of past cyber incidents.

Descriptive Statistics
CYBER INCIDENTS

Figure 3.1 breaks down each type of coercive method initiated by rival states from the years 2000 to 2014. Overall there has been a rise in cyber incidents since the turn of the century, with various peaks and valleys. While cyber incidents are increasing, this increase appears to be directly associated with espionage and disruption campaigns, not the more malicious degradation activities that many fear. In fact, currently the only type of cyber coercion on the rise is espionage, and, to a lesser extent, disruption.

An early spike in operations is witnessed around 2001, and operations held steady at a low level until 2008 with a dramatic rise after the Russian operation against

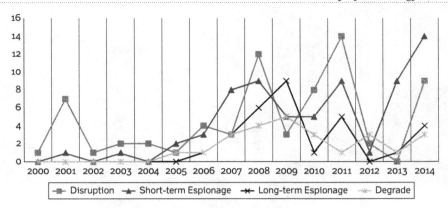

FIGURE 3.1 Yearly Cyber Incidents, Coercive Intent: 2000–2014

Estonia. We witness another spike around the Stuxnet operation in 2010, likely indicating the erosion of norms against the non-use of cyber operations around 2011 with a dramatic fall in 2012. The period after 2013 seems to highlight a new era of espionage operations, including the OPM hack by China. The US response was in some ways to suggest that these sorts of operations were expected and the normal course for espionage—remaining tense until a September 2015 agreement between China and the United States to limit cyber espionage for industrial purposes.

If the data were extended to 2017, we would probably witness a dip after 2014 with a dramatic rise in 2017 with a proliferation of low-level actions between regional rivals such as Vietnam versus the Philippines and United Arab Emirates (UAE) versus Qatar. Russia remains very active in the current period with China being remarkably restrained after 2015.

Table 3.2 provides an overview of the DCID 1.1 and rival-state use of cyber coercion between 2000 and 2014 and whether the incident under consideration led to a concession. The columns break down the initiating state and the form of cyber strategy (disruption, espionage, degradation), and code whether the incident met its implied objective (did it successfully breach the network as intended?) and achieved a concessionary behavioral change.

Table 3.2 is useful in determining the unique strategies of cyber actions used by each country. Based on publicly attributed cyber operations between 2000 and 2014, China is by far the most active cyber instigator in the international system. Espionage to acquire information appears to be China's method of action. Seen in this light, the Chinese elite may seek cyber means to catch up to the status quo hegemon, the United States. China has therefore has used much of its cyber capability in exploiting vulnerable information targets that could help narrow the technological gap with the United States. The problem, as discussed in chapter 6, is that

TABLE 3.2.

Cyber strategy by initiating state, 2000–2014

Country	Disruption Objective Achievement	Disruption Concessions	Disruption Attempts	Espionage Objective Achievement	Espionage Concessions	Esp Attempts	Degrade Objective Achievement	Degrade Concessions	Degrade Attempts	All Coercion Objective Achievement	All Coercion Concessions	Coercion Attempts
China	11 (100%)	0 (0%)	11	44 (92%)	1 (2%)	48	0 (0%)	0 (0%)	2	56 (92%)	1 (2%)	61
Russia	18 (95%)	0 (0%)	19	19 (95%)	0 (0%)	20	5 (83%)	0 (0%)	6	42 (93%)	0 (0%)	45
USA	0 (0%)	0 (0%)	0	6 (86%)	0 (30%)	7	9 (90%)	8 (89%)	10	15 (88%)	8 (47%)	17
N. Korea	10 (100%)	0 (0%)	10	2 (67%)	0 (0%)	3	3 (100%)	0 (0%)	3	15 (94%)	0 (0%)	16
Iran	2 (33%)	0 (0%)	6	2 (33%)	0 (0%)	6	2 (67%)	0 (0%)	3	6 (40%)	0 (0%)	15
Israel	1 (100%)	0 (0%)	1	7 (100%)	1 (14%)	7	1 (100%)	1 (100%)	1	9 (100%)	2 (22%)	9
India	6 (100%)	0 (0%)	6	1 (100%)	0 (0%)	1	–	–	–	7 (100%)	0 (0%)	7
Pakistan	6 (100%)	0 (0%)	6	1 (100%)	0 (0%)	1	–	–	–	7 (100%)	0 (0%)	7

S. Korea	4 (100%)	0 (0%)	4	3 (100%)	0 (0%)	3	–	–	–	7 (100%)	0 (0%)	7
Japan	3 (100%)	0 (0%)	3	–	–	–	–	–	–	3 (100%)	0 (0%)	3
Kuwait	1 (100%)	0 (0%)	1	–	–	–	–	–	–	1 (100%)	0 (0%)	1
Syria	1 (100%)	0 (0%)	1	–	–	–	–	–	–	1 (100%)	0 (0%)	1
Taiwan	–	–	–	1 (100%)	0 (0%)	1	–	–	–	1 (100%)	0 (0%)	1
Georgia	0 (0%)	0 (0%)	1	–	–	–	–	–	–	0 (0%)	0 (0%)	1
Lebanon	0 (0%)	0 (0%)	1	–	–	–	–	–	–	0 (0%)	0 (0%)	1
Total	63 (90%)	0 (0%)	70	86 (87%)	2 (2%)	97	20 (80%)	9 (36%)	25	169 (88%)	11 (6%)	192

Note: The table codes incident success, that is, whether it worked in accessing some aspect of the opponent's network. Coding objective success is potentially problematic for the following reasons. First, it risks being a tautology (i.e., it worked because it worked). Second, because we only can code publicly attributed incidents, we likely miss a disproportionately high number of unsuccessful cyber incidents. That is, usually only successful network penetrations or disruptions are reported.

it is difficult to achieve innovation and advancement by acquiring someone else's technology. China may be successfully altering the calculus regarding information asymmetries, but this perceived change is influenced more by the overreaction to Chinese activities than actual evidence of technological advancement.

For all states engaged in cyber espionage and information manipulation, it remains to be seen how effective these exploits are in terms of payoffs. For China, only one of these espionage attempts, the OPM hack, reaches a threshold that might warrant considering espionage a coercive instrument, because of the eventual agreement between China and the United States not to hack commercial systems and the move by the United States to change its behavior in terms of how it handles information and protects its operatives.[20]

The 2014–2015 Chinese OPM hack successfully stole terabytes of data on over 20 million people through access provided by a hack on a third-party contractor, KeyPoint. Stealing is one thing, but being able to turn this information into actionable intelligence is another. After a cyber incident is uncovered, a process that often takes over a year, the target can mitigate the damage and move assets to prevent further damage. There are also inherent technical challenges associated with processing millions of files. Finding a competitive advantage in terabytes of raw data is a monumental task that China is still faced with after this very public data breach. The shock value and surprise of cyber operations may also be overblown. At this stage, every government agency and critical infrastructure partner knows they are a target and invests in cyber defenses. Military exercises in multiple countries factor potential cyber effects through degraded command and control as well as Global Positioning System (GPS) disruptions that might come with war onset.

Russia appears to focus on low-cost, low-payoff cyber disruptions (primarily DDoS, website defacements) during active international disputes. Russia demonstrates this strategy of harassment and distortion, often veiled through third parties with connections to Russian nationalists and cyber-crime syndicates, in the 2007 attacks on Estonia, the 2008 events preceding the 5-day conflict with Georgia, and the ongoing civil war in Ukraine. Russia is also active in this regard with regional post-Soviet states (Maness and Valeriano 2015).

Of note, these high-profile incidents did not independently evoke concessionary behavioral changes. Rather, Russia uses cyber disruption as a signaling mechanism and to influence public opinion by undermining confidence in the target. Moscow disrupts networks and defaces websites with symbols connected to larger propaganda themes, but the effects are limited and temporary. More recently, the Russian advanced persistent threat (APT) groups such as "Fancy Bear" have used espionage coercive methods, most notably the hacks on the Democratic National Committee (DNC) during the 2016 US elections, the French elections in 2017, the German elections in 2017, and to infiltrate mobile apps used by the Ukrainian military in targeting for artillery pieces.

Yet, to date, Russia appears to fail in any degradation campaigns, unlike its rival, the United States. Chapter 5 explores Russian cyber coercion further and how the Kremlin applies cyber power as part of a broader information warfare construct. Our overall conclusion is that Russia is active and engaged in the cyber arena but has yet to demonstrate any clear effectiveness beyond sending cheap signals to adversaries that amplify its broader influence campaigns. Their effectiveness may have to be evaluated in a few years as Russia seeks to invade critical infrastructure networks with potent malware, preparing the battlefront for future conflagrations (Zetter 2016). These efforts are likely cheap demonstrations that will likely be eliminated before they become serious threats.

The United States succeeds in invoking a behavioral change through cyber degradation more often than any other rival state surveyed. This should not be surprising, since these incidents reflect a level of sophistication beyond Russian and Chinese efforts as well as unique approaches that emphasize precision strike and counterespionage. The Stuxnet operation was undoubtedly complex and expensive (Sanger 2012b), reflecting a form of sunk costs that increases signal strength. Degrade operations can be successful, but also show a remarkable degree of complexity that makes it difficult both for them to achieve results and to witness just how their actions influenced the target. The efforts to attack both the North Korean ability to launch ballistic missiles and attack ISIS are clear examples of this (Sanger 2016; Sanger and Broad 2017).

Likewise, the Snowden revelations demonstrated the global surveillance and intrusion capabilities of the Americans to a dramatic degree. Wikileaks's Vault 7 release and other information dumps also demonstrate the complex abilities of the American teams (Shane, Rosenberg, and Lehren 2017). Through operations such as Arrow Eclipse and Shotgiant, the National Security Agency has demonstrated a unique capability to undermine Chinese cyber espionage. That is, not only does the United States use cyber tools to target critical vulnerabilities but also US agencies turn rival states' intrusions into their own attack vectors and respond in kind. Chapter 7 explores these behavioral patterns further.

The political impact of Stuxnet as a stand-alone coercive incident should be questioned (Valeriano and Maness 2015: 145). Parallel to Stuxnet, there was a sophisticated negotiation campaign since 2006 involving diplomatic pressure and economic sanctions by the permanent members of the United Nations Security Council and Germany (P5+1) as well the looming threat of Israeli military intervention. Iran's eventual concession likely had more to do with these instruments of power and positive economic inducements than it did the cyber espionage and degradation campaigns that accessed Iranian networks and only temporarily limited uranium processing. Chapter 4 explores these combined incidents and how cyber power works alongside other instruments to achieve coercive effects.

EVENTS PRODUCING CONCESSIONSS

Table 3.3 lists the cases of concession for combined degradation operations. All the degradation incidents involve the cyber superpower, the United States, which was the initiator seven times. These events count six advanced defensive measures launched by the United States that successfully changed behavior, targeting Russia, China, and North Korea: Cisco Raider, Boxing Rumble, Buckshot Yankee, Arrow Eclipse, NSA Fourth Party countermeasures, and Shotgiant. Stuxnet, which is coded twice in the DCID with the United States and Israel being coded as dual initiators against Iran, is analyzed in chapter 4 as a combined coercive success. We unpack Stuxnet and other US cyber degradations in chapter 7.

CYBER CAPACITY

Table 3.4 compares the cyber capacity measure, as a proxy for power, for the top 10 active states in the cyber realm from 2000 to 2014. This power indicator is then compared with traditional measures of power from the international relations literature: economic size, military expenditures, and CINC. Scores in bold indicate the

TABLE 3.3

Degradation cyber incidents that produce concessions

Initiator	Target	Name	Start Date	Method
US	China	Cisco Raider	2/29/2006	Keystroke & Botnet
US	China & North Korea	Boxing Rumble	1/1/2008	Botnet
US	Russia	Buckshot Yankee	11/26/2008	Virus & Botnet
US and Israel	Iran	Stuxnet	6/1/2009	Worm
US	China	Arrow Eclipse	5/27/2007	Keystroke & Worm
US	China	NSA Fourth Party	7/1/2009	Keystroke & Worm
US	China	Shotgiant	3/10/2010	Trojan

TABLE 3.4

Different power dynamics: Top ten most active cyber states (2014 constant)

Country	Latent Cyber Capacity	Economic Power (GDP billion $)	Military Power (Total billion $)	CINC
S. Korea	**6.71**	1,378	21.3	0.0232826
United States	6.51	**17,950**	**706.9**	0.143291
China	6.07	10,870	200.9	**0.2181166**
Japan	5.86	4,123	41.1	0.0370358
Israel	5.32	296	16.6	0.0042498
Russia	5.03	1,326	61.6	0.0400789
Iran	4.53	425	10.1	0.0157625
India	4.35	2,074	48.4	0.0808987
Pakistan	4.11	270	8.1	0.0145536
N. Korea	4.01	25 (est.)	11.1	0.0132601

most powerful state for each category. Remembering the research design earlier in the chapter, the latent cyber power index captures two forms of cyber power: infrastructure and knowledge capital. Not surprisingly, the United States takes the top spots in economic and military power, while China is number one in CINC power measures. Population is an important measure for this index, which gives China the edge over the United States. It is these conventional power measures where we ensure that military power and economic capacity are controlled for when measuring concessions as a result of cyber action.

Surprisingly, South Korea has the most latent cyber power available, although it has only used this capability sparingly on its rival neighbors North Korea and Japan. This large figure reflects the high level of connectivity in the society and the fact that most measures extracted from the World Bank are measured proportionally, per 1,000 people. Therefore, in all probability the United States and China have more aggregate, as opposed to per citizen, cyber capacity. As South Korea is under the American umbrella of protection in East Asia, its need to use its latent cyber potential has yet to manifest, but this need may be more pressing in the future, as China asserts regional control. The finding also illustrates the difficulty of measuring capacity in the realm of covert action and concealed acts. Arguably, the United States will remain the world's cyber superpower for at least for the next decade. As a traditional great power, its investment in cyber capabilities should keep it the manifest cyber hegemon for years to come.

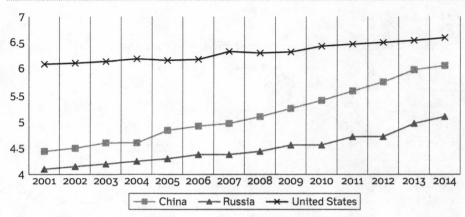

FIGURE 3.2 Latent Cyber Power over Time: China, Russia, United States

Figure 3.2 shows the differences in absolute cyber power between the three most active states in the cyber conflict domain. The United States has been the world's leading cyber power since 2000, compared to the other major cyber actors, Russia and China. There is a cyber hegemon, and this is very clear from the data. However, the gap between the United States and China is rapidly narrowing because of China's advances in nonmaterial indicators such as education and infrastructure. As on the military and economic fronts, China is a rising cyber power. As discussed in chapter 2, this change could produce escalatory dynamics, a subject we explore later in this chapter.

Russian cyber power is also rising relative to the United States but at a slower rate than China's. Russia's rampant political corruption, lack of economic diversity, and limited military budget has a lot to do with its lack of latent cyber power relative to its top two peers. This may partially explain Russia's lagged latent cyber power. However, Russia's goals in cyberspace do not dictate the need for more advanced cyber capabilities, as their strategies of low-level disruptions, political short-term espionage, and disinformation do not require highly technical malware. More about Russian cyber capacities and strategies is discussed in chapter 5.

CYBER ESCALATION

The overwhelming majority of the cyber incidents in the dataset are at a low severity level of 2 (43.2%) or 3 (27.6%). Table 3.5 illustrates the distribution. Examples of cyber incidents that register a severity score of 2 include targeted harassment, website defacing propaganda, or disruptive activities including denial of service attacks and botnets. These are usually easy to implement and to eradicate, hence their low severity coding. India and Pakistan lob these types of cyber incidents at each other

TABLE 3.5

Cyber incident severity frequency and concession distribution

		Frequency	Percent	Cumulative Percent	Concessions
Severity Level	1.0	9	4.7	4.7	0
	2.0	83	43.2	47.9	1
	3.0	53	27.6	75.5	0
	4.0	40	20.8	96.4	7***
	5.0	5	2.6	99.0	3***
	6.0	2	1.0	100.0	0
	Total	192	100.0	100.0	11

***$p < .01$, **$p < .05$, *$p < .10$

often, and much of Russian cyber action in post-Soviet countries is coded at this severity level. Cyber incidents that are coded with a severity score of 3 usually involve the theft or compromise of targeted critical information. The targeted thefts from US defense contractors by the Chinese People's Liberation Army (PLA) groups are prime examples of these incidents.

Table 3.5 also shows the distribution by severity score of cyber incidents that produce concessions. As the table indicates, level of severity is a good indicator to predict a concessionary outcome in the cyber domain. The severity level of 2 evoked concessions only once. However, cyber incidents that registered as a 4 and 5 evoked concessions seven and three times, respectively, and these are significant at the 99% confidence level. These cyber incidents are usually a widespread government or private sector theft of information, such as the OPM hack, or a counterespionage campaign with the intent to stop such a theft, such as Arrow Eclipse. Yet, while high, these incidents do not reach the upper thresholds. It seems the widespread impact of these incidents at this severity level are a good explanatory factor in predicting concessions. As the severity score scale ranges from 1 to 10, it would seem that the incidents on the higher side of the scale, if they ever happen, would also be able to evoke concessions. Appendix 1 describes the realm of possibilities in the DCID severity scale in more detail.

Table 3.6 shows the severity levels that led to a cyber response in the DCID 1.1 dataset. The severity levels tend to fall along stable lines and match the expected values for cyber responses. This said, interpreting cyber escalation must be considered in this context. An incident with a severity level of 1 for the initiating state has never led to a response. Severity level 2 incidents have led to responses 14 times. Severity level 3 incidents, have been met with retaliation five times, while severity level 4

TABLE 3.6

Cross-tabulations: Past attack severity and cyber response

			Cyber Response		
			No	Yes	Total
Severity	1.0	Count	11	0	11
		Expected Count	9.7	1.3	11.0
		z-score	.4	−1.1	
	2.0	Count	71	14	85
		Expected Count	74.8	10.2	85.0
		z-score	-.1	1.2	
	3.0	Count	51	5	56
		Expected Count	49.3	6.7	56.0
		z-score	.2	-.7	
	4.0	Count	30	3	33
		Expected Count	29.0	4.0	33.0
		z-score	.2	−.5	
	5.0	Count	4	1	5
		Expected Count	4.4	.6	5.0
		z-score	-.2	.5	
	6.0	Count	2	0	2
		Expected Count	1.8	.2	2.0
		z-score	.2	−.5	
Total		Count	169	23	192
		Expected Count	169.0	23.0	192.0

***$p < .01$, **$p < .05$, *$p < .10$

incidents have led to a response in the cyber realm three times. Only once has an incident coded as a severity 5 been met with a cyber response. That is, rivals tend to respond only to lower-level incidents and the response tends to check the intrusion as opposed to seek escalation dominance.

The majority of cyber escalation episodes are at a low severity threshold and are nonescalatory. These incidents are usually "tit-for-tat" type responses within one step of the original incident.[21] The average severity score for cyber incidents in the DCID is 2.7 out of 10, and as Table 3.7 indicates, most escalatory events stay within the severity scores of 3 and 4. Table 3.7 lists the target responses that are escalatory as a result of an incident from the initiator that was coded as less severe. To put this in context, escalation usually means stealing more information or extending the

TABLE 3.7

Cyber escalatory responses by targets

StateA	StateB	Name	Start Date	Initiator	Objective	Severity	Change
US	Iran	Iran network infiltration	3/14/2010	US	3	3	+1
US	China	Cisco Raider	2/28/2006	US	4	5	+1
US	China	Boxing Rumble	1/1/2008	US	4	4	+1
US	China	NSA Fourth Party collection	7/1/2009	US	4	4	+1
US	China	Shotgiant	3/10/2010	US	4	4	+1
US	China	Ocean Lotus	4/1/2012	US	4	4	+1
US	N Korea	NK Stuxnet	3/1/2010	US	4	5	+3
Iran	Israel	Stuxnet .5	11/1/2007	Israel	3	4	+2
Iran	Israel	Stuxnet	6/1/2009	Israel	4	5	+3
Iran	Israel	Israel Infrastructure Hack	3/2/2013	Iran	4	5	+2
Lebanon	Israel	Gauss	9/1/2011	Israel	3	3	+1
China	Taiwan	TooHash	9/1/2013	Taiwan	2	3	+1
N. Korea	S Korea	Government theft	9/8/2008	S Korea	2	3	+2
S. Korea	Japan	Dark Hotel	1/1/2008	S Korea	2	4	+2
S. Korea	Japan	Earthquake hack	3/11/2011	S Korea	2	3	+1

length of a network disruption, not destroying critical infrastructure or taking down power grids.

The retaliation exhibited is likely an ambiguous signal, a form of "tacit maneuver" to determine escalation potential and rival intention (Schelling 1960; Carson 2016; Carson and Kari-Milo 2017). The plausible deniability factor also allows the weaker state to be more brazen in the cyber realm, sending a signal to the more powerful initiating state that it also possesses cyber capacity to compel the aggressor should the exchange continue. All this can be done without having to claim responsibility publicly in a manner that would bring international condemnation or produce domestic opposition that limited freedom of action. The ambiguity of cyberspace shields decision makers from hawks, who will demand higher rates of escalation, and doves, who will demand appeasement.

Cyber operations in terms of retaliation events, therefore, are likely a vehicle to probe intentions, a form of competitive learning under uncertainty hypothesized in the bargaining literature discussed in chapter 2 (Schelling 1960; Axelrod 1984; Fearon 1995, 401; Powell 2004). Given their deniability, these probes have the added benefit of limiting risk by demonstrating that there are limits to provocations. The fact that we only have two events where the response to an initial attack moves up three notches, both under the Stuxnet context, suggests that dramatic escalation is rare.

Findings

H1. Confirmed in light of evidence: Degradation produces more concessions.

Table 3.8 summarizes each initiating state's cyber incidents by coercive method and whether or not the cyber action successfully achieved the goals of the operation for the years 2000–2014. Here we consider the total number of operations initiated along with figures regarding behavioral change. Overall, all four methods succeed in achieving their objective at the levels of expectation using cross-tabulation methods. In terms of the objective being met—that is, whether the cyber attempt breached the network of the intended target—all four categories do so at the expected frequency. The null hypothesis for objective achievement for all four coercive categories can therefore not be rejected.

One caveat regarding the data coding objective achievement is that unsuccessful operations are more difficult to discover. There are few incentives for attacking governments to report failed espionage attempts. Yet, there is an incentive for a state or private actor defending to demonstrate that such efforts have either been

TABLE 3.8

Cross-tabulations between cyber degradations and objective achievement and concessions

Cyber	Objective Achievement		Concession	
Objective	Yes	No	Yes	No
Disruption				
Count	63	7	0	70
Expected	61.6	8.4	4.0	66.0
z-score	0.2	−0.5	−2.0**	0.5
Short-Term Espionage				
Count	57	10	0	67
Expected	59	8	3.8	63.2
z-score	−0.3	0.7	−2.0**	0.5
Long-Term Espionage				
Count	29	1	2	28
Expected	26.4	3.6	1.7	28.3
z-score	0.5	−1.4	0.2	−0.1
Degrade				
Count	5	20	9	16
Expected	3	22	1.4	23.6
z-score	1.2	−0.4	6.3***	−1.6
Total				
Count	169	23	11	181
Percentage	88%	12%	5.7%	94.3%

***$p < .01$, **$p < .05$, *$p < .10$

stopped or have failed in their attempts because that brings confidence to the population. Critical network attacks are often reported for this reason. Israel commonly is able to thwart attacks before they even reach the target, but these are mainly initiated by nonstate actors and are not covered in our data. That said, the shape of our data demonstrates quite a bit of variation and evidence of cyber events of all types. Furthermore, higher objective failure rates imply even lower rates of cyber concessions, further reinforcing our central argument that cyber operations have limited coercive utility.

Table 3.8 also summarizes each initiating states' cyber incidents by coercive method (disruption, short-term and long-term espionage, or degradation) between 2000 and 2014 and whether the incident resulted in a concession in the target state. The table shows the cross-tabulation analysis that measures the difference between the actual counts of each political objective's concessionary success rate against the expected counts. The z-scores represent the standard deviations by which actual observations differ from the expected observations at either the 99% or 95% confidence level.

For concessions, *the form of cyber coercion matters*. As Table 3.8 indicates, the null hypothesis for long-term espionage fails to be falsified, implying that this coercive measure succeeds at about the expected rate, with the actual count being 28 when compared to the expected count of 28.3. However, short-term espionage and disruptive techniques, both of which have a zero-success rate, should have succeeded at least three times each according to expected values, but we witness no examples of success and these findings are significant at the 95% confidence level. Disruptions and short-term espionage appear to be cheap talk, and act more as signaling techniques that offer a form of tacit bargaining, or they establish more of an escalation threshold than a traditional compellent tool.

Alternatively, degradation techniques succeed over three standard deviations more than expected, and this is significant at the 99% confidence level. Degradations require a significant investment of time and resources; therefore, these cyber coercive measures are able to evoke a concessionary behavioral change in 36% of cases (9 of 25). While there is evidence these actions can work, a 36% success rate is not exactly indicative of a game-changing technology of coercion likely to alter strategic competition. In fact, the level is consistent with prior studies of coercion depicted in Table 3.2 (33%). In other words, cyber degradation works, but it is by no means a silver bullet, much less a common instrument of statecraft.

Table 3.9 compares the mean severity scores across the different forms of cyber strategies in relation to the overall distribution of severity scores between concessions and no concession events. Traditional approaches to denial forms of coercion, which are linked to our concept of degradation, suggest that the strategy works by attacking the adversary's military strategy (their objectives) as opposed to punishing their civilian population (Pape 1996: 12–20). The coercive strategy produces the concession, in theory, not the degree of punishment (incident severity). Therefore, cyber degradation should produce concessions at a severity level equal to or less than that of other forms of coercion.

What we do not know is whether it is the severity of the incident, the degradation strategy, or some other factor that is producing the observed concession. Either way, the cyber coercive incident is likely exhibiting a sunk cost. Cyber degradations and

TABLE 3.9

Severity and cyber degradations

	Concession	No Concession	Difference
Total Severity (mean)	3.45	2.65	0.8
Cyber Disruption Severity (mean)	N/A	2.07	N/A
Count	0	70	
Cyber Short-Term Espionage Severity (mean)	N/A	2.97	N/A
Count	0	67	
Cyber Long-Term Espionage Severity (mean)	4	3.25	0.75
Count	2	28	
Cyber Degradation Severity (mean)	4.11	3.19	0.92
Count	9	16	

higher severity cyber operations reflect more complex and costly actions. Therefore, they signal resolve and commitment. Consistent with studies on the signaling effects of covert action, sunk costs can signal resolve (Carson and Kari-Milo 2017) and, hence, should be more likely to produce concessions. Degradation events might also invoke concessions because the target may anticipate escalation risks based on the demonstrated resolve of the initiator, a phenomenon Carson and Yarhi-Milo (2017: 134) refer to as counterescalation risks.

Yet, is the concession a function of cyber degradation or latent power differences between rival states? The empirical findings of the directed dyads binary logistic regression find that latent cyber capacity, as a proxy measure of power, does not translate into coercive success in cyberspace. As seen in Table 3.10, cyber capacity appears to increase the implied rate of concession, but not at the level of statistical significance. The table calculates the odds ratio estimate, which measures the likelihood a concession will be achieved by each independent variable in the four rows for each dyadic difference in power for each of the initiator and the target states as an interval variable. However, more traditional forms of power, namely CINC and military, are statistically significant predictors of concessions as a result of cyber coercive degradation methods. The more powerful the initiating state in CINC and military terms, the more likely a target will capitulate as a result of cyber coercion through degradation operations.

TABLE 3.10

Power Differentials and the Odds of Concessions: Binary Logistic Regression

	Odds Ratio	Std. Error	z-score	p-value
Cyber Power Differential	1.976	1.268	1.06	.289
CINC Differential	1.140	.062	2.40	.016**
Economic Power Differential	.970	.021	−1.34	.180
Military Power Differential	1.008	.004	2.14	.032**
Constant	.006	.005	−6.86	.000***

***p <. 01, **p <. 05, *p <. 10
N=384

While these traditional power indicator results are significant, one actor likely drives the outcomes. The United States is responsible for 8 of the observed 11 concessions. This condition means we cannot tell whether it is the cyber capacity difference or the fact that the initiating state, the United States, has a power advantage relative to its rivals in every power category except CINC scores, and only China has a higher score in the latter category. We likely have an outlier driving these results. We hypothesize that cyber capacity should matter less to generating concessions than traditional measures of power. Yet, all power measures, except for the CINC power measure, where China is the top-ranked country, are associated with higher expected rates of concession, and the United States, given it has more economic and military power than its rivals, likely skews the results. The findings may also be a function of how the United States integrates multiple instruments of power in a combined approach, the subject of chapter 4, or the unique US approach to cyber strategy, the subject of chapter 7. A simple solution would be to remove the United States to see whether the state is driving the findings, but since the great majority of concessions involve the United States, this solution would produce no actual results.

If proxy indicators of cyber power are not associated with behavioral change, do demonstrated capability and intent produce concessions? Signals of credibility might influence concessions; these signals could either be past actions or the rival's current calculus (Press 2005). Table 3.11 shows the answers to this question and finds that past cyber incidents do not alter the rate of concession.[22] Furthermore, when compared to controls for regime type and CINC scores, past cyber operations appear to shape political behavior less than traditional measures. The statistically significant results in Table 3.11 show that traditional power measures, CINC scores, continue to explain how concessions are predicted with these controls. Furthermore, the Regime Type score shows that autocratic states are much less likely to achieve

TABLE 3.11

Cyber Power Differentials and the Odds of Concessions with Controls: Binary Logistic Regression

	Odds Ratio	Std. Error	z-score	p-value
Cyber Power Differential	.929	.460	−0.15	.882
CINC Differential	1.218	.111	2.16	.030**
Past Cyber	1.656	1.337	0.63	.532
Regime Type	205.134	360.708	3.03	.002***
Constant	.00017	.0004	-4.05	.000***

***p <. 01, **p <. 05, *p <. 10

N=384

concessions at the statistically significant level. The United States is again the outlier driving the results in Table 3.11. The United States is a democracy and has a power advantage over its rivals in the cyber, military, and economic domains.

Similar to overall concessions, this finding might be a function of ambiguity (i.e., the difficulty of credible signaling in cyberspace) or the limited effects of conflicts in cyberspace. Alternatively, the fact that revealed cyber incidents burn exploits and hence reduce the payoff of future intrusions may explain the findings. Once a cyber incident is revealed, the vulnerability is patched and the initiator has to find new ways of attacking a target in cyberspace. Targets know they could be compromised, but they also know the initiator has removed an exploit from their arsenal, which actually might be quite limited, according to investigators (Waterman 2017). In other words, unless you assume infinite exploits, every cyber incident reduces the number of available exploits for coercion. Therefore, Gartzke's (2013: 59) claim that revealing cyber capabilities degrades their usefulness and makes compellence marginal appears sound. In the end, credibility in cyberspace may hinge on coercive strategies that incorporate other instruments of power, such as diplomatic, economic, or military, and demonstrating the ability to employ sophisticated cyber operations like degradations. Just being able to penetrate or disrupt a network in the past is not sufficient to produce a concession on the next instance of attack. However, what strategy a state uses does have an impact, an issue we tackle in chapter 4.

H2. Mixed in light of evidence: Cyber coercion produces limited escalation.

Cyber operations appear to produce limited escalation in cyberspace but not in other domains. Table 3.12 reports the findings from four separate Cox regression survival analyses. At first glance, it appears that past cyber incidents, coded categorically,

TABLE 3.12

Escalation Hazards as a Result of Cyber Operations

	Cyber Escalation odds-ratio (z-score)	Diplomatic Escalation odds-ratio (z-score)	Economic Escalation odds-ratio (z-score)	Military Escalation odds-ratio (z-score)
Past Cyber	4.108**	.687	1.474	1.585
	(2.21)	(-.37)	(.94)	(1.60)
Regime Type	2.410	.206	4.725	.931
	(1.41)	(-.91)	(1.22)	(-.20)
Cyber Capacity	.681	2.046	.859	1.130
	(-1.03)	(1.13)	(-.70)	(.80)
CINC	.961	1.050	.981	.979
	(-1.18)	(.76)	(-.74)	(-1.07)
Military Power	1.003	1.019**	.999	.999
	(1.07)	(2.04)	(-.46)	(-.96)
Economic Power	.982	.898**	1.002	1.007
	(-1.51)	(-2.22)	(.19)	(1.10)

***$p < .01$, **$p < .05$, *$p < .10$
N=384
Hazard Ratio of Escalation reported with coefficients in parentheses
Categorical variables: Past Cyber (1=yes, 0=no); Regime Type (1=Democracy, 0=Autocracy)
Interval variables: Cyber Capacity, CINC, Military Power, Economic Power

increase the probability of cyber escalation within 3 months of the original incident. Remembering Table 3.7, only 6 of 15 of these escalations occurred above a one-step increase. Put in context, the majority of the cyber responses shifted from a severity level of 3 to a severity level of 4. A prime example of this is the US counterespionage efforts against Chinese efforts to steal information from government and private sector organizations. Thus, while escalatory, the responses appeared to be low-level "tit-for-tat" responses designed to signal resolve, end current cyber operations, or manage escalation risk.

Looking at the diplomatic domain in Table 3.12, more economic power reduces the odds that escalation will happen. More powerful economic countries employing cyber operations are less likely to evoke escalation from their less powerful targets. As China and the United States are the economic powers included in this analysis, leverage in the economic domain seems to have an impact on whether or not escalation in the cyber or diplomatic domains is probable. Furthermore, more military power increases the probability that the target state will escalate in the diplomatic realm, but only slightly.

With respect to cyber capacity and escalation potential, the results are definitive. Differences in cyber capacity between rival dyads, measured categorically, do not produce escalation in cyberspace or other domains. In fact, none of the power measures or regime type control variables produced a statistically significant escalation dynamic. Only past cyber incidents seem to matter, but tend to reflect a "tit-for-tat" logic and remain at lower levels of escalation.

There are also interesting temporal dynamics that emerge while analyzing escalation dynamics. There were 23 cases of cyber escalation out of 192 incidents. The majority of these 19 episodes occurred in cases where there was a past cyber incident, defined as the initiator previously conducting a cyber operation of any type against the target. These episodes tended to occur quickly, with 16 of the cases involving escalation within 30 days and the other 3 cases occurring between 30 and 60 days. Alternatively, in the four cases where there was cyber escalation absent a prior cyber incident only one occurred in less than 60 days. The other three cases occurred between 60 and 90 days. The temporal aspects of cyber escalation are statistically significant.[23]

Table 3.13 highlights that cyber degradations are associated with a higher rate of escalation than cyber disruption or forms of espionage. Rivals do not need to signal resolve and the risk of future escalation when they are subject to website defacements or basic DDoS attacks. They do appear to seek a "tit-for-tat" check when opponents penetrate their networks with more sophisticated cyber degradation.

There is likely a unique decision calculus in cyberspace. Responding to noise, low-level cyber incidents, risks jeopardizing network access. That is, *if you use it, you lose it*. Most cyber operations start as computer network exploitation, cyber espionage, and intelligence, surveillance, and reconnaissance (ISR) connected to mapping a rival's networks and finding vulnerabilities. Since there is not an infinite number of vulnerabilities, anytime you exploit one, you reveal you are in the network and jeopardize your access. The target responds by patching their network, thus limiting your access. Every decision in cyberspace therefore involves a shadow of the future. Escalating and responding to a hack now means you lose the ability to respond in the future. Therefore, states tend to only respond to more sophisticated incidents, like cyber coercive degradations.

There is a second interesting temporal dynamic. Table 3.14 below provides an overview of the descriptive statistics of escalation including the average time of response. The average length for a cyber response was 21 days. This compares with 12 days for economic, 8 days for diplomatic, and 9 days for military. The findings suggest that it may take longer to develop a cyber response than it does traditional

TABLE 3.13

Cyber escalation by strategic objective: Cross-tabulation

		Cyber Escalation	
		No	Yes
Disruption	Count	59	11
	Expected Count	61.6	8.4
	z-score	−.3	.9
Short-Term Espionage	Count	61	6
	Expected Count	59.0	8.0
	z-score	.3	−.7
Long-Term Espionage	Count	25	3
	Expected Count	24.6	3.4
	z-score	.1	−.2
Degrade	Count	24	3
	Expected Count	23.8	3.2
	z-score	.0	−.1
Total	Count	169	23
	Expected Count	168.0	24.0

$^{***}p < .01, {}^{**}p < .05, {}^{*}p < .10$

instruments of power used to signal a rival during an evolving crisis. Read alongside the above finding about cyber escalation's temporal dynamics, cyber coercion as a tool for escalation management requires time to access a network and develop the right malware. In all probability, firing a missile, though more escalatory, is a cheaper and faster response. Cyber operations are not as easy to use or rapid as they are made out to be.

It is tempting to conclude cyber operations result in escalation. As seen in Table 3.14, cyber incidents lead to some form of escalation 53.65% of the time. Furthermore, as seen in Table 3.12 past cyber incidents seem to increase the odds of cyber escalation. Yet, these responses must be analyzed in context. The majority of escalations that occurred 90 days after a cyber incident involved traditional instruments of strategy, not the cyber arena, which one would expect in exchanges between rivals. Furthermore, these acts tended to be limited. When one removes the Russia-Georgia and Russia-Ukraine dyads, all military escalation involved only threats and displays of force. Economic escalation similarly remained limited and often linked to larger rivalry dynamics. For example, take the early 2001 exchange between China

TABLE 3.14

Escalation dynamics as a result of cyber strategies

	Count	Percent of Episodes	Average Time
Response Dynamic			
Escalation	97	53.65%	
No Escalation	95	46.35%	
Domain Escalation			
Cyber Escalation	24	12.50%	21
Economic Escalation	37	19.27%	12
Diplomatic Escalation	18	9.38%	8
Military Escalation[a]	55	28.64%[b]	9
Multidomain Escalation[c]	36	18.75%	11[d]

N= 192

a = of the 55 instances only 14 involved an intentional battlefield death and were clustered in interstate conflict episodes (8 Russia-Georgia, 6 Russia-Ukraine). The remaining military escalations tended to be threats or displays.

b = removing the cases of wartime escalation, military escalation occurred in 21.35% of the instances.

c = three episodes had over two escalation vectors: India-Pakistan (2008), Russia-Ukraine (2014), and US-China (2009).

d = of the 11 instances, four were during wartime (Russia-Georgia 2008). The other episodes were India-Pakistan (4), DPRK-ROK (2), and US-China (2) and did not involve the intentional use of military force that resulted in battlefield deaths.

and Taiwan after Beijing hacked Taiwanese political parties. The cyber incident led to economic escalation. Yet, the resulting economic threats did not stop Beijing from overtaking the United States as Taiwan's largest trading partner the same year (Tanner 2007). The escalation observed after cyber incidents tends to be limited and consistent with rivalry dynamics.

Conclusion

Despite its "revolutionary" promise and bold claims by pundits, to date, cyber coercion produces few concessions. Rather, the utility of cyber operations appears to be an ambiguous signal that allows rivals to manage escalation risks. Cyber methods, like traditional covert action, can signal resolve but tend to produce few clear-cut concessions on their own.

Second, neither cyber capacity, as a proxy for power, nor past cyber incidents explain concessions. Rival states do appear to focus on power differentials, but this result is driven by the outlier of the United States and its unique power position. Past cyber incidents appear to matter less than measures of relative power. Rival states appear to focus more on current conditions than on past actions.

Lastly, there appear to be unique escalation dynamics in cyberspace. Cyber operations produce limited escalatory responses. Past cyber incidents, though not associated with concessions, do appear to increase the odds of escalation. These responses, though, are limited in severity and reflect a "tit-for-tat" logic. Cyber operations provide a means of probing rival resolve while seeking a position of advantage and limiting their ability to respond. Cyber operations, therefore, may be stabilizing and offer a means of avoiding military escalation or further damaging diplomatic and economic relationships.

This chapter covers the correlates of cyber coercive strategies as an isolated instrument of power launched by technologically savvy states against their rivals. However, it would be folly to assume, based on our results, cyber operations are working in isolation most of the time. We therefore now turn to how cyber operations are used in a combined sense, with other instruments of power (diplomatic, economic, military), which is the subject of chapter 4.

4

CYBER COERCION AS A COMBINED STRATEGY

Introduction

While cyber strategies take many forms, the public seems most interested in the digital domain's coercive potential. Perhaps the most famous example of cyber coercion is the Olympic Games operation: a series of cyber actions by the United States and Israel targeting Iran and popularly known as Stuxnet (Sanger 2012a). The operations were a complex, costly series of efforts designed to forestall Iranian nuclear proliferation efforts. These efforts were a classic coercive campaign. In both public and private, Iranian officials were threatened about the consequences of pursuing their nuclear ambitions.

While the Stuxnet episode has been unpacked comprehensively by many analysts (Farwell and Rohozinski 2011; Lindsay 2013; Slayton 2017), the episode has not been analyzed systematically as a coercive campaign combining a wide range of threats and positive inducements. In addition to US and Israeli cyber sabotage against the Natanz nuclear facility, covert operatives assassinated nuclear scientists (Peterson 2014) and recruited key figures as informants. Multiple regimes threatened Iran with further economic sanctions while the US and Israeli militaries threatened conventional military strikes against Iranian facilities. On top of this, there was an active internal effort for a change of leadership within Iran and diplomatic initiatives by the United States to reduce tensions and produce a settlement. Seen in this light, the Stuxnet infiltration is one action in a much wider coercive campaign. Cyber operations rarely occur in isolation of these broader overt and covert measures. To truly understand the process of cyber coercion, we must look at it in the additive, combined context. Failing to examine adjunct effects opens the investigator to bias with their blinders set toward finding evidence of cyber effects, when the picture is always much broader in scope.

This chapter explores how states integrate cyber degradations into larger coercive campaigns to compel their rivals. Cyber operations clearly do not occur in isolation, but analysts speak of these events as if they do. These options are among many that can be combined to achieve a strategic end. Building on the literature review in chapter 2 and findings in chapter 3, we posit an empirical question: *Are there unique combinations of power more likely to produce concessions?* To answer this question, we map how states combine cyber degradation, diplomatic, economic, and conventional military instruments to compel their rivals. We also examine the utility of achieving concession by target type, focusing on government or nonmilitary targets.

The investigation finds that, consistent with the findings of the previous chapter, cyber operations have a limited coercive utility. Even when cyber operations are combined with more traditional inducements like economic and military threats, they are unlikely to produce concessions. There is no magic combination of statecraft in rival relationships that tends to be highly coercive.

When cyber degradations involve a mix of positive and negative inducements and target noncivilian networks, the results suggest that concessions are more likely but still rare. The stick and carrot approach can translate to the digital domain, but the finding is limited due to the small number of concessions and a possible explanation is due to the outlier—the United States. The United States has more cyber capacity and economic and military power than its rival in each case. What is clear is that targeting civilian networks does not compel rival states. Similar to earlier studies on airpower (Pape 1996), punishment and risk strategies are not effective in the digital domain.

The chapter proceeds by first establishing a theoretical perspective for looking at coercive strategy, and foreign policy in general, from a combined perspective. From this vantage point, the chapter provides an introduction to qualitative comparative analysis using crisp sets (Ragin 2014) as a method for analyzing common properties associated with cyber compellence between rival states. Using crisp set methods, we then analyze the DCID data alongside common events data uncovered from the ICEWS dataset, both described in the previous chapter, to understand the combined context of cyber incidents. From this vantage point, we investigate the impact of cyber strategies on various target types.

These findings provide a more robust examination of the efficacy of cyber coercive campaigns. While cyber coercion is difficult and rarely produces rival concessions, there are combined strategies that appear to coalesce in the cases. Thus, cyber strategy is a means of amplifying larger campaigns to signal resolve and probe a rival's risk tolerance and the escalation potential. Cyber operations are an ambiguous signal, which as a form of covert action enables escalation management as opposed to independently compelling rivals.

Positive versus Negative Coercive Cyber Actions

Examining the combined context of cyber conflict is an important consideration often left out of the conversation regarding the utility of cyber methods. While cyberspace can be considered its own domain, and the language we use often invokes this framework, the reality is that it is more of a layer (Choucri 2012) that interacts with other diplomatic and military tools at the same time, often in the same place. Cyberspace includes the digital form of software and human capital needed to launch destructive cyber acts, but it also includes the physical hardware that is located within states and territories. The targets that are of interest to cyber hackers are located somewhere. Invoking the physicality of the Internet in many ways pushes us to think about the interactive context of cyber actions.

With the physical targets that are the goals of cyber operations, along with the personalities targeted for influence, we must consider the additive and combined context of cyber actions. There is a location, history, and personality inherent in all cyber actions that seek strategic impact. To properly understand how cyber works as part of a larger coercive campaign, we must understand the context of these interactions, including the positive and negative steps states take to achieve effects.

Distinguishing between the carrot and the stick has been a traditional conceptualization of punishment and reward in international relations. The conceptual origins are from the idea of choosing between the reward (carrot) or the punishment (the stick) to motivate a stubborn donkey. Applied to strategy, the question is whether you motivate a desired action in the target by offering them positive inducements or negative consequences. In coercion, it is important to remember that not all actions are punishments. Positive inducements can be more useful than punishment (Baldwin 1985), depending on the actor and their reward structures. That is, political actors often combine inducements to shape rival behavior.

An early conceptualization of the punishment–reward dynamic comes from Machiavelli (2008). His work articulated a view that it would be better to be loved but fear is the path toward progress and achieving results. The leader should not succumb to the instinct to be adored, but instead be firm and punish when needed. While some suggest this work is either satirical or tongue-in-cheek, it cannot be denied that generations of scholars have taken his advice as instructive of action. Its influence on realism is clear, appeals to morality or institutions are muted by the conjecture that material power is the best way to achieve results and security (Goertz and Diehl 1993).

As outlined in chapter 2, in analyzing cyber strategy we focus on a range of shaping activities designed to change the cost-benefit calculus of rival behavior and achieve a position of relative advantage. The majority of cyber operations act as ambiguous signals associated with tacit bargaining and covert action or help a rival state alter the balance of information through espionage as a means of gaining an intelligence advantage. The minority of cyber operations fall into more traditional coercive acts of degradation designed to compel adversaries. While the act is concealed, these incidents do not occur in a political vacuum. They tend to accompany a broader coercive campaign and what Alexander George called "tacit ultimatum" (Levy 2008) about what the target state needs to do to stop the pain. In Schelling (1960, 1966), compliance with demands will forestall punishment. The opposition must always be willing to unleash the power to hurt, but the goal is always achieving a bargained settlement short of war.

In our conceptualization of combined coercive actions, consistent with coercive diplomacy, we account for positive inducements in diplomatic, economic, or military categories alongside covert punishment in cyberspace. Diplomatic overtures, meetings, consultations, and summits are seen as positive steps forward where dialogue and a frank exchanges of ideas take precedence over threats. In economic maneuvers, negative sanctions are popular, but so are positive events like freeing up previously seized money, removing sanctions, or exchanging cash and goods to remove ill will. Military actions range from aid and cooperation, on the positive side, to displays of force and engagement on the negative side of the spectrum. That is, we take a combined approach and view cyber coercion, in the form of degradation incidents, as part of larger campaigns. Because successful degradation is not the norm, the question emerges as to the larger diplomatic and military context in which the concession occurred.

Table 4.1 lists the successful concessionary behavioral changing outcomes for cyber degradation actions using the combined approach for analysis. As there are only nine of these dyadic events, it is difficult to make many generalizations on this outcome variable at first sight. This is where the qualitative comparative analysis (QCA) method is the most useful and can produce generalizations with Boolean addition, multiplication, combinatorial logic, and minimization processes (Ragin 2000). However, looking at the events involving the high-cost, high-pain

TABLE 4.1

Crisp set truth table for combined cyber degradations, concessionary behavioral change

Event	Past Disruption	Past Espionage	Diplomatic Negative	Diplomatic Positive	Economic Negative	Economic Positive	Military Negative	Military Positive
Buckshot Yankee	0	1	1	1	1	0	0	0
Stuxnet (US)	0	1	1	0	1	0	1	0
Cisco Raider	0	0	0	0	0	0	0	0
Arrow Eclipse	0	1	1	1	1	0	1	0
Boxing Rumble (China)	0	1	1	1	0	0	0	1
NSA Fourth Party	0	1	1	1	1	0	1	1
Shotgiant	0	1	1	1	0	0	0	0
Boxing Rumble (NK)	0	0	1	1	0	0	0	0
Stuxnet (Israel)	0	1	0	0	0	0	0	1

degradation events that lead to concessions from the target, it is interesting that the initiators use a myriad of conventional foreign policy actions in combination. There appear to be three necessary conditions in this basic preliminary analysis that can predict concessions in our universe of cases: the presence of degradation and past espionage cyber activities and the *absence* of past cyber disruptions and positive economic inducements. All other independent variables that lead to successful concessions are thus sufficient but not necessary. Also, QCA gives us an analytical perspective through which to examine cyber campaigns and how they, as a layer, connect to other instruments of power. We are not interested in what does not lead to a concession, only what does, therefore only the concessionary events are displayed, with the negative outcomes (no concessions) omitted.

Coercive Signals in the Combined Form

H3. There are unique combinations of cyber operations and instruments of power that increase rival concessions.

The central question in this chapter is whether cyber campaigns produce concessions and, if so, what combinations of operations and instruments of power help rival states reach their objective. In a combined sense, manipulating the enemy is difficult without adjunct power considerations. Cyber espionage strategies involve being either secretive or using some sort of distraction with the target so that the cyber operation can infiltrate a network undetected. Since manipulative strategies are usually data-wiping or espionage campaigns, they need to be undetected before doing their malicious work. It is for this reason we focus on degradation, which can include punishment but concerns primarily denial coercive actions, combined cyber strategies in this chapter. However, we do add two new cyber variables to the analysis in this chapter—the presence or absence of past cyber disruptions or espionage campaigns within 1 year of the combined cyber degradation—to see whether there is a relationship between multiple-incident cyber campaigns and the probability of a concession being evoked. This helps us get at our notion of a cyber campaign seeking to alter behavior.

Since coercion requires the target be aware of the influence attempt, a state will employ many coercive tools alongside its cyber operations to send a clear signal. We can evaluate this prospect, as a robustness check, by examining the number of other coercive instruments combined with cyber degradations and whether together they achieve a concession. For Boghard and Lonergan (2017: 10), "coupling a cyber operation with a diplomatic message may be the least costly method to ensure ascription for the coercer, but it also must be credible." Using multiple tools enhances credibility and attribution of the attempt to change behavior in the target.

While risk strategies may be important for compellent behavioral change in coercive operations (Pape 1996), denial and punishment cyber operations present a particular challenge because of the high likelihood of involving civilians and committing gross international norm violations. Denial in cyber terms does not mean all-out destruction of infrastructure, but is as close as one can get when using cyber as a form of sabotage. Attacks on critical infrastructure such as the power grid, power plants, and other industrial control systems (ICS) or supervisory control and data acquisition (SCADA) systems important to a state's proper functionality would fall into this category of civilian harm and norm violation when attacked by sabotage, either with cyber means or conventional means.

There is also a clear pattern to how cyber concessions are produced. While we investigate all forms of additive power used alongside cyber operations, it is thought that specific operations such as economic sanctions and diplomatic overtures are best used in combination to produce a positive concession. On the other hand, using military means along with cyber methods is likely to harden the target and make them more resistant to coercive attempts. Changing the behavior of the enemy often requires more than just military threats, especially if the context is short of war, as is the case with cyber operations that function akin to covert action and traditional political warfare.

While there are inherent coordination challenges in combining instruments of coercion, rival states tend to assume the worst case. States struggle to integrate diplomatic action and economic measures with sensitive military operations and covert cyber activity. This challenge is especially acute in cyberspace, where operations tend to target special access programs (SAPs) restricting access. Yet, regardless of the degree of coordination rivals assume a unified signal from the aggressor.

Last, does the target type matter? For Borghard and Lonegran (2017: 14), there is a hierarchy of targets that are more likely to produce concessions: critical infrastructure (whether state or private), military command and control network, and private networks. In Pape's (1996) earlier study on airpower, risk and punishment strategies, both of which target civilians, are found to be less effective than denial strategies. We can evaluate this argument by examining whether there are discernable differences in the concession rate between operations involving government or civilian networks.

Public–private partnerships in cyberspace and questions about the level of state responsibility to protect civilian networks complicate these targeting questions. While protecting civilians from conventional military attack is a central task for the modern state, protecting civilian cyberspace might require the state to place itself directly between rivals and citizens. This positioning adds a layer of responsibility the state may not want and the civilian population may not necessarily desire due to privacy concerns. As it stands, in most states the government has no responsibility to protect private networks.

Methods and Measurements: Qualitative Comparative Analysis and the Crisp Set Method

To uncover the dynamics of cyber coercion with combined methods, next we turn to an introduction to the comparative method, specifically QCA using the crisp set method. QCA is not symmetrical, making it distinct from conventional statistical analysis (Ragin 2000, 2014). In other words, quantitative techniques using equal intervals that represent equal differences in the values of variables make it easier to conceptualize measurement and present logical and data analyses. The QCA process is able to analyze a limited number of cases with multiple independent variables, but these variables do not have to be used as controls as in quantitative analyses. Each independent variable is additive and has equal explanatory power for the solution outcomes. For a relatively small-N analysis such as the one in this research, crisp set QCA is the preferred method.

Other scholars (Chan 2003; Koenig-Archibugi 2004; Maat 2011; Thiem 2011) have used QCA to uncover important international relations phenomena that could have otherwise been missed—for example, important generalizations or case-specific details that might go unobserved in large-N statistical investigations. Chan (2003) uses the QCA crisp set approach to uncover the possible causes of war termination from the years 1945 to 1992. Koenig-Archibugi (2004) uses the fuzzy set approach to find the differing explanatory government preferences for institutional changes of the foreign and security policy of the European Union. Maat (2011) also uses fuzzy set QCA to find which territorial transgressions are more likely to lead to interventions by the international community. Thiem (2011) uses QCA to uncover specific conditions of intergovernmental cooperation regarding armaments in Western Europe for the years 1996–2006. This chapter continues this growing tradition of the use of QCA methods in international relations by uncovering the combined effects of state-initiated cyber coercion from the years 2000–2014. Next, we unpack what this method entails and why it is the appropriate one for answering the research questions at hand.

There are two basic forms of QCA: the crisp set analysis and the fuzzy set analysis. Crisp set analysis involves the coding of causal and outcome variables in binary form, or the mere presence or absence of a variable in a case that is in a dataset composed of a small to medium-sized number of cases (Ragin 2014). Causal and outcome variables are coded as either "1 (present)" or "0 (absent)" and are compiled into a dataset that researchers have collected to uncover certain conditions necessary or sufficient for outcome variables similarly coded as present or absent. A necessary condition means that a certain causal condition (x) must be present for an outcome variable (y) to be present (Ragin 2014). In other words, without x, we do not have y. However, x being necessary does not mean that y is guaranteed (Ragin 2014). A sufficient condition means that with a certain causal condition (x), an outcome (y) must follow (Ragin 2014). For a sufficient condition, x guarantees y.

Thus QCA is advantageous to selecting and unpacking case studies where generalizations can be made while still staying true to in-depth case study analysis for certain outcomes in the political arena (Ragin 2014). Boolean algebra is used to reduce the number of cases that contain the necessary conditions present in the small number of cases where they are present, and then the researcher can take these cases and do traditional qualitative in-depth analyses of these cases. Crisp set QCA is parsimonious in that it only deals with the presence or absence of causal and outcome variables, which are coded as either "0" or "1." To get a sense of what conventional foreign policy action when combined with cyber coercive action is successful in evoking a concessionary behavioral change, we apply this logic to membership for our conventional foreign policy actions and cyber strategies (causal variables) and to membership for our outcome (successful cyber action, behavioral change in target) variables and then uncover the necessary conditions for these scaled outcomes.

Crisp set QCA relies on the principles of Boolean algebra, where the use of binary data makes for simplified conditions based on the presence or absence of a variable in a case or event to be studied (Ragin 2014). These independent variables are then measured against the presence or absence of an outcome event, also coded as either "1" or "0." Truth tables are then developed to represent the data and the variables in nominal data form, so that the different combinations of independent variables are displayed against the presence of an outcome variable. In our study, this may show the presence of a positive diplomatic action combined with a negative military action with cyber espionage achieving the objective of breaching the targeted network, which in turn led to a concession with a cyber degradation, and how many times this particular combination of causal variables did so. These truth tables can then be used for Boolean addition, multiplication, combinatorial logic, and minimization.

Boolean addition is the simple concept of combinations of additive variables that may lead to an outcome variable that is present as a result. That is, if causal variables A and C are present, but causal variable B is not, and the outcome variable is coded as present, then we can conclude that variables A and C are conditions that cause the outcome to be present, but not B (Ragin 2014). In other words, $1 + 1 = 1$ for Boolean algebraic logic. Depending on how many times in a dataset this particular combination of independent variables leads to an outcome being present, a researcher will decide to include it for minimization and combinatorial logic analysis.

Boolean multiplication takes the addition one step further, and considers the combination of the presence and absence of particular causal variables and their effects on the presence of the outcome variable (Ragin 2014). For example, if A and C are present and B is not, we would write the multiplication as such: AbC, where the lower case "b" denotes the absence of a causal variable combined with the presence of the other two. Here instead of taking the numeric representations of the three variables and multiplying them ($1*0*1 = 0$), for Boolean multiplication we would simply drop the absent variable and write the new combined equation as AC. Different combinations of multiplied variables would be repeated to write a large equation of possible combinations of causal variables that evoke a positive outcome in the dataset. Boolean multiplication is useful for medium-sized datasets with many causal variables. For our purposes, we do not use this process and only stick to the more simplified additive effects of the combinatorial causes of our outcome variable of a behavioral change.

Combinatorial logic is the process of simplifying the main causal combinations of events with the outcome variables that are coded as present (Ragin 2014). Once it is found that certain combinations of causal variables happen the most frequently in the dataset under analysis, researchers can focus their algorithmic equations to determine which conditions are necessary and sufficient for an outcome variable to occur.

For this analysis of combined coercive strategies directed by state actors with successful cyber actions, we use the crisp set approach to assign membership scores to diplomatic, economic, and military action in the conventional foreign policy realm, as well as the presence or absence of past cyber disruptions and espionage, and membership in cyber degradations that were either part of or not part of a larger cyber campaign by the initiating state. These scores are combined with membership in the dependent variable: a concessionary behavioral change. Crisp set scores are binary; they are either coded as "0" (absent) or "1" (present). Here we build on earlier work of our categorical approach to the success of cyber strategies on their own and dig deeper by combining levels of successful cyber degradations and (Ragin 2000). Next, we turn to the research design to detail the logic and variable coding of our crisp set approach to combined cyber successful action by states.

RESEARCH DESIGN: INVESTIGATING COMBINED STRATEGIES

The goal of this portion of our research is to uncover the set relationships that would best explain rival state concessions. Our focus on cyber security is driven by the conjecture that cyber strategies are effective ways of leveraging power. The prior chapter suggests that concessions brought on by cyber activities are rare and depend more on strategy. The prospect of cyber power being leveraged in conjunction with other forms of power and influence is likely and should be investigated (Byman and Waxman 2002; Gartzke and Lindsay 2015). Therefore, we analyze the utility of additive strategies seeking to force the opposition to make a concession.

The unit of analysis is dyadic pairs of states where the cyber payload was part of a coercive effort targeting a rival state and resulting in a concession. Our selection on success is appropriate given the QCA method and our focus on observing the correlates of successful action in the foreign policy arena: success is measured by an observable concessionary behavioral change in the target state. While we are limited to concessions only evidenced during cyber actions, this limitation is proper given our focus on cyber means of influence.

The coding of the conventional causal variables is timed to be within a reasonable window of the impactful cyber action that allows for a cyber campaign to fulfill its malicious intent as well as evoke a behavioral change in the target state. We therefore use logical cut-points that attempt to capture how states initiate complex foreign policy actions against adversaries, and code any conventional foreign policy operation within 1 month of the start date of the cyber incident, which includes conventional action 1 month before and 3 months after the start date of the cyber incident. State decision-making and the subsequent implementation process of these complex and coordinated events take time, and 1 month before and 3 months after these cyber incidents allows for both enough time for these states to launch these combined strategies and logical cutoffs for our own coding efforts.

For the collection and truth table construction of the conventional foreign policy data, we use several datasets. The primary source of the events collection effort is derived from the Integrated Crisis Early Warning System Dataset (ICEWS), which is an events dataset that collects data for the years 1995–2015, includes events ranging from diplomatic meetings to military action, and includes initiations and targets from both state and nonstate actors (Boschee et al. 2015). Variables are coded as either negative or positive based on whether they are a "positive" inducing foreign policy action or a "negative" threatening one. Coded variables in this dataset can include diplomatic negotiations, which include high-level meetings between state diplomats and telephone conversations between leaders; economic reduction of trade, where bilateral deals are altered or terminated; and military usage, which includes all use of conventional military force by one state against another. This variety and the differing severity of foreign policy actions make the use of ICEWS data the most-suited and encompassing collection of noncyber variables for the purposes of this analysis.

As other datasets are up to the task, and can increase the reliability of the variables we collect for our purposes, we also use supplemental datasets that have been constructed over the decades. Supplemental datasets used for the conventional coding process include the Correlates of War (COW) Militarized Interstate Dispute (MID) dataset (Sarkees 2010; Palmer et al. 2015), which measures degrees of military action between states. Here we code variables that represent states' use of different military action against their targets. The MIDs are military events short of war, defined as fewer than 1,000 battle deaths. These can range from threats, displays, or the use of military force by one state against another, and help us verify the military events coded using ICEWS. Another supplemental dataset used is the International Crisis Behavior (ICB) dataset (Brecher and Wilkenfield 2000; Brecher et al. 2016), which measures escalatory foreign policy dynamics between states during international crises. Here we code variables that perpetuate crisis and include all variants of or conventional data (diplomatic, economic, military). These variables include those coding mediation, which could lead to compromise before a possible armed conflict breaks out between states, as well as escalation, which increases the dangers of armed conflict between states, especially in a crisis situation. The variables extracted from this dataset are used to verify those collected from ICEWS.

A final supplemental dataset used for consistency is the Threat and Imposition of Sanctions (TIES) dataset (Morgan et al. 2014), which collects data on economic sanctions imposed by states on target entities. Variables extracted from this dataset verified economic foreign policy events between states and added important context as to why certain sanctions were issued by the imitator in terms of issue type as well as salience. With these supplemental datasets assisting our primary ICEWS collection source, we are confident that all possible events are coded in conjunction with the cyber incidents in a specific time frame so that accurate measures of combined coercive action are captured and our results are robust.

For the collection and truth table construction of the cyber coercive variables, we use the DCID version 1.1, explained in detail in the previous chapter. We only use the 25 cases that are coded as degradation strategies and add the conventional variables to the model for this analysis. The previous cyber action (either disruptions or espionage) variable, which is measured as the presence or absence of previous cyber action within one calendar year of the case in question, is also an independent variable for this analysis. The QCA process goes through several minimization steps to find the necessary and sufficient conditions for concessions as a result of combined cyber actions. The QCA software (Drass and Ragin 1992; Ragin, Drass, and Davey 2016) starts with the 25 degradation cases and their coded independent binary variables covering cyber campaigns, diplomatic, economic, and military actions as well as the binary dependent variables of the presence or absence of a concession.

The Quine-McCluskey algorithm then reduces the dataset to only the combinations that produce concessions, the focus research endeavor. As we have a relatively moderate number of cases with only nine positive outcomes in terms of concessions for this particular analysis, all remainders, or combinations that do not produce concessions, are eliminated. There is also the possibility of what are called contradictory statements, or combinations that may produce concessions that simultaneously may also not produce concessions. Fortunately, we did not have any of these contradictory combinations appear in our minimization process. As we have eight independent variables predicting concessions, and the fact that we only have nine positive cases, the probability of having contradictory combinations is low.

To minimize the combinations to produce the least amount of necessary and sufficient conditions that predict concessions, decisions must be made as to certain cutoff points regarding frequency and consistency of combinations in the 25 cases in the QCA analysis. A frequency cutoff means that a minimum number of combinations of foreign policy actions that lead to concessions by target states must be present to avoid elimination from the minimization process. For this analysis, we set the frequency cutoff at one, as we only have nine cases evoking concessions and setting the cutoff higher would produce no results. Perhaps more important is the consistency cutoff process, which sets a minimum percentage of combinations of the independent and dependent variables to be present in positive outcomes, or combinations producing concessions. In other words, if the consistency cutoff percentage is set at 80%, and the independent variable of espionage does not appear in at least 80% of all cases with positive outcomes, in our case concessions, it is eliminated from the analysis.[1] This will be our logical cutpoint in the analysis that follows. This will allow for a minimized combination of necessary and sufficient conditions, so that we can make generalizations about which combinations of combined cyber actions lead to concessionary behavioral change. We now move to a description of the coding processes of the binary data for the QCA analysis of this chapter.

CODING CONVENTIONAL COERCION

Table 4.2 gives a brief summary of the coding scheme and definitions for the conventional foreign policy variables. The coding of the variables is based on Schrodt's (2012) Conflict and Mediation Event Observation (CAMEO) events data intensity scale and is simplified for the purposes of this crisp set analysis. The different foreign policy actions, categorized as diplomatic, economic, or military, are coded according to whether they are negative or positive inducements. For example, if an event involving cyber coercion has either a military usage, display, or threat present, that event would be coded as "1" under the negative military category, "0" if

TABLE 4.2

Conventional foreign policy action matrix

Diplomatic	Economic	Military
Threaten (−): Threaten to break up or withdraw from discussion, negotiation, or meeting	**Embargo/Sanction** (−): Stop or restrict commercial or other material exchange as a form of protest or punishment	**Usage** (−): All uses of conventional force and acts of war typically by organized armed groups not otherwise specified
Deny/Reject (−): This event form is a verbal act. The target for this event type is the party that introduces some accusation or charge against the source actor who denies responsibility	**Reduce trade** (−): Decrease or terminate provision of economic aid and/or trade with a country	**Display** (−): All military or police moves that fall short of the actual use of force, not otherwise specified
Negotiate (+): This event code should be used only when the report makes clear that negotiations, bargaining, or discussions are involved in the meetings or consultations in question. "Holding talks" and "discussions" are treated as negotiations	**Aid** (+): Offer, promise, agree to, or otherwise indicate willingness or commitment to provide economic support; Extend, provide monetary aid and financial guarantees, grants, gifts and credit	**Confidence building** (+): Provide peacekeepers or other military forces for protection, extend or expand their mandates; Extend, provide military and police assistance including arms and personnel.
Coordination (+): Initiate, resume, improve, or expand diplomatic, nonmaterial cooperation or exchange not otherwise specified.	**Trade increase** (+): Increase trade and/or sign bilateral/ multilateral trade agreement	**Cooperate** (+): Offer, promise, agree to, or otherwise indicate willingness or commitment to provide military support; Initiate, resume, improve, or expand military exchange or cooperation; Extend, provide military and police assistance including arms and personnel.

none of these negative military actions is present. If one of the 25 cyber degradation events have either a diplomatic praise, negotiation, or coordination present within the three-month period, that event would be coded as "1" in the positive diplomacy category, "0" otherwise.

Crisp sets are useful for parsimony and clear results regarding necessary and sufficient conditions, so simplifying these categories for this preliminary analysis is justified. The cyber coercive variables used in this QCA are limited to degradation tools and the presence or absence of past cyber disruptions or espionage in the dyadic cases. We now turn to the findings and data analysis of this crisp set method.

Findings: Explaining Concession with Combined Cyber Strategies

H3. Confirmed in light of evidence. There are unique combinations of cyber operations and instruments of power that increase rival concessions.

Table 4.3 below shows the results of the Quine-McCluskey algorithm to uncover the necessary and sufficient conditions for combined cyber strategies that evoke concession. After inserting our population of cases into the QCA software (Drass and Ragin 1992; Ragin, Drass, and Davey 2006) we focus on the puzzle of this chapter: are there any discernable patterns to evoking a concession from target states using combined strategies involving cyber? The combinations in Table 4.3 give us several possible sufficient conditions that will be combined and minimized using the Quine-McCluskey process. Necessary conditions imply that certain cyber and foreign policy actions must be present (or absent) for a concession to be observed. Looking at Table 4.3, there are

TABLE 4.3

| | The attributes of successful cyber coercive campaigns | |
| | Cyber Instruments | Non-cyber Instruments |
Conditions	(absence)	(absence)
Necessary	Degradation	(+ Economic)
	Past Espionage	
	(Past Disruption)	
Sufficient		+/− Diplomacy
		− Economic
		+ Military
		− Military

Notes: Solution coverage is 0.777778; solution constituency is 1 (see Table 4.4).
Reduced Boolean Addition Equation available in the endnotes.[4]

TABLE 4.4

Reduced Boolean addition for combined cyber campaigns

Cyber Instruments [a]	Non-cyber Instruments	Raw Coverage (Unique Coverage)	Episode Examples
Degradation	+/− Diplomacy	.222	Buckshot Yankee
Past Espionage	− Economic	(.111)	Arrow Eclipse
Degradation	− Diplomacy	.222	Arrow Eclipse,
Past Espionage	− Military	(.111)	Stuxnet (US)
	− Economic		
Degradation	+/− Diplomacy	.222	Arrow Eclipse
Past Espionage	− Military	(.111)	NSA Fourth Party
	− Economic		
Degradation	− Military	.111	Stuxnet (Israel)
Past Espionage		(.111)	
Degradation	+/− Diplomacy	.111	Boxing Rumble
Past Espionage	+ Military	(.111)	(NK)

Solution Coverage: 0. 777778

Solution Consistency: 1 (note: all coverages above have a consistency of 1)[a] All episodes selected on the presence of a successful cyber degradation

four necessary conditions that lead to a concession: the *absence* of past cyber disruptions and positive economic inducements, and the *presence* of past espionage events and degradation cyber techniques, which is implied given the construct of this model.[2] These conditions are present (or absent) in all parts of the addition equation broken into the five rows in Table 4.4 and are indicated in bold. The remaining different combinatorial cases are then given frequency consistency cutoffs. An example is the Buckshot Yankee counterespionage campaign against Russian hackers, where the Kremlin's espionage campaign was found and degraded out, halting all of these Russian operations targeting Department of Defense networks in 2008.

Our frequency cutoff is at 1, indicating that these causal variables must be present in at least one of the concessionary events. The frequency cutoff indicates that a certain combination of conventional scores must occur a minimum number of times. The consistency cutoff is also at 1, or 100%, and is the point where if consistency of certain combinations of combined events does not make up at least a percentage of the cutoff, they are dropped from the minimization process. In other words, if certain combinations of causal variables are present in at least all of the cases, they are not eliminated from the minimization process.

The raw coverage percentage scores associated with Table 4.3 measures the proportion of memberships in the outcome explained by each term in the solution for coercive actions involving the necessary condition of cyber degradation. Similarly, the unique coverage percentage measures the proportion of memberships in the outcome explained solely by each solution term. These coverage scores are all at 11%, which is not surprising, given that there are only 9 total concessions out of a population of cases of 25. The solution coverage score of over 77% indicates that all of the combinatorial actions in Table 4.3 explain about 78% of the outcome of objective concessionary combined actions. In other words, this is the percentage of equations that explain concessions. The solution consistency percentage of over 100% explains the degree to which membership in the different combinations of causal variables is a subset of membership in the outcome variables of behavioral change. Basically, the independent variables as individual units are present in 100% of all positive outcomes, or successful concessions. Two successful degradation campaigns are dropped from the minimization process because they do not meet this minimal threshold.

We can now start to minimize our Boolean addition equation with this in mind. Looking at Table 4.4, we keep all the past cyber espionage in our individual Boolean multiplication rows, as they are necessary conditions, and eliminate the absent necessary conditions, the absence of cyber disruptions and the absence of positive economic inducements to get a clearer picture of what it takes to evoke a concession from a target state with combined cyber actions. The presence or the absence of the remaining instruments of foreign policy options remain as they are either present or absent within each Boolean multiplication equation.

Looking at Table 4.4, the following combinations of degradation and past cyber espionage combine to produce outcomes:

- negative and positive diplomatic action, and negative economic action;
- negative diplomatic, economic, and military actions;
- negative diplomatic, economic, and military actions and positive diplomacy;
- negative military conventional instruments of power; and
- diplomatic negative action and diplomatic and military positive inducements.

Necessary conditions for evoking concessions in a combined sense include degradations, past cyber espionage, and the absence of past cyber disruptions and positive economic inducements. The remaining independent variables are sufficient conditions for combined cyber action and evoking concessions from a target state. Boxing Rumble and Arrow Eclipse meet these criteria, as well as the more well-known US and Israeli degradation incident, Stuxnet.

A prime example of successful combined action pressuring a state to concede was the Stuxnet worm. Stuxnet involved not just a degrade but also cyber espionage incidents such as Flame and Duqu that supported it, the combined actions of diplomatic and military threats, and economic sanctions by the United States on Iran.

The goal was to prevent the progress of Iran's uranium enrichment program that could have one day been weapons-grade. As Israel was pressuring the Bush administration in 2006 to endorse military action against Iran's nuclear facilities, Stuxnet was proposed by the NSA as a more covert and less escalatory option available for both Israel and the United States (Sanger 2012a). The Bush administration was losing popularity over the continued war in Iraq, military escalation with another Persian Gulf country was not a viable option. The lack of a viable military option pushed the administration to adopt the Olympic Games program, which included cyber incidents such as Stuxnet, Flame, and Duqu. This covert cyber operation continued when Barack Obama took over the US presidency in 2009 (Sanger 2012b).

Yet, while Stuxnet damaged centrifuges at the Natanz enrichment facility, Lindsay (2013) argues the cyber operation alone was insufficient to push Iran to the negotiating table. Occurring alongside the cyber covert action, the United States used diplomatic engagement and economic inducements alongside the threat of military action to get Iran to concede (BBC News 2016). It was not until the initial secret meetings with the new Iranian president, Hassan Rouhani, that the offer of releasing assets held by the United States (totaling in the billions although the exact number is disputed) and lifting of sanctions were offered between March and June of 2013. After these moves were offered, the concession was quickly made and in November of 2013 a Joint Plan of Action was signed between Iran and the key negotiating partners known as P5+1. This combination of the cyber action plus economic inducements led to the Iranian concession. What we cannot measure is the timeline associated with positive economic inducements since these were associated with secrete deliberations between Iran and the United States (BBC News 2013).

The findings in Table 4.4 also demonstrate that it is not the number of coercive instruments that produces concessions. Rather, degradations, past cyber espionage, and the absence of positive economic inducements are necessary conditions for producing concessions, and certain combinations with these three necessary conditions are sufficient for producing concessions. The average number of instruments used per successful concession is 3.33.[3] Yet, there are episodes that had only one instrument and others that had six. There appear to be particular combinations of positive and negative inducements that matter more than the sheer number.

With respect to positive inducements, they are a sufficient but not necessary condition of producing rival concessions in cyber campaigns. Looking at Table 4.4, positive diplomatic and military instruments, when combined with high-cost, complex cyber degradation operations, tend to produce concessions. Yet, these attributes are only sufficient conditions. The only necessary condition is the use of cyber degradation and the absence of positive economic inducements.

Another interesting aspect of this subset of concessions is that the United States appears to integrate positive inducements with its cyber degradation efforts while other actors do not. The only other successful degradation initiators, Israel, relied on negative inducements. Israel's threats to bomb Iranian nuclear facilities factored into Tehran's decision calculus in 2014–2015. Though we have a limited number of cases and the United States skews the sample, there may be a larger-state–small-state dynamic at play. That is, great powers have enough bargaining space to include positive inducements while smaller states have less room to concede in their exchanges with rivals.

Last, target selection in cyber campaigns matters. Consistent with findings in the air power (Pape 1996) and terrorism literature (Abrahms 2006), targeting civilian networks does not produce a concession, indicated in Table 4.5. Concessions appear to be more likely when the target is a government network. In fact, the only successful concession where the primary target is civilian involved the United States targeting the Chinese search engine Huawei in 2010, which is seen as a retaliatory response to the Chinese attack on Silicon Valley companies the previous year and primarily involved the US giant Google. The United States reached out to protect its private sector by using a not escalatory tit-for-tat retaliatory response to Chinese cyber malice in order to compel the Chinese to stop the widespread hacking of the US private sector.

TABLE 4.5

Predicting concessions by target type

| | | | Concession | | |
			No	Yes	Total
Target Type	Civilian	Count	41	1	42
		Expected Count	39.6	2.4	42.0
		z-score	.2	−.9	
	Government	Count	140	10	150
		Expected Count	141.4	8.6	150.0
		z-score	−.1	.5	
Total		Count	181	11	192
		Expected Count	181.0	11.0	192.0

$***p < .01, **p < .05, *p < .10$

The combined findings amplify this insight. Negative and positive diplomatic actions tend to target government officials or facilities not civilians. While economic threats tend to impact civilians, the target of the threat is the government or elites, not the average civilian. The same applies to military inducements, which are military threats targeting governments.

The utility of punishment strategies directed toward civilians are clearly questionable. Since we are all dependent on digital connectivity, attacking civilian, public targets causes fear of cyber–Pearl Harbor. When civilian attacks have occurred, the reality is that the population quickly adapts and moves on. Russian attacks against Estonia in 2007 did not lead to any concessions. In fact, Estonia temporarily severed its connection to shield itself from Russian operations. The response was not to return fire but to bunker down.

The fact still remains that governments need to prepare the population for eventual civilian targeted attacks on such facilities as power plants or basic Internet connectivity. Cyber espionage seems to be necessary for future degradations to succeed. With the move away from past technologies such as cable communication, radio, and other forms of connection, we have become dependent on the Internet for media and information. When this is attacked, there will certainly be consequences, but concessions appear unlikely.

Conclusions

Based on these results, it seems the future of cyber conflict and combined campaigns lies with degradations. Though the least frequently used form of coercion in the DCID 1.1, when combined with other instruments of power these complex operations are the most successful in changing a rival state's behavior. The United States again is the outlier and skews the sample. Washington appears to have mastered the art of combining complex degradations with economic threats and diplomatic inducements, as well as reconnaissance via cyber espionage. This said, smaller states have begun to use similar methods. Israel has generated concessions with combined military and diplomatic threats and cyber espionage with cyber degradations.

Other coercive forms produce less concession than degradation. Espionage actions have only evoked concessions at a rate of 2% (2 out of 97) in our universe of cases, yet we may see payoffs in the future as the information stolen may begin to foster comparative advantage, especially among major powers. Yet, this chapter finds that they serve as a necessary condition to allow for future cyber degradations to evoke concessions. Espionage therefore plays an important auxiliary role in modern-day combined coercion. However, our research on the China case introduces significant questions about the process of success through espionage. Stealing is no method to achieve innovation and adaptation. Disruptions achieve their objectives and will probably continue to be used to signal displeasure about policies with rivals, yet they are not coercive enough to produce concessions, even in the combined sense.

This chapter illustrates a process of competitive learning as rival states combine cyber instruments with traditional tools of statecraft. New technologies create new challenges but not necessarily new advantages. Cyber degradation works more as a multiplier than a single decisive blow that forces a state to capitulate. We now turn to chapters on the leading cyber rivals and see this process of learning in context.

5

COMMISSARS AND CROOKS

Russian Cyber Coercion

Introduction

While ranked sixth in latent cyber capacity (chapter 3), Russia is the second most active state when it comes to going on the offense in cyberspace. From early disruptive actions against Estonia and Georgia, to degrading attacks on critical infrastructure in Ukraine, and finally, complex espionage actions and propaganda purchased through social media sites seeking to bring down the democratic process in the United States (2016), France (2017), and Germany (2017), Russia has been one of the most aggressive and destructive actors in cyberspace. Yet, its efforts focus on breaking norms and disrupting the system rather than cyber violence. When it comes to evaluating the efficacy of Russia hacking activities, we question the conclusion that Moscow achieves its ends in cyberspace. More often than not, Russia fails, doubles down, and fails again.

Russia's recent cyber actions show that there is a distinct and evolving pattern to Russian cyber coercion. Cyber operations offer Moscow a new domain to weave a web of lies and half-truths designed to shape public opinion and signal resolve. Episodes such the 2016 US presidential election hacks and disinformation campaigns illustrate how Russia integrates cyber operations into diplomatic and propaganda efforts to gain a position of advantage relative to its rivals. The net effect is not a compellent success. Rather, Moscow uses low-cost, deniable cyber actions to amplify broader propaganda efforts, sowing discontent within the governments and populations of the targeted state, while signaling the risk of escalation.

This chapter shows that Russian cyber strategies demonstrate a similar pattern in peacetime as in wartime. In peacetime, Russia seeks to isolate adversaries, distort perceptions through propaganda, and undermine adversaries from within. In times of conflict, as in Georgia and Ukraine, Russian cyber actions complement the broader military and information campaign, but in a very restrained manner. Disruptions that enable propaganda and isolate rivals shape broader coercive campaigns. In peacetime, the effect of cyber operations has often given Moscow a strategic advantage in line with its national interest when it invokes chaos and discontent in the broader populations of its targets. Putin is a rational actor seeking to enhance his domestic position by showing strength externally (Maness and Valeriano 2015).

This chapter unpacks how the Russian state engages in cyber disruption, espionage, and degradation alongside larger coercive campaigns to advance its interests. Through analyzing the empirical distribution of attributed Russian cyberattacks in relation to the overall sample of cyber events, the chapter offers a qualitative review of the book's hypotheses. These case-specific findings reinforce the results of the macro tests in chapters 3 and 4. To this point, Russia has yet to find a way to evoke concessions from its target. Rather, the goal of Russian cyber operations appears to reside in sowing discontent and chaos in targeted populations in rival states as a means of pressuring decision makers and bolstering larger propaganda efforts.

The chapter proceeds by first introducing case-specific attributes to Russian-initiated cyber actions important for contextualization of these incidents. We find that there are two state-specific dynamics that shape the Russian strategic logic and employment of cyber capabilities as a form of political warfare. First, there is a Soviet ghost in the machine. The way Russian operatives approach cyber reflects a preference for manipulation through disruption and distortion, consistent with active measures and reflexive control doctrines from the Cold War, alongside an operational interest in deception and surprise. Therefore, Russia fails to produce cyber-specific compellent outcomes, but does integrate cyber strategies into broader propaganda efforts and influence operations. Specifically, multimedia propaganda efforts reflect the doctrine of reflexive control, "a means of conveying to a partner or an opponent specially prepared information to incline them to voluntarily make the predetermined decision desired by the initiator of the action" (Thomas 2004). Russian information warfare is perpetrated through this lens; the goal is to sow confusion, discontent, and division in an opponent's government and population. This information effect has been Russia's doctrine in Western countries recently, with little success in achieving results beyond general chaos and mistrust.

The second state-specific dynamic shaping Russian strategic logic in cyberspace concerns third-party relationships. The cyber ecosystem in Russia is integrated into an extensive criminal network. In other words, there is a symbiotic relationship between Kremlin cyber operatives and cyber criminals. Russia tends to use third-party intermediaries, especially criminal networks, to mask the origins of attacks and lower the costs of developing capabilities. While this approach theoretically lowers the effort required in advancing Russian cyber capabilities, with the state contracting out expertise, software, and systems, it does not guarantee concessions or further development of capabilities through internal talent development. In this case, we witness restrained Russian action, even under the context of active war situations, and see a wider distribution of targets as Russia moves from one failed foreign policy adventure to another.

Using data from the DCID 1.1, this chapter identifies patterns of Russian cyber coercion and uses these observations to elaborate on the central claims of the book. The chapter isolates Russian cyber incidents and compares their disruption relative to the sample of all rival exchanges. From this vantage point, this chapter details Russian cyber incidents and what they tell us about cyber strategy, signaling, and coercion.

The Context of Russian Cyber Operations
UNIQUE ORIGINS: THE SOVIET GHOST IN THE MACHINE

Russian approaches to cyber coercion reflect larger strategic preferences that emerged during the Soviet Union and a reliance on criminal elements to mask cyber intrusions. Russia also has a long tradition of integrating information operations aspects into military activities. The Soviet Army held that changing material conditions would lead to a military employing surprise and deception to evolve (Glantz 1988). Starting in the 1970s, Soviet authors started to explore what they termed "the initial period of war" (Ivanov 1974). The opening stages of a conflict were critical to shaping the campaign, both in terms of achieving a position of advantage and controlling escalation. According to Kir'ian (1985: 123), the military would need to "achieve considerable results in the initial period of war in order to be able to exercise greater influence over the future course of war." Glantz argues these strategic preferences grow out of the experience of the Red Army and the fight against internal and external enemies to consolidate power between 1918 and 1921. The fledging Red Army used deception to weaken its adversaries (Glantz 2016).

Deception and distorting information as a means of manipulation were central features of the Soviet foreign policy. The Soviets had a well-established concept for integrating deception, surprise, and propaganda into broader coercive efforts.

With respect to military operations, Russia would achieve surprise and the ability to exercise greater influence through the following mechanisms: misleading the enemy to one's intentions (disinformation), concealing information about your own intentions, using new forms of combat to enhance deception, conducting active deception campaigns, and planting seeds of doubt through false flag operations (Kir'yan 1976: 163).

The importance of disruption and manipulating information had informed the Soviet concept of active measures. Active measures embodied a wide array of political warfare measures, including both covert and overt psychological operations aimed "at the pollution of the opinion-making process in the West" (Metzl 1974: 921). These influence operations included activities designed to undermine a rival's populations in political leaders and institutions, shape policy, disrupt relations between rivals and their allies, and discredit opponents (Schultz 1988). Under Putin, this strategy extends to increasing Russia's leverage in post-Soviet space as a counter to the Color Revolutions that swept through George, Ukraine, and Kyrgyzstan (Saari 2014). The connectivity, web of global networks, and velocity of cyberspace likely amplify efforts to use disinformation to undermine rivals.

The central role of surprise, deception, and information persist in modern Russia, where "in government and academic circles, information is understood to be a form and source of power" (Jaitner 2015: 88). In this rendering, cyber actions are subordinate to a larger Russian "information space" that leverages broadcast and print propaganda, cyber and electronic warfare, covert action, and any other means available to "disorganize governance, organize anti-government protests, delude adversaries, influence public opinion, and reduce an opponent's will to resist" (Jaitner 2015: 88).

The Kremlin uses cyber strategies as part of a broader information warfare concept designed to confuse its enemies and leverage the disruption to compensate for its declining power (Snegovaya 2015: 11). This strategy of confusion and manipulation has additional antecedents in the Soviet concept of reflexive control. Reflexive control is about influencing your enemy to make suboptimal decisions that benefit you (Thomas 2004). Rather than attack the enemy's decision cycle, it seeks to manipulate it through misinformation and deception.

The concept first appears in the Soviet military literature during the 1960s (Thomas 2004). In fact, Russian thinkers after the fall of the Soviet Union held that the Strategic Defense Initiative (SDI) was a US reflexive control campaign designed to get the Soviets to spend money they did not have on countering futuristic weapons that did not exist (Thomas 2004). Reflexive control operates at the strategic level, as seen in the SDI example, but also at the operational and tactical level. At lower echelons, reflexive control aligns with Soviet ideas about the importance of *maskirovka* (deception) and the use of disinformation to "the enemy's decision-making processes" (Snegovaya 2015: 12).

Following the Cold War, mirror imaging heightens this preference for manipulation. Russian thinkers see themselves as victims of a sustained unconventional, information warfare campaign by the United States (Jaitner 2015: 89). According to Inkster (2016), since the 1990s Russian nationalists have been "increasingly seized by the conviction that the West is out to undermine [Moscow] through the use of soft-power tools such as the internet and social media, and the use of NGOs to promote Western values." For example, in 1998 the Russian foreign minister Igor Ivanov (1998) wrote a letter to the United Nations expressing Moscow's concerns over the "the creation of information weapons and the threat of information wars, which we understand as action taken by one country to damage the information resources and system of another country while at the same time protecting its own infrastructure."

Russian strategists see a constant war of influence capable of destroying great powers. Russian elites refer to the Cold War as the "first information war" and argue that the West was also behind the Arab Spring (Jaitner 2015: 89). These views are shared by elites in the Kremlin who shutdown nongovernmental organizations they saw as waging a war against the Russian state through democracy promotion, human rights advocacy, and other civil society programs that threaten elite influence (Alexeeva 2013).

This view finds particular resonance in the Gerasimov doctrine, which explores how to integrate military and nonmilitary means to achieve political objectives.[2] For General Gerasimov (2013: 5), "[The] method of conflict has altered in the direction of the broad use of political, economic, informational, humanitarian, and other nonmilitary measures—applied in coordination with the protest potential of the population. All this is supplemented by military means of a concealed character, including carrying out actions of informational conflict and the actions of special-operations forces."

Though Russians have always discussed combining multiple instruments of power, the concept envisions a new ratio of 4:1 nonmilitary—often influence operations, cyber and covert action—to military action. New forms of operations would seek to wage almost constant war in a unified information space, seeking to undermine adversaries from within by reducing the military, economic, and political power of the state (Bartel 2016: 36). In this manner, the Gerasimov Doctrine collapses

traditional distinctions between war and peace and between military and civilian domains. In one sense, information warfare is as a lineal descendent of the active measures (aktivnyye meropriyatiya) conducted during the Soviet era, a significant portion of which involved putting into the public arena news stories that sought to portray the West in a negative light. The best-known example of this was the planting in an Indian newspaper in 1984 of a story that the AIDS virus, then sweeping through Sub-Saharan Africa, was the outcome of US genetic-engineering experiments. (Inkster 2016)

For Russians, the Gerasimov doctrine continues the process of turning "the West's playbook against it via an approach characterized as non-linear war" (Inkster 2016).

This logic extends to the cyber domain. Russian cyber operations, as part of a broader propaganda campaign, undermine an adversary's will to fight through influencing public opinion and disorienting both public and government perception. According to Lewis (2015: 48), "cyber-attacks that produce strategic or military effect can include the manipulation of software, data, knowledge and opinion to degrade performance and produce political and psychological effect. Introducing uncertainty into the minds of opposing commanders or political leaders is a worthy military objective." Moscow uses cyber operations not just to steal information or disrupt a network, but to manipulate public opinion once the initial events occur. Weedon (2015: 66) states, "computer network operations are tools to be integrated into broader efforts to maintain political and military dominance in a given theatre and, more broadly, in the domestic and global courts of public opinion." Achieving a concession from the target state is but one of many strategic goals for Russia.

THE CYBER ECOSYSTEM: THE CRIMINAL UNDERWORLD

Another key feature of the Russian approach to cyber strategies is the historic connection between intelligence services and criminals. Over the past 20 years, Moscow has used cyber criminals either as proxy "hackers-for-hire" or a means of hiding Russian attacks that target governments could attribute to the Kremlin. While the United States tends to avoid this practice, China will use criminals if necessary, but tends to mainly rely on promoting a duty to the motherland for foreign nationals living abroad and working in the technology sector.

For Russia, there is a symbiotic relationship between the cyber-criminal underworld and the Russian intelligence services as well as other agencies involved with conducting cyber operations. Russian hackers, if arrested, tend to be let off on technical grounds based on government connections or their ability to pay a bribe (de Carbonnel 2013).

Haarmo (2017), in her interview with F-Secure founder Mikko Hypponen, finds that when his firm outed the Dukes hacking group, the Russian network did not change its mode of operations to throw the scent off. This lack of fear or need to veil criminal activities indicates that the Russian government, or at least elements therein, supported and protected the group. Criminal groups operating in other countries would change IP addresses, rework their coding, and cease activity for a prolonged amount of time. The Dukes group did none of these actions when caught.

After the collapse of the Soviet Union, Russia and Eastern Europe emerged as the epicenter of cybercrime (Glenny 2009). The former Soviet space became the primary market for cybercrime tools and stolen data. Russia led the world in quality malware (Ablon, Libicki, and Golay 2014: 7). Hacker forums tended to be dominated by Russians and Ukrainians (Albon, Libicki, and Golay 2014: 8). Diverging from Chinese hackers, who focused on stealing intellectual property, Eastern European groups used malware to target financial institutions (Albon, Libicki, and Golay 2014: 8). In a 2008 study, McAfee Avert labs linked many of the major cybercriminals in Russia to the state (McAfee 2008). That same year, Russia passed China as the leading originator of malware (Fried 2008).

Russian cyber campaigns against other states are dependent on this criminal ecosystem for talent and to maximize deniability. For example, malware first created to steal bank credentials was used to launch distributed denial of service (DDoS) attacks in Georgia in 2008 (Zetter 2012) during the short military conflict in August of that year. In June 2014, the US Department of Justice launched Operation Tovar to take down a peer-to-peer botnet, GameOver Zeus, ransoming money from banks and other institutions. This botnet infected an estimated 500,000 to 1 million computers globally (Krebs 2014). In 2017, the US Treasury sanctioned Mikhalovich Bogachev, a Russian criminal wanted in conjunction with GameOver Zeus, for suspected involvement in the US election hack (Graff 2017).

The Russian Business Network (RBN), a cyber-criminal organization active since 1996, was founded by individuals with direct connections to the Russian military and Federal Security Service of the Russian Federation (FSB). The founder of RBN, "Flyman" has family members active in St. Petersburg politics, the same networks that gave rise to President Vladimir Putin (Warren 2007). Other RBN members were former FSB members (McQuaid 2008). The organized crime syndicate was implicated in a 2003 attack against the US Department of Defense (Howard 2009).

What explains the emergence of Russia and eastern Europe as the epicenter of cybercrime? According to Kostyuk (2015: 113), countries in the region, such as Ukraine, have few cyber regulations, a society home to highly educated programmers, a struggling economy, and permissive norms surrounding stealing copyright and intellectual property. Similarly, according to Maurer (2015: 79), "there was no shortage in the region of labor skilled in information technology and hacking while a mature industry was missing and government salaries of a few thousand dollars a year pale in comparison to reports of thousands or millions of dollars in the latest cyber heist."

The Soviet Union's collapse saw the Russian state left with a large number of highly trained, underemployed scientists. In addition to the nuclear proliferation risks this situation presented, there were less-appreciated cyber proliferation risks.[3] Since at least the late 1960s, Soviet computer pioneers began championing broad-based computer literacy for Soviet citizens as a means of "cyberneticize the economy" (Afinogenov 2013: 574). During perestroika in the mid-to-late 1980s, these ideas led to the emergence of an amateur computer culture. The combination of this amateur computer culture and high levels of mathematics education and out-of-work scientists created an ecosystem ripe for the growth of cybercrime. Though difficult to pin down the origins of illicit networks, some historians have suggested that "the hackers and malware-creators for whom the Russian computing scene is known today are offshoots of late Soviet amateur computer culture: the first internationally known Russian computer hacker, Vladimir Levin, who stole over $12 million from Citibank in 1994, was one of these self-taught hobbyists" (Afinogenov 2013: 584).

Early hubs of cyber-criminal activity parallel former Soviet hubs for scientific research. The RBN—a front for illicit web activity—set up in another knowledge hub: St. Petersburg (Krebs 2007). Before it vanished, RBN sold criminal groups web-hosting services and created a hub for cybercrime, specializing in stealing personal information for resale (Krebs 2007). The RBN even engaged in retaliatory acts of cyber disruption, such as crashing the National Bank of Australia's home-page for 3 days after the bank took measures against Rock Phish, a $150-million-dollar RBN spear-phishing campaign (The Economist 2007).

This combination of the amateur computer culture and high levels of STEM education alongside lax digital piracy laws and a culture of "covert entrepreneurialism" has made Russia the epicenter for a cybercrime network that reaches across eastern Europe (Null 2015). In addition to these path-dependent effects, the sheer size of the cybercrime market creates its own gravity. According to Galeotti, "for a lot of the Russian techies [crime] became very lucrative. . . . They began to recruit top graduates from universities who could earn 10 times what they would get in Russia and twice what they would get in the west" (Warren 2007). The Russian state finds low-cost, abundant cyber talent in criminal circles.

Data Analysis: Russian Cyber Coercion

Between 2000 and 2014, publicly documented cyber coercive exchanges between Russia and its rivals reveals the strategic preference for simple disruption operations likely set off by the ecosystem of professional intelligence operatives and criminals. During this time Russia conducted 45 cyber coercion operations (see Table 3.2 in

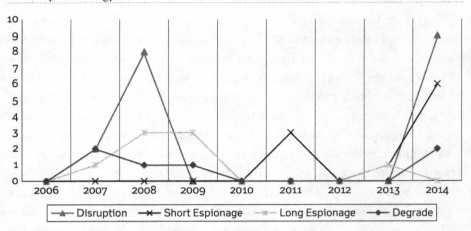

FIGURE 5.1 Russia Yearly Cyber Incidents, Coercive Intent: 2000–2014

chapter 3). These episodes included 19 disruptions (42.2%), 20 espionage incidents (44.4%), 12 being short-term (26.7%) and 8 long-term espionage (17.8%), and 6 degradations (13.3%). Of note, Figure 5.1 shows that Russia had no direct coercive success in cyberspace. None of the Russian cyber operations evoked a concessionary behavioral change. This said, Russia did integrate cyber operations into wartime campaigns to compel Georgia and Ukraine. Limited success in these cases likely reflects larger military instruments of power, not cyber-enabled coercion.

Russian use of cyber coercion against rival states peaked in 2008 and 2014, coinciding with combined campaigns in the military conflicts of Georgia and Ukraine, respectively. There is a continuous use of espionage throughout the period under observation. These operations comprise mostly disruptive and short-term espionage techniques, indicating that Russian strategic doctrine of implementing chaos and disinformation are present against these former Soviet states. For example, in the early stages of the Georgia campaign, Russia defaced government websites, which coincided with a barrage of DDoS attacks on government and private networks. The Ukrainian government was constantly under siege from Russian-backed DDoS and website defacement attacks. In both cases, mainly website defacements and disruption tend to reflect the dominant Russian narrative, inserting language and symbols that painted Georgian and Ukrainian politicians as fascists.

Table 5.1 shows that Russia uses no distinct coercion pattern when compared to the rest of the universe of initiating rival states in the DCID 1.1 dataset. Looking at the cross-tabulation analysis, Table 5.1 shows that the cross-tabulation comparison to the rest of the world's imitating states in cyber space are all around the expected level. Although Russia uses disruptive techniques as well as short-term espionage more than other coercive objectives, this is at the expected level when compared to the rest of the world. Russia will use whichever coercive objective fits the particular

TABLE 5.1

Cyber objective differentials between Russia and global cyber initiators

		Disruption	Short-term Espionage	Long-term Espionage	Degrade	Total
Russia	Count	19	12	8	6	45
	Expected Count	16.4	15.7	7.0	5.9	45.0
	z-score	.6	−.9	.4	.1	
World	Count	51	55	22	19	147
	Expected Count	53.6	51.3	23.0	19.1	147.0
	z-score	−.4	.5	−.2	.0	
Total	Count	70	67	30	25	192
	Expected Count	70.0	67.0	30.0	25.0	192.0

[***]$p < .01$, [**]$p < .05$, [*]$p < .10$

task at hand, which for the most part is limited disruptive objectives and short-term espionage campaigns that are flipped into disinformation operations against the target state within a short period of time.

Figure 5.2 indicates that Russian cyber disruptions tend to involve a mix of vandalism and DDoS. These methods are overwhelmingly used in its ongoing conflicts in the former post-Soviet space with rivals such as Georgia and Ukraine. Russia uses intrusions, specifically short-term espionage campaigns, and intrusion methods to steal information in order to launch information operations in Western rival states to distort public opinion and undermine confidence in the target government's institutions. Examples of this include the covert data theft operations and subsequent

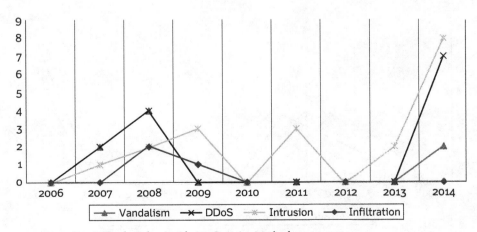

FIGURE 5.2 Russia Yearly Cyber Incidents, Coercive Method: 2000–2014

TABLE 5.2

Cyber method differentials between Russia and global cyber initiators

		Vandalism	DDoS	Intrusion	Infiltration	Total
Russia	Count	8	13	21	3	45
	Expected Count	7.3	7.7	20.6	9.4	45.0
	z-score	.3	1.9*	.1	−2.1**	
World	Count	23	20	67	37	147
	Expected Count	23.7	25.3	67.4	30.6	147.0
	z-score	−.2	−1.0	.0	1.2	
Total	Count	31	33	88	40	192
	Expected Count	31.0	33.0	88.0	40.0	192.0

***$p < .01$, **$p < .05$, *$p < .10$

overt political information dumps at specific times in the Ukrainian elections as well as the 2009 cyber espionage campaigns on the Lithuanian Parliament.

Table 5.2 displays the cross-tabulation analysis that compares the distributions of the use of cyber operations by Russia when compared to the rest of the universe of cases of initiating rivals. The distribution of cyber methods reveals a higher than expected Russian preference for DDoS at a statistically significant level. The unique feature of Russian cyber is how these disruptions factor into larger influence campaigns. Russia rarely uses more sophisticated cyber methods, infiltrations, which include worms and viruses, at the statistically significant level. This distribution is indicative of Russian strategic practice, leveraging cyber operations as part of broader active measure campaigns designed to influence targeted populations and undermine a rival state from within.

Figure 5.3 indicates that the primary targets of the Russian government in the cyber domain are those of the private sector as well as the nonmilitary sections of

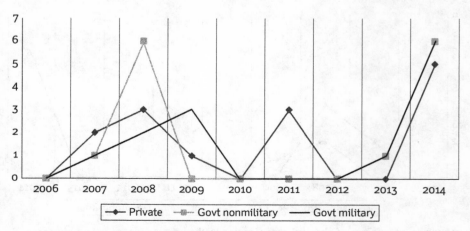

FIGURE 5.3 Russia Yearly Cyber Incidents, Target Type: 2000–2014

TABLE 5.3

Target type differentials between Russia and global cyber initiators

		Private	Govt. Non-military	Govt. Military	Total
Russia	Count	14	24	7	45
	Expected Count	9.8	27.4	7.7	45.0
	Std. Residual	1.3	−.7	−.3	
World	Count	28	93	26	147
	Expected Count	32.2	89.6	25.3	147.0
	Std. Residual	−.7	.4	.1	
Total	Count	42	117	33	192
	Expected Count	42.0	117.0	33.0	192.0

***$p < .01$, **$p < .05$, *$p < .10$

target governments. Only during the military conflict with Ukraine do we see a significant uptick in military targets from Russia. This indicates that Russia is largely attempting to avoid escalation and adhering to its strategic doctrine of causing chaos and implementing disinformation campaigns on its targets, without targeting the military for the most part. Only in times of military conflict do we see evidence of extensive military targeting.

Table 5.3 furthers the findings of Figure 5.3, showing that Russia overwhelmingly targets the private sector and nonmilitary sections of target governments. Russia shows a greater propensity for attacking private corporations, recently seen with the NotPetya attack of 2017, when they attacked financial and business institutions in Ukraine with a wiper virus.[4] Their propensity to attack civilian targets is not statistically significant, but they were expected to attack 10 private targets and they attacked 14 over the time span.

ESCALATORY RESPONSES TO RUSSIAN CYBER ACTIONS

Table 5.4 shows the cyber incidents initiated by Russia that led to escalation by the targeted state in any of the four foreign policy domains under examination in this volume. When the target is United States and other Western countries, we see escalation in the diplomatic and economic domains. Diplomatic threats and overtures have long been a part of US responses to Russian coercive actions, and the economic responses can largely be attributed to the economic sanctions placed on Russia by Western states as well as Ukraine for Russia's controversial involvement in the

TABLE 5.4

Russian cyber actions: Target escalatory responses

Name	Date	Method	Target	Target type	Objective	Response			
						Cyber	Diplomatic	Economic	Military
US embassy hack	8/6/2008	Virus	US	Govt. nonmilitary	Disruption	0	1	1	0
CyberBerkut NATO	3/15/2014	DDoS	US	Govt. military	Disruption	0	0	1	0
Operation Pawn Storm	6/2/2014	Intrusion	US	Govt. military	Short espionage	0	1	1	0
Operation Pawn Storm	6/3/2014	Intrusion	US	Private	Short espionage	0	1	1	0
US Banks hacked	6/4/2014	Intrusion	US	Private	Disruption	0	1	1	0
White House hack	10/26/2014	Intrusion	US	Govt. nonmilitary	Short espionage	0	0	1	0
State Dept hack	11/15/2014	Intrusion	US	Govt. nonmilitary	Short espionage	0	0	1	0
CyberBerkut NATO	3/15/2014	DDoS	Canada	Govt. military	Disruption	0	1	1	0
CyberBerkut NATO	3/15/2014	DDoS	UK	Govt. military	Disruption	0	1	0	0
Operation Pawn Storm	8/11/2014	Intrusion	Poland	Govt. nonmilitary	Short espionage	0	0	1	0
Sandworm	1/1/2009	Intrusion	Ukraine	Govt. nonmilitary	Long espionage	0	1	0	0
CyberBerkut Telecom	3/1/2014	DDoS	Ukraine	Private	Degrade	0	0	1	1
CyberBerkut Ukraine	5/22/2014	DDoS	Ukraine	Govt. nonmilitary	Disruption	0	1	1	1
Operation Pawn Storm	6/1/2014	Intrusion	Ukraine	Govt. nonmilitary	Short espionage	0	0	1	1
CyberBerkut DDoS	10/1/2014	DDoS	Ukraine	Govt. military	Disruption	0	0	1	1

Name	Date	Action	Country	Target	Objective				
Fancy Bear Android Malware	10/6/2014	Intrusion	Ukraine	Govt. military	Degrade	0	0	1	1
CyberBerkut Billboard Hack	11/20/2014	Deface	Ukraine	Private	Disruption	0	0	0	1
Fancy Bear	1/1/2007	Intrusion	Georgia	Govt. nonmilitary	Long espionage	0	0	0	1
Duke Series	4/8/2008	Intrusion	Georgia	Govt. nonmilitary	Long espionage	0	0	0	1
Before the gunfire	4/20/2008	DDoS	Georgia	Govt. nonmilitary	Disruption	0	0	0	1
VoiP	8/4/2008	DDoS	Georgia	Private	Degrade	1	0	0	1
Russo-Georgia Conflict	8/5/2008	DDoS	Georgia	Govt. nonmilitary	Disruption	1	0	0	1
Russo-Georgia Conflict	8/5/2008	DDoS	Georgia	Private	Disruption	1	0	0	1
Russo-Georgia Conflict	8/5/2008	Deface	Georgia	Govt. nonmilitary	Disruption	1	0	0	1
Georgia Government deface	8/7/2008	Deface	Georgia	Govt. nonmilitary	Disruption	0	0	0	1

annexation of Crimea and the Ukrainian conflict. It is therefore difficult to attribute the responses in the diplomatic and economic domains primarily to Russia's cyber actions. Rather, it seems that the responses coincide with the timeline of Russia's actions in other domains as well as cyber. Russian cyber interactions with the West, therefore, are relatively nonescalatory, which indicates evidence for hypothesis 2 in chapter 3.

Cyber responses and military escalation overlap militarized disputes, making it difficult to discern escalation dynamics. That is, Georgia and Ukraine were under attack by Russia, both in cyberspace and militarily, and would use all available means to counter Moscow. With respect to cyber escalation, only in the Georgian military conflict do we see a cyber response from the target, which was quickly eradicated by Russian Advanced Persistent Threat (APT) groups and had no impact on the outcome of the military effort in August 2008. What we can say is that military escalation in response to Russia cyber activity appears to be limited to the post-Soviet space and regional rivals, not the West.

CYBER DISRUPTION: INFLUENCE, MANIPULATION, AND SIGNALING

Moving beyond the data, Russian cyber operations against Estonia and Lithuania illustrate how Moscow uses the digital domain aggressively. Russia does not achieve concessions through cyber operations as much as it uses disruptions to signal escalation risk and conduct larger propaganda campaigns. In this respect, Moscow can signal escalation risks in crises with NATO members as a means of achieving leverage. Of note, Russia could harass smaller rivals without triggering their alliance commitments, but still achieve escalation dominance.[5] In these campaigns, targeting civilians does not appear to be an effective strategy for producing concessions.

Russia employs cyber disruption as a low-cost form of signaling escalation risks when they have a limited ability to achieve concessions through conventional means, and as an adjunct to larger influence campaigns designed to discredit and isolate adversaries. Russia employed cyber disruptions in the 2007 Bronze Solider campaign in Estonia as a means of harassment, demanding better treatment of Russian ethnic nationals in the state and more respect for Estonia's Soviet past. These harassing probes are more concerned with creating fear and uncertainty in Estonian leaders and NATO member states about the prospect of Russian military intervention. In other instances, such as the cyber effort against Lithuania in 2008, Russia sought to integrate cyber disruption with propaganda efforts designed to influence public opinion in favor of Russian interests. Cyber disruptions, both through DDoS actions that are designed to harass the target and website defacements that are used for propaganda to manipulate opinion, can be means of isolating a rival and creating conditions favorable for Russia in the long run.

In Spring 2007, Russia escalated a conflict with Estonia over the treatment of ethnic Russians and the placement of a World War II–era statue, launching a multifaceted cyber disruption campaign.[6] The campaign paralleled propaganda seeking to shape world opinion that Estonia was a fascist regime (Bloomfield 2017; Koschev 2007). Nashi, a Kremlin-backed nationalist youth group, emerged as a central actor, leading protests at the Estonian embassy in Moscow parallel to riots in Tallinn (Miller 2007).

The crisis revolved around a Soviet-era grave marker known as the Bronze Soldier in the central square of Tallinn. The Estonian government decided to remove one of the few remaining memorials from what it perceived as over 60 years of Soviet occupation. The Russian government protested this decision. Between April 26 and May 19, the dispute erupted, resulting in two waves of cyber disruptions targeting civilian and government networks.

Estonia was especially vulnerable to cyber disruption due to the high dependence the state had on digital interactions. Based on Implementation Plan 2007–2008 of the Estonian Information Society Strategy, the government had been making gains in migrating the economy and government services online (European Communities 2009). Ninety-five percent of all banking operations had been moved online and a range of Estonian government services were largely electronic, including voting and state exam results by 2005 (Tikk, Kaska, and Vihul 2010: 17–18). Estonia was a ripe cyber target.

The DDoS originated worldwide, and such a move is consistent with concealing origins, a deception tactic, and means of maximizing surprise consistent with Russian doctrine. This cyber disruption campaign also had attributes of proxy sponsorship. Internet forums had been used to distribute target lists and instructions for how to connect a computer to a botnet as well as how to rent a server farm to increase the strength of DDoS attacks (Tikk, Kaska, and Vihul 2010: 19). At a 2009 panel, Sergei Markov, a State Duma deputy from Putin's United Russia Party told the audience, "about the cyberattack on Estonia . . . don't worry, that attack was carried out by my assistant. I won't tell you his name, because then he might not be able to get visas" (Radio Free Europe/Radio Liberty [RFE/RL] 2009). According to a 2010 study, "log analyses affirm that the second phase of the cyber-attacks involved coordination resources unavailable to ad hoc regular citizen protest. As was observed, the second phase attacks had the features of central command and control attacks . . . came in (often precisely timed) waves, and required both financial and intellectual resources" (Tikk, Kaska, and Vihul 2010: 23).

The Russian government might not have been involved in the first wave of attacks, popularly dubbed a "cyber riot" (Tikk, Kaska, and Vihul 2010: 18). The incidents were primarily pinging attacks (such as checking the availability of the targeted computers using MS Windows commands) using a global network of botnets routed through proxy servers to conceal their origin. However, the Kremlin was involved in the second wave. The cyber disruption campaign escalated between April 30 and May 18 of 2007. During this phase, more sophisticated DDoS disruptions emerged, targeting the commercial sector and government websites. Estonian Banks were a prime target. Between May 9 and 15, Estonia's largest banks were hit by DDoS attacks knocking the largest commercial bank, Hansapank, offline for hours on May 9 (Espiner 2007). On May 15 a botnet of 85,000 hijacked computers flooded government websites (Tikk, Kaska, and Vihul 2010, 20). Mobile phone networks and Estonia's six largest news organizations were also affected by DDoS attacks. The highly digitized government, in which all personnel's contact information was available online, allowed hackers to spam government ministries and often overwhelmed servers.

The wave of cyber disruption incidents from May 9 to 11 involved both DDoS and website defacements. The websites of the Estonian president, prime minister, and Parliament, and of multiple government ministries, were overwhelmed by DDoS floods, forcing them to shut down, or they were defaced with propagandist messages. For example, hackers put a Hitler mustache on the face of prominent Estonian politicians on their website, a theme consistent with Russian propaganda that Estonian was a fascist state (Finn 2007). This incident shows how cyber disruptions, in the form of website defacements, function as adjuncts to larger propaganda campaigns designed to discredit adversaries.

Similar use of cyber disruptions to overwhelm actors to signal political opposition occurred in 2008 when DDoS attacks hit RFE/RL and Lithuanian government websites. Coinciding with coverage of the 22nd anniversary of the Chernobyl meltdown, on April 28, 2008, 55,000 fake hits overwhelmed RFE/RL websites covering the event (RFE/RL 2008).

Following a controversial amendment banning public displays of the Soviet insignia, in June 28, over 300 Lithuanian websites were defaced by suspected Russian hackers (Hamilton 2008). Similar to the Estonia campaign, the so-called patriotic hackers received instructions on web forums outlining how to launch mass website defacements against Lithuania by overwhelming the Internet service providers (ISPs), where a large number of sites were hosted (Danchev 2008). Also, as with the Estonian defacements, Russian propaganda condemned the Lithuanians as fascists.

Russian disruption operations were typical and common during the era of cyber conflict we highlight, but we also note the limited coercive impact of each event. The campaign in Estonia resulted in Estonia pulling its own networks offline to forestall further attack, but no overall change of behavior toward Russian nationals or ethnic individuals. According to Davis (2007), "web sites around Estonia had resorted to a siege defense by cutting off international traffic." The Estonian government moved the Bronze Soldier statue just outside of Tallinn, where it remains. Instead of pushing Estonia closer to Russia, the attacks only pushed Estonia deeper into NATO and entrenched the housing of the Cyber Center of Excellence in the Baltic nation.

CYBER ESPIONAGE: ACCESS, MANIPULATION, AND CONTROL

The Russian approach to cyber espionage involves not just stealing critical information but also leveraging it for propaganda value and signaling resolve as a means of changing the trajectory of future crises. By itself, cyber espionage does not achieve concessions. Rather, it is an additive means of accessing networks for future coercion and stealing sensitive information. Used in conjunction with broader propaganda campaigns, espionage can gain access to influence public opinion. These shaping actions do not achieve independent concessions but set the conditions for future crisis bargaining.

Espionage often runs parallel to broader manipulation efforts or set the conditions for follow-up actions. One of Russia's cyber espionage tool kits, known as Snake/Uroburo/Tula, first appeared in 2005, targeting systems in the United States, United Kingdom, and other Western European countries (BAE Systems 2014). The tool kit used malware that had previously attacked Pentagon classified systems (Agent.bz) and appeared again in Ukraine in 2013 (Sanger and Erlanger 2014). The tool kit could also access systems through other threat vectors including Abode exploits, watering hole attacks through Java exploits, and social engineering tricks to have users run a flash player that installed malware (Kaspersky 2017).

Since May 2007, the tool kit dubbed Red October infiltrated diplomatic and government agencies in multiple countries including the United States, but was primarily discovered in post-Soviet space. The kit used exploited code vulnerabilities in Microsoft Word and Excel to steal data "from mobile devices, such as smartphones (iPhone, Nokia, Windows Mobile), enterprise network equipment (Cisco), removable disk drives (including already deleted files via a custom file recovery procedure)" (GREAT 2013).[7] Other reporting links the cyber espionage tool kit to the RBN (Carr 2013).

Beginning in mid-2013, Operation Armageddon, a cyber-espionage campaign that relied predominantly on spear-phishing, targeted Ukrainian security services. The timing of the attack coincided with the final negotiations between Ukraine and the European Union Association Agreement (Prince 2015). Espionage efforts such as these reflect how cyber espionage has dual use as a signaling mechanism. The intrusion both accesses critical information, which may aid in future cyber coercive incidents as a crisis escalates, and signals ambiguously enough to limit retaliation, to promote Russian interests in external actors.

Another Russia-linked cyber-espionage campaign from a group known as Sandworm surfaced in 2009 based on zero-day exploits affecting Windows operating systems (Zetter 2012). According to one study, Sandworm "focused on nabbing documents and emails containing intelligence and diplomatic information about Ukraine, Russia and other topics of importance in the region" and stole "SSL keys and code-signing certificates" to help breach other systems (Zetter 2012). In October 2014, Sandworm used BlackEngery 3 for multiple intrusions in Ukraine, focusing on power companies and media outlets (Hultquist 2016). In 2016, Ukrainian power companies, along with the finance and defense ministries, reported temporary disruptions linked by iSight Partners and attributed them to Sandworm (Polityuk 2016). These incidents similarly demonstrate the dual purpose of cyber espionage as setting conditions but signaling the risk of crisis escalation. These campaigns can sow doubt into target policy makers, contemplating what other networks Russia may have access to. Cyber espionage in this respect can be destabilizing.

A Russian group known as APT28, or Fancy Bear, similarly used malware to target groups of interest to the Russian state, including security ministries and journalists across the Caucasus region, the Polish and Hungarian governments, NATO, and the Organization for Security and Cooperation in Europe (OSCE) (Threat Intelligence 2014). Unlike traditional Russia cyber-criminal groups, "APT 28 does not exfiltrate financial information from targets and it does not sell the information that it gathers for profit" (Scott and Spaniel 2016). FireEye contrasts APT28 with China-based threats optimized for widespread intellectual property theft for economic gain. Threats such as APT28 can mask their activity through "satellite-based internet links (particularly IP addresses in Middle Eastern and African countries) to hide their operational command and control" (Weedon 2015: 67). According to FireEye, cyber espionage campaigns by groups like APT28 demonstrated that "Russia has been more effective at integrating cyber espionage into a geopolitical grand strategic campaign—not just a military one, but economic and political" (Jones 2017).

First discovered in 2011, Energetic Bear is a team that uses a common malware suite to infiltrate networks in the commercial space with economic or defense interests. Initially, the malware appeared on the networks of firms associated with the aviation industry and major defense contractors in the United States and Canada (Scott and Spaniel 2016: 29). In 2013, the malware appeared on major energy firms such as Exxon-Mobil and British Petroleum (MSS Global Threat Response 2014). Of note, Energetic Bear is "uniquely positioned to assist in a combination of digital and physical warfare for military or political purposes" (Scott and Spaniel 2016, 29). Energetic Bear uses tools that mimic aspects of the Stuxnet worm. The exploitation kit reflects a new approach "compromising the update site for several ICS software producers" through a remote access toolkit (RAT) type malware (Symantec 2014). The tool kit uses three primary infection methods: spear-phishing using PDF with embedded flash exploits, trojanized software installers, and waterhole attacks (Kaspersky 2014). The malware appears to have been adapted from the source code of malware and Trojans available in the cyber black market, but updated for state-based espionage (Symantec 2014).

Cyber espionage is also a means of manipulation and undermining the institutions of opponents. According to F-Secure, since 2008 MiniDuke, along with the CosmicDuke APT group, has acted as a state-sponsored espionage organization (Peters 2015a). The Duke series first appeared after an April 5, 2008, speech by US President Obama advocating for a missile defense shield in Poland (Scott and Spaniel 2016). These groups were a "well resourced, highly dedicated and organized cyberespionage group," the Dukes have mixed wide-spanning, blatant 'smash and grab' attacks on networks with more subtle, long-term intrusions that harvest massive amounts of data from their targets, which range from foreign governments to criminal organizations operating in the Russian Federation" (Gallagher 2015). In 2013, the group was linked to a spear-phishing campaign targeting the Ukrainian Ministry of Foreign Affairs (Gallagher 2015).

Another Duke variant dubbed CozyDuke/CozyBear/APT29 appeared after 2014. These Russian government-backed cyber-espionage groups "typically target entities to steal information that is closely linked to Russian geopolitical interests and priorities . . . this includes: Western governments (particularly foreign policy and defense-related targets); international security and legal institutions; think tanks; and educational institutions" (Weedon 2015: 78). In 2014, the CozyDuke series appeared, using a spear-phishing campaign that breached targets to either connect to malicious websites or open Flash video attachments exposing their device to an attack vector (Paganni 2015). Some of the most successful spear-phishing efforts relied on invitations to view a video, "Office Monkeys LOL.zip" blended with malware (Hackett 2015). This type of attack helped Russian hackers access the unclassified White House computer network in 2014 (Frizell 2014).

The group focused on targeting individuals with access to critical organizations through socially engineered spear-phishing campaigns that trick users into downloading malware. For example, in November 2016 an APT29 spear-phishing campaign compromised multiple e-mail accounts in the Norwegian Intelligence Agency PST (Paganni 2017). In early 2015, the group used an especially stealthy malware, HAMMERTOSS, to relay commands and extract data via Twitter, GitHub, and cloud storage services while remaining hidden by mimicking user behavior (FireEye 2015).

The style and content of Russian-enabled cyber collectives reflect two logics of cyber espionage and its coercive potential. First, accessing target networks sets the conditions for follow-up operations. In military parlance, you prepare the environment for future action. Not only do you access critical networks and steal information, altering the balance of information in a crisis, but also, even if the intrusion is revealed, the target is left wondering what else was stolen and what other networks are compromised. Second, they demonstrate the utility of cyber espionage as a low-cost means of manipulating public opinion. In this respect, the actions are classic political warfare. Cyber is a tool both to manage crises indirectly and to subvert public opinion and political will.

Beyond disputes with rivals, Russian cyber espionage is also increasingly a critical means of controlling populations through punishment or manipulation. Russia fields dual-use espionage tool kits that both hack foreign networks and enable domestic surveillance. Operation Pawn Storm, a cyber espionage campaign ongoing since as early as 2004, targeted a wide variety of organizations including Polish government sites, US military and civilian targets including a nuclear fuel dealer, and multiple NATO sites (Trend Micro 2016).

The same campaign targets more diffuse actors as well. In December 2014, "a well-known military correspondent for a large US newspaper was hit via his personal email address in December 2014, probably leaking his credentials. Later that month, Operation Pawn Storm attacked around 55 employees of the same newspaper on their corporate accounts" (Hacquebord 2015a). Linked to APT28, Pawn Storm infiltrated and disrupted TV5 Monde in France. In October 2015, Pawn Storm set up a fake VPN and fake Outlook Web Access (OWA) server to conduct spear-phishing attacks against the Dutch Safety Board investigating the Malaysian Airlines Flight 17 commercial airline flight that was shot down by a Russian Buk surface-to-air missile over Ukraine (Hacquebord 2015a).

The Pawn Storm case also "builds a case for domestic spying" against targets including "peace activists, bloggers and politicians" (Hacquebord 2015b). Some of the targets, such as the antiestablishment punk band Pussy Riot, critical of the Russian government, and journalists reflect traditional approaches to domestic surveillance. Other targets, including a Russian military attaché in a NATO country, could reflect a dual use of Pawn Storm as a counterintelligence vehicle as well. Berserk Bear, another cyber front group, not only repurposed its malware for the 2008 Georgia campaign but also has a long history targeting nonstate groups of interest to the Russian state including nonprofits and political dissidents (CrowdStrike 2015).

The Manipulation of the 2016 US Election

The 2016 US election hack demonstrates how Russian leverages cyber espionage as part of broader active measures campaign (Hulcoop et al. 2017). These campaigns do not lay the groundwork for future strikes as much as they focus on altering the perceptions of targeted domestic populations. As such, this event deserves extensive coverage as a crucial case of Russian cyber activities. The goal of the 2016 election hack was to achieve a broader psychological impact on American society while demonstrating to a Russian audience the corrupt nature of democratic institutions (Valeriano, Maness, and Jensen 2017b).

The event serves as a demonstration of the utility of espionage as a tool of manipulation. Often termed "reflexive control" or "active measures," and now being associated with the idea of hybrid warfare, this form of espionage tries to influence the adversary through information control and manipulation aided by propaganda, operations all conducted short of war. As demonstrated throughout this chapter, the strategy of political warfare remains a tool in Russian politics handed down from the Soviet era.

The Soviet approach to manipulation and disinformation to shape rival behavior continues to be a key aspect of Moscow's playbook in its near abroad during the post–Cold War period. There have been activities directed toward Poland, Serbia, Ukraine, Estonia, and Georgia since 2000 (Maness and Valeriano 2015). Rid (2017: 4–5) notes that since 2015, the Russian Army (GRU) have set up five front bodies to disseminate information: the Yemen Cyber Army, Cyber Berkut, Guccifer 2.0, DC Leaks, Fancy Bear, and ANPoland (Rid 2017). There is also Russia Today (now simply RT) and Sputnik, Russian media conglomerates that amplify and disseminate Russian propaganda under the veil of objective news outlets.

This return to political warfare and the use of indirect measures to undermine adversaries from within appears to have caught US officials, often overly focused on dramatic cyberattacks, off guard. As the *New York Times* notes, "American officials did not imagine that the Russians would dare try those techniques inside the United States. They were largely focused on preventing what former Defense Secretary Leon E. Panetta warned was an approaching 'cyber Pearl Harbor'" (Lipton et al. 2016). The focus on the spectacular rather than the mundane blinded the United States to a critical insidious threat to the stability of the American system. At the same time, the United States was a vulnerable target, since trust in the media reached a low in 2016, with only 32% of the population saying they trusted the media a "great deal" (Swift 2016).

Political warfare as articulated by Keenan (1948) is an effort to use all methods short of war to convince the enemy to back down or change position. Fused with Russia's corresponding decline in material and economic power, political warfare can be a tool used by the desperate and disadvantaged to fight an unconventional battle and level the playing field. *Wired* magazine notes, "Russian active measures represent perhaps the biggest challenge to the Western order since the fall of Berlin Wall" (Graff 2017).

There are three main methods used as Russia fuses cyber strategies with information warfare. First, gain access to critical and private systems through hacking or using previously cultivated insider access. Two, exfiltrate information and disseminate politically sensitive content to public sources, manipulating or altering such information if needed. Finally, spread and amplify the message with trusted news sources and bot networks. This process, what can be termed as the "acquire, release, and spread method," allowing the aggressor to target the enemy and manipulate critical audiences through digital means.

Furthermore, Russia perfected this practice against its own population. The Citizen Labs report on Russian activities around the time of the election hack, dubbed Tainted Links, also highlights the "domestic roots" of Russian external operations (Hulcoop et al. 2017). A significant and virtually unnoticed component of the cyber intrusions was their target preference: civil society partners such as activists and journalists. Russian elites see foreign NGOs, which they shut out of the country in 2015, as threats and acceptable targets for political warfare (Luhn 2015).

The Russian political warfare operation that culminated in the election hack started in 2015 before Donald Trump entered the presidential race. During the summer of 2015, Russia started the process by sending out thousands of phishing e-mails trying to get their targets to click on malicious links. Thomas Rid during Senate testimony notes that about 2.4% of the attacks were successful in producing information (Rid 2017).

The breaches by Russia were not discovered until June 2016 with the *New York Times* noting that two different groups of Russian hackers (Cozy and Fancy Bear) penetrated the Democratic National Committee's computer systems (Sanger and Corasaniti 2016). The goal was to both monitor the DNC's communications while also exfiltrating their files, including opposition research on Donald Trump. This information, in the tradition of KGB, could be used to either augment larger influence operations or as future blackmail material to gain leverage.

Perhaps the most devastating information grabs were the e-mails taken from Hillary Clinton's staff, further exacerbating a long-standing issue surrounding the question of stored e-mails on her personal home server. Campaign Chairman John Podesta's e-mails were stolen as a result of a typo on advice from an IT consultant to not answer a phishing e-mail (illegitimate was corrected to legitimate). The DNC staffer Billy Rinehart entered his e-mail password into a phishing e-mail at 4 a.m. while in Hawaii (Lipton et al. 2016). These two events highlight the comedy of errors and misfortunes evident during the operation, with Russian hackers getting lucky at a few critical moments.

The Dukes group, or Cozy Bear, as the Information Security (InfoSec) community calls them, had previously been caught operating in unclassified White House systems, the State Department, and various other US organizations (Lipton et al. 2016). By the summer of 2015, they started to penetrate both DNC and Republican National Committee files (Greenberg 2017b).

In March 2016, Fancy Bear or APT28 piled on. This intrusion thus demonstrates the uncoordinated nature of Russian cyber operations, with duplicate processes occurring. Both actors were attacking the same targets, seemingly under the same mandate without overall coordination under similar instructions (Lipton et al. 2016). Podesta's e-mails were released the same day as damning audio tape of Trump remarking on his ability to grab women hit the news cycle (the Billy Bush bus tape incident). Coordinated drops of information went on until late in the election cycle, potentially demonstrating collaboration between the brokers of information and the Trump campaign. Russian activities seemed to continue until a meeting between Obama and Putin at the G20 on September 5, where Obama warned against further attempts to influence the election. The information dumps stopped, but Russian hackers continued to probe state-level election voting systems looking for weaknesses as well as use bots to sow social media with propaganda.

In July 2016, Clinton's campaign suggested that Russia might be trying to sway the election (Lipton et al. 2016). Yet, it was not until October 7 that the Obama administration formally accused Russia of interfering with the election (Sanger and Savage 2016). A bipartisan statement was drafted, but the Senate Republicans would not sign on to the general statement supporting attribution of interference in the election to Russia suggesting it would tip the scales for the Democrats (Waddell 2016).

The issue was more complicated than simple Russian interference though; the main candidate encouraged the intrusions and information dumps. That Trump was "embracing an unlikely ally" in Wikileaks was certainly a troubling development (Healy et al. 2016). Julian Assange, the leader of the organization, blames Hilary Clinton for his predicament and has openly sided with the Russian government, refusing to publish e-mail troves of Russian documents (Healy et al. 2016). *Think*

Progress counts 164 mentions of Wikileaks by Trump during campaign events (Legum 2017).

The coordination through information dumps, botnets supporting the releases, and the mentions by Trump himself demonstrates the power and collaboration needed to make political warfare insidious. As Clint Watts noted in Senate testimony, "part of the reason active measures have worked in the U.S. election is because the Commander-in-Chief has used Russian active measures at times against his opponents" (Legum 2017). Watts went on to note the many times fake information was released, passed, and amplified by bot networks, and then parroted by the Trump campaign itself.

In September 2017, Facebook announced that the company had sold at least $150,000 in ads to Russian operatives after being called into private questioning by the House of Representatives (LoBianco 2017). "The Agency," a well-known Russian Troll farm, is linked to the ad buys (Knake 2017). These ads seemed to seek to influence divisive internal conflict by amplifying issues such as Black Lives Matter (Shinal 2017).

The ads ran from June 2015 to May 2017. As it stands, the *Daily Beast* estimates that, at a minimum, 23 million people saw the ads with a high-end estimate of 70 million (Collins et al. 2017). The figure is based on an average of six dollars in ad buys resulting in 1,000 views, with estimates increasing through targeting and voluntary sharing of the information.

Speculation that Russia was behind the attacks and information releases has been consistent since the issue was first reported in June 2016. A plethora of sources have indicated that the operation was sophisticated and bore the hallmarks of a Russian influence operation, starting with Crowdstrike, a prominent cyber security firm to which the DNC turned (Alperovitch 2016). News organizations including the *New York Times*, the *Washington Post*, and, later, *Politico*, all released investigative reports on the operation (Lipton et al. 2016; Nakashima 2016; Watkins 2017). Thomas Rid notes in *Esquire* that researchers connected the command server for the malware targeting the DNC to a prior attack on German Parliament in 2015 (Rid 2016).

In January of 2017, the entire US Intelligence Community as a collective offered their assessment that Russian operations sought to "undermine public faith in the US democratic process, denigrate Secretary [Hillary] Clinton, and harm her electability and potential presidency" (Office of the Director of National Intelligence [ODNI] 2017). The report finds motive in Putin's blaming Clinton personally for the release of the Panama Papers (a series of information dumps locating illicit banking methods) and protests in Russia in 2011 and 2012. Methods to aide sourcing the attribution claim were both an extensive review of the digital forensics and traditional human intelligence methods, resulting in the intelligence organizations assessing with high confidence that the operation was Russian led and directed by Putin himself.

While Putin denies Russian involvement, Russia also publicly arrested three nationals in December of 2016 claiming they were traitors to the United States (Shane et al. 2017). These officials likely were sources for the IC report, and this should give us added confidence in the sourcing of the attack. In June of 2017 Putin offered the most he has on the issue by stating, "the hackers are the same, they would wake up, read about something going on in interstate relations and if they have patriotic leanings, they may try to add their contribution to the fight against those who speak badly about Russia" (Calamur 2017).

Cyber coercion is difficult, costly, and time consuming. The Russian operation against the election started well before 2016 and continued past the actual vote. While there is no clear impact that can be detailed, the operation likely reinforced negative opinions of Hillary Clinton already held by Republican voters and supporters of Bernie Sanders. There is no evidence the operation changed minds, no poll has ever been released that showed support for Trump was generated through Wikileaks. The question is, did the hacks motivate individuals to reject Clinton and turn out to vote for Trump?

It appears likely that dozens of strategic mistakes led to Clinton's loss, including not giving sufficient attention to the Rust Belt, the inability to counter the fears of immigrant threat, James Comey's note that Clinton's e-mails were under review again, and persistent gender bias (Yglesias 2017). Yet, not having an effective counter to the information warfare waged by Russia and its convenient allies was a costly mistake.

From the strategic perspective, the benefit to Russia was in causing chaos in its target. This classic tactic of Russian disinformation campaigns continues to wield unforeseen benefits for Russia. These manipulation strategies engage on all fronts, seeking to achieve effects in situations where Russia has few advantages. Changing the direction of the US Government, or weakening the new president before they even take office, is an enormous benefit to Russia in that it confuses policy toward Ukraine, delays any action against Syria for human rights violations, and allows Russia's operations to continue in a similar fashion against Germany and France during their 2017 elections.

Yet, overall, the greatest benefit was likely a bit more subtle; American alliances are fractured and confused. The United States paradoxically offers military hardware to its allies while also threatening trade wars with these very same countries, as in the case of South Korea. If confusion was the goal, Russia succeeded to dramatic effect.

While the benefits are clear, impact is not. The reality is that we have a difficult time in social science dealing with what might be called a second-order effect. A second-order effect is something that happens through linkages and other nondirect, nonlinear connections. Research on second-order or nonlinear impacts is rare in social science, with Alker (1966) making an early effort.

It is even more unclear whether social media has an impact on the voter. Researchers for Google and Facebook determined that there is a very thin line at which a campaign might have a positive effect on a viewer. Even with trials of more than 10 million subjects randomized, it is nearly impossible to determine at what point advertising investments are profitable (Lewis and Rao 2013).

Examining voter turnout methods is just about as complicated as pinpointing the effect of marketing campaigns. Green et al. (2013), in a meta-analysis, note the majority of effects that can be delineated require personal contact or the strong influence through social bonds and networks. Following this insight, Teresi and Michelson (2015) note an 8.2% increase in turnout when subjects are exposed to personal political messages about voting from friends on their Facebook feed. While this demonstrates an impact can happen, we also know that the information disseminated by Russia through Facebook and Wikileaks lacked a personal touch. Unless this information was conveyed by a trusted source once initially advertised, targeted ad buys rarely seem to have a clear impact.

The crux of the possibility of impact relies on trusted sources and complex dissemination methods that cut through the noise of the 2016 election campaign and direct the voter to alter their perceptions of a candidate. This is a difficult process and Russia likely had a very minor impact on an already divisive election. With such a close election, minor impacts can matter greatly.

Cyber operations can have a clear and coercive effect, but it is rare, contingent on many factors, and depends on the target's lack of trust in critical sources of information to achieve results. By preparing for massive global catastrophes that might be a cyber 9/11 scenario, observers miss the more persuasive and insidious impact of Russia's complex attack and dissemination strategies.

Most episodes of Russian cyber espionage demonstrate mixed utility. Cyber espionage does not independently produce concessions. As a bargaining instrument, cyber espionage typically augments larger propaganda efforts. There are also signs cyber espionage, as a form of covert action, helps Russian manage escalation and signal resolve. That Russian operatives have infiltrated American critical infrastructure demonstrates the potential utility of espionage operations for future operations (Nakashima 2017) but has no operational effect on limiting American action in the present because the United States has done the same (Miller, Nakashima, and Entous 2017).

Ukraine: A Case Study of Combined Effects

The ongoing conflict in Ukraine offers a portrait of how Russia combines cyber coercion with other instruments of conventional power. This is also a critical case in that it goes beyond the US election hack with the use of actual force to support information operations. Specifically, cyber campaigns in Ukraine seek to disrupt and delegitimize the country as a means of isolating Kiev and demonstrating the futility of the Ukrainian state.

Russia seeks more than manipulation, it seeks domination. According to Giles, "unlike Georgia . . . Russia already enjoyed domination of Ukrainian cyberspace, including telecommunication companies, infrastructure, and overlapping networks" (Giles 2015b). This access allowed them to wage a more comprehensive coercive campaign. That said, there is no evidence to suggest the Russian campaign is at all sophisticated. Rather, the digital domain played a supporting role to Russian proxy military operations and propaganda efforts. Outside of Russia's fait accompli seizure of Crimea, these operations have produced no concessions beyond creating a frozen conflict. In this respect, cyber combined coercion on the front demonstrated the restraint the country operates under even during war. The limited disruptive campaign is simply a testing ground for new operations, but the fact that few operations have been conducted of any sophistication makes the opposition question resolve (Greenberg 2017a).

In late 2013, activists set up a protest camp in Kiev's independence square (Maidan), calling for an end to rampant corruption and deeper European integration (Greenberg 2017a). The events escalated after over 100 protesters were killed in 48 hours by a special police unit, the Berkut, causing the protests to escalate and pro-Russian President Viktor Yanukovych to flee. By February 27, 2014, reports of Russian operatives and "local militias" in Crimea started to appear, paving the way for a March referendum for Crimea to join Russia. In early May, two regions dominated by ethnic Russians, Donetsk and Luhansk, held referendums, declaring independence.

Paralleling the escalating crisis in late 2013, Ukrainian officials noted that "network vandalism had given way to a surge in cyber espionage, from which commercial cyber security companies developed a list of colorful names: RedOctober, MiniDuke, NetTraveler, and many more" (Koval 2015: 55). Koval claims that Russia conducted constant, low-level disruption campaigns against Ukraine using "botnet-driven" DDoS attacks, often "in retaliation for unpopular government initiatives" (Koval 2015: 55). Glib Pakharenko offers an insider's account of the cyberattacks during the Maidan protests:

the cyber attacks began on 2 December 2013 when it was clear that protesters were not going to leave Maidan. Opposition websites were targeted by DDoS attacks, the majority of which came from commercial botnets employing BlackEngery and Dirt Jumper malware. . . . As Ukrainian opposition groups responded with their DDoS attacks, cyber-criminal organizations proactively reduced their use of the Ukrainian Internet Protocol (IP) space rerouting their malware communications through Internet Service Providers (ISP) in Belarus and Cyprus, which meant that, for the first time in years, Ukraine was not listed among the leading national purveyors of cybercrime. (Pakharenko 2015: 50)

In early 2014, Ukrainian civilian and government networks were subject to a barrage of DDoS attacks. Cyber Berkut, a pro-Russian hacktivist group, a major proxy group with links to the Russian government, organized the incidents. The threat actor took their name from the former special police unit disbanded in the wake of the Maidan protests, producing an illusion that pro-Moscow Ukrainians were rebelling against Kiev. CrowdStrike has linked the group to the Russian government based on forensic data and parallels between messages put out by CyberBerkut and "messaging delivered by Russia-owned state media" (CrowdStrike 2015). According to reporting by the firm, "there are significant parallels between the current techniques employed by CyberBerkut and those used in previous conflicts associated with Russia, namely the conflict in Estonia in 2007. These techniques, leveraging Soviet-style deception, propaganda, and denial tactics, suggest a process in which the first iterations of online warfare implemented in Estonia are now being perfected in Ukraine" (CrowdStrike 2015).

Cyber Berkut's actions range from disrupting mobile phone networks as a means of complicating Ukraine's response to the ongoing crisis to more complex, foreign disruptions designed to isolate and delegitimize Kiev (Masters 2014). In March 2014, Cyber Berkut claimed credit for a DDoS attack targeting three NATO websites (ABC 2014). In October of that same year, the group was linked to a DDoS attack against the German Ministry of Defense (Trend Micro 2015). In January 2015, a DDoS attack against the German Parliament and Chancellor Angela Merkel's websites was attributed to the group (Wagstyl 2015).

Over the course of 2014, Cyber Berkut also conducted prominent website defacements, placing narratives and symbols that matched Russian propaganda linking the Ukrainian conflict to fascism. In August 2014, the group hacked Polish websites, including the stock exchange, and defaced them with images of the Holocaust (Bennett 2014). In November 2014, during US Vice President Joe Biden's visit to Kiev, the group defaced several Ukrainian government websites with messages stating, "Joseph Biden is the fascists' master" (Shevchenko 2014). In December 2014, the group hacked multiple electronic billboards in Kiev and replaced advertisements with videos showing graphic images of civilian casualties and portraying Ukrainian officials and anti-Russian activists as war criminals (VK 2014).

The most significant disruptive effort involved combining cyber espionage and disruption alongside propaganda to undermine the legitimacy of the Ukrainian election in 2014. According to Ian Gray, an analyst at Flashpoint, Russia seeks to achieve a low-cost disruption "by organizing a disinformation campaign attacking confidence in the election itself" (Waterman 2016). In May 2014, CyberBerkut "infiltrated Ukraine's central election computers and deleted key files, rendering the vote-tallying system inoperable. The next day, the hackers declared they had 'destroyed the computer network infrastructure' for the election, spilling e-mails and other documents onto the web as proof" (Clayton 2014). Compounding the intrusion, the group installed malware that attempted to manipulate the results, showing a victory by ultranationalists, a key theme reinforced by broader Russian propaganda reflecting the Maidan as a fascist revolution (RFE/RL 2014). According to Ukrainian cyber security experts, "preparation for such an attack does not happen overnight; based on our analysis of Internet Protocol (IP) activity, the attackers began their reconnaissance in mid-March 2014—more than two months prior to the election" (Koval 2015: 60).

Another combined strategy on display in Ukraine was the use of false flag operations designed to not only hide attribution but also discredit the target, a tactic consistent with Soviet practices. False flags are a form of covert action designed to manipulate perception with deep historical roots. The term refers to making it seem as if an act was carried out under another nation's flag. A group attempts to conceal its involvement by creating the perception that a separate group carried out some act of sabotage, subversion, or physical attack. Under the handle Anonymous Ukraine, in March 2014, Russia released fabricated documents claiming to show evidence that the US Army attaché was coordinating a series of false flag attacks designed to look like Russian Special Forces with the Ukrainian Army (Carr 2015). In March 2015, CyberBerkut released documents said to be hacked from US defense contractors and the Ukrainian government showing US plans to move weapons into Ukraine (Smith 2015). Later that month, the group also released documents said to be hacked from the Ukrainian military showing the government in Ukraine supplied weapons to the Islamic State (Stone 2015). The group also released documents said to be hacked from the Soros Foundation, showing that George Soros was pressuring American officials to provide lethal assistance to Ukraine (Durden 2015).

In all cases, these false flag operations were picked up and broadcast through Russian media outlets and operatives on social media sites. Russia uses troll factories to shape how its public digests Western media and distort unfavorable stories for foreign audiences (Giles 2015a). For example, in March 2015 a false flag operation citing evidence that the Ukrainian state-owned defense conglomerate Ukroboronprom collaborated with the Qatari government to supply surface-to-air missiles was reported on outlets such as *Sputnik International*, a state-controlled Russian media outlet (Sputnik 2015).

This disinformation and delegitimizing campaign built on earlier network exploitation and cyber espionage. Access to Ukrainian information networks allowed them to spear-phish Ukrainian officials. Hackers use typosquatting, registering a domain with just a misplaced letter, to spear-phish users accessing the website of Ukrainian President Petro Poroshenko (Tucker 2016). Similar social engineering hacks were used as part the US presidential election hack, where the two groups CozyBear and Fancy Bear spear-phished Democratic operatives at the DNC (Stone 2016). The same groups were also linked to spear-phishing attacks on DC-area think tanks after the US presidential election (Kan 2016).

As the Ukrainian crisis continued, Russia found new ways of combining cyber effects with irregular and conventional military operations. First, Russia employed traditional military operations to isolate information objectives. For example, in November 2014, Russian operatives sabotaged cables connecting the Crimean Peninsula to Ukraine (Baraniuk 2015). Conventional operations helped isolate a target. Russia used cyberspace for intelligence and reconnaissance as well as cheap means of recruiting fighters. According to Glib Pakharenko:

> Russian signals intelligence (SIGINT) including cyber espionage, has allowed for very effective combat operations planning against the Ukrainian Army. Artillery fire can be adjusted based on location data gleaned from mobile phones and Wi-Fi networks. GPS signals can also be used to jam aerial drones. Ukrainian mobile traffic can be rerouted through Russian GSM infrastructure via a GSM signaling level (SS7) attack; in one case this was accomplished through malicious VLR/HLR updates that were not properly filtered. Russian Security Services also use the internet to recruit mercenaries. (Pakharenko 2015: 55)

Second, Russia employed cyber methods to degrade Ukrainian military capabilities. In 2016, the cyber security firm Crowdstrike reported that Russia used an Android-based malware to infect apps Ukrainian units were using to target artillery. These infections enabled digital reconnaissance and helped Russian units geolocate Ukrainian artillery formations and preemptively strike them (Myers 2016). While there is some debate as to the effectiveness of this operation, with Crowdstrike altering the estimates from 80% effectiveness in targeting Ukraine to 15%–20%, that Ukrainian artillery was using basic apps for targeting demonstrates the potential vulnerability that cyber operations introduce to conventional military operations (Kuzmenko 2017).

Third, Russia employed earlier cyber espionage campaigns to activate malware capable of degrading Ukrainian critical infrastructure. In October 2014, Sandworm used BlackEngery 3 to gain access to power plants and then insert KillDisk malware, a program similar to destructive systems used during the 2014 Ukrainian election (Hultquist 2016). Soon after the intrusion, some Ukrainian power plants went offline, though analysts still cannot draw a direct connection to KillDisk (Hulquist 2016). Blackenergy 2015 (Zetter 2012) and new CrashOverride 2016 (Goodin 2017) are other critical infrastructure-targeting strands of malware that have been found in Ukrainian power plants.

Fourth, Russia integrated their operations with cyber disruption efforts paralleling broader disinformation campaigns. Russia weaponized social media to promote its narrative (Nielsen 2015). Russian groups built redirects to steer users away from websites to Russian propaganda. For example, in 2015, "cybercriminals help[ed] spread pro-Russia messaging by artificially inflating video views and ratings on a popular video website. The campaign began with the infamous Angler exploit kit infecting victims with the Bedep trojan. Infected machines were then forced to browse sites to generate ad revenue, as well as, fraudulent traffic to a number of pro-Russia videos" (Kogan 2015). Analysts linked the same malware to Russian cyber-crime groups, who used it to steal $45 million dollars from banks (Biasini 2016).

In effect Russia, practices a new style of information operations designed "not to rebut but to obfuscate" (Inkster 2016). These operations rely "on the fact that Western governments simply lack resources that would be required systematically to refute or debunk the huge number of stories put out, and on the Western media's professional obligation to report both sides of the story, thereby giving a veneer of legitimacy to Russian fabrications" (Inkster 2016).

Conclusion

Russia is a rogue actor in the digital domain, not a cyber superpower. Despite Moscow's frequent use, not to mention the sheer audacity and high-profile character of targets, the Kremlin fails to generate rival concessions when it uses cyber aggression. Russia has a preference for cyber disruptions that harass and sow discontent, which fail to coerce in a direct manner. The Russian approach to cyber coercion appears to be more about ambiguous signaling and amplifying propaganda than it does direct compellence. Russian cyber activities continue the Soviet approach to active measures, political warfare optimized to manipulate target populations and disrupt rivals from within. Due to these strategies, degradation efforts do not generate the concessions in a manner similar to the cyber superpower, the United States.

The Russian case offers insights into how states combine cyber operations with military instruments of power and information operations. Moscow tends to use cyberattacks in three waves: 1) prior to the conflict to delegitimize and district their rivals; 2) during the conflict to support combat operations; and 3) after the initial fighting to create chaos that, consistent with active measures, undermines the legitimacy of the target state. However, Russian use of cyber operations during conflicts does not appear to alter the outcomes or make concessions more likely. Of note, the operations in both Georgia and Ukraine have resulted in frozen conflicts, not decisive victories.

When Russia employs cyber coercion against Western rivals outside of its former Soviet space, these states tend to counter with diplomatic and economic instruments. These counters are consistent with a "tit-for-tat" logic, limited horizontal escalation designed to check Moscow and limit a dangerous conflict spiral. When cyber coercion is used against targets in the Baltics, the states counter by strengthening their ties to NATO and enhancing their domestic military.

Finally, Russian cyber strategy, in addition to reflecting tenets of Soviet-era active measures, focuses on soft targets, including civilian networks. These methods have largely been unsuccessful beyond the debatable example of the US election hack in 2016. As opposed to the United States, Russia tends to amplify propaganda with bots and troll farms rather than positive diplomatic coercion. To date, these operations have yet to produce concessions. In the end, Moscow acts more like a rogue state undermining the norm against targeting critical infrastructure than it does like a responsible actor in the digital domain.

Russia still has not unleashed the full potential of cyber operations against critical energy targets. They have not resorted to direct cyber violence, destroying infrastructure that results in immediate death such as blowing up a power plant, digitally sabotaging vital public infrastructure like sewers or water treatment, or hacking personal medical devices. Rather, Moscow's network intrusions on the battlefield in Ukraine indirectly helped military units increase their lethality (Myers 2016; Kuzmenko 2017).

Russia's aggressive, albeit unsuccessful cyber operations, threaten stability in cyberspace by targeting critical systems and illustrate how political warfare has extended into the digital domain. This case demonstrates the futility yet also the opportunities of cyber strategies; not much has been achieved, but the state has served notice that it is capable and dangerous, especially when it targets a susceptible internal population. We now turn to a case study approach to the most active cyber state in the international system to date, China.

> Information war is a product of the information
> age which to a great extent utilizes information
> technology and information ordnance in battle.
> It constitutes a "networkization" [wangluohua]
> of the battlefield, and a new model for a complete
> contest of time and space. At its center is the
> fight to control the information battlefield, and
> thereby to influence or decide victory or defeat.[1]
>
> —WANG PUFENG

6

CHINA AND THE TECHNOLOGY GAP

Chinese Strategic Behavior in Cyberspace

Introduction

The discourse on Chinese cyber security practices often fails to match the reality of actual behavior. The fear of a vibrant and aggressive China in the international stage is so prevalent that scholars and observers may have missed the key development in cyber security: the shift from a state seeking to use cyber espionage to catch up to its adversaries to a state focused on maintaining dominance in the Asia Pacific region and within China itself. Sovereignty is the key goal for Chinese foreign policy behavior, and this now extends to cyberspace. How did the fear of China become the dominating feature of the cyber security discourse?

The implosion of the Soviet Union and the ensuing decline of Russian relative power sparked a debate about which actor would emerge as the next challenger to the United States. Academic and policy assessments gravitating toward power transition and offensive realism (Fravel 2010) envisioned a new great power competition that would shape the 21st century playing out between the United States and China. In cyber security, this China threat narrative continues to manifest as the coming challenge of Chinese cyber dragon (Cheng 2016).

China remains the prime threat for many. For example, Mearsheimer (2001) argues that China is the only realistic security threat to the United States and the Chinese quest for hegemony will eventually lead to war. Concerns about China's long-term military potential drove the 2001 Quadrennial Defense Review and studies by the Office of Net Assessment on defense transformation (Silove 2016; Jensen 2017) long before the vaunted Pacific Pivot (Meijer 2015). For these defense thinkers, China is the pacing threat the United States could use to prioritize its defense modernization portfolio (Krepenvich and Watts 2015). More recently, Allison (2017) makes the case that the United States is locked in a Thucydides trap, where the growth of Chinese power and the fear that this provokes in the West will result in war. The fictional scenario painted by Singer and Cole in the book *Ghost Fleet* (2015) suggests that the coming global conflagration will involve China with a heavy focus on cyber tactics winning, and potentially losing the day. While this is a work of fiction, Singer and Cole claim it has prompted policy changes and influenced strategic doctrine (Prine 2017).

The industry that advances the China threat narrative is entirely too pessimistic about future interactions with China and locates the source of agitation in the growth of Chinese power and the fear it causes, as opposed to the specific issues of disagreement that tend to drive conflicts (Vasquez 1993). This fear is perhaps why the growth of Chinese cyber power is so troubling in the international system. Cyber operations are a means of adding to the capabilities of great powers (Valeriano and Maness 2015), not a new way for small powers to challenge larger states. China's ability to leverage cyber tools for economic, commercial, and technological advantage only confirms the pessimist's worst fears: a war with China that starts in the digital domain but ends in World War III.

Using evidence to evaluate China's cyber rise in power is key to assessing accurately the level of threat between rival great powers in the digital domain. An empirical account of China's many covert cyber intrusions helps scholars and policy makers cut through the rampant threat inflation associated with China's rise as a great power. This perspective helps the international community understand and regulate cyber behavior in a more meaningful way as opposed to incentivizing cyber security dilemmas and threat spirals. As Lindsay (2015a: 8) notes, "exaggerated fears about the paralysis of digital infrastructure and growing concerns over competitive advantage exacerbate the spiral of mistrust."

For our theory of cyber strategy, *how China uses cyber espionage against rivals is a crucial example of the process of information manipulation as a limited form of coercion and ambiguous signaling.* Cyber espionage seeks to alter long-term power balances while also casting a shadow on the present, leaving uncertainty about what one's rival knows or does not know about one's own plans and vulnerabilities. It also serves as a possible path to innovation, although this path is also uncertain. This leverage shapes bargaining between rivals. Seen in this light, the rise of China will come with a corresponding rise in Beijing's ability to gather information and knowledge to compete with the United States if cyber espionage is a useful means of acquiring power, leverage, and signal escalating costs.

Through documenting and analyzing rival attempts at cyber strategic moves, a picture of the Chinese cyber dragon starts to emerge along these lines. China is primarily engaged in cyber espionage that acts to both steal valuable information, altering either its short-term bargaining position or long-term economic and military balance and sending a signal that, as deception (Gartze and Lindsay 2015) or covert action (Carson and Yarhi-Milo 2017), probes a rival's resolve in a crisis. The distribution of publicly attributed cyber exchanges between rivals reveals that 78% of cyber exchanges (48 of 61) between Beijing and its rivals takes the form of cyber espionage.[2] Seen in a comparative perspective, China accounts for 59.70% (40 of 67) of all publicly attributed short-term cyber espionage incidents between rivals between 2000 and 2014 and 26.67% (8 of 30) of all long-term cyber espionage campaigns. This distribution makes China the largest user of both forms of espionage in the dataset.

There are unique logics in each form of manipulation. China uses short-term cyber espionage, like other rivals, to gain access that helps in larger coercive bargaining games. This access may be to enable a future attack or point of leverage—the shift from cyber intelligence, surveillance, and reconnaissance (ISR) and exploitation to offensive action and degradation—or it may function as an ambiguous signal that demonstrates resolve and signals the risk of escalation. China uses long-term cyber espionage to erode the disadvantages the state has in information technology, a project that began in the 1980s. This project expanded in the 1990s as China began to use cyber espionage to steal intellectual property in an effort to increase its relative power.

While pessimists see a cyber dragon, characterizing Chinese strategic moves in the digital domain as destabilizing, Beijing's actions tend to be predictable and restrained. They operate in cyberspace to seek economic and research advantages, maintain a position of control over their population, promote regime stability, and sometimes activate national sentiment over common issues such as rights to shipping lanes and the treatment of North Korea.

Rather than seeing cyber rivalry as adding to an already unstable US-China competition to shape the international order, we witness a competitive but stable great power relationship. Since the mid-2000s, China and the United States have entered into a predictable period of (1) cyber challenge, (2) conventional or counter-espionage responses by the United States, (3) retrenchment by China, and (4) new challenges advancing the new issues that emerge once the players have reset. This characterization of Chinese cyber behavior defies typical predictions of escalatory cyber conflict. The Chinese cyber dragon, as the literature so colorfully invokes, is instead a rolling wave of expected, but not accepted, aggressive behavior. Chinese cyber behavior is driven by a national project to maintain power in Asia and achieve balance with the United States.

Our coverage of Chinese cyber behavior examines how Beijing uses the digital domain in rival interactions. First, we unpack the literature on how China uses cyber conflict to shape the international system and enable its rise as a great power, highlighting how threat inflation crowds out empirical perspectives that demonstrate stability and predictability. Second, we situate Beijing's approach to the digital domain in Chinese strategic theory illustrating its early focus on innovation and preemption and its evolution toward using digital power to control the domestic population and seek information advantages. Third, we use these insights to analyze empirically all publicly attributed Chinese cyber incidents. This investigation offers a case-specific contextualization of the larger findings of chapters 3 and 4. We offer a portrait of how one power uses cyber strategies. This portrait highlights the unique leverage, and limitations, of cyber espionage as a form of strategic bargaining between rival states.

Contextualizing China's Approach to Cyber Conflict: Rising Power, Hidden Vulnerability

RISING POWER

Concerns about shifts in relative power tend to distort how analysts interpret the actions of leading states in the international system. Whether power transitions (Organski and Kugler 1980) and associated rivalry risks (Thompson 2003), domestic log-rolling coalitions (Snyder 1991), legitimation strategies (Goddard 2009), or cognitive psychology (Goldgeier and Tetlock 2001), there are multiple vectors through which changes in power can distort how policy makers and pundits assess threats.

China's status as a rising power distorts how analysts portray Beijing's actions in cyberspace. China operates as a lightning rod in cyberspace. There is a tendency toward worst-case biasing prevalent in think tank reports (Lieberthal and Singer 2016), academic treatments (Brenner 2015), and public commentary (Swaine 2013). These accounts tend to exaggerate the danger. There are conflicting trends that make China as vulnerable as it is threatening. Beijing is both the target of rival cyberattacks and the originator of the majority of espionage operations. It is also a leading digital authoritarian (Tsai 2016) for activists who see the Great Firewall of China as the future of digital oppression. In reality, the Great Firewall is less a bulwark and more a flowing stream, in that, while it can interrupt information acquisition, it is penetrable and often bypassed by activists (Tai 2016). Furthermore, the

main threat for Chinese political elites, who seek to carefully orchestrate state
is not external attackers getting in through the Great Firewall, but the ideologica
challenge that might result if Chinese actors get out (Lindsay 2015a: 19).

The reality is that China is not an aggressive actor intent on promoting cyber
violence and there is little evidence of shifting strategies through time. Instead, the
state employs thousands of cyber hackers to defend the digital domain and state
interests, target internal actors, and catch up in technological sectors where the state
is not permitted acquire technology legally. While concerning for the West, the
Chinese view is they are protecting their regime from leading powers like the United
States, guarding their citizens from malign influences, and completing a civilization-
defining modernization process after being hindered by Western powers for hundreds of years. Understanding the motivations, constraints, and drivers of each side
is key in conflict analysis, and Chinese cyber scholars often undervalue factors when
evaluating Chinese cyber operations.

The actions of the Chinese state are clear; based on evidence, Beijing prefers
cyber espionage and is often on the receiving end of cyber degradation operations originating in the United States. As they steal information, China likely faces
challenges converting it into actionable intelligence, and in the process, becomes
a target for US precision cyber operations that erode Beijing's confidence in their
own capabilities. These rounds of espionage attack and counter by Western states
have produced a perplexing stability. While cyberspace is inherently lawless, despite
the Tallinn Manual II (Schmitt 2017), there is a clear behavioral expectation where
liberties are taken by the Chinese state, but when called out by the opposition, the
state backs down and tries again later. There is tacit bargaining even in the ambiguity
of cyberspace.

This summary defies conventional wisdom about Chinese cyber behavior. China
has generally avoided using the digital domain for offensive cyber degradation, pre-
ferring to conduct covert operations to leverage sufficient deniability to steal information to ambiguously signal resolve and alter the long-term balance of power.
It is also important to note how critical the Edward Snowden revelations were to
the Chinese, with his escape to Hong Kong in 2013 and confirmation of extensive
NSA activities directed against China (Inkster 2015) including surveillance of text
messages (Helm, Boffey, and Hopkins 2013). The confirmation that they had been
a target and a victim as much as an aggressor allows for the Chinese to continue operating as they had been in the past, a process that was only restrained after the 2015
diplomatic agreement between Obama and Xi, a likely watershed moment in cyber
security relations.

Proclaiming overall innocence and shock due to the Snowden revelations is a bit
too much for China, though, since they are active against both internal threats (King

nnon 2011) and external challenges. China hosts and plays a part in
meant to punish members of the international community who
ording to Chinese dictates. In this way, China also uses disruption
to express to the opposition that deviant behavior has not gone
without notice. The wide range of targets Chinese cyber operatives focus on displays
a variety not evident in other states in the data. There is a clear Chinese way of cyber
conflict that enables friction below the threshold of war (Lindsay 2015: 9), but it is
not a process of violence so much as punishment, denial, and seeking to alter the dynamics of information asymmetries.

HIDDEN VULNERABILITIES

Chinese thinkers are as aware of their vulnerabilities in cyberspace as they are their
opportunities of using the domain to catch up to the West and undermine rivals. For
China, risk and vulnerability can motivate action in cyberspace. Inkster (2015: 34)
notes, "an awareness of the risk posed by the cyber domain has deepened an in-
grained sense of insecurity—a sense that to outside observers seems at odds with the
country's economic power, growing military capacity and general aura of stability."
An op-ed in the *People's Liberation Army Daily* in August 2009 noting the sub-
versive threat of the Internet and the hardware and software dominance of the West
(Inkster 2015: 41) also seems to have spurred greater motivation for action in cyberspace. The first major step toward moving away from this subjugation by foreign
powers is the development of a Chinese operating system to bypass the need for
Microsoft Windows. NeoKylin, a Unix-based system, was authorized in 2013 and
has started to come into operation as of 2015 (Jain 2015). While this system will help
move the state beyond the perceived tyranny of the Windows operating system, it is
also likely prone to hacking and intrusions, given its untested development. A new
operating system is no assurance of security for any motivated aggressor. In fact,
new operating systems bring with them new zero-day vulnerabilities previously unknown and without defensive patches.
Paradoxically, the digital realm is at once a critical capability and vulnerability
for China. As scholars have noted, "the cyber domain has been a powerful enabler
of China's rise, and will be a critical avenue through which the country's emerging
power is expressed and exercised" (Inkster 2015: 47). Lindsay and Cheung (2015: 78)
go further: "cyberspace is an enabler of China's emergence as a great power in the
twenty-first century." If China is to become an active hegemon with global interests,
it will need to assert itself in the cyber domain. Yet, Lindsay (2015a: 78) also offers
caution, noting that information, and the data stored on information networks, become powerful targets in cyberspace.

While China is emboldened in some ways by cyber power and has made it a key component of its strategic plans, like any other connected state, it is vulnerable in the digital domain. Stealing intellectual property does not guarantee long-term economic growth. The growth engine of Silicon Valley did not emerge based on secrets the United States stole from Soviet labs. Often a focus on replication and reproduction can stifle domestic production and a make a state dependent on external advances. Steal mass amounts of information and you risk becoming dependent on another state's innovation. This vulnerability extends to the security sector. What can be stolen can be infected through honey pots and traps, and cyberspace lends itself to more complex games of spy versus spy and deception (Gartzke and Lindsay 2015).

THE EVOLUTION OF CHINESE STRATEGIC THEORY ON CYBERSPACE

To understand Chinese cyber activity, we also must understand the history of Chinese political thought around cyber coercion and the actual behavior evident in the data. We need to see the opportunities and risks inherent in the digital domain for a rising power like China. The possibilities offered by digital technology can be liberating (Livingston and Walter-Drop 2014). The connectivity of the modern world changes the character of strategic interactions (Khanna 2016) and enables China to focus on not just traditional military targets but also a broader range of social, political, and economic targets. Combining subjective and objective factors, psychological warfare, and cyber intrusions gives China a unique perspective as a cyber actor due to its targeted focus on seeking an information advantage after falling behind.

The December 2016 "Chinese National Cyberspace Security Strategy" is organized around three "grave threats": political stability, economic progress, and culture solidarity (Creemers 2016). The strategy mentions that competition is expanding online, and that a small number of nations are aggravating a cyber arms race. The strategy develops a less aggressive face forward by noting, "We must persist in positive use, scientific development, management according to the law, and enhancing security, persist in safeguarding cybersecurity, use the development potential of cyber to the greatest extent, let it extend to China's 1.3 billion people even better, enrich all of humankind, and persist in safeguarding global peace."

Despite the recently developed national strategy for cyber security, actual cyber security doctrines developed by China differ vastly, with an obvious difference between declared intentions versus empirical realities evident in behavior. This is a typical challenge when evaluating the cyber security strategies of most states, and it is no different in China. Inkster (2015: 33) notes this duality of defensive strategy but overt offensive behavior. Pollpeter (2015: 139) describes an active policy of attacking first and offensively orientated strategies in Chinese doctrine despite the desire for defense strategies in communications with multinational players.

Active Chinese doctrine in cyberspace intrinsically links to information warfare doctrines. In fact, until the 2016 National Strategy, there was little to distinguish information warfare from cyber conflict in official doctrine because the terminology was different in China. Wang Pufeng, noted as the founding father of Chinese cyber security doctrine, writes, "information war is a product of the information age which to a great extent utilizes information technology and information ordnance in battle" (Foxman 2013).

This perspective evolved from earlier Chinese writings on information warfare that integrated classical and Communist strategic theory. In 1985, another noted earlier architect of Chinese cyber security policy, Shen Weiguang, proposed a new form of warfare, "take home battle," in which networks across society mobilized to wage information warfare on behalf of the nation (Thomas 1998). The concept bridged Mao's idea of People's War with emerging capabilities.

A People's War, best articulated in Mao Tse Tung's (1967) *On Protracted War*, called for mobilizing popular support and waging a protracted guerrilla struggle before transitioning to conventional operations. With respect to information warfare, Shen Weiguang saw networks of citizens and businesses mobilizing in cyberspace. Modern connectivity would increase the mobilization potential and create new attack surfaces for guerrilla campaigns designed, whether through lethal or nonlethal means, to wear down an enemy over time.

This connectivity offered a new means to employ a classical concept: attacking *Shih*. Shih is best of thought of as similar to the concept, center of gravity in Western military theory. Shih is strategic power. *Shih* is defined variously as "momentum, potential energy, force, the strategic configuration of power, strategic advantage" (Yuen 2014: 45). It is the source of one's strength. According to Tai-tsung, in war "cause the enemy's strategic power [shih] to constantly be vacuous, and my strategic power to always be substantial" (Yuen 2014: 25). In the book of *Campaign Stratagems*, Shih is the "combination of the friendly situation, enemy situation, and the environment; as the sum of all factors impacting the performance of the operational efficiency of both sides; and as the key factor determining the rise and fall of operational efficiency" (Thomas 2013: 5).

Looking back at Mao's *On Protracted War*, the inherent potential is the strategic depth of China (i.e., Japan could attack coasts but had trouble in the interior) and its sheer size (i.e., importance of unifying the population). For Sheng Weiguang, as he pondered cyber warfare in 1985, it was the ability to accelerate and decentralize mobilization for people's war in cyberspace. According to leading Chinese cyber thinkers writing 10 years later, these guerrilla attacks in cyberspace would target "the enemy's weak parts and dead angles ... [using] network special warfare detachments and finding some computer experts to form a shock brigade of network warriors who specialize in looking for critical nodes and controls centers on the enemy network and sabotaging them" (Thomas 1998: 6).

If classical theory provides the lens through which to think about cyber effects, the 1991 Persian Gulf War, specifically the capabilities the United States displayed in destroying Iraqi military power, provide the strategic context for shifting from theory to practice. Leading People's Liberation Army (PLA) thinkers saw the first Persian Gulf conflict as the harbinger of a new way of warfare.[3] Whereas US analysts tend to highlight this revolution in military affairs focusing on how satellite positioning technology, command networks, and stealth aircraft enabled precision military strikes, Chinese thinkers take a broader view that focuses on information and cyber warfare. The Chinese belief that Desert Storm had been won by cyber warfare, assuming that the United States had attacked Iraq's computer systems, helped direct strategic policy (Mulvenon 1999: 178). The US victory was instrumental in pushing Chinese doctrine forward and helping them conceive of offensive cyber war.

As Mulvenon (1999) notes, the early focus on preemption in Chinese strategy was influenced by the assumption that Iraq could have defeated their more capable adversary if they had only struck early, while the United States was gathering forces in Saudi Arabia. This was a belief in the strategic utility of rapid strikes designed to degrade American lodgments and prevent full mobilization and deployment. China could carry out rapid attacks, a lightning-fast informationized war, that caused capitulation in Taiwan before the United States could respond (Mulvenon 1999: 185). Planners envisioned not just ballistic missile raids, but a full range of cyber actions directed against military targets and critical infrastructure.

The strategic utility of multidomain raids made sense until the United States countered with the AirSea Battle doctrine in 2010 (Van Tol et al.). Under AirSea Battle, the United States threatened blinding strikes in the cyber, air, sea, and land domains against Command, Control, Communications, Computers, Intelligence, Surveillance and Reconnaissance (C4ISR), designed to limit Chinese ability to escalate a crisis beyond the initial attack. Mutual threats of strategic raids short of protracted war in cyberspace seem to have produced a strategic equilibrium.

Rather than seeking a Schlieffen Plan–like, preemptive blow against US forces, China is likely striving for a coercive effect. The term "weishe" in Chinese is said to invoke both deterrence and compellence (Pollpeter 2015: 147). Pollpeter (2015: 147) argues weishe as a concept means to "defend legitimate interests without resorting to actual hostilities." Beijing is engaging in classic bargaining, using a mix of threats and limited coercive diplomatic acts, including cyber, in order to limit strategic escalation.

Even offensive actions, whether in the digital domain or more traditional military threats and displays, can play a defensive and deterrent role. Pollpeter (2015: 148) notes that Chinese thinkers believe their strategic measures are different due to the legitimacy of their interests and as a response to historical aggression by the West. What the defense officials in the United States view as offensive actions are often viewed as justifiable by Beijing, with information warfare the key to success.

Information as the key to a theory of victory is a theme similarly captured in Wang Houqing and Zhang Xingye's (2000) *The Science of Campaigns*. Houqing and Xingye argued, "integrated combat operations directed at the battlefield sources from which any enemy probes for information, his information channels, and his information processing and decision-making systems, so as to disrupt an enemy's ability to control information and seize and maintain battlefield information superiority" (Houqing and Xingye 2000: 134). For early Chinese strategists, in this new world offense is easier than defense. The side that disrupts their rival's information first gains a position of advantage. Pollpeter (2015: 144) notes, "information supremacy is the precondition for achieving supremacy in the air, at sea, and on the ground."

According to Thomas (2013: 2), for Chinese thinkers, "a cyber strategy is the result of the creative use of subjective thought to manipulate or guide objective cyber conditions, which are the dynamic new aspects of the strategic environment." Thomas (2013: 2) finds that Chinese cyber thinkers with "a packet of electrons can execute a stratagem such as 'rustle the grass to startle the snake,' that is, cause firewalls to alert and thus expose defense capabilities when probed." Overall Chinese cyber doctrine specifically focuses on three tasks: (1) identify vulnerabilities and exfiltrate data, (2) target communications networks to constrain the adversary, and (3) serve as a force multiplier (Pollpeter 2015: 157).

Task 1, espionage, is perhaps the key to Chinese strategy. It follows the strategic priority given to information advantages in crises as well as the belief that long-term power depends on intellectual property. Innovation is the key to growth, and central to innovation and increasing productivity in the information age are intellectual property and trade secrets. Constraining the adversary and multiplying force (tasks 2 and 3) cannot happen without success achieved through task 1, achieving information dominance on the battlefront.

At its core, the objective factor driving cyber security strategy in the modern world is the relationship between information and power. The Chinese strategic community's "view of the relationship between information and power has crystalized in the past half century, as the world economy has globalized, and as information has become even more integrated with development" (Cheng 2016: 1). This objective condition underlies the concept of "informationized war" in the PLA textbook *The Science of Military Strategy* (Guangqian and Youzhi 2001, 2005). In the text, the authors maintain the objective of informationized warfare is "to achieve strategic goals through information control and information attack, including conducting soft sabotage or hard destruction of the infrastructure, basic information sources or battlefield information systems, the armed forces of a country rely on for survival through information network in order to achieve its strategic goals" (Guangqian and Youzhi 2001: 21, 2005: 18).

The relationship between information and power as an objective factor creates new strategic models. With respect to information warfare, the new model means attacking the enemy's decision cycle along multiple fronts. In 1995, Shen Weiguang defined information warfare as "decision control warfare, where information is the main weapon designed to attack the enemy's cognitive and information systems and influence, contain or change the decisions of enemy policy makers and their consequent hostile actions. The main target of information warfare is the enemy's cognitive and trust systems, and the goal is to exert control over his actions" (Thomas 1999: 5).

The information advantage is clearly a goal and defines how China operates in cyberspace (Hannas et al. 2016: 219). Seeking advances through the manipulation and extraction of information is obviously quicker than seeking to develop research and development capabilities in new areas. But technological acquisition is not so simple that one could steal it and apply it to new markets. Stealing technology requires adaptation, analysis, and demonstration of active prototypes that behave as expected.

Rather than coerce through a show of objective force, "a cyber show of force can involve actually mapping and showing an opponent his strategic cyber geography, thereby deterring an opponent due to the exposure and exploitability of his key nodes and infrastructure" (Thomas 1999: 5). The Shih inherent in cyberspace enables indirect forms of coercion through espionage. This logic is key, as it alters the long-term information balance as it relates to economic growth, political advantage, and military options. More importantly, in the short term, consistent with work on covert action (Carson and Yarhi-Milo 2017), espionage—through revealing vulnerability—can act as an ambiguous signal in competitive interactions between rivals. Stealing information or burning vulnerabilities reminds adversaries just how vulnerable they are in the information age.

This process was key for the Office of Personal Management (OPM) hack in 2014, which resulted in the acquisition of 21.5 million records of US government employees, applicants, and those seeking security clearances (Koerner 2016). A hack by the same Chinese group into the United Airlines (a commonly used airline for government employees) systems had a similar goal, to map, investigate, and gather as much information as possible about the trends, flows, and course of American government systems (Chew 2015). By attacking key nodes, the Chinese attackers were able to alter the balance of information between the two sides in favor of the attacker. They signaled American vulnerability as way of demonstrating resolve and highlighting the risks associated with escalating any dispute with Beijing.

Manipulation of information clearly forms a key component of modern information warfare. Murawiec (2004: 187–188) notes, "just as in Sun Zi's times, the aim of war—or the aim of China's regional strategy—is not to 'destroy the enemy' but to 'convince' him. China will play to its own strengths, of which its psycho-political manipulation, mind games, and actions at a distance are the most honed."[4] Despite the rather presumptuous nature of the quote, the connectivity of the modern world gives new vectors for influence and manipulation.

What capabilities China actually has to achieve its goals of information manipulation and control varies according to the investigator. Inkster (2015: 37) notes that cyber militias in China likely have a membership of 10 million individuals, while Sheldon and McReynolds (2015: 193) put the number at 8 million. It seems likely that Chinese defensive posturing is influenced by the possibility that these militias could drag China into a conflict not of its choosing (Inkster 2015: 35). But Sheldon and McReynolds (2015: 201) note that the main task of militias during a conflict would be civil defense akin to the national guard in the United States.

That civil defense is the key task of the Chinese militias might be surprising for some who consider their offensive power, but the reality is that China is just as vulnerable in cyberspace when compared to every other advanced nation. Mutual vulnerability, with China only beginning to research how to protect critical information facilities (Pollpeter 2015: 146), is a key consideration skipped when considering the capabilities of the Chinese cyber attackers.

In terms of conventional cyber power, a report from the Mandiant cyber security firm notes that Unit 61398 is linked to the 2nd Bureau of the PLA and operates out of Shanghai. The report notes, "the sheer scale and duration of sustained attacks against such a wide set of industries from a singularly identified group based in China leaves little doubt about the organization behind APT1" (Mandiant Report 2014). Mandiant also suggests that there are 20 other ongoing advanced persistent threat groups operating in China. In 2010, the Chinese established the Information Safeguards Base as a direct response to the establishment of Cyber Command in the United States (Inkster 2015: 34). The operations are directed out of the 3/PLA group that organizes signals intelligence (Stokes 2015: 170).

Understanding the Chinese view on cyber warfare requires us to understand China's position in this world, its vulnerabilities, and possibilities. Chinese perspectives on information warfare emerges from the intersection of Chinese strategic theory, and the emphasis on *Shih* and People's War, adapted to modern conditions to defeat a technologically superior adversary, the United States. China prefers mapping US networks to gain access and signal the risks associated with future crises to more short-term, offensive cyber degradation. In both its short-term access (i.e., leverage intrusions) and long-term IP theft designed to alter power balances over decades, Beijing demonstrates the unique, albeit weak and indirect ways, espionage can be a form of gaining bargaining advantage in cyberspace.

This logic implies more restraint and strategic patience than an impending cyber war between the leading cyber powers. Beijing is engaging in classic bargaining, using a mix of threats and limited coercive diplomatic acts, including cyber action, in order to limit strategic escalation.

Data Analysis: Chinese Cyber Strategies

An empirical examination of Chinese cyber operations illustrates the ways in which cyber espionage functions more as an ambiguous signal of resolve in crises than a stand-alone instrument. The primary rival exchange of interest in this regard is the United States and China dyad. Table 6.1 is indicative of the cyclical interactions between China and the United States. China usually casts out global espionage campaigns in search of intellectual property, and the United States will counter with a sophisticated degradation action to persuade the working PLA hackers or other Chinese entities and proxies into ceasing operations, regrouping, and beginning another espionage campaign until the United States shuts that campaign down as well. That is, China steals, burning a vulnerability in the short term and gaining long-term intellectual property of questionable value, only to be subject to higher-severity, complex counterattacks.

These retaliatory degradation actions against China achieve their objective at higher rates than the espionage campaigns. The NSA launched Cisco Raider against the PLA to stop the tide of counterfeit Cisco software being downloaded and spreading spyware in many private sector networks. The NSA Fourth Party incident in 2009 piggybacked the Chinese Byzantine series, which means it spied on the targets through the Chinese effort. Arrow Eclipse was another "man in the middle" campaign that spied on Chinese espionage campaigns in order to better defend US military networks in the future. The Shotgiant US incident is a retaliation against the Aurora campaign, where one of the victims included tech giant Google, and aimed to exploit vulnerabilities on the largest Chinese search engine, Huawei.

All of these incidents produced concessions from China. Consistent with the concept of sunk costs as demonstrating resolve, these American efforts were time consuming, expensive relative to other cyber forms, and capable of achieving seemingly

TABLE 6.1

Cyclical cyber interactions between China and the United States

Initiator	Cyber Incident	Start Date	Objective
China	Hainan Island incident	4/29/2001	Disrupt
China	Titan Rain	9/1/2003	Espionage
US	Cisco Raider*	2/28/2006	Degrade
China	State Department theft	5/28/2006	Espionage
China	Shady RAT	8/1/2006	Espionage
China	Fred Wolf espionage	8/1/2006	Espionage
China	Commerce disable	10/1/2006	Disrupt
China	Naval War College disable	12/1/2006	Disrupt
China	750,000 American zombies	3/1/2007	Disrupt
China	GhostNet	5/27/2007	Espionage
US	Arrow Eclipse*	5/27/2007	Degrade
China	Commerce Secretary hack	12/1/2007	Espionage
China	2008 Campaign hack	8/1/2008	Espionage
China	Hikit	9/1/2008	Espionage
China	Byzantine series	10/30/2008	Espionage
China	FAA hack	2/4/2009	Espionage
China	Senator Nelson theft	3/1/2009	Espionage
China	Lockheed F-35 plans stolen	3/29/2009	Espionage
China	Aurora	6/1/2009	Espionage
US	NSA Fourth Party collection*	7/1/2009	Degrade
China	Night Dragon	11/1/2009	Espionage
China	Commerce theft	11/1/2009	Espionage
China	Htran	1/1/2010	Espionage
US	Shotgiant*	3/10/2010	Degrade
China	US National Security E-mail hacks	4/1/2010	Espionage
China	FDIC hack	10/1/2010	Espionage
China	Energy Department hack	2/1/2011	Disrupt
China	Pentagon raid	3/1/2011	Espionage
China	Operation Beebus	4/12/2011	Espionage
China	White House theft	11/7/2011	Disrupt
US	Ocean Lotus	4/1/2012	Degrade

*Chinese Concessions

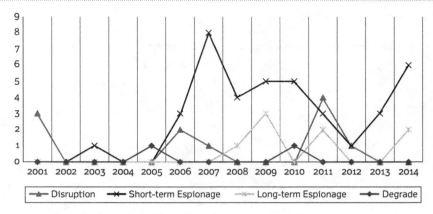

FIGURE 6.1 China Yearly Cyber Incidents, Coercive Intent: 2000–2014

unstoppable network access. That is, the United States appeared to escalate in cyber-space through precision degradation campaigns designed to alter the cost-benefit calculation of future Chinese cyber espionage efforts.

Figure 6.1 demonstrates the yearly figures for Chinese cyber operations since 2000. They seem to have ramped up aggressive actions in 2006–2007. Since then, the ebbs and valleys view of Chinese cyber action appears clear, there are no stable trends besides starts and restarts, which result in the valleys evident in the data. While these levels indicate only publicly documented incidents between rival states, they are likely indicative of the whole of cyber operations. Looking at Figure 6.1, we can see that, overall, China is most likely to engage in an espionage attack, both short- and long-term, over disruption and degrade operations. This pattern is not surprising when one considers the extensive discourse and concern over Chinese espionage operations. China rarely uses other methods besides information manipulation tactics; this fits with its doctrines and strategic goals discussed earlier.

Overall, Lindsay (2015b: 21) predicts the shape of our data quite well when he notes an "interesting thing about kinetic cyber disruption is that there is little evidence of it in the historical record. Stuxnet and a few other reported instances of military cyber operations (mostly by the United States) might suggest the shape of things to come, or they may be outliers." To code disruption, our data looks for harassment campaigns and other short-term attack methods. Lindsay (2015b) more likely means degrade operations in our conception and it is clear these are rare events in the China data sample, with only two instances (see Table 6.2).

Remembering the macro analysis in chapter 3, China has been the most active cyber actor in our data sample. Looking at Table 6.2, the Chinese government has conducted 61 total operations from 2000 to 2014, including the great majority of espionage incidents (48% of all espionage cases in the data sample; 40% short-term

TABLE 6.2

Cyber objective differentials between China and global cyber initiators

		Disruption	Short-term Espionage	Long-term Espionage	Degrade	Total
China	Count	11	40	8	2	61
	Expected Count	22.2	21.3	9.5	7.9	61.0
	z-score	−2.4**	4.1***	−.5	−2.1**	
World	Count	59	27	22	23	131
	Expected Count	47.8	45.7	20.5	17.1	131.0
	z-score	1.6	-2.8**	.3	1.4	
Total	Count	70	67	30	25	192
	Expected Count	70.0	67.0	30.0	25.0	192.0

***$p < .01$, **$p < .05$, *$p < .10$

and 8% long-term) when compared to the behavior of Russia (20%) and the United States (10%). Specifically, compared to the rest of the universe of cases of cyber initiators, China conducts short-term espionage more than what would be expected if the null hypothesis were true at the 99% confidence level, indicating that this is China's preferred method when attempting to achieve its foreign policy goals in the cyber realm. China uses degradation and disruption techniques less than the expected null value at the 95% confidence level, indicating that the use of cyber weaponry has yet to be folded into Chinese cyber strategy at this time. China uses long-term espionage at around the expected null value. These findings are consistent with Chinese strategic theory and the idea of using espionage as a cheap instrument to signal a rival about the risks of escalation.

Figure 6.2 shows China's preference for nonmilitary targets. The distinction between penetrating civilian systems and military systems is clear; Hannas et al. (2013: 222) write, "DoD classified networks, on the other hand, are an attractive but less accessible target for the Chinese." This view might explain why China tends to avoid targeting military systems when compared to their propensity for attacking government offices that are not directly connected to military operations. Even the OPM attack was perpetrated through access provided by a third-party contractor rather than a direct attack on government systems. Chinese cyber strategy appears to prefer soft targets to minimize risk as it seeks to alter the balance of information and probe rival resolve.

Examining the targets typical in Chinese operations reveals interesting patterns, with China by far accounting for most of the attacks on government nonmilitary

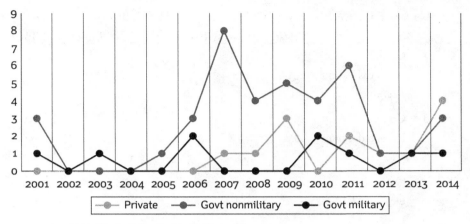

FIGURE 6.2 China Yearly Cyber Incidents, Target Type: 2000–2014

targets when compared to Russia and the United States. As Table 6.3 demonstrates, 39 times we have witnessed China attack nonmilitary targets to steal information, harass the opposition, and target dissidents. Finally, like Russia, China is quite apt to attack private targets not associated with government operations but which have a tangential connection (such as targeting United Airlines data because it is used heavily by government employees).

Figure 6.3 uncovers the different cyber methods preferences by cyber actors and produces some interesting results. Compared to Russia, China is very unlikely to use vandalism and DDoS methods. These tactics are common in disruption actions, which would explain the general dearth of their use, but the results are also fairly surprising, given the prolific number of militia hackers (numbering 8–10 million). Espionage and the theft of intellectual property is the primary strategic preference of the Chinese government.

Table 6.4 further illustrates the breakdown in attack methods through raw data and compares Chinese cyber method use preferences with the rest of the world. Intrusions are the most used method, as consistent with China's overall strategic preference for espionage exploits to gain competitive advantage as it rises to superpower status on the world state. Intrusions are used more than the expected value if the null hypothesis were true at the 99% confidence level. More sophisticated infiltrations are used at about the expected rate, with low-level vandalism and DDoS methods being used less than what is expected at the 95% confidence level. China's rise is predicated on catching up to the United States in economic and military domains, and it sees the theft of Western technologies and intellectual property as a shortcut to this goal.

In our data, China only generated an observable concession once out of the 61 cyber incidents it has launched against rival states. This coercive success was the

TABLE 6.3

Cyber target differentials between China and global cyber initiators

		Private	Govt. Nonmilitary	Govt. Military	Total
China	Count	13	39	9	61
	Expected Count	13.3	37.2	10.5	61.0
	z-score	−.1	.3	-.5	
World	Count	29	78	24	131
	Expected Count	28.7	79.8	22.5	131.0
	z-score	.1	−.2	.3	
Total	Count	42	117	33	192
	Expected Count	42.0	117.0	33.0	192.0

***$p < .01$, **$p < .05$, *$p < .10$

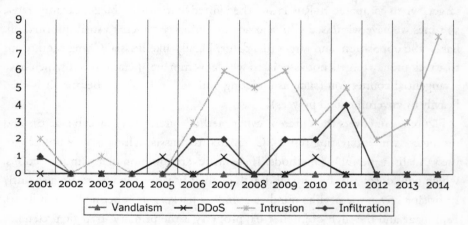

FIGURE 6.3 China Yearly Cyber Incidents, Coercive Method: 2000–2014

TABLE 6.4

Cyber method differentials between China and global cyber initiators

		Vandalism	DDoS	Intrusion	Infiltration	Total
China	Count	1	3	44	13	61
	Expected Count	9.8	10.5	28.0	12.7	61.0
	z-score	−2.8**	−2.3**	3.0***	.1	
World	Count	30	30	44	27	131
	Expected Count	21.2	22.5	60.0	27.3	131.0
	z-score	1.9*	1.6	−2.1**	−.1	
Total	Count	31	33	88	40	192
	Expected Count	31.0	33.0	88.0	40.0	192.0

***$p < .01$, **$p < .05$, *$p < .10$

OPM hack, which was combined with conventional foreign policy actions of positive and negative diplomatic actions as well as a military threat. A concession was met when then-president Barack Obama made coming to a diplomatic solution to the ceasing of Chinese espionage campaigns a primary topic of the Chinese President Xi Jingping's state visit in 2015. Since this meeting, Chinese intellectual property theft has slowed significantly.

Of note is the tendency of China to attack its regional neighbors over divergent interests. It should not be surprising to the observer of rivalry relations that China also targets Japan, Taiwan, India, Vietnam, and the Philippines. While the conflict with Taiwan is clearly based on national status and the territorial claim China holds over the state, its interactions with other states are based on control of the South China Sea and other associated problems. Since our data only covers interactions between rivals, we would not be able to capture tensions between China and nonrival states like North Korea.

ESCALATORY RESPONSES TO CHINESE CYBER ACTION

Table 6.5 uncovers the escalation dynamics as a result of Chinese cyber actions. It must be noted that only one-third (23 of 61) of China's cyber actions evoke an escalatory response at all and the preponderance of these are low-level, consistent with a "tit-for-tat" type response. Cyber responses, unlike other domains, tend to exhibit limited escalation confined to the digital domain. Cyber responses to Chinese action are exclusively from the United States, and are usually precision degradation responses to Chinese espionage campaigns. These escalations, which exhibit sunk costs signaling resolve and the risk of further escalation, tend to cause a cessation of action rather than conflict spirals. Diplomatic responses are rare, with economic action being more frequent with counteraction in this domain coming not only from the United States but also from China's Asian rivals Taiwan and Japan. We see military responses to Chinese cyber incidents from the United States, Taiwan, Japan, and India, and these responses are mostly in the context of territorial disputes with Asian neighbors or the United States backing their allies in the Asian region with military threats. All military threats were limited in scope and duration and did not produce battlefield casualties.

As with Russia, escalation as a result of Chinese cyber strategic actions are rare and usually between its great power rival, the United States, and with its regional neighbors that have the backing of US military might. As with our macro finding, China is relatively non-escalatory in cyberspace. Outside of US cyber degradation, responses tend to be "tit-for-tat" and a means of competitive learning as rivals determine resolve and escalation risk.

TABLE 6.5

Chinese cyber actions: Target escalatory responses

Name	Date	Method	Target	Target Type	Objective	Response			
						Cyber	Diplomatic	Economic	Military
Hainan Island incident	4/29/2001	Deface	US	Govt. nonmilitary	Disrupt	0	0	0	1
Titan Rain	9/1/2003	Intrusion	US	Govt. military	Short espionage	0	0	1	0
State Dept theft	5/28/2006	Intrusion	US	Govt. nonmilitary	Short espionage	0	0	0	1
Commerce disable	10/1/2006	Wiper	US	Govt. nonmilitary	Disrupt	0	1	0	0
750,000 American zombies	3/1/2007	DDoS	US	Govt. nonmilitary	Disrupt	0	0	1	0
GhostNet	5/27/2007	Intrusion	US	Govt. nonmilitary	Short espionage	1	0	1	1
Commerce Sec hack	12/1/2007	Virus	US	Govt. nonmilitary	Short espionage	1	0	0	0
Aurora	6/1/2009	Intrusion	US	Private	Long espionage	1	0	1	0
Energy Dept hack	2/1/2011	Intrusion	US	Govt. nonmilitary	Disrupt	1	0	0	1
White House theft	11/7/2011	Keystroke	US	Govt. nonmilitary	Disrupt	0	0	0	1
Iron Tiger	1/15/2013	Intrusion	US	Govt. military	Short espionage	0	0	1	0
OPM hack	3/15/2014	Intrusion	US	Govt. nonmilitary	Long espionage	0	0	0	1
Premera Blue Cross breach	5/5/2014	Intrusion	US	Private	Short espionage	0	0	0	1
DHS employee hack	11/6/2014	Intrusion	US	Govt. nonmilitary	Long espionage	0	1	1	0
USPS breach	11/8/2014	Intrusion	US	Govt. nonmilitary	Short espionage	0	0	1	0
DPP hack	3/1/2001	Intrusion	Taiwan	Govt. nonmilitary	Disrupt	0	0	1	0
GhostNet	5/27/2007	Intrusion	Taiwan	Govt. nonmilitary	Short espionage	0	0	1	1
Hikit	9/1/2008	Intrusion	Taiwan	Govt. nonmilitary	Short espionage	0	0	0	1
Htran	1/1/2001	Keystroke	Japan	Govt. military	Short espionage	0	0	1	1
WWII Memorial	1/6/2005	DDoS	Japan	Govt. nonmilitary	Degrade	0	1	1	0
Hikit	9/1/2008	Intrusion	Japan	Govt. nonmilitary	Short espionage	0	1	0	0
East China Sea Dispute	9/14/2010	DDoS	Japan	Govt. nonmilitary	Degrade	0	0	0	1
Shady RAT	7/1/2007	Intrusion	India	Govt. nonmilitary	Short espionage	0	0	0	1

Cyber Espionage as a Unique Chinese Tool

The major concern about Chinese cyber espionage resides in how stolen data can change relative power in the international system. While we see stability in the shape of the data's ebbs and flows, analysts and policy makers are not so sanguine about Chinese activities. The quote by General Keith Alexander, Commander of US Cyber Command and the NSA, invoking Chinese cyber espionage as the "greatest transfer of wealth in history" is illustrative of both how China operates in the domain and the hyperbole attached to actions by the state. Hannas et al. (2013: 1) start their volume by writing, "this book is about how a third world country used the technology of the world's greatest superpower to dominate it economically and—perhaps—strategically as well." Richard Clarke, former White House official, made a parallel claim in that the true danger from the cyber domain is not a digital Pearl Harbor, but "death by a thousand cuts. Where we lose our competitiveness by having all our research and development stolen by the Chinese" (Business Report Staff 2012). Such quotes are obviously quite bombastic in asserting that China dominates the United States economically.

While China retains its trade surplus with the United States, this is greatly aided by the positive terms of trade the United States gains in the relationship, including access to cheap labor aided by a beneficial exchange rate (Chun 2014). The debt China once held against the United States has long since been sold off without great consequence (Mullen 2017). The United States remains strong while China continues to grow; parity may come, but it certainly will not be constructed through stealing technology. Both states are in transition, with the United States becoming a service economy and China having to deal with increased purchasing power of the middle and upper class, setting off vast inequalities within the state and jeopardizing further growth.

Strategic dominance some observers credit to the rising power is vastly overstated by most observers of China. While there has been a large transfer of technology, it is unclear how much China has strategically gained from such transfers. They still depend on Russia for military hardware. It is even unclear whether their strategic planning still assumes a quick victory in a conflict over Taiwan.

Yet, our focus is on cyber espionage launched by China. The economic motivations of the practice are clear and long-standing. In the comparative context, it is questionable whether the practice of digital technology extraction is more useful than either traditional technology theft of foreign companies seeking to operate in China or Chinese students who go to study in the West and return with skills and knowledge of Western practices (Hannas et al. 2013). There is a clear spike in the data regarding Chinese cyber espionage in 2013, but this is not the nadir that Lindsay

(2015b: 2) expected given the heights reached in 2006, 2009, and 2011. In fact, there have been several peaks and valleys. What is evident is public notice of the issue became very clear in 2013 with attacks by the Chinese on news organizations reporting corruption in the Chinese state (Perlroth 2013).

Hannas et al. (2013: 216) locate the public acceptance of cyber espionage by China directed against United States as coming in 2006 with follow-up reviews in 2007 supporting this view. Escalation of activity is dated around 2009 and 2010 with attacks on Google and others (Hannas et al. 2013: 217).

While much is made of the attribution problem in cyber security, there is clear attribution of the exfiltration of information to China. What is lacking is identifying responsibility for such extractions. Are they government directed? Are they primarily focused in the private sector? How involved is the military in such technological escapes?

In terms of planning directed from the state, the plan articulated early in the era of information warfare sought to increase Chinese research and development capacity by illicit means. For example, the 1986 Plan 863, "sought to eliminate dependence on foreign technologies" (Inkster 2015: 34). The goal was to move past the need to rely on technology transfers to increase abilities, techniques, and equipment because of concentrated efforts in the West to deny China access to advanced technology.

The challenge of information acquisition only got worse after the Tiananmen Square attacks in 1989 and subsequent sanctions. George H. W. Bush suspended military sales and the US Congress voted to uphold Bush's executive order until human rights progress is made in China and to suspend all trade missions and talks (Glass 2011). The measures also banned licenses for technology and enhanced export controls for dual use technology (Dui-Hua 2010).

The Chinese reaction to sanctions and condemnation at what they considered an internal affair was swift. The national plan to acquire technology by any means necessary was swiftly accelerated throughout the 1990s to the 2000s. Inkster (2015: 47) notes that "some Western analysts have interpreted the new, more assertive China as a product of a decades long strategy to replace the US as the leading global power by 2049, the hundredth anniversary of the People's Republic. In this view, the ground for China's rise has been prepared through deception and concealment designed to lull the West into a false sense of security." Lindsay and Chueng (2015: 54) note, "China uses espionage to support its interests in national security, maintenance of the Communist Party's rule on power, and economic development."

Not all espionage is digital in nature, with traditional methods still critical in leading to infiltrations. Insider threats are common avenues of attack for cyber violations. Inkster (2015: 37) writes about the targets of such influence, "such individuals were susceptible to the proposition that while their mainland compatriots had suffered,

they had enjoyed comfortable lives and that this placed on them a moral obligation to assist China, a poor developing country, to catch up with the West." This
obligation posed to Chinese migrants in the United States was a potent force for
conversation.

Yet, Chinese deception and espionage operations have not gone unnoticed, and
led to significant reciprocation by the United States and condemnation by the international community. Australia took the step of banning Hauwei from competing for
government contracts lest the Chinese company insert backdoors (Lu-YueYang 2012).

The actual progress in Chinese espionage operations is interesting to highlight.
Inkster (2015: 36) writes, "China's intelligence agencies appear to have relatively limited political influence—the MSS, for example, is not regarded as a power ministry."
So, their direct influence on policy and events is suspect. There is also a clear division
of labor between infiltration teams and exploitation teams in Chinese espionage operations (Inkster 2015: 45). This would mean that there is little direct coordination
between targets exploited and how the process of extracting data and information
is conducted.

While there is a coordination problem, there is also evidence that Chinese efforts
are not very successful and prone to replication, suggesting that there is little overlap
between teams that break into systems and future teams that break into the same organizations years later. As Inkster notes (2015: 46), "the fact that exploits designed to
collect information on one interaction of a technology are repeated against its subsequent versions suggest that in many cases, China has failed to identify the under-
lying principles of that technology." Cyber espionage is difficult, especially if there
are coordination and learning challenges. Stealing technology is no sure way to learn
how to use and further develop this technology (Gilli and Gilli 2017). The history
of innovation is filled with failures following industrial theft and even failures when
direct collaboration is conducted.

Lindsay and Chueng (2015: 68) note, "overreliance on economic espionage may
become an impediment in China's quest to become a leading industrial superpower."
Failing to develop domestic industry can be catastrophic. The parallel concern is the
inability of the state to manufacture new technologies once stolen. The innovation
process is often divorced from the production process and introducing an unnatural
connection can "create dependency through investment in a large-scale absorption
effect" (Lindsay 2015a: 26).

While there is rampant speculation that Chinese espionage activities have led to
rapid jumps in technology, with the F-35 being cited as the prime example, there is
little evidence that this is true across the board or that turning IP theft into combat
power is as straightforward as many imagine. The F-35 itself has been prone to extensive problems with development, design, and implementation in the West. There

is no guarantee the J-20, the plane likely built based on the stolen plans, will escape these challenges (Gertler 2014). Just because you steal plans for an F-35, it does not mean you know how to best use them or integrate them with the larger infrastructure required to use fifth-generation platforms. The F-35 is as much a flying server connecting multiple air, ground, cyber, sea, and space platforms as it is as weapon. Replicating its combat power therefore requires infrastructure and trained personnel that takes at least a generation to develop.

China itself has been able to defend against Western incursions, despite the speculation introduced by the Snowden files. Aggressive counterespionage activities by China had their impact too, with numerous CIA sources reportedly eliminated in 2010–2011. The *New York Times* reports that moles and leaks were thought to be a prime cause of the unmasking of sources later confirmed by hacking into electronic communications and surveillance devices at meeting points (Mazzetti et al. 2017).

On the American side, there have been extensive efforts to unmask China's own agents with a few examples recently uncovered and removed from the spying game. Clearly the height of activity came in 2014 with the surprising move to indicit five officers from PLA Unit 61398—a bold step to counter the proliferation of Chinese espionage and make known that the United States could provide evidence of specific actions in cyberspace (DOJ 2014).

What is clear is that grandiose claims surpass the empirical record. For example, Hannas et al. (2013: 216) write, "cyber espionage is the latest and perhaps most devastating form of Chinese espionage, striking at the heart of American military advantage and technological competitiveness." There is an opposing side to this story that could be reassuring, but also concerning. Inkster (2016: 46) notes, "meanwhile, the developing world is increasingly wired by China, almost certainly in circumstances that will give the country's intelligence community access to the information transiting those networks."

While it is evident that Chinese espionage operations are increasing over time, and problematic for the targets, there are also clear patterns. According to Figure 6.1, we see spikes in 2006–2007, a spike again in 2009, a spike in 2011, a sharp decline in 2012–2013, and another spike in 2014 that is stopped after 2015 with the agreement between Xi and Obama.

A report by the cyber security firm FireEye demonstrates the decline in Chinese espionage operations after 2014 (FireEye 2016). The report notes a "noticeable decline" after 2014, citing governmental reforms in China and unprecedented action in the United States (the indictment of Chinese military officers). There is a clear and dramatic decline in activity among 72 suspect Chinese intelligence groups after July 2015, suggesting the combination of internal changes, the diplomatic exchanges between the countries, and American legal aggression all had a cumulative impact in halting the exploitation of data by China.

While there has been a clear decline in Chinese cyber operations since 2014, the contention is that China has moved to using more sophisticated operations in cyberspace. But this conclusion is based on hunches with no actual evidence that the lack of recent discovery of operations is guided by better practice. Instead, China might have concluded that a more stable cyberspace in is in the interest of all, especially with a violent domestic population and criminal actors.

China appears to have moved toward focusing on conventional espionage operations due to the extensive network of Chinese nationals in the United States and susceptible targets (Mazzetti et al. 2017). The agreements signed between China and the United States (2015) and Canada (2017) both demonstrate a stated willingness to avoid espionage for commercial advantage. This shift likely demonstrates China's interest in shaping the normative system in cyberspace, directing allowed action away from commercial espionage because it achieves no clear gain for China, and focusing instead on allowing for the continuation of hacking activities to achieve a military advantage in case of future conflict.

China's Other Actors: Criminals and Patriots

Any discussion of Chinese cyber activities cannot leave out coverage of the criminal element in the state and the role of third-party nationalist groups. For Lindsay (2015a: 17), "rampant cybercrime is a result, in part, of China's below average cyber defense." These weak defenses make the Chinese state vulnerable to external attacks, but more importantly vulnerable to internal destabilizing threats.

Kshetri (2013: 57) argues China's early shift toward cybercrime was influenced by the change from a Marxist-Leninist approach to economic progress to a capitalist turn that focuses on economic growth. This then encouraged and emboldened criminals to act in cyberspace. This rather simplistic paradigm betrays the advantage of cybercrime in China in the early stages of the Internet, its utter deregulation, lack of interest by the state (which only seemed to be rectified in 2015), and the societal acceptance of wealth acquisition.

Due to a lack of regulation and attention early on, the cybercrime market proliferated quite quickly. There was a retrenchment with renewed interest by the state to reassert control after 2009 (Kshetri 2013: 56), and a more forceful focus after that. Seeking to harness the particularly aggressive form of Chinese nationalism, Chinese hackers were encouraged to "fight for the honor of their motherland" (Kshetri 2013: 59).

Criminal behavior in cyberspace has distinctly different motives, and criminal actors have vastly inferior capabilities when compared to state actors. Where criminal behavior and state behavior collide is of interest to our study, with Russia demonstrating a close linkage between criminal actors and government operatives. China does not operate at such a level consistently, but the practice of co-opting criminals is not unheard of. Inkster (2015: 37) calls them partial state actors. Add to this the typical practice in the 1980s of military operatives setting up criminal and illicit businesses to bring money into the military, we have a firm foundation for criminal aided cyber aggression in China. A PLA officer moonlighting is common, or was common until recently (Inkster 2015: 36).

The nationalism evident in Chinese cyber activism can be and has been funneled externally by Beijing. Lindsay (2015b: 5) suggests these actors will be the wild cards in any cyber conflict. In an effort to maintain control over the domestic population and flow of information, a 2015 bill mandated that service providers give up encryption information to the state, with a measure to provide backdoors for all software and hardware (Inkster 2015: 34). This backdoor is mainly to control domestic actors, not external action.

The true focus of many Chinese information operations is to control the impulses of their own population. External threats are a problem that might generate undue influence, but China seeks to maintain control over the population through the subtle accumulation of control over their digital systems. Instead of emboldening a People's War, the fear is really that the population will be unleashed against the Communist State. In some ways, the focus on external disruption and espionage has further encouraged this development and might be a source for limiting future cyber conflict launched externally.

Another source of control is the newly devised Strategic Support Force (SSF), thought to rival the US Cyber Command (Bing 2017b). This force can compel both domestic and military actors to organize under a unified command. While the force is significant, the most unique aspect is the public nature of the shift within China (DoD 2017). The move toward recognizing and standing up a powerful force in response to other states' own developments is not unexpected, but moving out of the shadows is, and this process will likely continue as we come to terms with just what is allowed and forbidden in cyberspace.

Conclusion

China takes a unique approach to cyber strategy, and ambiguous signaling is evident in its preference for espionage. This strategic preference emerges from a combination of central ideas about the role of information warfare in disputes, Chinese doctrine, and an imperative to alter the calculation of relative power between Beijing and Washington. However, in these cyber exchanges, the digital domain appears to be less coercive than many pundits imagine, tending toward tacit bargaining between rivals and predictable patterns of action-reaction that stabilize rather than escalate great power competition.

How China operates in cyberspace is also influenced by their views of how the domain should be governed. They advocate a multilateral model where each state makes the rules for their territory based on the principle of sovereignty, differing from the multistakeholder model typically advocated by Western actors (Inkster 2015: 44). This view would suggest a limited utility of attacking externally but does not preclude the utility of espionage in order to protect sovereign interests. These themes are reinforced in their newly developed National Cyber Security Strategy, posted in December of 2016 (Creemers 2016).

The National Cyber Security Strategy introduces a community view of cyber security since the dependence China has on the Internet is similar to the dependence exhibited in the West. All countries engaging in digital communication, except maybe North Korea, depend on digital connectivity and are vulnerable to violations.

The need for innovation rather than imitation might have provoked a retrenchment in Chinese activity around 2015 and the diplomatic agreement with the United States. In fact, a leading source of cyber security news recently declared that China is now the active source for cyber security norms after they followed up the US agreement with similar agreements with Canada, the UK, and Europe (Bing 2017c).

Moving forward, we are at an interesting time where China seems subdued after the indictment of Chinese military officers by the United States and satisfied after the agreement between Xi and Obama in 2015. Reducing the practice of commercial espionage would be a key strategic change for China's behavior in cyberspace, suggesting a new era that might emerge after 2015. We hope we are not too optimistic in projecting stability in Chinese cyber behavior, at least in terms of espionage for advantage. Evidence would suggest that the process of information transfer through cyber means is fraught with complications and might have overall degraded internal Chinese industry by stifling innovation. While cyber activity in China may continue to express national interests, it is questionable whether China will still maintain cyber espionage at previous levels. We do know that it is difficult for states to change behavior wholesale and there might be a transition period before a new path to stability.

Inkster (2016: 35) notes that China's "interest in global connectivity makes it more prone to compromise with the like-minded. Indeed, diplomats attending the 2015 UN/GGE commented on the difficulty Russia experienced gaining China's approval for some of its positions." This would suggest that China is more interested in stability than disruption, which contrasts with Russia cyber conflict behavior and their reliance on cheap signals.

As the United States further withdraws from international diplomacy regarding cyber security issues, China seeks to take its place. China is now seeking to be the leader in cyber security norms for the international system. The June 2017 agreement signed between China and Canada signals the continuing shift away from aggressive hacking activities toward establishing a clear normative agenda for China in the cyber landscape (Fife and Chase 2017). After the failure of the 2017 GGE in the UN, China now advocates a regional ASEAN cyber security agreement that leaves out the United States. China's geopolitical engagement of global institutions, on their terms, now extends the idea of a "peaceful rise" (Bijian 2005), but now exhibited in digital space.

As long as Russia and China differ on how to counter the West, we can expect stability to dominate in cyberspace. Russia uses cheap signals and disruption to achieve strategic goals while China moves away from espionage to focus on maintaining domestic control and shaping Internet governance in an image that supports control over actions within its borders. We now turn to uncovering the cyber strategy of the most successful compelling state in the international system, the United States.

What can be seen can be hit; what
can be hit can be destroyed.
—GENERAL WILLIAM DEPUTY

7

THE UNITED STATES

The Cyber Reconnaissance-Strike Complex

Introduction

In June 2013, *The Guardian* and *Washington Post* reported the first leaked documents
from a low-level NSA contractor, Edward Snowden (Greenwald et al. 2013; Gellman
and Markon 2013). The prior month, Snowden fled the United States for Hong Kong,
where he passed information about covert US cyber activities to multiple journalists
and state agents. The Snowden leaks revealed programs such as TreasureMap, an operation that would create a "near real-time interactive map of the global internet" and
enable covert implants, such as Turbine, to launch precise "cyber-assaults" (Bamford
2015). The leaks also illuminated the sheer scale of these espionage-turned-degrada-
tion campaigns, reflecting a "clandestine campaign that embraces the Internet as a
theater of spying, sabotage and war" (Gellman and Nakashima 2013).

Revelations in the Snowden documents, though an initial shock, reflect a consistent
strategic logic that connects US cyber operations with a preference for precision strikes
against adversary command and control systems that emerged at the end of the Cold
War. This approach to strategic competition, the *reconnaissance-strike complex*, translates
into degradation and espionage operations, to include offensive counterintelligence,
designed for strategic competition between rivals in the digital domain. In these covert
actions, information is everything: the ends, the ways, and the means of achieving a
position of advantage between rivals.[1] The United States relies on complicated, costly,

and time-intensive cyber operations meant to achieve success, debilitating surprise, and altering the cost-benefit calculus of rivals challenging US interests.

These covert actions are not without costs. While the United States achieves coercive success far more often than other cyber powers in the DCID 1.1, 53% (9 of 17), these sophisticated cyber degradation operations also tend to produce unintended proliferation. What starts as a precision strike against critical systems, such as Iranian nuclear centrifuges, ends up spilling into the public domain. According to Symantec (Falliere et al. 2011), Stuxnet spread to 155 countries. Cyber covert action begets digital proliferation as rivals and criminals adapt the malware for their own ends. Cyber instruments, once used, often become "instantly democratized" and available on the open market (Hudson 2012). This dynamic erodes their coercive potential and generally contributes to cyber restraint. States seeking the proverbial quick win in cyberspace balance this choice with losing access to their rival's network once the attack occurs (i.e., the patch problem) and the risk of having their attack turned against them. Aggressive degrade actions also damage efforts to establish stable cyber norms against aggressive attacks on critical facilities.

This chapter analyzes US cyber coercion against rival states. First, the chapter situates the US approach to cyber in the larger intellectual history surrounding a preference for precision strike and how it alters the character of war for US strategists. Second, the chapter connects this logic to the emergence of information warfare concepts in the early 1990s, when US practitioners began to integrate cyber into larger visions of precision strike. Next, the chapter shifts to outline how the United States approaches cyber strategy for coercive effect. This investigation offers a case-specific contextualization of larger findings in chapters 3 and 4. We offer a portrait of how the leading cyber power uses covert coercive cyber actions to shape rival behavior in the digital domain.

These insights highlight the importance of the reconnaissance-strike as a strategic construct. They also demonstrate the US approach toward cyber espionage and turning defensive measures into attack vectors through deception, a process first proposed by Gartzke and Lindsay (2015). That is, precision strike translates into counterintelligence options in the digital domain. The conclusion discusses how cyber degradation fits within a broader, combined approach to coercion and the overall limits of cyber strategies.

A Preference for Paralyzing Precision: The Reconnaissance-Strike Complex

In the 1970s, Soviet theorists carefully studied US operations ranging from Linebacker in Vietnam to Assault Breaker, a program established to study technological offsets.[2]

In these experiments, the Soviets saw the outline of the future. The character of war was changing. Dispersed sensors and precision strike munitions able to reach deep into enemy territory, connected by new computers created a counter to massed tank formations. For Adamsky (2010: 58), this preference for an "engineering approach to security" and the central "role of technology" reflects enduring aspects of American strategic culture. These ideas were the foundation of what defense practitioners and scholars would later call revolution in military affairs (RMA).

Much of defense discourse in the 1990s, an era of shrinking budgets and strategic realignment, deals with the RMA: how the combination of information technology and precision strike called for new systems, organizations, and doctrine fundamentally altering warfare. The larger genealogy of the RMA term can be linked back to a series of Russian doctrinal publications in the 1970s analyzing US experiments with laser-guided and precision weapons as well as space systems. These publications, including the *Scientific-Technical Progress and the Revolution in Military Affairs* and the writings of Marshal N. V. Ogarkov were translated by the US Air Force and disseminated throughout the Defense Department by the Military Publishing House. Much of the research emphasized an automated reconnaissance-strike complex that would make it possible to use conventional weapons to achieve effects similar to those offered by escalatory nuclear payloads (Watts 2007).

This vision drove debates beyond operational innovation. In the 1990s, the Office of Net Assessment and other defense transformation acolytes were using the idea of a new era of information dominance to propose concepts about realigning defense priorities focusing on the concept of "offsetting." The case had been made that the weapon systems displayed in the Gulf War were a byproduct of a larger strategy in which the United States could use advanced technology to offset Soviet mass.[3] Disruptive technologies, including stealth fighters, more unmanned systems, and Joint Surveillance Target Attack Radar (JSTAR) would enable the United States to use less forces when confronting an adversary with superior numbers. Information stood at the center of these visions of future war. To quote Army General William Depuy (Jensen 2016: 25), there was a "new lethality" emerging in weapons technology that meant "what can be seen can be hit; what can be hit can be destroyed."

In the 1990s, these earlier visions of a technological offsets, systems-of-systems, and a reconnaissance-strike complex comingled into a defense transformation program. The United States would sustain a hegemonic position through fielding the first military that integrated these systems, alongside new concepts, with the hope of ensuring a conventional deterrent for generations.

The "system of systems" concept became a central aspect of efforts to usher in the RMA. Three areas became critical: intelligence, surveillance, and reconnaissance (ISR); command, control, communication, computer systems, and intelligence processing (C4I), and precision strike (Blaker and Manning 1997). Through integrating these subsystems, US forces would penetrate the competitors' decision-making cycle and be able to rapidly find targets, process the information, select the appropriate weapon system, and engage it with a high level of accuracy before the enemy even knew they were being tracked. Parallel to these efforts, John Boyd explored what he calls the first cybernetic theory of war (Osinga 2007; Lawson 2013).[4] Of note, information was the focal point. The state that best integrated information into a system that prioritized targets and engaged the enemy with precision fire would collapse the enemy's will. Whether through attacking command and control systems or blinding the adversary, a state achieved a position of advantage.

This defense transformation thesis and idea of a reconnaissance-strike complex resonated with emerging airpower doctrine and the concept of effects-based operations (EBOs). The near-zero miss and strategic effects from tactical strikes were key components of John Warden's targeting philosophy.[5] According to Warden (1992: 65):

> Wars through history have been fought to change (or change the mind of) the command structure—to overthrow the prince literally or figuratively or to induce the command structure to make concessions. Capturing or killing the state's leader has frequently been decisive. In modern times, however, it has become more difficult—but not impossible—to capture or kill the command element. At the same time, command communications have been more important than ever, and these are vulnerable to attack. When command communications suffer extreme damage . . . the leader has great difficulty in direct war efforts. In the case of an unpopular regime, the lack of communications not only inhibits the bolstering of national morale but also facilitates rebellion on the part of dissident elements.[6]

Beyond airpower, Warden's logic of paralyzing an enemy system paralleled the emerging idea of EBOs. A RAND (Davis 2001: xiii) study defined EBOs as "operations conceived and planned in a systems framework that considers the full range of direct, indirect, and cascading effects; effects that may, with different degrees of probability, be achieved by the application of military, diplomatic, psychological, and economic instruments." Targeting different instruments of power against key nodes in a system could lead to collapse.

A 2003 study by the Defense Science Board linked EBOs to a new paradigm called discriminate use of force, "new precision and 'nonlethal' weapons and emerging capabilities such as information dominance now enable the discriminate use of force" and as such, heralded a new way of war (DoD 2003: 1). These concepts overlapped the emerging joint concept of rapid decisive operations (Hogg 2002: 348), which envisioned simultaneously massing effects against critical targets to "have the maximum impact on breaking not only the enemy's coherence, but also his will, ending the war or conflict in a single stroke." Key to these desired end-states were efforts that blinded adversary systems in order to limit their ability to visualize the battlefield. The actor best able to map the network and deliver precision effects could collapse the enemy system with minimal force and without assuming significant risk to their own military. Information dominance, to include blinding enemy intelligence, and precision effects were clarion calls and the organizing feature of a new theory of victory in the United States.

THE EMERGENCE OF INFORMATION WARFARE

Early ideas about information warfare in US strategy reflected the dominant features of the reconnaissance-strike complex: near-zero miss and seeking strategic effects through targeting C4ISR. This theory of victory had influenced the way defense practitioners and analysts viewed cyber capabilities. After the Cold War and parallel to the rise of the RMA, scholars began to focus on the role of information in warfare.[7] These pioneers broadened the scope of information warfare beyond traditional interests in intelligence and reconnaissance and propaganda to include emergent information pathways such as the use of cyber tactics. This early body of scholarship and practitioner reflections stressed how the ability to accumulate and to process information faster than your adversary changed warfare. Advocates defined information warfare as "actions intended to protect, exploit, corrupt, deny or destroy information or information resources in order to achieve a significant advantage, objective or victory over the adversary" (Alger 1996). Achieving these effects required lines of effort, "to know, to deny knowledge, and to manipulate information" (Thayer 2000: 47). For these thinkers, information warfare implied collecting and processing information about the enemy, denying them access to critical information about one's own forces, and deceiving them through manipulating information. A key aspect of denying access took the form of cyber counterintelligence often in the form of honeypots that lured in digital spies only to attack their networks.

Conceived along these lines, the US strategy for information warfare was "based upon the defense and attack of information and information systems" (Bunker 2002: 101). While military forces have always tried to defend and attack information systems, especially in the form of the enemy's commanders understanding of the situation, "the importance of this form of conflict has been magnified many times over with the computer and Internet revolutions" (Bunker 2002: 101). The rival state best able to increase their information access while limiting the enemy's access achieves a position of advantage in the digital domain.

For proponents of the emerging information warfare movement, the connectivity of the digital age changed the ways and means associated with the objective of attacking an adversary's information system and their internal cohesion (Cronin and Crawford 1999: 258):

> A typical goal of conventional warfare is to destroy or degrade the enemy's physical resources, whereas the aim of IW is to target information assets and infrastructure, such that the resultant damage may not be immediately visible or detectable to the untrained eye: These strikes are called soft kills. In practical terms, cyberwarfare means infiltrating, degrading, or subverting the target's information systems using logic bombs or computer viruses. But it also extends traditional notions of psychological warfare: an IW goal may be silent penetration of the target's information and communications system in order to shape community perceptions, foster deception, or seed uncertainty.

This interest in information warfare as it relates to the broader RMA movement paralleled after action reviews from the Persian Gulf War and the emergence of the Internet. The dotcom boom of the 1990s occurred while military theorists had been assessing how the US-led coalition achieved victory against Iraq in Desert Storm. Though the coalition had been using few precision weapons, the dramatic television footage of laser-guided bombs heading to their target and interest in new platforms such as the stealth fighter reflected for some the first shots of a new form of warfare. According to Feaver (1998: 88), in these optimistic accounts:

> Desert Storm was a preview of a new era, with prototypes and first-generation systems hinting at the likely course of conflict in the next century. Under the new form of warfare, called information warfare (IW), information-processing ability becomes each side's center of gravity and therefore the focus of military effort, both offensive and defensive. Conflicts will turn on whether one side can control the other side's ability to process information while protecting its own information processing from the efforts of the enemy to control it. The side that can conquer its opponent's information while preserving its own information from enemy attacks will prevail. The side that loses control over its information will lose.

This view of information warfare as the "manipulation or disruption of information distribution networks" along offensive and defensive lines found its way into military doctrine (Feaver 1998: 90). The US Army Information Operations (2003: v) manual stated, "Information operations (IO) encompass attacking adversary command and control (C2) systems (offensive IO) while protecting friendly C2 systems from adversary disruption (defensive IO). Effective IO combines the effects of offensive and defensive IO to produce information superiority at decisive points." The US Air Force (1998) drew a direct connection between information superiority and gaining air and space superiority. Using the emerging information domain to gain a position of advantage relative to the enemy became a key component of US Air Force doctrine. This doctrine (1998) prioritizes information superiority as the key aspect of achieving victory:

> The Air Force believes that to fully understand and achieve information superiority, our understanding of information operations must explicitly include two conceptually distinct but extremely interrelated pillars: information-in-warfare—the "gain" and "exploit" aspects of other information-based processes—and information warfare—the "attack" and "defend" aspects. Information warfare involves such diverse activities as psychological operations, military deception, electronic warfare, both physical and information ("cyber") attack, and a variety of defensive activities and programs. It is important to stress that information warfare is a construct that operates across the spectrum, from peace to war, to allow the effective execution of Air Force responsibilities.

In joint doctrine, employing instruments of power in the information environment required "the ability to securely transmit, receive, store, and process information in near real time. The nation's state and nonstate adversaries are equally aware of the significance of this new technology, and will use information-related capabilities (IRCs) to gain advantages in the information environment, just as they would use more traditional military technologies to gain advantages in other operational environments" (Joint Chiefs of Staff [JCS] 2014: ix). In this reading, information operations became the employment of these IRCs to "influence, disrupt, corrupt, or usurp the decision making of adversaries and potential adversaries while protecting [your] own" (JCS 2014, ix). Through manipulating information, one could achieve a strategic position of advantage.

Thinkers began to see more conventional uses for cyber manipulation in the early 1990s. Paralleling the RMA, advocates argued that cyber created new battlefield dynamics and expanded the space-time boundaries of conflict.[8] Specifically, the cyber domain had unique spatial and temporal characteristics (Bunker 1998). First, it led to a spatial expansion by enabling, through computer networks, attackers to extend the depth of battlefield. Second, in relation to civilian audiences, it enabled increased reach and access. Communications networks connected domestic audiences to war in a new way, allowing adversaries to manipulate the media and deny civilian support for military action. Third, cyber capabilities led to the idea of temporal acceleration. The speed of attack became the speed it took to circulate images or send malicious code through computer networks.

This vision of using the digital domain to achieve a position of advantage, how information superiority enabled a reconnaissance-strike complex, shaped concepts beyond crises and conventional war. The core aspects of the reconnaissance-strike complex found their way into a 2013 conventional concept for fighting a limited war with China, the Air-Sea Battle. The concept (Department of Defense [DoD] 2013: 4) described how to shape anti-access area denial (A2AD) environments to enable power projection. The central idea (DoD 2013: 4) was to develop an integrated network "capable of attack-in-depth to disrupt, destroy and defeat adversary forces (NIA/D3). A joint force would simultaneously attack an adversary in multiple domains, a network integrated attack." According to the Air-Sea Battle Office (DoD 2013: 7), the attack would occur along three lines of effort: (1) disrupt adversary command, control, communications, computers, intelligence, surveillance, and reconnaissance (C4ISR); (2) destroy adversary A2/AD platforms and weapon systems; and (3) defeat adversary formations.

The concept supports the Joint Operational Access Concept (DoD 2012). According to Lieutenant General George Flynn (2012), that concept addressed challenges associated with maintaining "operational access and freedom of maneuver" and translated them into the requirements for Joint Force 2020, such as future capabilities, force structure, and procurement decisions. The Joint Operational Access Concept (2012) outlined 30 operational capabilities "needed to gain and achieve access." According to DoD officials, this concept and Air-Sea Battle were part of the rebalance and efforts to develop and update "operational concepts and plans to conduct a broader array of missions" in the Asia-Pacific (House COAS 2014; Jensen and Shibuya 2015). The reconnaissance-strike complex and achieving information superiority were central to emerging DoD ideas about containing Chinese military power in the Western Pacific. What started as a hypothesis about future war by thinkers in the Office of Net Assessment, largely based on the writings of Soviet generals, came to fruition as a vision for countering China through information superiority.

There has been a consistent interest in precision strike and how it alters warfare since the late 1970s in the United States. This vision of a reconnaissance-strike complex defined major defense debates and shaped successive operational concepts. From hunting down high-value individual targets as part of counterterror contingencies, to developing concepts for blinding strikes against Chinese C4ISR, the idea of using cyber capabilities to infiltrate command networks, often through counterintelligence honeypots, and paralyze them at an opportune moment became dominant features of the American way of war. These attributes are empirically observable in US cyber operations against rival states between the years 2000 and 2014.

Data Analysis: US Cyber Coercion

Figure 7.1 highlights the fact that the United States uses cyber operations at a much more sparing rate than its top rival competitors, China and Russia. This fits the strategic narrative of the United States, where covertness and surgical strikes in the cyber domain are the preferred approach. The United States also significantly reduced its cyber activity after the revelations of the Stuxnet worm, where this highly advanced cyber sabotage operation spread to networks worldwide and cast the United States as a violator of international law and norms. Concerned about other states being more aggressive in cyberspace as a result of this degrading operation on Iran's nuclear program, the United States appears to have since used cyber operations more sparingly against rivals, usually in the form of counterespionage campaigns against China or Russia or dormant probing of networks to enable future action. The Shadow Brokers NSA zero-days dump makes apparent that the digital spy agency has invested significant time and resources to give it the ability to launch shorter-notice cyber actions than its rivals.

Cyber coercion and covert action associated with degradation and espionage appear to be the only forms used by the United States and at a much lower rate than Russia or China. As the United States has historically overmatched its adversaries in

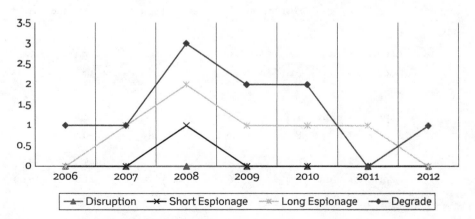

FIGURE 7.1 United States Yearly Cyber Incidents, Coercive Intent: 2000–2014

both latent cyber capacity and demonstrated capabilities, it could be that many clandestine American cyber incidents stay classified and not available for open source data sources. However, the collection of incidents covered in Figure 7.1 fits how the United States conducts its operations according to strategic doctrine: gain information superiority, identify the optimal targets, and conduct a precision strike at the right moment.

This approach may not be unique to the United States for much longer. As China gains latent cyber capacity and working expertise, they may similarly shift to focusing on network access and precise degradation efforts. However, based on observations from the DCID, this inflection point has not yet been reached. As discussed in chapter 6, China to date prefers espionage and access to degradation and destruction. There are unique, empirical differences between how the two cyber superpowers approach achieving effects in the digital domain.

Table 7.1 shows the cross-tabulation analysis of US cyber coercive choices in relation to other cyber initiators in the DCID dataset covering 2000–2014. The United States has initiated no disruptive action, which are low-cost low-pain actions that predominantly affect civilian and commercial networks. This absence is no surprise, as disruptions do not fit with the strategic logic of the reconnaissance-strike complex. These operations target lower-value targets as opposed to the critical nodes and command and control type targets favored by precision strike (Kaplan 2016: 41). The United States also uses short-term espionage well below the expected rate, and only once has the cyber superpower used this method. However, long-term espionage is

TABLE 7.1

Cyber objective differentials between US and global cyber initiators

		Disruption	Short-term Espionage	Long-term Espionage	Degrade	Total
US	Count	0	1	6	10	17
	Expected Count	6.2	5.9	2.7	2.2	17.0
	z-score	-2.5^{**}	-2.0^{**}	2.1^{**}	5.2^{***}	
World	Count	70	66	24	15	175
	Expected Count	63.8	61.1	27.3	22.8	175.0
	z-score	.8	.6	$-.6$	-1.6	
Total	Count	70	67	30	25	192
	Expected Count	70.0	67.0	30.0	25.0	192.0

$^{***}p < .01, ^{**}p < .05, ^{*}p < .10$

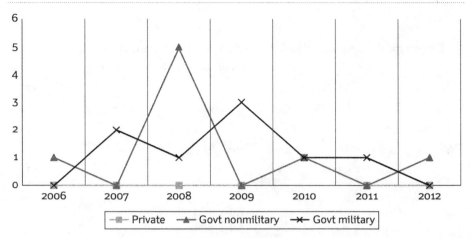

FIGURE 7.2 United States Yearly Cyber Incidents, Target Type: 2000–2014

used more than what would be expected at the 95% confidence level. These cyber espionage cases appear to reflect attempts to gain a position of advantage required to collect information and launch precision degradation efforts against rivals when needed. The United States' preferred coercive method is to degrade its adversaries, as it uses these objectives more than what would be expected at the 99% confidence level, which is consistent with the preference for precision strikes that erode critical capabilities.

Figure 7.2 shows that US targeting of government military and nonmilitary networks ebbs and flows over the years at about the same rate. This indicates that when US cyber operations are engaged, that they are most likely coordinated with the NSA and other Pentagon divisions tasked with offensive cyber operations. US cyber actions are more coordinated, sophisticated, and controlled when compared to the cyber operations coming out of Russia and China. In this respect, the coercive success of the United States in cyberspace makes sense. Complex, highly coordinated, costly, and sophisticated cyber operations have sunk costs that demonstrate resolve to rival states once revealed.

Table 7.2 uncovers the cross-tabulation analysis of the differential targets of choice between the United States and the other two cyber powers. Only the United States' choice of targeting military targets is statistically significant at the $p < .05$ level. This preference is consistent with the targeting logic of the reconnaissance-strike complex. The United States has targeted the network of a private entity only once, the Chinese search engine Huawei in retaliation for China's part in hacking Google and other Silicon Valley giants (New York Times 2014). The restraint from targeting private networks and near exclusivity of government networks is indicative of American mode of operations in the cyber domain.

TABLE 7.2

Target type differentials between US and global cyber initiators

		Private	Govt. Non-military	Govt. Military	Total
US	Count	1	8	8	17
	Expected Count	3.7	10.4	2.9	17.0
	z-score	−1.4	−.7	3.0***	
World	Count	41	109	25	175
	Expected Count	38.3	106.6	30.1	175.0
	z-score	.4	.2	−.9	
Total	Count	42	117	33	192
	Expected Count	42.0	117.0	33.0	192.0

***$p < .01$, **$p < .05$, *$p < .10$

Figure 7.3 shows the scale of limited cyber actions the United States launched when compared to its competitors in the digital domain. The overwhelming methods of choice apparent in US operations are the more advanced infiltrations, which includes viruses, worms, keystroke logs, and logic bombs. These surgical and advanced methods fit the strategic doctrines unpacked in the narrative earlier in this chapter. Though the United States is linked to fewer cyber exchanges between rivals, the incidents tend to be more severe and targeted. Consistent with the reconnaissance-strike complex and its emphasis on blinding an adversary, as well as destabilizing their system, these actions often take the form of sophisticated counter-intelligence operations that lure in unsuspecting digital spies only to spring the trap.

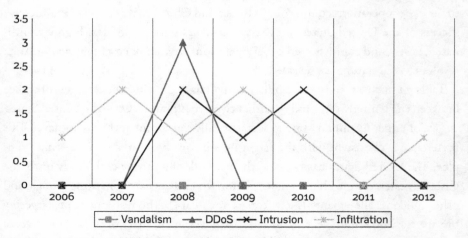

FIGURE 7.3 United States Yearly Cyber Incidents by Method: 2000–2014

TABLE 7.3

Cyber method differentials between US and global cyber initiators

		Vandalism	DDoS	Intrusion	Infiltration	Total
US	Count	0	2	6	9	17
	Expected Count	2.7	2.9	7.8	3.5	17.0
	Std. Residual	−1.7	−.5	−.6	2.9***	
World	Count	31	31	82	31	175
	Expected Count	28.3	30.1	80.2	36.5	175.0
	Std. Residual	.5	.2	.2	−.9	
Total	Count	31	33	88	40	192
	Expected Count	31.0	33.0	88.0	40.0	192.0

***$p < .01$, **$p < .05$, *$p < .10$

Table 7.3 coincides with the findings of the other data analyses and finds that the United States' overwhelming cyber method of choice is infiltrations. Washington uses these methods at three standard deviations above the expected null value and this is statistically significant at the $p < .01$ level. The United States has never used harassing vandalism methods and rarely uses DDoS techniques, which are usually used to target civilian networks and reflect a less sophisticated form of cyber coercion. These disruptions are not in line with US doctrine, where the more precise infiltration techniques to degrade military networks or disrupt rival cyber spies are usually the goal. If information superiority and gaining a position of advantage are the objective, you would not trade network access for a limited harassing effect.

ESCALATORY RESPONSES TO US CYBER COERCIVE ACTIONS

Table 7.4 lists the responses from target states as a result of US cyber actions. Russia responded to American network infringement with cyber actions of their own, which is indicative of Russia's willingness to counter US cyber action with action in the same domain. Iran and China have also responded to US cyber coercion once each, which can be seen as tit-for-tat responses that have been the norm for each dyad for years. While the China cyber response level seems low, it reflects China's unique approach to cyber strategy. Beijing is more interested in gaining access and stealing information than they are achieving a near-term coercive effect. When they do, it tends to be a low-level signal or a response in another domain.

Diplomatic threats have been seen from Iran and North Korea. Iran threatened the United States economically by promising to forbid American companies from

TABLE 7.4

US cyber actions: Target escalatory responses

Name	Date	Method	Target	Target Type	Objective	Response			
						Cyber	Diplomatic	Economic	Military
Reign	2/1/2008	Intrusion	Russia	Govt. nonmilitary	Long-term espionage	1	0	0	0
QWERTY keystroke	2/1/2008	Keystroke	Russia	Govt. nonmilitary	Short-term espionage	1	0	0	0
Flame	6/1/2009	Virus	Iran	Govt. military	Long-term Espionage	0	1	1	0
Iran network	3/14/2010	Intrusion	Iran	Govt. nonmilitary	Long-term Espionage	1	0	0	0
Cisco Raider	2/28/2006	Keystroke	China	Govt. nonmilitary	Degrade	1	0	0	0
NSA Fourth Party	7/1/2009	Intrusion	China	Govt. military	Degrade	0	0	0	1
NK Stuxnet	3/1/2010	Worm	N. Korea	Govt. military	Degrade	0	1	0	0

investing in Iran if continued cyber aggression continued after the revelations of the Flame virus in 2011. Limited military threats and displays have happened only once as a result of US cyber coercive actions, from China following the revelations of the NSA conducting counterespionage on People's Liberation Army (PLA) actions.

A few caveats must be noted regarding the preceding data analysis. By focusing on rival states, we purposely miss two other important targets: partners and non-state actors. US espionage campaigns targeting partners, such as the 2014 revelation that Washington was spying on German President Angela Merkel, are not captured (Castle 2013). The United States has also conducted a wide range of cyber espionage and degradation campaigns against nonstate actors such as ISIS (Sanger 2016a). Actions against partners and nonstate actors would require different theories of cyber action. We must evaluate empirically what we can see and draw inferences from these actions, bounding our claims based on data limitations. The fact that US cyber behavior is consistent with the evolution of US strategic thought since the end of the Cold War demonstrates that the DCID captures the outline, if not the detail, of how rivals seek a position of advantage in the digital domain. We now turn to the qualitative comparative analysis (QCA) that uncovers the necessary and sufficient conditions of US combined cyber actions.

NECESSARY AND SUFFICIENT CONDITIONS OF SUCCESSFUL US COMBINED CYBER ACTION

Table 7.5 displays the crisp set truth table of the combined foreign policy actions of US cyber endeavors that have produced concessions from rival states. Concessions evoked from the targets of the United States are all degradations, with no espionage or disruptive techniques evoking concessions from target states.[9] The United States uses all of its instruments of power in many of these cyber operations, indicating that cyber operations alone are not sufficient to evoke concessions and are only useful in an additive context. Only once does a US degradation evoke a concession on its own.

Cisco Raider was launched against the PLA to stop the tide of counterfeit Cisco hardware that was being downloaded online and spreading spyware in many private sector networks (Cooney 2008). Chinese hackers were then able to access networks once this counterfeit software was installed and intellectual property as well as secretive government information was accessed and stolen. US agencies intervened directly in these operations and launched the degradation operation, as a covert counterespionage campaign, against these Chinese entities, flooding them with crippling botnets as they tried to access networks through the counterfeit software. The operation decreased these espionage operations and left the crafty counterfeit software unusable, as users patched the zero-day vulnerability.

TABLE 7.5

Crisp set truth table for combined US cyber degradations, concessionary behavioral change

Event	Past Disruption	Past Espionage	Diplomatic Negative	Diplomatic Positive	Economic Negative	Economic Positive	Military Negative	Military Positive
Buckshot Yankee	0	1	1	1	1	0	0	0
Stuxnet (US)	0	1	1	0	1	0	1	0
Cisco Raider	0	0	0	1	0	0	0	0
Arrow Eclipse	0	1	1	1	1	0	1	0
Boxing Rumble (China)	0	1	1	1	0	0	0	1
NSA Fourth Party	0	1	1	1	1	0	1	1
Shortgiant	0	1	1	1	0	0	0	0
Boxing Rumble (NK)	0	0	1	1	0	0	0	0

Another example of using cyber degradation as a covert signaling mechanism linked to counterespionage is Boxing Rumble. Boxing Rumble was the NSA/Cyber Command answer to PLA attempts at penetrating several secure DoD networks (InfoSec Institute 2015). The operation would seek out and find these spear-phishing and other Trojan techniques and fool Chinese hackers into thinking that they had broken through to highly classified DoD networks. However, the Boxing Rumble campaigns actually were sending either bogus information that the Chinese thought was legitimate intelligence, or wiper malware that sabotaged the PLA centers back in China. The costs of attempting to penetrate DoD networks became so great that operations ceased, and many PLA centers had to be burned as a result of the sophisticated malware infecting their computers.

The Boxing Rumble incident involved diplomatic, economic, and military inducements and a clever reactionary botnet to several Chinese espionage Advanced Persistent Threat (APT) groups targeting civilian DoD networks (InfoSec Institute 2015). Whenever certain strands of codes known to be of the PLA variant were launched against these networks, a successful denial of service barrage would be launched back at the source, effectively shutting the hackers' network down until the botnet could be removed. The United States usually does not hack back as a matter of doctrine, however since this involved military networks on both sides, the hack back was deemed legitimate. More discussion on the incidents in Table 7.5 appears later.

The US use of cyber degradation demonstrates how covert action can still signal resolve through sunk costs and escalation risks. In addition to the sophisticated and costly nature of the intrusion, the ability to coordinate other instruments of power demonstrates the ability to escalate both horizontally and vertically. That rare concessions are more likely in these cases is not surprising. For the infamous Stuxnet worm, the presence of diplomatic threats, economic sanctions, and military threats by the United States combined to demonstrate resolve and compel Iran to acquiesce to the 2013 Joint Plan of Action ending their nuclear program.

Table 7.6 shows the results of the Quine-McCluskey algorithm that uncovers the necessary and sufficient conditions for US combined cyber strategies that successfully achieve concessions from target states. Remembering the results of chapter 4, necessary conditions mean that particular foreign policy actions must be present (or absent) for a US-induced concession to be observed. Looking at Table 7.6, we find four necessary conditions that are indicated in bold: the presence of cyber degradation and past espionage techniques and the absence of cyber disruptions and economic positive inducements.[10] The frequency cutoff of 1 indicates that the causal conditions in Table 7.6 must be present in at least one of the successful concessionary

TABLE 7.6

The attributes of US successful cyber coercive campaigns

Conditions	Cyber Instruments (absence)	Non-cyber Instruments (absence)
Necessary	Degradation Past espionage (Past disruption)	(+ Economic)
Sufficient		+/− Diplomacy − Economic − Military

Note: Solution coverage is 1; solution constituency is 1 (see Table 7.7)

US actions. The consistency cutoff is at 100%, which allows for certain combinations remaining in the minimization process to find necessary and sufficient conditions.

The raw coverage measures the proportion of memberships in the successful concession outcome explained by each term in the solution for US coercive actions with the intent to degrade. Unique coverage percentage measures the proportion of memberships in the successful concession outcome explained solely by each part of the equation, indicated in each row of Table 7.7. Raw coverage scores are at either 75%, 25%, or 12.5%. The solution coverage score of over 1% indicates that all of the combinatorial actions in the Boolean equation explains 100% of the outcome of objective of successful US cyber combined actions—the percentage of equations that explain concessions. The solution consistency percentage means that the variables in Table 7.7 as individual units are present in 100% of successful concessions.

Table 7.7 reports the complete reduction of the Boolean addition equation into three minimized sections. The elimination of the absence of the remaining conventional foreign policy instruments that are sufficient reduce and minimize the equation to its simplest form. Looking at Table 7.7, the combinations of degradation, past cyber espionage, and negative and positive diplomatic action, make up 75% of the solution term; degradation and past espionage with negative diplomatic, economic, and military action; and degradation and past cyber espionage with all conventional instruments of power except positive economic and military inducements, compel rivals.

The event that used the most instruments of US power was the NSA Fourth Party operation. This degradation event was a covert counterespionage effort that undermined other countries' efforts to spy on the NSA and the broader defense and intelligence networks by botnets. Here the United States used all instruments

TABLE 7.7

Reduced Boolean addition for US combined cyber campaigns

Cyber Instruments[a]	Non-cyber Instruments	Raw Coverage (Unique Coverage)	Episode Examples
Degradation Past Espionage	+/− Diplomacy	.750 (.500)	Shotgiant, Boxing Rumble (NK) Buckshot Yankee
Degradation Past Espionage	− Diplomacy − Military − Economic	.250 (.125)	Arrow Eclipse, Stuxnet
DegradationPast Espionage	+/− Diplomacy − Military − Economic	.250 (.125)	Arrow Eclipse NSA Fourth Party

Solution Coverage: 1

Solution Consistency: 1 (note: all coverages above have a consistency of 1)

[a] All episodes selected on the presence of a successful cyber degradation.

of power with the exception of positive economic inducements. According to the Snowden leaks, the NSA would detect attempts to penetrate the nonsecure network and reroute them to servers controlled by the Tailored Access Operations unit. Specifically, "a DNS spoofing attack tricked the botnet into treating the spies as trusted command and control agents. The NSA then used the bot's hooks into other victims to foist its own custom malware" (Pauli 2015). For example, when PLA hackers used the accounts of Chinese and Vietnamese dissidents to create a botnet targeting DoD unclassified networks, the NSA was able to hijack the attack and use it to bolster its own data collection efforts.

According to the *New York Times*, starting in 2007 and peaking in 2010, the NSA conducted a series of intrusions under the codename Shotgiant designed to penetrate Huawei's networks (Sanger and Perlroth 2014). Positive and negative diplomatic action was taken in tandem with this cyber degradation. The penetrations had two objectives. First, they sought to identify any linkage between Huawei and the PLA. Huawei built network infrastructure, including undersea cables and routers purchased by China and countries such as Iran, Pakistan, and Cuba. Getting inside Huawei's networks enabled broad-based surveillance and attack vectors.

Second, Shotgiant turned Huawei into a spying mechanism for the United States. According to the *New York Times* and based on the Snowden leaks, "when [Huawei] sold equipment to other countries—including both allies and nations that avoid buying American products—the NSA could roam through their computer and telephone networks to conduct surveillance, and if ordered by the president, offensive cyber operations" (Sanger and Perlroth 2014). According to *Der Spiegel*, Shotgiant was so successful that the NSA accessed Huawei source code, leading to a situation in which, in the words of an NSA official, "we currently have good access and so much data that we don't know what to do with it" (Der Spiegel 2014). Of note, the operation was an interagency effort, involving the FBI, NSA, and multiple other agencies in "combined economic, counterintelligence, military" surveillance efforts targeting telecommunications infrastructure (Der Spiegel 2014). Demonstrating the ability to coordinate multiple instruments of power and launch costly degradation campaigns signals resolve and should, in theory, increase the probability of generating a concession despite the fact that most of the action was covert.

The Art of Cyber Espionage and Counterespionage

The United States relies on an open Internet not just for commerce and economic growth but also to facilitate extensive espionage and counterespionage campaigns. This use is consistent with the fight for information at the core of the reconnaissance-strike complex. Washington has key terrain that gives it an intelligence advantage, leading to more targeted and higher-payoff cyber espionage campaigns than its rivals.

The majority of the world's Internet traffic passes through 32 fiber-optic cable landing points that act as a hub for another 56 systems and account for roughly 80% of all traffic (Aid 2015). The NSA relies on a mix of voluntary compliance, paid access, and covert action to gain access to Internet traffic. Some of these efforts include corporate-partners projects run out of the Special Source Operations group, which spent between 200 and 300 million dollars per year between 2011 and 2013 to buy access (Timberg and Gellman 2013). Voluntary cooperation is even older, dating back to the 1970s under the cover name BLARNEY, a program to access "the "backbone" providers of global communications" (Timberg and Gellman 2013). AT&T supposedly cooperated with the NSA between 2003 and 2013 to provide access to "billions of emails," even though they flowed across domestic networks, as well as "technical assistance in carrying out a secret order permitting the wiretapping of all Internet communications" (Angwin et al. 2015).

Under PRISM, the NSA expanded these access initiatives to access communications from Microsoft, Google, Yahoo, Facebook, PalTalk, YouTube, Skype, AOL, and Apple (Lee 2013). These new access vectors, under FISA warrants, allow the NSA to access not just e-mails but also voice over internet protocol (VoIP) systems, instant messaging, text messaging, chat rooms, and social media sites (Aid 2015). These operations are aided by key allies such as the United Kingdom, who as part of operation Tempora placed intercepts at the landing points for over 200 fiber-optic cables (Zetter 2013). Using undersea cables to access information and deny your adversary is an old tactic. During the Spanish-American War (1898), the US Navy destroyed undersea cables connecting Cuba with the rest of the Spanish Empire as a means of isolating the island and limiting the ability of the Spanish to coordinate their forces (Winkler 2009).

Since as early as 2012, an APT suspected of being a front for a covert US cyber activity, OceanLotus, targeted entities linked to maritime traffic and intelligence from China (Segal 2015). Initially, the group used watering hole attacks and then shifted after February 2014 to spear-phishing (Peters 2015a). The APT installed trojans that allows them to intercept confidential documents and correspondence. According to Segal (2015), "over 90% of the infections were in China, most in Beijing and Tianjin." While the initial infect was targeted, subsequent reporting showed significant slippage. According to SkyEye Labs, "more than 100 OceanLotus Trojan program samples of four different types were used and spread over 13 countries" (Rafati 2015).

Another cyber espionage effort connected to the United States is the Flame virus, which conducted precision intrusions to extract information of intelligence value. Similar to Stuxnet, Flame targeted networks in Iran and the Middle East (Lee 2012). According to Zetter (2012), Flame had been "designed primarily to spy on the users of infected computers and steal data from them, including documents, recorded conversations and keystrokes. It also opens a backdoor to infected systems to allow the attackers to tweak the toolkit and add new functionality." Flame could turn on microphones and record conversations, access Skype calls, use Bluetooth to access contact lists and send all of the captured information via secure sockets layer (SSL) channels covertly back to command and control servers (Zetter 2012).

THE EQUATION GROUP

In August 2016, a group known as Shadow Brokers released source code linked to the secretive group in the NSA, the Tailored Access Operations (TAO) unit. According to the *New York Times*, "most of the code was designed to break through network firewalls and get inside the computer systems of competitors like Russia, China, and Iran. That, in turn, allowed the NSA to place implants in the system, which can lurk unseen for years and be used to monitor network traffic or enable a debilitating computer attack" (Sanger 2016b).

The source code appeared to link the NSA to the Equation Group, one of the most capable Advanced Persistent Threat (APT) actors. Operating since as early as 1996, the Equation Group produced the most sophisticated malware documented by cyber security firms. The group built and deployed a "suite of surveillance platforms, which they called EquationLaser, EquationDrug, and GrayFish" that made them "the most complex and sophisticated spy system uncovered to date" (Zetter 2015a). The malicious code gave "the attackers complete and persistent control of infected systems for years, allowing them to siphon data and monitor activities while using complex encryption schemes and other sophisticated methods to avoid detection" (Zetter 2015a).

EquationDrug and GrayFish acted as digital scouts seeking out key access points and information consistent with the earlier idea of information dominance in service doctrines. Once the malware infected a machine, "the firmware flasher module [got] deposited onto the system and reach[ed] out to a command server to obtain payload code that it then flash[ed] to the firmware, replacing the existing firmware with a malicious one" (Zetter 2015b). These scouts were built to cover wide areas. According to reporting by tech journalists, "the firmware flasher module [could] reprogram the firmware of more than a dozen different hard drive brands, including IBM, Seagate, Western Digital, and Toshiba" (Zetter 2015b). Hiding in the firmware allowed these digital scouts to remain concealed from even the most advanced antivirus scanners.

Designers built this malicious firmware to remain concealed and report back information of value for long periods of time. Demonstrating advanced capabilities, and hence sunk costs, the developer built the firmware to survive even complete updates. According to tech journalists, "if a victim, thinking his or her computer is infected, wipes the computer's operating system and reinstalls it to eliminate any malicious code, the malicious firmware code remains untouched. It can then reach out to the command server to restore all of the other malicious components that got wiped from the system" (Zetter 2015b). The compromised firmware has unique features that allowed it to store encrypted documents and files it steals on the hard disk unbeknownst to the user hiding in "the service area of the hard drive disk . . . needed for internal operation" (Zetter 2015b). Similar exploits have been published by *Der Spiegel* in 2013 and its overview of the NSA catalog of implants (Appelbaum et al. 2013). These implants included a number of different malware packages that embed on the "computers BIOS and disk drive firmware" as well as use "packet injection and hardware interception" (Schneier 2015).

Packet injection works by shooting exploits into Internet traffic as its passes through servers (Weaver 2013). This method was on display in the QUANTUM program (Schneier 2013). According to Weaver (2013), the technique demonstrated how "the internet backbone—the infrastructure of networks upon which internet traffic travels—went from being a passive infrastructure for communication to an active weapon for attacks."

Hardware injection involves covert action and intercepting routers before they shipped to unsuspecting customers and installing code. As part of the Snowden leaks, Glenn Greenwald detailed how the NSA, "intercepts servers, routers, and other network gear being shipped to organizations targeted for surveillance and install covert implant firmware onto them before they're delivered" (Gallagher 2014). Though the NSA intended the surveillance to be targeted, the risk was threefold. Even targeted surveillance in an open, interdependent information space can cascade through the system, infecting others, and end up in the wrong hands. Just how targeted is targeted surveillance? According to Kaspersky Labs, based on an analysis of infections in 2008, they conclude that the Equation Group hit approximately 2,000 users per month (Kaspersky 2015: 20). In other words, even targeted intrusions slip over in the digital domain producing potential constraints on using cyber coercion for actors concerned about proliferation or their designed malware being used against them.

Cyber security analysts also linked the Equation Group to Fanny, a computer worm distributed through the Middle East and Asia since at least 2008 (Constantin 2015a). Fanny used "two zero-day exploits, which were later uncovered during the discovery of Stuxnet. To spread, it uses Stuxnet LNK exploit and USB sticks . . . [and] a vulnerability patched by Microsoft bulletin MS09-025, which was also used in one of the early versions of Stuxnet from 2009" (GReAT 2015a). The highest infection rates by country were in Russia, Pakistan, Afghanistan, India, China, and Mali, with targets ranging from governments and military networks to commercial networks associated with telecommunications, aerospace, energy, nanotechnology, cryptographic technology, and financial institutions, even Islamic activists and scholars (Menn 2015a).

In 2010, researchers from Kaspersky and Microsoft linked the Equation Group through zero-day exploits to Stuxnet. The famed worm used the same zero-day exploit, the LNK exploit (CVE-2010-2568) "to propagate through USB drives and infect even machines that had Autorun disabled," as Fanny (GReAT 2015b). In fact, Fanny used the vulnerability first. According to Kaspersky Labs (2015: 13),

It's important to point out that these two exploits were used in Fanny before they were integrated into Stuxnet, indicating the EQUATION group had access to these zero-days before the Stuxnet group. Actually, the similar type of usage of both exploits together in different computer worms, at around the same time, indicates that the EQUATION group and the Stuxnet developers are either the same or working closely together.

A reconnaissance-strike complex requires first identifying targets. What the Equation Group's suite of malware did, unparalleled for over a decade, was gain access to targeted systems to enable precision degradation attacks like Stuxnet. *The art of precision warfare is not hitting the target, it is finding the target and denying the enemy's ability to scout your networks.*[11] According to Costin Raiu, director of Kaspersky Lab's Global Research and Analysis Team, the "Equation Group are the ones with the coolest toys . . . every now and then they share them with the Stuxnet group and Flame group, but they are originally available only to the Equation Group people. Equation Group are definitely the masters, and they are giving the others, maybe, bread crumbs. From time to time they are giving them some goodies to integrate into Stuxnet and Flame" (Goodin 2015). Consistent with literature on covert communications and signaling, demonstrating that degree of sophistication (sunk costs) is an ambiguous signal of resolve to rivals. Covert network penetrations, beyond their intrinsic intelligence value, have coercive effects that can shape rival behavior, leading to outright concessions or minimized escalation risks.

Cyber espionage requires gaining access and finding a means of exhilarating information to be effective and demonstrate resolve once outed. For example, take Reign, another cyber operation linked to the United States. Reign was a backdoor Trojan used for "systematic spying campaigns against a range of international targets since 2008" (Symantec Security Response 2015). Reign was customizable depending on the target and can enable mass surveillance. According to Symantec, Reign reflected a "technical competence rarely seen and has been used in spying operations against governments, infrastructure operators, businesses, researchers, and private individuals" (Symantec Security Response 2015). In another study, analysts observe:

> Reign is different to what are commonly referred to as "traditional" advanced persistent threats (APTs), both in its techniques and ultimate purpose. APTs typically seek specific information, usually intellectual property. Reign's purpose is different. It is used for the collection of data and continuous monitoring of targeted organizations or individuals.

Technical details led cyber security analysts to link Reign to Flame, Stuxnet, and Duqu (Symantec Security Response 2015). According to reporting by *Der Spiegel*, aspects of the Reign source code matched files released by Snowden and indicated links between Reign and the QWERTY keystroke (Rosenbach et al. 2015). QWERTY allowed intruders to log keyboard strokes and record what a user types

(Cyber Defense 2015). Subsequent analysis by Kaspersky linked QWERTY source code to a Reign plugin (Raiu and Soumenkov 2015). Cricket references and other signs in the code led multiple cyber security analysts to link QWERTY to a broader Five Eyes intelligence collection effort codenamed WARRIORPRIDE (Constantin 2015b). That is, the United States maintained an allied cyber network (with the UK, Canada, Australia, and New Zealand) that its rivals lack. This network both increased Washington's reach and resulted in less reporting attributing cyber espionage to the United States. Through alliance mechanisms and liaison activity like this, the United States can amplify its already sizable advantages in cyber power to gain access to target networks. Therefore, both the sophistication of US cyber operations and its alliance network, as sunk costs, demonstrate resolve and produce coercive effects.

According to Kaspersky, Reign had additional features of interest. Whereas most cyber espionage involved "extracting sensitive information such as emails and other electronic documents, we have observed cases where the attackers compromised telecom operators to enable the launch of additional sophisticated attacks" (Kaspersky Labs 2014). These Global System for Mobile (GSM) attacks allowed Reign to penetrate and monitor cellphone communications in multiple countries (Kaspersky Labs 2014). The largest concentrations of intrusions were in Russia, at 28%, and Saudi Arabia, at 24% (Symantec Security Response 2015). The malware had an "extensive command-and-control infrastructure" that used "Reign-infected computers" to enable a "peer-to-peer" network that stores stolen data, allows exfiltration, and even allowing additional attack vectors (Symantec Security Response 2015). Furthermore, like the Equation Group suite of malware, Reign encrypts stolen data. Through sheer sophistication, these covert, cyber campaigns act as ambiguous signals to rivals.

TURNING DEFENSE INTO AN ATTACK VECTOR

Another unique feature of US cyber espionage is the documented efforts of turning defenses into attack vectors as a form of counterintelligence and sabotage. For Gartzke and Lindsay (2015), network defenders can use deception to lure in unsuspecting attackers and subject them to either counterespionage intrusions or sabotage. In this form of active defense, "cyber-attacks can be foiled not just by blocking intrusions, but by converting the penetration into something that confuses or harms the attacker" (Gartzke and Lindsay 2015, 336). This approach to blinding an adversary is consistent with the reconnaissance-strike complex.

A series of files released by Shadow Broker in 2016 illustrated additional NSA efforts to penetrate Chinese networks. Between 2000 and 2010, it appears that the NSA gained access to servers running Solaris, a UNIX-based operating system using the Extremepar and Ebbisland intrusions. The agency used these servers as "staging servers" to mask intrusions and "make attribution harder" (Fox-Brewster 2016). The targets tend to be disproportionately Chinese. According to Matthew Hickey, co-founder of Hacker House, these "NSA exploits are works of art, robust, reliable, anti-forensic, network IDS evasion techniques . . . beautiful" (Rashid 2017). Of note, US cyber espionage intrusions demonstrate the potential for coercion. According to Jacobs (2014), following the Shotgiant intrusions, the Chinese government reached out to the United States to seek limits on "the practice of cyberespionage."

The United States has also proved adept at cloaking infections. Through operation DEFIANTWARRIOR, the United States hijacked "botnet computers and use them as 'pervasive network analysis vantage points' and 'throw-away non-attributable' CNA [computer network attack] nodes." This means that if a user's computer is infected by cybercriminals with some malware, the NSA might step in, deploy their own malware alongside it and then use that computer to attack other interesting targets. Those attacks couldn't then be traced back to the NSA" (Constantin 2015c).

Through implants, when connected to other US databases like Xkeyscore and Tutelage, allowed the NSA to "identify the components involved in the attack and take action to block it, redirect it to a false target to analyze the malware used in the attack, or do other things to disrupt or deceive the attacker" (Gallagher 2015). This technique, commonly referred to as fourth-party collection, turns other actor's espionage efforts into new surveillance and attack vectors. According to Gallagher (2015), "by discovering an active exploit by another intelligence organization or other attacker on a target of interest, the NSA can opportunistically ramp up collection on that party as well, or even use it to distribute its own malware to do surveillance."

The United States demonstrated mastery in baiting adversaries into accessing its networks, such as offering a honey pot, and then infecting rival systems. Through operation Buckshot Yankee, the NSA countered the 2008 Russian intrusions into multiple US networks through the agent.biz malware by, among other things, banning USB drives and establishing Cyber Command (Nakashima 2011). According to Lynn (2010), these "active defense" operations represented a turning point in DoD cyber strategy.

Turning intrusions into attack vectors is a particularly sophisticated form of counterintelligence and covert action. In many respects, it is old wine in a new bottle. During the Cold War, the CIA conducted a covert industrial sabotage campaign setting up Soviet front companies to buy defective equipment and software that undermined their energy infrastructure (Weiss 1996).

These mass intrusions demonstrate the cascading risk of infections. Even near-zero miss malware in cyberspace has the potential to create opportunities for criminals and other nefarious actors. For example, the May 2017 massive ransomware attack that hit multiple countries and companies was based on NSA zero-day exploits released by Shadow Brokers (Farrell 2017). The short-term benefits of precision access and degradation collide with the long-term risk of malware proliferation and being subject to increasingly sophisticated attacks by rivals. Put another way, when the US military fires a tomahawk cruise missile in a limited use of military force, the target cannot take the missile and use it against the United States. Unlike military coercive instruments, cyber operations live on after their use and can be adapted by rivals.

Cyber Degradation: Digital Strikes

The reconnaissance-strike complex Soviet generals feared in the late Cold War came to life online after the USSR's collapse. The clearest illustration of the extension of RMA-related strategic thought to practice is the US preference for cyber degradation and honeypots (i.e., counterintelligence and turning enemy spies into attack vectors). As seen in Table 7.1 earlier in the chapter, the US use of degradation is statistically significant at a higher percent of observed cyber exchanges between rivals than other actors. These complex intrusions often involve obtaining covert access to the target's critical networks and using this information advantage to destabilize the adversary from within. The strategic logic is evident in the Stuxnet campaign.

Stuxnet is the World War I of cyberspace—extensively covered in the trade press and academic press without consensus on its efficacy. Popular accounts focus on how Stuxnet has ushered in a new era of cyber offensive campaigns that reflected the ease of offense and potential for escalation in cyberspace (Zetter 2014; Sanger 2012a). The minority of academic accounts echo this perspective.[12] The majority of security studies scholarship finds that Stuxnet was either more costly than initially purported or had limited effects.[13]

Yet, the Stuxnet story is more complex and illustrates the findings on combined coercive effects highlighted earlier. Developers in the United States began working on the Stuxnet worm as early as 2005 (MacDonald et al. 2013). Development accelerated after Israel requested US assistance for limited military strikes against Iranian nuclear facilities in Natanz. Stuxnet began more as a means of delaying military action during complex negotiations than a plan to decisively cripple Iranian enrichment. In this respect, the operation was more an example of covert action and sabotage than a conventional precision strike (Lindsay 2013; Valeriano and Maness 2015: 149). These operations rely on significant intelligence preparation to find a critical vulnerability.

In 2009, developers modified Stuxnet by shifting the attack vector from targeting valve pressure to stress centrifuge rotation frequency in an effort to increase its destructive potential (MacDonald et al. 2013). Four zero-day vulnerabilities were used, plus a host of other associated methods to achieve a destructive event inside the plant (Lindsay 2013). The malware had to be inserted into the plant since it was not networked, it then had to map the plant, report back, and then return to seek damaging intent, likely aided by human intelligence sources (Valeriano and Maness 2015: 152). As Sanger notes in interviews, the intention was to confuse the plant operators to think the destruction was caused by bad parts, not malware (Sanger 2012a: 188).

Sanger (2012a: 204) notes that 984 centrifuges were eventually taken offline, one-fifth of the plant's total capacity. Damage estimates range from 6 months to 5 years, and Sanger's (2012: 206) sources reveal the CIA estimate at 1–2 years with the majority of the time being spent on enhancing defenses to prevent a repeat of the operation. The International Atomic Energy Agency notes that Iran actually sped up uranium production during this time by overworking other centrifuges.

Barzashka (2013: 48) argues the impact of the worm was "circumstantial and inconclusive." Instead the legacy of the impact has become mythical through time with the idea of this attack being a norm-breaking event that changed the shape of cyber conflict. Stuxnet was not a low-cost, high-payoff offensive success. Subsequent studies suggested the degradation effort was much costlier in terms of time, people, and resources on the attacker than originally estimated. Slayton's (2017: 94) case study highlights that Stuxnet produced a situation in which the offensive cost more than the defense, and Sanger's (2012) reporting backs up estimates of a high-cost investment with little payoff.

For comparison, the cost of a tomahawk land attack cruise missile is $1.59 million (DoD Comptroller 2014). The 59 missiles launched at the Syrian air base in April 2017 cost approximately $93 million.[14] For the estimated cost of Stuxnet, and with it no guarantee of success, the United States and/or Israel could have launched three cruise missile offensive strikes, totaling over 150 precision warheads and 177,000 pounds of high explosive. Furthermore, these strikes would have had higher confidence and easier battle damage assessments but would also produce an increased chance of escalation to war, a situation avoided by using cyber means.

A more apt comparison for the cost of Stuxnet is other covert action programs. Take the US efforts, largely orchestrated through the CIA, to fund Syrian rebels in 2015 (Wright 2015). The cost was somewhere between $250 and $500 million—comparable to Stuxnet's estimated cost. Admiral Bobby R. Inman, deputy director of the CIA in 1982, famously challenged Congress on the cost per year of fielding a covert, paramilitary force in Nicaragua, saying "I would suggest to you that $19 million or $29 million [$49 million inflation adjusted] isn't going to buy you much" (Taubman 1982). The cost per year to support the Mujahedeen in Afghanistan rose from $30 million in 1980 to $630 million in 1987 (Bergen 2001: 68). Covert action is not cheap, nor is it guaranteed, but it does help rivals signal each other and manage escalation risks by enabling backstage tacit bargaining between states (Carson 2016).

Of note, cyber methods are equal to or more expensive than traditional forms of covert action. Furthermore, there are additional risks associated with covert cyber coercion. Cyber intrusions proliferate in criminal malware and are replicated by smaller states and rivals. The United States sought to degrade North Korea's missile development and nuclear programs through a degradation campaign similar to Stuxnet (Sanger and Broad 2017). The intent was to gain access and sabotage the system from the inside. Both Iran and North Korea used P-2 centrifuges obtained through the nuclear black-market set up by the Pakistani scientist A. Q. Khan (Menn 2015b). These systems used a Siemens AG control software. The same vulnerability that Stuxnet exploited existed in North Korea. Yet, according to officials the attack was "stymied by North Korea's utter secrecy, as well as the extreme isolation of its communications systems" (Menn 2015b).

Beyond access channels, the strategic logic of cyber degradation requires amplifying coercive instruments. In both the Stuxnet campaign and efforts against North Korea, cyber degradation occurred as part of a larger system of coercion. Similar to the "system of systems" logic highlighted in EBOs, the United States exhibits a preference for combining cyber coercion with other effects. This preference is empirically captured in Table 7.7 and confirms earlier theses from the coercive diplomacy literature (Byman and Waxman 2002; George 1991).

Beyond mere technological mastery or skill in covert action demonstrating resolve through sunk costs, degradation campaigns require integration with other instruments of power. Strategy matters. Despite analysts' claims of dysfunction in Washington, the US national security enterprise can, on occasion, coordinate its effects to achieve coercive outcomes. In these campaigns, the whole is greater than the sum of the parts. Like combined arms, what Biddle (2004) calls the modern military system at the core of military power, strategic power requires combined effects.

Conclusion: The Cyber Hegemon

This chapter demonstrates how the United States uses cyber strategy to compel rivals and its affinity with the theoretical underpinnings of precision and winning the fight for information. There has been a sustained discourse in US defense circles arguing that information superiority and precision alters warfare since at least the late 1970s. The introduction of cyber capabilities emerged in an environment already prone to see its utility in operations designed to access critical military and intelligence networks and degrade their high-value capabilities.

This preference for precision and targeted strikes resonates with empirical findings that show a statistically significant penchant for using cyber degradation against military-grade targets. Furthermore, these precision strikes and counterintelligence activities overlap larger efforts to integrate different instruments of power and positive inducements to alter an adversary system. The United States emerges, despite the recent coverage given to Russian efforts to manipulate elections and engage in gray-zone conflicts, as the most sophisticated strategic actor, able to integrate cyber operations with a range of diplomatic offers, economic sanctions, and military threats. That the United States does not exploit its position more, despite the Snowden revelations, reveals the inherent benefits being the cyber hegemon affords and hence a distinct strategic logic in limiting disruptive acts that might undermine that position (Rovner and Moore 2017).

What we cannot say is whether these preferences are a function of the United States' unique, historical advantage entering the information age or the byproduct of the history of ideas in the defense epistemic community. All we can say empirically is that the United States is the cyber hegemon, for now. We also can infer, based on the findings in chapter 3 that translating this latent cyber capacity to concessions against rivals is more about strategy than sheer capability alone. The crisp sets and chi-square results for degradation show that the United States' coercive advantage comes more from how it operates than from its latent power. Did the strategy emerge from this natural advantage? That is, you could fill the ranks of the NSA because you had more connected youths and the top schools for computer science. Is the dominant position the United States currently holds a function of its strategic choices or contingent on history and the development of its technological education foundations?

These findings have important implications for the future of US cyber strategy. First, the United States should be able to sustain its relative advantage in the digital domain even as China closes the power gap. Keeping a comparative advantage will require mechanisms that sustain combined approaches to coercion. There are no guarantees grand strategy works in a connected age (Meijer and Jensen 2017), much less that it can be sustained among domestic turmoil and competing influence (Brands 2015).

Second, while the strong do what they will and the weak suffer what they must, even in cyberspace, there is a rationale for restraint (Valeriano and Maness 2015). The greatest risk to a cyber security dilemma (Buchanan 2017) may lie not in the inherent capabilities of cyber operations but in the corresponding threat inflation wrought by an academic and policy community eager to capture headlines and imagine future war. Pundits and cyber security analysts who profit from overstating the cyber threat to the United States risk producing crises where none need exist. They inflame a series of rivalries engaged in tacit bargaining and prone to limited escalation and stability.

Third, the US case demonstrates the proliferation risks inherent in cyber conflict even if the intent was precision. Successful cyber degradation efforts often spill into the public domain for criminals and rivals to copy. This proliferation risk, along-side the fact that once you convert initial network access into an attack vector you lose access, likely further restrains rivals' use of cyber methods. Cyber coercion may be more stabilizing than the concern around election hacks, critical infrastructure attacks, and massive IP theft in the headlines leads us to believe.

8

CONCLUSION

Cyber Political Warfare with Limited Effects

THIS BOOK EMERGES from a critical gap in the cyber security literature. Scholars and policy makers alike have struggled to examine cyber operations empirically. Despite limitations inherent in collecting data on covert action, which are surmountable, without systematically examining cyber exchanges we will struggle to understand contemporary strategic competition. What cyber strategies emerge in competitive interactions? How do rival states align ends, ways, and means? Does it work? This book answers these questions. We provide insights into how rival states use cyber operations as a modern form of political warfare.

We build on the cyber coercive turn in scholarship by empirically testing claims about cyber coercion using a database of all known cyber exchanges between rivals from 2000 to 2014. Whereas most of the early cyber coercion literature, consistent with theory development efforts, involves individual case examples or deductive reasoning, we seek a broader, inductive approach based on observing a larger sample of cyber exchanges and expand the scope to consider objectives like disruption and espionage. The dataset allows us to test key claims in the cyber coercion literature as well as the broader body of coercion scholarship.

Unpacking the strategic logic of cyber conflict as a new means of coercing political opponents demands that we understand the realities and limits of this innovation. There are constraints and challenges in applying new methods of influence to coerce a target to change their behavior. Compellence is difficult and costly, and requires an accumulation of efforts to achieve effects. This finding suggests we should take an evolutionary perspective on the utility of new weapons and their ability to leverage power and influence.

We urge caution. States seeking to leverage cyber actions to achieve decisive effects are likely to be disappointed. There is little evidence these operations produce concessions in exchanges between rivals. When concessions do occur, they tend to take the form of degradations associated with the United States. Yet, even these successes come at a cost. Cyber degradations are complex and expensive, and require other diplomatic and military threats. Furthermore, cyber degradations have a history of spilling into the global commons.

Major Findings

There are three sets of propositions on cyber operations and its efficacy, cyber signaling, and cyber strategy. Through analyzing the DCID 1.1 dataset and comparing the findings to case studies on the three major cyber rival actors (Russia, China, United States), we assess the hypotheses in Table 8.1 below.

First, only cyber degradation is coercive, and these operations tend to produce concessions at rates consistent with other instruments. As detailed in chapter 2, using existing studies on coercion as a guide, to be effective cyber operations would need to produce concessions in over 33% of the cases; cyber degradation matches this threshold. As discussed in chapter 1, if you add all cyber strategies reviewed here, that figure drops to less than 5%. This distribution makes sense. Only cyber

TABLE 8.1

Cyber strategy hypotheses

Cyber Coercion

H1. Cyber degradation is more likely to achieve a concession.
Confirmed in light of evidence. Degradation produces more concessions than the expected rate relative to other cyber coercive methods.

H2. Cyber operations produce limited escalation.
Mixed in light of evidence. Past cyber incidents increase the odds of escalation but at low levels and confined to the cyber domain.

H3. There are unique combinations of cyber operations and instruments of power that increase rival concessions.
Confirmed in light of evidence. There are necessary and sufficient conditions associated with combined coercive campaigns involving cyber operations.

degradation, due to sunk costs, produces a sufficiently costly signal. These precision strikes are often costly to develop and risk spilling into the wild for rivals and criminals alike to adapt.

Furthermore, the preponderance of successful cyber degradations observed in the dataset originate in the United States raising the possibility that US capabilities, resolve, or skill, more than the style of attack, produce the findings. This problem extends to assessing whether or not latent cyber capacity, as a proxy for power, produces rival concessions. Because the United States is also the leading economic and military power, we cannot say if it is cyber power or more traditional relative power measures that are producing an increased rate of concessions in exchanges between rival states. What the US case does show is that the sunk costs of even ambiguous actions can demonstrate resolve and signal escalation risks as a means of managing a crisis while shaping behavior short of a concession. These are findings echoed in recent literature on covert action (Carson 2016; Carson and Yarhi-Milo 2017). Counterespionage campaigns such as Cisco Raider and Boxing Rumble send signals to rivals China and North Korea and alter short-term behavior, but they have not stopped future cyber intrusions by these US rivals. Even concessions can be transitory in cyberspace.

Rival states also appear to focus more on the current strategic calculus (Press 2005) than on past actions in cyberspace. The form of cyber coercion—whether it was a costly degradation campaign or a low-cost disruption—appears to shape outcomes. Rivals use cyber operations, as an extension of covert action, seeking to reveal information about capabilities and intentions that helps them manage long-term competition.

Cyber operations offer rivals an ambiguous signaling mechanism that helps them manage escalation risks. Cyber exchanges between rivals, outside of wartime episodes in Georgia and Ukraine, are not associated with significant crisis escalation thus far. The new game of spies and intrigue takes place in the digital domain. Russian operatives use digital "active measures" in the form of website defacements and DDoS attacks alongside more traditional propaganda to manipulate information and undermine the legitimacy of rivals. Chinese units look for soft commercial targets to steal information that helps them manage a long-term economic and military modernization program. US agencies deploy sophisticated malware capable of penetrating hardened networks, hiding in plain sight, and mapping vulnerabilities for future sabotage actions. Much like the game of spies in the Cold War, these covert actions do not lead to war. There is an accepted, albeit painful, dimension of long-term competition between historical antagonists. Escalation remains limited to tit-for-tat type responses designed to check a rival, and does not force a government's hand and set the stage for a dangerous standoff.

We also demonstrate that campaigns matter in cyberspace. How states combine cyber measures with other instruments of power alters the efficacy. There are distinct combinations that appear to produce concessions at a higher rate. In addition to using higher cost degradation operations, cyber operations tend to occur alongside positive inducements, that are shown in chapter 4 to be a sufficient but not necessary condition through qualitative comparative analysis. Furthermore, targeting civilian networks does not work. For all the website defacements and propaganda campaigns that Russia launches, consistent with the Soviet concept of active measures, these disruptive events do not produce political concessions. They certainly have created fear and disorder, but they do not have a tangible coercive effect beyond their influence value in psychological warfare.

Future Research Directions
HISTORY AND DECISION-MAKING EXAMINATIONS

Few have sought to document the process of decision-making in cyberspace. Brantly (2016) builds an expected utility model based on rational choice and capability considerations to theorize when states will leverage cyber tools. Others will need to dive a bit deeper; what are specific decision-makers thinking when they decide to leverage cyber action for coercive effect? What are the goals and constraints that determine behavior? The account by Sanger (2012b) of the Obama administration's decision to launch the Olympic Games attacks (including Stuxnet) on Iran stands out as one of the few investigative documents of the process of cyber action being waged as political warfare.

There also needs to be more work on the psychology of cyber effects. How do cyber actions affect the target's stress level and overall perception of threat? Gross et al. (2017) demonstrate with a series of experiments and biological tests for stress levels that cyber terrorism scenarios provoke a physiological response in the target. This response may be the reason cyber actions are so feared and produce rampant threat inflation. That is, cyber effects are not just objective. Their subjective attributes change how individuals assess threats. In other words, emerging digital technologies, from malware to social media manipulation, increase an individual's sense of vulnerability and likely skew rational decision-making.

Perception matters, and we have done little as a field to dive into the psychology and biological markers (i.e., stress levels) of cyber actions as they affect nation-states and their populations. This critical step will give us more confidence in estimating the impact of cyber actions and how decision makers with a heightened sense of vulnerability manage responses. Experiments on cyber scenarios that test individual psychological state and biological response, along with wargames supporting these efforts, are a potential pathway toward research progress.

Another promising avenue to assess cyber decision-making resides in formal modeling. Just as early work on deterrence relied on game theory to extract predictions about rival behavior, the emerging cyber character of political warfare needs a clearer logical framework. Specifically, formal models could help clarify some of how states bargain during cyber disputes. These models could help highlight how covert interaction in cyberspace can produce important risk dynamics that constrain inadvertent escalation.

CYBER BEHAVIOR: POWER DYNAMICS OR STRATEGIC CULTURE?

Not all actors engage in competition in cyberspace. While most should maintain at least a defensive posture, and keep in touch with the continually shaping strategic environment, there are clear variations of engagement by state. Understanding country- and region-specific patterns should be a future task for scholars.

Our findings suggest that the most powerful states in the system are simply trying to maintain power and the status quo. The behavior of these states is predicated on maintaining position. This would suggest that these states are unlikely to use disruptive strategies because the more powerful state is trying to maintain order, not disrupt the system. States seeking to maintain power in cyberspace mainly rely on cyber degradation options meant to target an adversary and compel them to change behavior toward the direction of the interests of that initiator.

States rising in power would avoid attempting degradation operations because they cannot manage the risks introduced by operating in cyberspace in a destructive manner. Instead, states rising in power would mainly use espionage for economic, military, or commercial gain in order to reach parity with the target and alter the balance of information.

States declining in power are flailing in the international system. Their actions increasingly have little influence on the course of events unless they wage outright war. They are simply trying to maintain influence in a system. These states use disruption as the primary method because it is a form of cheap signaling, as they can afford little else. Declining-power states will conduct espionage, but this would be done to disrupt and cause chaos in the target state and also to erode confidence.

Future research should compare these inferences about relative power and the trajectory of leading states with case-specific portraits of how states use cyber operations, as a modern form of political warfare, to shaping rival competition. Our case studies offer a step in this direction.

There do appear to be unique strategic preferences at the country level. Through comparative case studies of how Russia, China, and the United States use cyber strategies, we show that each country has a distinct approach. Whether these approaches are the result of strategic opportunities and constraints implied by how changing dynamics comingle with domestic institutions to shape foreign policy or an enduring strategic culture, we cannot say.

The Russian approach to cyber strategy emphasizes disruption and finding ways to manipulate public opinion through website defacements and DDoS incidents conducted through shadowy third parties. These disruptive efforts are designed to undermine confidence in the rival state. Russia employs this low-cost, low-payoff form of coercion more than either China or the United States. This strategic preference likely reflects how codependent the evolution of cybercrime and state-based cyber capabilities unique to the Russian state that emerged after 1991. Overall, Russia uses disruption as a form of cheap signals when they can do little else.

The Chinese approach to cyber efforts emphasizes espionage as a way to achieve a superior position in their region and in the system. Between 2000 and 2015, China conducted covert intrusions more than Russia or the United States. Furthermore, power differentials did inform Chinese strategic preferences and objectives. China does disrupt weaker actors when they challenge their position in Asia, but it mainly employs espionage against its stronger rival, the United States. The complication is that the path to innovation through stealing technology is to this point mainly unsuccessful. Progress comes from leveraging skill and talent domestically, a point likely known to China, and this could be a cause of its decline in cyber activities after 2014.

The United States is a more prudent actor that mainly relies on counterespionage and degradation strategies. The US approach to cyber strategy is consistent with doctrine on precision warfare and paralyzing strikes. Timing matters. The United States began a broader strategic dialogue about information warfare in the early 1990s, at the same time as the broader discourse emphasized the revolutionary in military affairs and benefits of precision strike. Cyber strategies were path-dependent on this set of preferences. The United States does not use disruption, demonstrating instead a preference for targeted, severe attacks against hardened government targets as a way to avoid serious conflagrations.

Future research should examine what factors, if any, produce distinct national approaches to cyber strategy and statecraft. For example, are the clear differences established in the case studies a function of politics, power, or culture? Do domestic influences, such as log-rolling coalitions and how states translate cyber capacity into coercive power, produce distinct strategies? Alternatively, are national approaches to cyber operations a function of the rise and decline of leading states in the international system? Last, does strategic culture and enduring preferences shape the use of cyber coercion? In all likelihood, each of these perspectives offers important variables that can be assessed in a strategic rivalry context. Policy makers need a better predictive framework to help then judge future cyber operations and develop appropriate responses.

The Policy Context: We Were Promised Cyber Bombs!

Networked means of attack have long been promised as a possible avenue of coercive diplomacy that would dramatically alter the battlefield. More recently, in the war against the Islamic State, multiple members of the Obama administration noted that the United States was going to be "dropping cyber bombs" (Martin 2016). The term even appears in official statements. Assistant Secretary of State Robert Work states, "so for example, we are dropping cyber bombs. We have never done that before." He then notes, "it sucks to be ISIL" (Clark 2016).

The promise of a dramatic and visible means of networked cyber war do not match the reality of what the United States is doing against the Islamic State. Their activities are mostly limited to intercepting communications and altering information, sometimes in the hopes of finding terrorists in one location for targeting purposes (Valeriano et al. 2016). While cyber operations certainly supported US and Coalition attacks against the Islamic State, the actual bombs dropped were rather old fashioned. The promise of cyber bombs is a distraction from the more mundane aspects of cyber conflict. With a focus on dramatic effects, we miss the often-unpredictable outcomes of cyber operations and their relationship to coercive success.

As the book highlights, cyber operations have yet to deliver a decisive victory. Digital effects have been slow to emerge and tend to amplify rather than replace traditional instruments of power. Even heralded cyber units reflect this limited utility. As Nakashima and Ryan (2016) note, "CYBERCOM has not been as effective as the department [Department of Defense] would expect them to be, and they're not effective as they need to be." While cyber units have achieved some level of success against ISIS, they can be thwarted by a nimble adversary that can move from computer to computer or server to server to avoid attacks. This limitation is the downside in attacking small and flexible targets such as terrorist groups. Their limited cyber ambitions, nonexistent hardware, and ability to communicate outside of computer networks makes them a difficult target to coerce in the digital domain.

The challenge is even greater for a large state attacking a rival power. While Russia and China are fixed in location and offer a plethora of hardened networks and critical infrastructure to attack, they are not as dependent on the digital domain as the United States. That is, every cyber operation Washington, DC, launches against its rivals opens the country to a counterattack. There is a risk imbalance. The more connected the state, the more vulnerable they are. This logic is behind the saying often used by policy makers to describe US vulnerability in cyberspace: *don't throw rocks in a glass house*. For example, in 2015 James Clapper, the director of national intelligence, told Congress, "I think it's a good idea to at least think about the old saw about people who live in glass houses shouldn't throw rocks" (US Congress 2015). For Clapper, cyberspace should remain a covert backstage (Carson 2016) for tacit maneuvers and tit-for-tat actions signaling escalation risks. According to Clapper, "we spy, they spy back" (US Congress 2015).

Yet, the throwing rocks in a glass house metaphor is ignored by those seeking to respond aggressively to cyber provocations. In a US Senate hearing on January 5, 2017 to discuss the 2016 election hack, Senator Lindsay Graham noted that the United States should respond to Russia, stating, "It is time now not to throw pebbles, but to throw rocks. . . . Putin is up to no good and must be stopped" (Sullivan 2017).

The discourse of dramatic cyber effects raises the shadow of unrealistic expectations. Policy makers, as highlighted earlier, risk advocating starting cyber wars where we currently have an uneasy, stable domain of competition. We need to move the discourse toward the reality of what cyber tools are good for, how they work, and how they achieve effects. We need to talk about coercion, not war. Policy makers would be wise to stop offering cyber bombs and start focusing on the more mundane task of building network defenses and resiliency. There are no rocks to throw, only information to steal and digital spies to catch.

Compellence operations might have limited impact because through time the proper response is not to concede but to bolster defenses (Libicki 2016: 199). This suggests that the proper course of action for any actor operating in cyberspace is to ramp up their defenses rather than focusing on the offense. Like second-wave deterrent nuclear strategies (Jervis 1979), the primary goal should be on resiliency and protecting networks rather than singularly bolstering the United States' already considerable offensive advantage.

COMPETITIVE RISK TAKING AND DIPLOMACY

There is also the question of how rivals should engage in competitive exchanges, often predicated on getting the other side to reveal capabilities and intentions without assuming the full risk of escalating into war. Deterrence scholars first identified this balancing act. In his review of the first three waves of deterrence theory, Jervis (1979: 303) notes, there is a "tension between the desire to increase risks in order to make the other side retreat and the desire to lower them in order to make the situation safer; between the incentive to let things get a bit out of hand and the need to maintain control; between the desire to foreclose one's own options and so leave to the other the 'last clear chance' to avoid war and the desire to preserve flexibility."

Because rivals, whether competing in cyberspace or more traditional domains, will seek a continuous position of advantage, this balancing act can be precarious. We should not rely on the prudence of national security decision makers and their advisers alone to moderate risky gambles in the digital domain. Like earlier periods of strategic rivalry, such as the Cold War, we need multilateral frameworks that delegitimate certain activities beyond the scope of ambiguous signals designed to demonstrate resolve. Coercion has to come out of the shadows as diplomats and international institutions negotiate what is an acceptable level of intrusion and manipulation in the 21st century. Though states are sure to break these rules, institutional and legal efforts will sufficiently increase the costs of action to keep cyber strategy at more moderate levels of competition.

In this light, the Trump administration's decision to close the US Department of State's Office of the Coordinator for Cyber Issues, essentially folding some aspects into the Bureau of Economic Affairs, is a step in the wrong direction (Fidler 2017). Downgrading the importance of cyber issues alongside continued refusals to acknowledge the significance of the failed Russian bid to influence American elections alters the risk level associated with 21st-century political warfare. The United States sacrifices flexibility and emboldens rivals with these decisions.

The United States should return to being a champion of an open, multilateral cyber order that encourages the free exchange of data and ideas. While these ideas run contrary to tenets of the "America First" agenda, they ensure a stable digital domain, a 21st-century *Mare Liberum*, "free sea," that supports a liberal order.

Rather than close key diplomatic offices, the United States should create focal points for public–private cooperation with respect to cyber security. Unlike the Cold War, the private sector plays a vital, stabilizing role in cyberspace. There are market incentives for startups and established businesses to expose the cyber strategies states use to achieve a position of advantage relative to rivals. Firms like CrowdStrike and Fireeye identify new threats and, in the process, bolster state intelligence and help the public respond in a manner that limits coercion and escalation risk. There is a potential for a private sector–based arms control regime in cyberspace that governments and international institutions should further incentivize. By revealing threats these firms help reduce private information and allow rival states to better determine how much risk to assume in a competitive exchange.

Ensuring cyber restraint and stability despite the relentless friction of covert intrusions requires that the public and private spheres alike deal with the problem of threat inflation. Threat inflation reflects how narrow interests undermine rational foreign policy. Historical examples range from log-rolling coalitions leading states to engaging in dangerous overseas expansion (Snyder 1991) and nationalist violence following partial democratization processes (Snyder 2000) to elite manipulation and the 2003 Iraq invasion (Kaufmann 2004). According to Kaufmann (2004: 6),

> threat inflation . . . can be defined as (1) claims that go beyond the range of ambiguity that disinterested experts would credit as plausible; (2) a consistent pattern of worst-case assertions over a range of factual issues that are logically unrelated or only weakly related—an unlikely output of dis-interested analysis; (3) use of double standards in evaluating intelligence in a way that favors worst-case threat assessments; or (4) claims based on circular logic, such as Bush administration claims that Hussein's alleged hostile intentions were evidence of the existence of weapons of mass destruction (WMD) whose supposed existence was used as evidence of his intentions.

Treating cyber capabilities as a revolutionary change in conflict processes produces unappreciated strategic risks. Between media pundits searching for influence, eager generals seeking to demonstrate new capacity, and self-interested policy makers fearing the underappreciation of the threat, there are many incentives for exaggerating threats and effects. Threat inflation gives way to insecurity that can force the development of inefficient policy outcomes and horrible strategies unsuited for the new coercive instrument. A state is left either at the doorstep of inadvertent escalation or great strategic mismatch, bringing the wrong strategic capabilities and force posture to the competition because they might not understand the best uses of the new capability.

Minimizing threat inflation requires continued investments in empirical research and public–private partnerships that provide objective reporting on the actual use of cyber coercion. Knowledge and transparency can help minimize the tendency of narrow interest groups, whether cyber security firms and technology journalists seeking to grab headlines or military services and intelligence agencies competing for budgets, to subvert the marketplace of ideas. These reporting mechanisms will only be strengthened if connected to multilateral efforts to support an open, digital order.

Our Likely Cyber Future: Renewed Political Warfare

What do the insights in this book tell us about the future of cyber exchanges between rivals? To paraphrase the acclaimed science fiction writer William Gibson, the future is already here, it is just not evenly distributed. The next 10 years will likely see an acceleration in the use of what Soviet thinkers called active measures and what George Kennan called political warfare. We are not optimistic that the current US administration will be able to sustain, much less lead, a multilateral cyber order that constrains the worst tendencies of rivals engaged in strategic competition. Yet, given the unique nature of cyber operations, we still assess minimal risks to covert action in cyberspace unleashing inadvertent escalation in the military domain.

The world is witnessing the reawakening of an old strategic practice: *political warfare*. The connectivity of the modern world puts a premium on coercive diplomacy in the shadows. From election tampering and fake news disseminated across multimedia in Ukraine (2014), the United States (2016), and France (2017), states such as Russia use cyber operations to enable covert influence campaigns short of war.

These operations extend beyond undermining democracies, and are also creating rifts among autocratic allies. In June 2017, an APT group linked to the United Arab Emirates (UAE) triggered a diplomatic crisis in the Persian Gulf by taking control of a Qatari news website. After hacking the online news feed, the group planted false information showing the emir praising Iran and calling for good relations with Israel while (contradictorily) backing Hamas and the Muslim Brotherhood (Bing 2017a). The intrusion was followed by a massive DDoS attack on Al-Jazeera, the Qatari owned media outlet (Kirkpatrick and Frankel 2017). In effect, UAE operatives conducted a classic psychological warfare operation that undermined the integrity of an alliance network. The news agencies in multiple Gulf States ran with the false story, leading to a diplomatic and economic blockade of Qatar by Saudi Arabia, Bahrain, Egypt, Jordan, and the UAE.

Cyber incidents like these show how states are mixing the old with the new. Much like the early Cold War, emerging cyber operations combine espionage, propaganda, economic warfare, and sabotage in an effort to signal resolve and shape adversary foreign policy (Valeriano, Maness, and Jensen 2017). The character of war and strategic competition is changing. The new Cold War is online.

The connectivity of the digital domain amplifies the effects of political warfare. Social media helps rival states reach key constituencies in their competitor's domestic populations, a phenomenon on display in the Russian purchases of ads on Facebook and Twitter during the 2016 US election. The extension of commerce and governance online creates vulnerabilities for states. Rivals can target economic capacity in a manner that used to require states to wage open, economic warfare. They can conduct sabotage through malicious code, as opposed to explosive satchel charges.

The question that remains is, why are we not seeing more concessions as a result of cyber coercion? The answer lies in the unique character of cyber operations. *Cyber instruments are a use-it-and-lose-it coercive instrument that come with an inherent amount of risk.* To gain network access for higher-cost and compellence-producing degradations, states must first infiltrate and map their rival's networks. This access gives them a position of advantage. They can extract information and monitor their rival, even if imperfectly. The decision on whether or not to execute a follow-up attack has to be balanced with the costs of losing network access. Once you convert your initial infiltration into an attack vector, you lose the access. In theory, this additional cost shifts the cost-benefit calculus associated with cyber operations in favor of restraint or using lower-level cyber disruptions that do not burn exploits because to do otherwise is quite risky. This "use it and lose it" dynamic is amplified by the shadow of the future unique to political warfare in the digital domain.

For leading powers such as United States that have multiple cyber rivals (Russia, China, Iran, North Korea), the cost associated with burning a vulnerability is increased. Once a cyber operation is outed, states and the private sector move to patch the vulnerability. There are not an infinite number of vulnerabilities. Therefore, every attack, in theory, decreases the number of future attacks you can launch against a rival. For the United States, this condition means that if it chooses to launch a cyber degradation action against China, that specific attack vector will likely be lost in exchanges with Russia.

Therefore, while the world is likely to see an increase in election hacking, false flag operations, DDoS attacks targeting key companies, and ransomware, there is unlikely to be an increase in political concessions. The risk of 21st-century cyber disruption and intrigue lies more in proliferation risks. A further constraining feature on launching cyber operations is the fact that, unlike a limited missile strike, the rival can copy the code and increase its own cyber capabilities. Rivals learn from and can emulate cyber coercive instruments at a faster rate than they can from military competition. States find it is easier to replicate code associated with a rival's cyber offensive operation than they do building a fifth-generation aircraft based on stolen plans.

The proliferation risk extends to criminal activity. As discussed in chapter 7, complex, but covert, US cyber degradation campaigns found their way into criminal malware. Rogue regimes like North Korea use the new disorder to seek ways of accessing illicit finances that help them survive isolation and sanctions as well as build nuclear devices (Perlroth 2017). Even when these attacks do not gain funds, which is likely, they allow revisionist regimes to undermine the digital order.

In the end, state use of cyber instruments to achieve a position of relative advantage will continue. Rival states will use the ambiguity of the digital domain to engage in long-term competition. Just as Cold War spies rigged elections, funded smear campaigns, and supported unrest against their rival's interests, so too will states like the United States, Russia, and China use the complex nature of digital connections to shape rival behavior. Political warfare online will be frightening, but likely stabilizing as well, just as it was in the past before the advent of the Internet. States like Russia will seek to hack elections and influence populations through active measures, but this form of competition is preferable to nuclear exchanges.

The key for states seeking to avoid dangerous escalation is to create new norms, share information on attacks and vulnerabilities, and encourage public–private multilateral frameworks that help restrain our worst tendencies. Leading actors like the United States need to play a constructive role (Rovner and Moore 2017) that helps ensure global, digital connectivity as a path for research, education, communication, and economic markets rather than conflict.

The Dyadic Cyber Incident and Dispute Dataset Version 1.1

Overview

This appendix presents a point of reference for variables for dyadic rival states that are in Dyadic Cyber Incident and Dispute Dataset (DCID) v 1.1 for the years 2000–2014. This builds on the previous version 1.0 released by Valeriano and Maness (2014, 2015). The DCID is primarily focused on rivals for data construction purposes, simplifying the complicated process of identifying cyber events. This dataset can be modified in many ways, including removing the dyadic component to make it monadic—then it is called the Cyber Incident and Dispute dataset (CID). Here we are focused on observable incidents between international nation-states, since interactions between criminal elements and other nonstate actors would require different data collection strategies and theories. Version 2.0 of our data will expand the data collection to all states and nonstate actors.

Rival dyads are extracted from the Klein, Diehl, and Goertz (2006) enduring rival dataset as well as Thompson's (2001) strategic rival dataset. Each pair of states engaged in cyber conflict has two states involved, on opposite sides of the cyber incidents and disputes. For individual cyber conflicts, we use the phrase "cyber incident." Incidents may include thousands of events, but accounting for every single intrusion or attack made is impossible and unwieldy. For a series of cyber incidents between two states over a limited period of time, we use the term "cyber disputes." This appendix pertains to research involving only incidents and only the description of coding efforts for these individual events is discussed.

For the coding of the variables for all pairs of states added to the dataset (nonstate actors or entities can be targets but not initiators as long as they critical to state-based systems, or if the original hack escalates into an international incident in the noncyber domain), the initiation must come from a government or there must be evidence that an incident or dispute was government sanctioned (see what follows for responsibility confirmation). For the target state, the object must be a government entity, either military or nonmilitary; or a private entity that is part of the target state's national security apparatus (power grids, defense contractors, and security companies), an important media organization (fourth estate), or a critical corporation (Saudi Aramco). The dataset does not include multilateral cyber incidents; these types of incidents are coded only at the dyadic level. Third parties are noted and coded as an additional variable in the data.

Version 1.0 of DCID uncovered 126 active rival dyads in the data (Valeriano and Maness 2014, 2015). Valeriano and Maness (2014) identified 110 cyber incidents within 45 overall disputes among 20 of the 126 pairs of states. (The Valeriano and Maness (2015) modification contained 111 incidents among 45 disputes, where an espionage dispute between China and India was added.) Version 1.1 has expanded to 192 incidents within multiple disputes from the years 2000–2014. It includes new variables and coding methods and expands the inclusiveness of relevant non-state targets to include national security contractors, media organizations, and other relevant corporations such as banks, technology companies (Google, Apple), and utility companies for the years 2000 to 2014. We do not code nonstate initiators in this dataset; the initiators must be state entities. Groups such as the Syrian Electronic Army, cyber jihadists such as the Islamic State, or hacktivist groups such as Anonymous are not included, as this would expand the purpose and scope of this data beyond measure.

Specific Procedures

The Cyber Conflict Data Project was developed to produce a replicable and reliable dataset for all cyber incidents and disputes between rival states and relevant nonstate targets. The coding method specifically follows the Correlates of War (COW) procedures in examining sources throughout history, in the media, and, new for cyber conflict, from government or critical cyber security firm reports.

An example of a Correlates of War dataset is the Militarized Interstate Disputes (MID) collection, which records cases of conflict between states "in which the threat, display or use of military force short of war by one member state is explicitly directed towards the government, official representatives, official forces, property, or territory of another state" (Jones, Bremer, and Singer 1996). It uses historical and diplomatic sources to isolate and codify each isolated incident. Cyber conflict is a more recent phenomenon than militarized disputes, as we demark the beginning of widespread international cyber conflict to begin with the year 2000. Therefore, we are able to access information on cyber incidents and disputes using search engines as our uniform data extraction tool, in addition to the other sources mentioned. In the future, automatic events data searches will be undertaken, but for now we are confident we can maintain an active dataset using focused search methods.

For the purposes of this study, electromagnetic pulses (EMPs), radar jamming, laser jamming/deception, and other measures/countermeasures traditionally considered electronic warfare (EW) are not defined as cyber incidents. Cyber incidents require the manipulation of computer code for malicious purposes. Electronic manipulation either damages or destroys circuitry through electronic (i.e., radio waves) and/or directed energy. We focus on cyber conflict as the manipulation of code through networks.

We focus on the following search terms to start our investigation. These search parameters are not exclusive, and the coder should endeavor to examine computer security reports and government information after incidents are identified to aid in coding the supplemental variables. In a search engine, enter "participant A eg. Iran" AND "participant B eg. Israel" AND "cyber" OR "internet attack" OR "infrastructure attack" OR "government cyber attack" OR "network breach" OR "hack" and customize the date range for 1/1/2000 to 12/31/2014.

After an incident is identified, computer security firm reports (Kaspersky, McAfee, Symantec, Crowd Strike, Fire Eye, among many) and government reports (Office of the Director of National Intelligence, Federal Bureau of Investigation, Department of Homeland Security, among many) are used to further code each incident. The following is advice we provide to coders to guide their efforts in data collection.

WHAT IS SEARCHED FOR AND RECORDED

A. The dyad (states involved), only two states recorded per incident
B. Start and end date of interaction
C. Method of interaction/incident, 1–4 with decimal denotations for infiltrations (methods are listed later) for incidents: defacements are vandalism; DDoS, zombies, botnets, and the like are denial of service; any incident that uses social engineering techniques is an intrusion, which includes Trojans, trapdoors, spear-phishing techniques, and backdoors. Intrusions are used in most theft/espionage operations; infiltrations are usually worms or viruses, but can also be logic bombs and keystroke loggings.
D. Type of interaction (nuisance, defensive, offensive)
E. The type of target (private/nonstate, government nonmilitary, government military)
F. The initiator of the interaction
G. The specific coercive strategy of the cyber incident (disruption, short- or long-term espionage, degradation)
H. Whether or not the incident successfully achieved its objective; whether it breached the target's network and fulfilled its intended purpose
I. Whether or not the political objective evoked a concessionary change in behavior of the target state
J. Whether or not a third party was involved in the initiation (other state, rebel group, corporation) 1 = yes, 0 = no. Sometimes, but not often, third-party states are involved in the initiation of a cyber incident. Look for explicit evidence that a third party was involved. Israel was a part of the United States' Stuxnet operation, for example.
K. Whether or not a third party was a target of the interaction 1= yes, 0 = no. This is more commonplace, especially for espionage campaigns (intrusions).
L. Whether or not an official government statement was issued by the initiator, 0 = no comment, 1 = denial, 2 = acceptance, 3 = multiple; this will help in the responsibility coding; although most of the time governments will deny or not comment about their part in cyber incident initiation.
M. Severity level on the 0–10 scale level, given below for both incidents and disputes
N. Damage type (1. Direct and immediate, 2. Direct and delayed, 3. Indirect and immediate, 4. Indirect and delayed)

O. A key source for the cyber incident

P. Any special notes pertaining to the incident

Once these procedures are finished, responsibility is the next and very important step in the coding process. To verify that the initiator was in fact the government or a government-sanctioned activity, the coding process goes through another process of verification. Attribution of cyber incidents can be a problematic issue; therefore, we focus on responsibility (Goodman 2010: 128). One of the advantages of a cyber incident is deniability. In this dataset, states that use information warfare must be fairly explicit and evident. If the responsibility of an incident is in serious doubt, we do not code it as a state-based action. We do not take conventional wisdom at its word for operations; instead, we analyze the history of relations, the intent of the action, and the likelihood of government complacency, and code disputes from this perspective. Therefore, simple news stories extracted by search engines such as "Google News" are not enough to make the dataset. Responsibility must be verified by government statements, policy reports, Internet security firm reports, white papers from software security firms (Symantec, McAfee, Kaspersky), or cyber security agency sources.

CODING FOR CYBER INCIDENTS

For individual cyber conflicts, we use the phrase "cyber incident." Incidents such as ShadyRat include thousands of intrusions, but accounting for every single intrusion the operation made is impossible and unwieldy. Therefore, ShadyRat and other multiple-intrusive incidents are coded as just one incident per dyad as long as the goals and perpetrators remain stable. Each cyber incident is directed by one state or on behalf of the state against another state or state's national security apparatus or relevant multinational corporations.

I. Methods of cyber incidents

Many news sources will report cyber incidents as viruses, because they do not have the technical know-how to categorize these types of interactions. It is important that coders be aware of this and make sure to code these incidents properly by finding additional reports. The news search is the primer to find cyber incidents; the latter documents are what you will need to code these incidents properly.

1. *Vandalism*: Website defacements: Hackers use Structured Query Language (SQL) injection or cross-site scripting (forms of command code) to deface or destroy victims' web pages. Although rather benign, these attacks may have important psychological effects.

2. *Denial of Service* (DDoS, distributed denial of service): DDoS attacks flood particular Internet sites, servers, or routers with more requests for data than the site can respond to or process. The effect of such an attack effectively shuts down the site, thus preventing access or usage. Government sites important to the functioning of governance are therefore disrupted until the flooding is stopped or the attackers disperse. Such attacks are coordinated through "botnets," or a network of computers that have been forced

to operate on the commands of an unauthorized remote user. The primary impact of DDoS attacks via botnets is the temporary disruption of service.

3. *Intrusion*: "Trapdoors" or "Trojans" and Backdoors: Trapdoors or Trojans are unauthorized software added to a program to allow entry into a victim's network or software program to permit future access to a site once it has been initially attacked. The purpose of trapdoors is to steal sensitive information from secured sites. Spear phishing is used to inject these cyber methods into networks. Here the initiator sends e-mails to employees or contractors of the targeted network, and if the e-mail is opened, the intrusion is introduced to the system. The botnet technique is another option, where a human being injects the intrusion from a portable drive such as a USB or disk.

4. *Infiltration*: Examples of attacks include logic bombs, viruses, packet sniffers, and keystroke logging. These methods force computers or networks to undertake tasks that they would normally not undertake: (1) Logic bombs are programs that cause a system or network to shut down and/or erase all data within that system or network. (2) Viruses are programs that attach themselves to existing programs in a network and replicate themselves with the intention of corrupting or modifying files. (3) Worms are essentially the same as viruses, except they do not need to attach themselves to existing programs. (4) Keystroke logging is the process of tracking the keys being used on a computer so that the input can be replicated in order for a hacker to infiltrate secure parts of a network.

General infiltrations, packet sniffers or beacons, are not coded in this dataset, as most of the time no act of cyber malice is committed. They are monitoring techniques that search for certain information. If a potential incident is labeled as a packet sniffer or beacon, do not code it.

When infiltration is found, please try to delineate the type and decimal the number with the 4 (.1 logic bombs, .2 virus, .3 worm, .4 keystroke logging)

II. Interaction type
  1. Nuisance (probing, disruption, chaos); most vandalism and denial of service incidents, intent is disrupting the day-to-day operations of a network, easily removable by target
  2. Defensive operation (Cisco Raider, Buckshot Yankee, Israeli operations against cyber jihad); the initiator must be the victim of a cyber incident first; these are defensive measures launched by a target, where it becomes the initiator
  3. Offensive strike (GhostNet, ShadyRAT, Stuxnet); intent is usually theft or espionage or to disrupt a specific national security strategy of a target, most intrusions and infiltrations

III. Target type
  1. Private/nonstate (financial sector, power grid, defense contractor, media organization, multinational corporation)
  2. Government nonmilitary (US State Department, government websites, government member website)
  3. Government military (US Defense Department, US Cyber Command, US Strategic Command)

IV. Severity scale

10—Massive death as a direct result of cyber incident

Example—NORAD hacked and missiles launched, Air traffic control systems manipulated, commercial airliner hacked and brought down

Notes—For this measure to be coded, a state must direct a cyber incident against another state's or private organizations' network where the system is manipulated and massive loss of life is a result (over 100 deaths).

9—Critical national infrastructure destruction as a result of cyber incident

Example—power grid hack, hydroelectric dams shut down, indirect death

Notes—For this measure to be coded, a state's critical infrastructure must be breached and the network manipulated so that widespread functionality is disrupted for a significant period of time. These efforts have to be massive, impactful, and clearly intentional.

8—Critical national economic disruption as a result of cyber incident

Example—stock market price manipulation, critical e-commerce shut down for extended periods

Notes—For this measure to be coded, a sophisticated infiltration must be responsible for the manipulation of prices that affect stock market indexes and prices for extended periods of time. Another example would be a cyber incident being responsible for the slowing or shutting down commerce online. This attack must be severe and critically threatening beyond compromising payment systems.

7—Minimal death as direct result of cyber incident

Example—Auto hacked, pacemaker hacked

Notes—Here a state-sponsored cyber incident would be responsible for the death of an individual or group of individuals of another state by either hacking into the automobile of the victim(s) and causing it to crash or, if the victim is dependent on a pacemaker to live, hacking this device, leading to that person's death.

6—Single critical network widespread destruction

Example—(Shamoon, DoD taken offline, Lockheed Martin database wiped out)

Notes—For this measure to be coded, a single network that is critical to national security must be breached and widespread destruction must be successful. Critical stored information is destroyed or unrecoverable or functionality of the network must be limited to nonexistent for a period of time.

5—Single critical network and physical attempted destruction

Example—(Stuxnet, Flame, DoD secure network intrusion)

Notes—This measure entails the successful breach of a network where damage is done, however the breached network is left intact in terms of functionality and recoverable losses.

4—Widespread government, economic, military, or critical private sector theft of information

Example—(US OPM hack, DoD employee records stolen, IRS hack)

Notes—Phishing and intrusion espionage campaigns that successfully steal large troves of critical information, such as the OPM hack.

3—Stealing targeted critical information

Example—(Chinese targeted espionage, government-sanctioned cyber crime, Sony Hack)

Notes—This involves the use of intruding on a secure network and stealing sensitive or secret information. The theft of Lockheed Martin's F-35 jet plans or the US Department of Defense's strategy in the Far East are examples. This is also coded if the target was critical to national security or the objective of the attack had national security implications. The piggy-back method is another example of this severity type. The United States' NSA was able to piggy back on China's Byzantine Series undetected and spy on the targets that the original espionage was spying on.

2—Harrassment, propaganda, nuisance disruption

Example—(Propagandist messages in Ukraine, vandalism, DDoS in Georgia, Bronze Soldier dispute)

Notes—Mainly vandalism or DDoS campaigns, this measure is coded when pockets of government or private networks are disrupted for periods of time and normal day-to-day online life is difficult, but recoverable.

1—Probing without kinetic cyber

Example—(US NSA dormant infiltrations)

Notes—Using cyber methods to breach networks but not using any malicious actions beyond that. Hacking a power grid but not shutting it down, planting surveillance technology within networks, and unsophisticated probing methods are examples of this severity level.

0—No cyber activity

V. Damage type (conceptualized from Rid and Buchanan 2015)

1. *Direct and immediate*: The term "direct" in this context means that the damage done by the cyber incident was what was intended by the initiator and the costs of the cyber incident are felt immediately. The Russian DDoS attacks on Estonia's government and private networks in 2007 is an example, as the effective shutdowns cost millions of dollars in lost revenue for the Baltic country.

2. *Direct and delayed*: Stuxnet was intended to disrupt Iran's nuclear program by damaging the centrifuges at the Natanz plant, and it succeeded. The impact of this attack took a number of months if not years to slowly disrupt and damage these centrifuges through code manipulation.

3. *Indirect and immediate*: "Indirect" in this context means that the damage done by the cyber incident was not the original intent of the initiator. The stealing of confidential information from a bank or a breach in the Wall Street system is an example of this. The costs of these incidents are felt immediately. Reputational damage or loss of confidentiality is what to look for when coding this damage.

4. *Indirect and delayed*: If intellectual property is stolen by an initiator and it becomes publicly available, this may result in improved competition for states or private companies that did not have this technology or advantage prior. China stole the American company's F-35 jet plans, and if it gave these plans to Russia, the effects of this cyber incident would be indirect and the costs would be felt at a future point in time.

VI. Coercive objectives for initiators

1. Disruption: take down websites, disrupt online activities, usually low-cost, low-pain incidents such as vandalism or DDoS techniques
2. Short-term espionage: gains access that enables a state to leverage critical information for an immediate advantage example; a being Russian theft of DNC e-mails and publicly releasing them in a disinformation campaign.
3. Long-term espionage: seeks to manipulate the decision-calculus of the opposition far into the future through leveraging information gathered during cyber operations to enhance credibility and capability, an example being China's theft of Lockheed Martin's F-35 plans
4. Degrade: attempt physical degradation of a targets' capabilities, Example: USA's Stuxnet against Iran; create chaos in a country to invoke a foreign policy response

VII. Specific political objective

Here we decipher as to why the cyber incident was launched in the first place. For example, for the Sony Hack the objective was to stop the release of the movie *The Interview*. A maximum of two political objectives are allowed.

VIII. Did the objective achieve its goal?

Did the cyber incident achieve its intended purpose? For example, did the disruptive attack successfully shut down a website via denial or service? Did an espionage technique breach the intended network and steal the information it sought to acquire? Did the degradation achieve damaging its intended target?

IX. Did the incident evoke a concessionary behavioral change?

Did the objective of the initiator evoke a concessionary behavioral change? That is, did the target state concede in some way to the initiator as a result of the cyber incident? Where processes or procedures changed? Did the direction of the state's foreign policy change?

Reliability Checks

For version 1.1 of the data, rigorous reliability checks were undertaken to investigate the reliability of our coding of the compellence variables. Experts from the professional military education (both students and instructors) system were recruited to help with the subjective coding of the two key variables of interest. Objective achievement and concessions could vary by the individual; because there is no objective measurement of such issues, obtaining reliable variable coding is paramount. We held multiple sessions where coding was done independently and then majority opinion decided on the variables' values. Intercoder reliability tests were then estimated to establish the success of our efforts in ensuring trust and verification of the coding effort. For the objective achievement dependent variable, we obtained a Fleiss' Kappa score of .496. Fleiss' Kappa tests are appropriate for intercoder reliability when there are three or more coders. This score can be interpreted as finding to what extent the observed amount of agreement among raters exceeds what would be expected if all raters made their ratings completely randomly. The score of .646 denotes substantial agreement, which is to be expected, as there were 15 different examiners involved in this effort. For the concessionary behavioral change dependent variable, we obtained a .589 Fleiss' Kappa score using the same amount of coders, which is also within the substantial threshold. For the independent variables of compellence type, the three authors coded these variables and then came to agreement on the final values, obtaining a substantial agreement with Fleiss' Kappa score of .759.

x. Variables for the Dyadic Cyber Incident and Dispute (DCID) Dataset, Version 1.5

Variable Number	Variable Name	Variable Description
1	Cyberincidentnum	Cyber incident number
2	DyadPair	State Pair ID (COW codes)
3	StateA	First state in dyad
4	StateB	Second state in dyad
5	Name	Name of cyber incident:
6	interactionstartdate	Cyber incident start date
7	Interactionenddate	Cyber incident end date
8	Interactiontype	Type of cyber interaction for incidents 1- Nuisance 2- Defensive operation 3- Offensive strike
9	Method	Cyber method utilized 1- Vandalism 2- Denial of Service (DDoS) 3- Intrusion 4- Infiltration 4.1 - Logic bomb 4.2 - Virus 4.3 - Worm 4.4 - Keystroke logging 5- Vandalism and Denial of Service (disputes only) 6- Intrusion and Infiltration (disputes only)
10	APT	Advanced Persistent Threat? 1- Yes, 0- No

Variable Number	Variable Name	Variable Description
11	Targettype	Type of target by cyber incident or dispute 1- Private/nonstate 2- Government nonmilitary 3- Government military
12	Initiator	State that initiated the incident or dispute (COW code)
13	Coercive objective	Objective of the initiating state (disputes only) 1- Disruption 2- Short-Term Espionage 3- Long-Term Espionage 4- Degrade
14	Political objective	Statement of political objective of initiator
15	Objective success	Did the objective succeed? 1-Yes, 0-No
16	Concession	Did the target concede? 1- Yes, 0- No
17	3rdpartyinitiator	Third party involved with initiating state? 1- Yes, 0- No
18	3rdparty target	Third party involved as a target? 1- Yes, 0- No
19	Govtstatement	Statement from the initiating state? 0- No comment, 1- Denial, 2- Acceptance, 3- Multiple statements
20	Severity	Severity level of incident or dispute (for disputes code the highest incident severity 1- Probing without kinetic cyber 2- Harassment, propaganda, nuisance disruption 3- Stealing targeted critical information 4- Widespread government, economic, military or critical private sector theft of information 5- Single critical network and physical attempted destruction 6- Single critical network widespread destruction 7- Minimal death as a direct result of cyber incident 8- Critical national economic disruption as a result of cyber incident 9- Critical national infrastructure destruction as a result of cyber incident 10- Massive death as a direct result of cyber incident
21	Damage type	1. Direct and immediate
22	Source	2. Direct and delayed 3. Indirect and immediate 4. Indirect and delayed The news source for the cyber interaction
23	Notes	Any special notes pertaining to the interaction

Cyber Strategy Policy Summary

Purpose of Book

- In the age of cyber conflict, coercion (the exploitation of potential force) combines with disruption, cyber espionage, overt propaganda manipulation, and covert psychological warfare to shape the behavior of antagonists. The goal of this work is to empirically access the efficacy of cyber instruments of power to pressure opposition states.
- We advance the position that cyber operations offer limited forms of coercion. These strategies are not likely to produce concessions, rarely invoke escalation, and exhibit tit-for-tat dynamics.

Three Forms of Cyber Strategies

- Our project codes three distinct types of cyber strategies. We define *cyber disruption* as low-cost, low-pain initiatives that harass a target to influence their decision calculus.
- *Cyber espionage* involves efforts to alter the balance of information or manipulate perceptions by digital means in a manner that produces bargaining benefits.
- *Cyber degradation* refers to high-cost, high-pain efforts that seek to degrade or destroy critical capabilities through computer networks. These operations destabilize the target, highlighting critical vulnerabilities.

Empirical Results

- Cyber incidents are increasing, this increase is directly associated with espionage (52%) and disruption (35%) campaigns, not the more malicious degradation activities (13%) that many fear.

- The results of the data analyses suggest that cyber operations rarely produce concessions (5.7%).
- A state's latent cyber capacity, as a proxy measure of power, is not a significant predictor of coercive potential.
- The majority of cyber escalation episodes are at a low severity threshold and are nonescalatory. These incidents are usually "tit-for-tat" type responses within one step of the original incident and are confined primarily in the cyber domain.
- Even when cyber operations are combined with more traditional inducements like economic and military threats, they are unlikely to produce concessions. There is no magic combination of statecraft in rival relationships that tend to be highly coercive. Degradations that do compel require a previous cyber espionage campaign to succeed.
- The US style of cyber operations flows from the precision strike complex developed after the Cold War. The focus is on degrade options that specifically target structures to compel the adversary to back down when facing a more advanced competitor.
- China has relied on cyber espionage to balance with an enemy in the past but seems to be abandoning these efforts because they do not lead to innovation. Instead, China is now focused on extending its view of sovereignty to cyberspace institutions in order to maintain control over its domestic population.
- Russia uses low-cost, deniable cyber actions to amplify broader propaganda efforts, sowing discontent within the governments and populations of the targeted state, while signaling the risk of escalation. No Russian operation has been successful to date.

Functions of Cyber Strategies

- We find that the utility of cyber strategy is as a form of political warfare optimized for the 21st century that relies on tacit bargaining and ambiguous signaling to help rival states achieve a position of relative advantage in long-term competition.
- Ambiguous signals are covert attempts to demonstrate resolve that rely on sinking costs and raising risks to shape rival behavior.
- Cyber actions can stabilize a crisis by communicating information about resolve and capabilities. These strategies enable learning and offer a form of limited communication during disputes.
- This does not mean that cyber strategies are useful, they are typically costly in terms of bleeding information about capabilities, destructive of norms, and harmful to civilians.

Why Are Cyber Strategies Limited?

- Lack of coercive impact: We demonstrate that cyber power is unlikely to change the behavior of the opposition without the application of significant military force or positive inducements like economic concessions.
- Norms: States do not want to be the first to open Pandora's box and use the weapons before anyone else does.

- Strategic uncertainty: Cyber operations are risky because they are untested and represent ambiguous signals.
- Spillage: While cyber strategies they can serve as a signal to the opposition, these capabilities can also be easily reproduced and spread once used.

Policy Options Moving Forward

- The discourse of dramatic cyber effects raises the shadow of unrealistic expectations.
- There is a danger in threat inflation, we fail to understand the often-unpredictable outcomes of cyber operations and their relationship to coercive success, which is limited.
- Need to prepare for the mundane, which includes basic information security and defenses against information warfare before a state gears up for offensive cyber war.
- Rather than close key diplomatic offices, the United States should create focal points for public–private and international cooperation with respect to cyber security to manage future escalation risks.
- There is a clear need to promote resiliency in the form of psychological recovery in order to withstand the sure-to-come future attacks.

The Dyadic Cyber Incident and Dispute Dataset (DCID), Version 1.1, Summarized Version

The Dyadic Cyber Incident and Dispute Dataset (DCID), Version 1.1, Summarized Version

Cyberincidentnum	Dyadpair	StateA	StateB	Name	interaction start date	interaction end date
1	2365	US	Russia	Reign malware campaign	2/1/2008	3/1/2011
2	2365	US	Russia	QWERTY keystroke log	2/1/2008	3/11/2011
3	2365	US	Russia	Duke Series	4/8/2008	9/17/2015
4	2365	US	Russia	US govt employee in Georgia hacked	8/6/2008	8/12/2008
5	2365	US	Russia	CENTCOM\ DOD (linked to APT 28)	10/1/2008	10/15/2008
6	2365	US	Russia	Buckshot Yankee	11/26/2008	11/28/2008
7	2365	US	Russia	Sandworm	1/1/2009	10/14/2014
8	2365	US	Russia	Power grid hacked, traced to Russia	8/24/2009	8/24/2009
9	2365	US	Russia	Energetic Bear/ Dragonfly/ Crouching Yeti	1/1/2011	7/1/2014
10	2365	US	Russia	Operation Pawn Storm	9/30/2013	10/22/2014
11	2365	US	Russia	CyberBerkut NATO websites	3/15/2014	3/26/2014
12	2365	US	Russia	Operation Pawn Storm: military networks (fake OWA)	6/2/2014	2/1/2015
13	2365	US	Russia	Operation Pawn Storm: Nuclear power plants, newspapers	6/3/2014	12/1/2014
14	2365	US	Russia	US Banks hacked	6/4/2014	7/8/2014
15	2365	US	Russia	White House hack	10/26/2014	10/28/2014
16	2365	US	Russia	State Dept hack	11/15/2014	11/17/2014
17	2630	US	Iran	Stuxnet .5	11/1/2007	61/2010
18	2630	US	Iran	Snowglobe	4/2/2008	12/1/2011

interactiontype	method	targettype	initiator	cyber_objective	objective_achievement	Concession	severity	damage type
3	3	2	2	3	1	o	4	2
3	4.4	2	2	2	1	o	4	2
3	4.2	2	365	3	1	o	4	2
1	4.2	2	365	1	1	o	3	1
3	3	3	365	3	1	o	4	1
2	4.2	2	2	4	1	1	4	1
3	3	2	365	3	1	o	4	2
1	4.2	1	365	4	o	o	1	1
3	3	1	365	2	1	o	3	2
1	3	2	365	2	1	o	4	2
1	2	3	365	1	1	o	2	1
3	3	3	365	2	1	o	4	2
3	3	1	365	2	1	o	4	2
1	3	1	365	1	o	o	3	2
1	3	2	365	2	1	o	3	2
1	3	2	365	2	o	o	3	2
3	4.3	3	2	3	1	o	3	2
3	3	2	2	3	o	o	4	2

(Continued)

Cyberincidentnum	Dyadpair	StateA	StateB	Name	interaction start date	interaction end date
19	2630	US	Iran	Stuxnet	6/1/2009	10/1/2010
20	2630	US	Iran	Flame	6/1/2009	12/2/2012
21	2630	US	Iran	Twitter hack	12/18/2009	12/18/2009
22	2630	US	Iran	Iran network infiltration	3/14/2010	3/14/2010
23	2630	US	Iran	Comodo hack	3/25/2011	3/27/2011
24	2630	US	Iran	Operation Newscaster	4/15/2011	5/26/2013
25	2630	US	Iran	Duqu	9/11/2011	12/1/2011
26	2630	US	Iran	Operation Ababil	12/28/2012	1/2/2013
27	2630	US	Iran	NMCI hack	9/23/2013	9/25/2013
28	2630	US	Iran	Saffron Rose	10/23/2013	3/15/2014
29	2652	US	Syria	Hama visit	7/9/2011	7/9/2011
30	2710	US	China	Hainan Island incident	4/29/2001	5/1/2001
31	2710	US	China	Titan Rain	9/1/2003	4/1/2006
32	2710	US	China	Cisco Raider	2/28/2006	5/6/2010
33	2710	US	China	State Dept theft	5/28/2006	7/72006
34	2710	US	China	Shady RAT	8/1/2006	1/1/2010
35	2710	US	China	Fred Wolf espionage	8/1/2006	8/1/2006
36	2710	US	China	Commerce disable	10/1/2006	10/07/2006
37	2710	US	China	Naval War College disable	12/1/2006	12/07/2006
38	2710	US	China	750,000 American zombies	3/1/2007	9/23/2010
39	2710	US	China	GhostNet	5/27/2007	8/1/2009
40	2710	US	China	Arrow Eclipse	5/27/2007	6/13/2013
41	2710	US	China	Commerce Sec hack	12/1/2007	12/5/2007
42	2710	US	China	Boxing Rumble	1/1/2008	7/19/2010
43	2710	US	China	2008 Campaign hack	8/1/2008	8/04/2008
44	2710	US	China	Hikit	9/1/2008	10/27/2014
45	2710	US	China	Byzantine series	10/30/2008	6/30/2011
46	2710	US	China	FAA hack	2/4/2009	2/10/2009

interactiontype	method	targettype	initiator	cyber_objective	objective_achievement	Concession	severity	damage type
3	4.3	3	2	4	1	1	5	2
3	4.2	3	2	3	1	0	3	2
1	1	1	630	1	0	0	2	1
3	3	2	2	3	1	0	3	2
1	3	1	630	2	0	0	1	1
1	3	1	630	2	1	0	2	2
3	3	3	2	3	1	0	3	2
1	2	1	630	1	0	0	2	1
1	3	3	630	2	1	0	1	2
1	3	1	630	2	0	0	1	2
1	1	2	652	1	1	0	2	1
1	1	2	710	1	1	0	2	1
3	3	3	710	2	1	0	4	1
2	4.4	2	2	4	1	1	5	1
3	3	2	710	2	1	0	2	1
3	3	2	710	2	1	0	4	1
3	3	3	710	2	1	0	2	1
3	4.1	2	710	1	1	0	2	1
3	4.1	3	710	1	1	0	2	1
3	2	2	710	1	1	0	2	2
3	3	2	710	2	1	0	4	1
2	4.4	3	2	4	1	1	4	3
1	4.2	2	710	2	0	0	3	1
2	2	3	2	4	1	1	4	3
1	3	2	710	2	1	0	1	2
3	3	2	710	2	1	0	4	2
1	3	1	710	3	1	0	4	1
1	3	2	710	2	1	0	3	2

(*Continued*)

Cyberincidentnum	Dyadpair	StateA	StateB	Name	interaction start date	interaction end date
47	2710	US	China	Senator Nelson theft	3/1/2009	3/1/2009
48	2710	US	China	Lockheed F-35 plans stolen	3/29/2009	4/1/2009
49	2710	US	China	Aurora	6/1/2009	1/1/2010
50	2710	US	China	NSA Fourth Party collection	7/1/2009	6/13/2013
51	2710	US	China	Night Dragon	11/1/2009	2/11/2011
52	2710	US	China	Commerce theft	11/1/2009	11/5/2009
53	2710	US	China	Htran	1/1/2010	2/1/2010
54	2710	US	China	Shotgiant	3/10/2010	6/13/2013
55	2710	US	China	US Top National Security E-mail hacks	4/1/2010	8/10/2015
56	2710	US	China	FDIC hack	10/1/2010	2/2/2012
57	2710	US	China	Energy Dept hack	2/1/2011	1/1/2014
58	2710	US	China	Pentagon raid	3/1/2011	3/10/2011
59	2710	US	China	Operation Beebus	4/12/2011	2/7/2013
60	2710	US	China	White House theft	11/7/2011	11/8/2011
61	2710	US	China	Ocean Lotus	4/1/2012	5/1/2014
62	2710	US	China	Penn State Engineering breach	9/1/2012	5/15/2015
63	2710	US	China	Wen Jiabao retaliation	10/26/2012	12/31/2012
64	2710	US	China	Iron Tiger	1/15/2013	9/16/2015
65	2710	US	China	Black Coffee	4/1/2013	5/12/2015
66	2710	US	China	UConn Engineering hack	9/24/2013	3/9/2015
67	2710	US	China	Operation SnowMan	2/1/2014	2/12/2014
68	2710	US	China	Regsiter.com breach	3/1/2014	3/18/2015
69	2710	US	China	OPM hack	3/15/2014	3/17/2015

interactiontype	method	targettype	initiator	cyber_objective	objective_achievement	Concession	severity	damage type
I	3	2	710	2	0	0	2	I
3	3	I	710	3	I	0	3	I
3	3	I	710	3	I	0	3	I
3	3	3	2	4	I	I	4	3
3	4.2	I	710	3	I	0	4	I
3	4.4	2	710	2	I	0	3	I
3	4.4	2	710	2	I	0	3	I
3	3	I	2	4	I	I	4	2
3	3	3	710	2	I	0	4	2
3	3	2	710	2	I	0	2	2
I	3	2	710	I	I	0	3	2
3	4.4	3	710	3	I	0	3	I
3	3	I	710	3	I	0	4	2
3	4.4	2	710	I	I	0	3	I
3	4.3	2	2	4	I	0	4	4
I	3	2	710	2	I	0	3	2
I	3	I	710	I	I	0	2	2
3	3	3	710	2	I	0	4	2
I	3	I	710	2	I	0	I	2
I	3	2	710	2	I	0	3	2
3	3	3	710	2	I	0	I	2
I	3	I	710	2	I	0	3	2
I	3	2	710	3	I	I	4	2

(*Continued*)

Cyberincidentnum	Dyadpair	StateA	StateB	Name	interaction start date	interaction end date
70	2710	US	China	Premera Blue Cross breach	5/5/2014	1/29/2015
71	2710	US	China	UCLA Health system breach	9/1/2014	7/25/2015
72	2710	US	China	DHS employee hack	11/6/2014	11/7/2014
73	2710	US	China	USPS breach	11/8/2014	11/10/2014
74	2710	US	China	Anthem breach	12/10/2014	1/27/2015
75	2731	US	N Korea	Boxing Rumble	1/1/2008	7/19/2010
76	2731	US	N Korea	Fourth of July	7/4/2009	7/7/2009
77	2731	US	N Korea	NK Stuxnet	3/1/2010	4/30/2010
78	2731	US	N Korea	March defacement	3/1/2011	3/4/2011
79	2731	US	N Korea	December defacement	12/7/2011	12/7/2011
80	2731	US	N Korea	Sony Hack	11/24/2014	11/25/2014
81	20365	Canada	Russia	Energetic Bear/ Dragonfly/ Crouching Yeti	1/1/2011	7/1/2014
82	20365	Canada	Russia	CyberBerkut NATO websites	3/15/2014	3/27/2014
83	200365	UK	Russia	Energetic Bear/ Dragonfly/ Crouching Yeti	1/1/2011	7/1/2014
84	200365	UK	Russia	CyberBerkut NATO websites	3/15/2014	3/25/2014
85	290365	Poland	Russia	Sandworm	1/1/2009	10/14/2014
86	290365	Poland	Russia	Operation Pawn Storm	6/1/2014	6/30/2014
87	290365	Poland	Russia	CyberBerkut Polish Stock Exchange	10/23/2014	10/24/2014
88	365366	Russia	Estonia	Defacement of govt websites	4/27/2007	5/10/2007
89	365366	Russia	Estonia	Defacement of private websites	4/27/2007	5/10/2007

interactiontype	method	targettype	initiator	cyber_objective	objective_achievement	Concession	severity	damage type
I	3	I	710	2	I	0	3	2
I	3	I	710	2	I	0	3	2
I	3	2	710	3	I	0	3	2
I	3	2	710	2	I	0	3	2
I	3	I	710	2	I	0	3	2
2	2	2	2	4	I	I	2	3
I	2	2	731	I	I	0	2	I
3	4.3	3	2	4	0	0	5	2
I	I	2	731	I	I	0	2	I
3	I	2	731	I	I	0	2	I
3	3	2	731	4	I	0	4	I
	3	I	365	2	I	0	3	2
	2	3	365	I	I	0	2	I
I	3	I	365	2	I	0	4	2
	2	3	365	I	I	0	2	I
	3	2	365	3	I	0	4	2
I	3	2	365	2	I	0	3	2
	I	I	365	I	I	0	2	I
3	I	2	365	I	I	0	2	I
3	I	I	365	I	I	0	2	I

(*Continued*)

Cyberincidentnum	Dyadpair	StateA	StateB	Name	interaction start date	interaction end date
90	365366	Russia	Estonia	DDoS of govt websites	4/27/2007	5/10/2007
91	365366	Russia	Estonia	DDoS of private websites	4/27/2007	5/10/2007
92	365368	Russia	Lithuania	Snake	1/1/2005	5/8/2014
93	365368	Russia	Lithuania	Lithuanian Parliament	6/28/2008	7/2/2008
94	365368	Russia	Lithuania	Lithuanian Parliament	6/28/2008	7/2/2008
95	365369	Russia	Ukraine	Snake	1/1/2005	5/8/2014
96	365369	Russia	Ukraine	Sandworm	1/1/2009	10/14/2014
97	365369	Russia	Ukraine	Duke Series	2/1/2013	9/17/2015
98	365369	Russia	Ukraine	CyberBerkut UKR govt site hack	1/1/2014	12/31/2014
99	365369	Russia	Ukraine	CyberBerkut Telecom disruption	3/1/2014	3/15/2014
100	365369	Russia	Ukraine	CyberBerkut Ukraine election intrusion	5/22/2014	5/26/2014
101	365369	Russia	Ukraine	Operation Pawn Storm	6/1/2014	2/1/2015
102	365369	Russia	Ukraine	CyberBerkut UKR MOD DDoS	10/1/2014	10/30/2014
103	365369	Russia	Ukraine	Fancy Bear (also APT 28 linked)	10/6/2014	7/15/2016
104	365369	Russia	Ukraine	CyberBerkut billboard hack	11/20/2014	11/21/2014
105	365372	Russia	Georgia	APT28/Sofacy Group/Sednit Group/Tsar Team/Fancy Bear	1/1/2007	7/15/2016
106	365372	Russia	Georgia	Duke series	4/8/2008	9/17/2015
107	365372	Russia	Georgia	Before the gunfire	4/20/2008	8/6/2008
108	365372	Russia	Georgia	Osinform	8/4/2008	8/4/2008

interactiontype	method	targettype	initiator	cyber_objective	objective_achievement	Concession	severity	damage type
3	2	2	365	4	1	0	2	1
3	2	1	365	4	1	0	2	1
	3	2	365	2	1	0	4	2
	1	1	365	1	1	0	2	1
	1	2	365	1	1	0	2	2
	3	2	365	2	1	0	4	2
	3	2	365	3	1	0	2	2
	3	2	365	3	1	0	2	2
	2	2	365	1	1	0	2	1
	2	1	365	4	1	0	2	1
	2	2	365	1	1	0	2	1
	3	2	365	2	1	0	3	2
	2	3	365	1	1	0	2	1
	3	3	365	4	1	0	4	2
	1	1	365	1	1	0	2	1
1	3	2	365	3	1	0	4	2
	3	2	365	3	1	0	3	2
1	2	2	365	1	1	0	2	1
3	2	2	372	1	0	0	2	1

(Continued)

Cyberincidentnum	Dyadpair	StateA	StateB	Name	interaction start date	interaction end date
109	365372	Russia	Georgia	VoiP	8/4/2008	8/8/2008
110	365372	Russia	Georgia	Russo-Georgia cyber actions	8/5/2008	8/5/2016
111	365372	Russia	Georgia	Russo-Georgia cyber actions	8/5/2008	8/5/2016
112	365372	Russia	Georgia	Russo-Georgia cyber actions	8/5/2008	8/5/2016
113	365372	Russia	Georgia	US-Georgia government defacements	8/7/2008	8/16/2008
114	630666	Iran	Israel	Electronic jihad	9/1/2000	9/1/2000
115	630666	Iran	Israel	Cyber jihad	8/1/2001	8/1/2001
116	630666	Iran	Israel	Antisemitic response	2/7/2006	2/7/2006
117	630666	Iran	Israel	Lebanese action propaganda	10/27/2006	10/27/2006
118	630666	Iran	Israel	Stuxnet .5	11/1/2007	6/1/2010
119	630666	Iran	Israel	Cast Lead retaliation	12/27/2008	12/27/2008
120	630666	Iran	Israel	Stuxnet	6/1/2009	10/1/2010
121	630666	Iran	Israel	Flame	6/1/2009	12/2/2012
122	630666	Iran	Israel	Nuclear Facilities virus	7/7/2009	1/1/2010
123	630666	Iran	Israel	Duqu	9/11/2011	12/1/2011
124	630666	Iran	Israel	Israel infrastructure hack	3/2/2013	6/8/2013
125	630666	Iran	Israel	Duqu 2.0	6/1/2014	6/30/2015
126	630666	Iran	Israel	Iranian multiple espionage	7/1/2014	6/14/2015
127	630670	Iran	Saudi Arabia	Shamoon	8/15/2012	8/16/2012
128	630670	Iran	Saudi Arabia	RasGas attack	8/20/2012	8/21/2012
129	630670	Iran	Saudi Arabia	Iranian multiple espionage	7/1/2014	6/14/2015
130	645690	Iraq	Kuwait	Iraq hack	12/13/2002	12/13/2002

interactiontype	method	targettype	initiator	cyber_objective	objective_achievement	Concession	severity	damage type
3	2	1	365	4	1	0	2	1
	2	2	365	1	1	0	2	1
	2	1	365	1	1	0	2	1
	1	2	365	1	1	0	2	1
1	1	2	365	1	1	0	2	1
1	2	2	630	1	1	0	2	1
1	2	2	630	1	1	0	2	1
1	1	2	666	1	1	0	2	1
2	2	2	630	1	0	0	2	1
3	4.3	3	666	3	1	0	4	2
1	2	2	630	1	0	0	2	1
3	4.3	3	666	4	1	1	5	2
3	4.2	3	666	3	1	0	3	2
3	4.2	3	666	3	1	0	2	2
3	3	3	666	3	1	0	3	2
3	4.2	2	630	4	0	0	5	4
1	3	2	666	3	1	0	3	2
1	3	2	630	2	0	0	1	2
3	4.1	2	630	4	1	0	6	1
3	4.1	2	630	4	1	0	6	1
1	3	2	630	2	0	0	3	2
1	1	2	690	1	1	0	2	1

(*Continued*)

Cyberincidentnum	Dyadpair	StateA	StateB	Name	interaction start date	interaction end date
131	652666	Syria	Israel	Mossad Trojan leads to Operation Orchard	12/10/2006	12/11/2006
132	660666	Lebanon	Israel	Cyber jihad on Israel	7/15/2001	8/1/2001
133	660666	Lebanon	Israel	Gauss	9/1/2011	8/8/2012
134	710713	China	Taiwan	DPP hack	3/1/2001	3/3/2001
135	710713	China	Taiwan	Prosecutor hack	11/17/2001	11/18/2001
136	710713	China	Taiwan	GhostNet	5/27/2007	8/1/2009
137	710713	China	Taiwan	Shady RAT	9/1/2007	1/1/2010
138	710713	China	Taiwan	Hikit	9/1/2008	10/27/2014
139	710713	China	Taiwan	Election hack	8/4/2011	8/6/2011
140	710713	China	Taiwan	TooHash	9/1/2013	11/3/2014
141	710740	China	Japan	Htran	1/1/2001	2/1/2001
142	710740	China	Japan	WWII Memorial	1/6/2005	5/15/2005
143	710740	China	Japan	Hack and extort	12/27/2007	6/1/2008
144	710740	China	Japan	Hikit	9/1/2008	10/27/2014
145	710740	China	Japan	Earthquake hack	3/11/2010	3/14/2010
146	710740	China	Japan	East China Sea dispute	09/14/2010	9/17/2010
147	710740	China	Japan	Mitsubishi Hack	09/01/2011	11/4/2011
148	710740	China	Japan	Icefog	9/1/2011	9/23/2013
149	710740	China	Japan	Parliament hack	10/25/2011	11/2/2011
150	710750	China	India	GhostNet	5/27/2007	8/1/2009
151	710750	China	India	Shady RAT	7/1/2007	1/1/2010
152	710750	China	India	Prime Minister's office hacked and info stolen	12/15/2009	12/15/2009
153	710750	China	India	Indian military classified files stolen	4/2/2010	4/7/2010
154	710816	China	Vietnam	Shady RAT	3/1/2007	1/1/2010
155	710816	China	Vietnam	Vietnam Hack	7/3/2011	7/6/2011
156	710840	China	Philippines	Philippines hack	3/28/2009	3/30/2009
157	731732	N Korea	S Korea	Dark Hotel	1/1/2008	11/9/2014

interactiontype	method	targettype	initiator	cyber_objective	objective_achievement	Concession	severity	damage type
3	3	3	666	3	1	1	4	4
3	4.3	2	660	1	0	0	2	1
1	4.2	1	666	3	1	0	3	2
1	3	2	710	1	1	0	2	1
1	3	2	710	1	1	0	2	1
3	3	2	710	2	1	0	4	1
3	3	2	710	2	1	0	4	1
3	3	2	710	2	1	0	4	2
1	3	2	710	1	1	0	2	1
1	3	2	713	2	1	0	3	2
3	4.4	3	710	2	1	0	3	1
3	2	2	710	4	0	0	2	1
3	4.2	1	710	2	0	0	3	1
3	3	2	710	2	1	0	4	2
3	3	2	710	2	1	0	3	1
3	2	2	710	4	0	0	2	1
3	4.4	1	710	2	1	0	3	1
1	3	2	710	2	0	0	3	2
3	3	2	710	2	1	0	3	2
3	3	2	710	2	1	0	3	2
3	3	2	710	2	1	0	3	2
3	3	2	710	2	1	0	3	2
3	4.2	3	710	2	1	0	3	1
3	3	2	710	2	1	0	3	2
3	4.2	2	710	1	1	0	3	1
3	3	2	710	2	1	0	3	3
1	3	2	732	2	1	0	4	2

(Continued)

Cyberincidentnum	Dyadpair	StateA	StateB	Name	interaction start date	interaction end date
158	731732	N Korea	S Korea	Un retaliate	6/1/2008	9/2/2008
159	731732	N Korea	S Korea	Government theft	9/8/2008	9/8/2008
160	731732	N Korea	S Korea	Government shutdown	7/6/2009	7/9/2009
161	731732	N Korea	S Korea	Web portal defacement	6/1/2010	6/2/2010
162	731732	N Korea	S Korea	Anti-Kim	1/4/2011	1/10/2011
163	731732	N Korea	S Korea	NK retaliation	1/4/2011	1/10/2011
164	731732	N Korea	S Korea	March DDoS	3/7/2011	3/8/2011
165	731732	N Korea	S Korea	Bank shut down	4/3/2011	4/3/2011
166	731732	N Korea	S Korea	June DDoS	6/7/2011	6/7/2011
167	731732	N Korea	S Korea	December defacement	12/7/2011	12/7/2011
168	731732	N Korea	S Korea	Telecom shut down	12/20/2011	12/20/2011
169	731732	N Korea	S Korea	South Korea nuclear facility hack	12/9/2014	12/12/2014
170	731740	N Korea	Japan	Fourth of July	7/4/2009	7/7/2009
171	732740	S Korea	Japan	Textbook hack	4/1/2001	4/1/2001
172	732740	S Korea	Japan	South Korea Patriotic	1/7/2004	1/14/2004
173	732740	S Korea	Japan	Japan Patriotic	1/7/2004	1/14/2004
174	732740	S Korea	Japan	Island Dispute	3/20/2005	3/20/2005
175	732740	S Korea	Japan	Dark Hotel	1/1/2008	11/9/2014
176	732740	S Korea	Japan	SK hack	3/1/2010	3/1/2010
177	732740	S Korea	Japan	Japan retaliation	3/1/2010	3/1/2010
178	732740	S Korea	Japan	Earthquake hack	3/11/2011	3/14/2011
179	750770	India	Pakistan	October 2001 defacements	10/22/2001	10/24/2001
180	750770	India	Pakistan	Worm infiltrates Pakistan govt	3/1/2003	3/13/2003
181	750770	India	Pakistan	July 2003 defacements	7/12/2003	7/13/2003
182	750770	India	Pakistan	November 2008 defacements	11/15/2008	11/27/2008

interactiontype	method	targettype	initiator	cyber_objective	objective_achievement	Concession	severity	damage type
3	4.2	3	731	2	0	0	1	1
3	3	2	731	2	1	0	3	1
3	4.2	2	731	4	1	0	2	1
1	1	1	731	1	1	0	2	1
1	1	2	732	1	1	0	2	1
1	1	2	731	1	1	0	2	1
1	2	1	731	1	1	0	2	1
1	4.2	1	731	4	1	0	2	1
1	2	1	731	1	1	0	2	1
3	1	2	731	1	1	0	2	1
1	3	1	731	1	1	0	2	1
3	3	1	731	3	1	0	2	2
1	2	2	731	1	1	0	2	1
1	2	2	732	1	1	0	2	1
1	2	1	732	1	1	0	2	1
1	2	2	740	1	1	0	2	1
1	1	2	740	1	1	0	2	1
1	3	2	732	2	1	0	4	2
1	2	2	732	1	1	0	2	1
1	2	2	740	1	1	0	2	1
3	3	2	732	2	1	0	3	1
1	1	2	770	1	1	0	2	1
3	4.3	2	750	1	1	0	2	1
1	1	2	750	1	1	0	2	1
1	1	2	750	1	1	0	2	1

(*Continued*)

Cyberincidentnum	Dyadpair	StateA	StateB	Name	interaction start date	interaction end date
183	750770	India	Pakistan	November 2008 defacements	11/15/2008	11/27/2008
184	750770	India	Pakistan	Transportation defacements	12/24/2008	12/25/2008
185	750770	India	Pakistan	September 2010 defacements	9/2/2010	9/12/2010
186	750770	India	Pakistan	September 2010 defacements	9/2/2010	9/12/2010
187	750770	India	Pakistan	PCA defacements	12/1/2010	12/3/2010
188	750770	India	Pakistan	PCA retaliation	12/1/2010	12/3/2010
189	750770	India	Pakistan	ICID defacement	10/1/2011	10/1/2011
190	750770	India	Pakistan	Tranchulas incident	2/1/2013	7/2/2013
191	750770	India	Pakistan	Telenor Pakistan incident	3/17/2013	3/17/2013
192	750771	India	Bangladesh	Terrorist warning	3/19/2010	3/20/2010

interactiontype	method	targettype	initiator	cyber_objective	objective_achievement	Concession	severity	damage type
1	1	2	770	1	1	0	2	1
3	1	2	770	1	1	0	2	1
1	1	2	770	1	1	0	2	1
1	1	2	750	1	1	0	2	1
1	1	2	770	1	1	0	2	1
1	1	2	750	1	1	0	2	1
3	1	2	770	1	1	0	2	1
3	4.2	3	770	2	1	0	3	1
3	4.2	1	750	2	1	0	3	1
3	1	2	750	1	1	0	2	1

Notes

CHAPTER I

1. For a critical overview of major works in this camp, see Gartkze (2013) and Lindsay (2013).

2. Major academic contributions to the literature on cyber coercion include Libicki (2009), Healey (2013), Liff (2012), Rid (2011), Gartzke (2013), Gartzke and Lindsay (2015), Thayer (2000), and Feaver (1998).

3. For overviews of the evolving definitions of strategy in military and diplomatic history, see Heuser (2010) and Freedman (2015).

4. On coercion diplomacy, see George, Hall, and Simons (1971), George and Simons (1994), George (1991), and Art and Cronin (2003).

5. On the original conceptualization of cheap talk, as empty threats, see Fearon (1995, 1997).

6. On how covert action can signal resolve through sinking costs, see Carson and Yarhi-Milo (2017).

7. For additional perspectives on rivalry, see: Bennett (1998), Colaresi (2001), Goertz and Diehl (1993, 1995), Thompson (1995, 2001), and Vasquez (1993, 1996).

8. Brantly (2016), Healey (2013), Romanosky (2016), Pytlak and Mitchell (2016), Gomez (2016), Axelrod and Iliev (2014), and Rid and Buchanan (2015).

9. The analysis focuses on cyber coercive incidents. Cyber incidents, such as a disruptive website defacement targeting commercial networks, likely contain multiple individual events. We do not code each website defaced or computer taken offline during a DDoS. Rather, our approach looks at the attack method and the dyadic interaction bound by a limited time period. In subsequent chapters we also control for the accumulation of these incidents through constructing a past cyber incident variable. In the case studies we use these data points to approximate select campaigns between major cyber rivals (i.e., Russia, China, and the United States).

CHAPTER 2

1. This definition is based on the work of Schelling (1966), George (1991), Byman and Waxman (2002), and Haun (2015).

2. Key works include Pape (2003), Kydd and Walter (2002, 2006), and Abrahms (2006, 2012).

3. This wide level of variation emerges from different study designs. Key differences include the definition of success (i.e., whether success is a binary variable or an ordinal ranking), different types of actors (i.e., state, nonstate), and different definitions of coercion and the range of coercive instruments observed (e.g., whether the study looked just at terrorism, all coercive diplomacy, or just militarized threats).

4. These insights are based on Pape (1996: 13) and Sescher and Fuhrmann (2017: 24).

5. For an overview of the leadership targeting literature, see Johnston (2012), Byman (2006), Steven (2002), Frankel (2010), Jordan (2009), and Price (2012).

6. See also Snyder and Borghard (2011).

7. Looking at Byrant's (2016) outcomes, success seems to be realized only in cases where the attacker has a huge advantage over the defender, such as in the case of Russia versus Georgia in 2008. All other cases generate low-level objective achievement scores—the only other cases with clear objective achievement are North Korea's attacks on South Korean banks and government systems in 2011 and 2013 (Bryant 2016: Appendix B), cases where the defender had no target to attack in order to retaliate.

8. In this respect, cyber operations can be thought of as closer to Alexander George's conceptualization of coercive diplomacy and the use of many instruments to manage competition while still seeking an advantage. Whereas for George, these actions are strictly defensive, we follow Jack Levy and extend the logic to offensive actions short of war as well (Levy 2008).

9. For an overview of cost-imposing strategies, see Mahnken (2014) and Erkman (2014).

10. This statement applies to most classical and contemporary forms of realist inquiry including classical, neorealism, offensive realism, and neoclassical. The logic only partially applies to approaches in the English School perspective, in which patterns of interaction create a more predictable set of conventions and institutions, loosely defined, that stabilize expectations.

11. Private information is a central concept in the bargaining literature. For an overview of the bargaining literature, see Powell (2002) and Reiter (2003). In discussing bargaining theory, we only partially address commitment issues and do not address issue indivisibility.

12. For studies on power differential as they relate to strategic competition between rivals, see Geller (1993, 2000).

13. The original concept is in Schelling (1966: 4); for an overview, see Knopf (2002).

14. Major works include Smoke (1977), Huth and Russett (1990), Geller (1990), Brecher (1993), Holsti (1972), Brecher and Wilkenfeld (2000), Colaresi and Thompson (2002), Kinsella and Russett (2002), Leng (1993), Lebow (1981), and Brecher, James, and Wilkenfeld (2000). For an overview of literature on crisis escalation as it relates to democratic peace, issue salience, domestic political structures and processes, and power transition, see Braithwaite and Lemke (2011).

15. This insight is based on Russell Leng's characterization of the strategic choice model and realist perspectives (1983). This perspective is often contrasted with psychological perspectives that stress how the stress of a crisis creates misperception, attribution errors, and amplifies cognitive limitations (Leng 2004: 52; Jervis 1976; Holsti 1989; Rubin, Pruitt, and Kim 1994).

16. Leng (2004: 52–53) characterizes the psychological perspective on crisis escalation, stating "misperceptions of intentions resulting from the distrustful evaluation of the adversary's

behavior, "lock-in" to a pattern of escalating coercive tit-for-tat influence attempts, self-reinforcing commitments to coercive tactics that are exacerbated by expectations of audience costs associated with behavior that suggests weakness, and a breakdown in communication."

17. Fearon (1995: 401) and Powell (1999: 407; 2006). This treatment does not address important differences between Fearon and Powell regarding the source of bargaining failures. Rather, we draw on each author's work to propose some research hypotheses about cyberattacks as a form of coercion.

18. For examples, see Fearon (1995: 401), Powell (1999), and Acemoglu and Robinson (2000, 2001).

19. On offensive advantages, see Fearon (1995: 402–405), Powell (1999: 82–114; 2006), and Sechser (2007). On shifting power, see Fearon (1995: 405–406) and Powell (1999: 115–148).

20. The offense–defense balance is a robust literature. See Jervis (1979), Lynn-Jones (1995), Van Evera (1998), Glaser and Kaufmann (1998), and, on cyber conflict, Slayton (2017).

21. For an overview of audience costs, see Schultz (1998, 2001, 2012). For critiques of the audience costs literature, see Snyder and Borghard (2011), Downes and Sechser (2012), and Trachtenberg (2012).

22. In all likelihood, nonstate actors, who carry out the preponderance of cyber acts, will face fewer constraints on their actions, thus altering patterns of cyber coercion. For a discussion on constraints and nonstate actors, see Betz (2015).

CHAPTER 3

1. Note, machine learning methods could be used to scrape new corpuses for data, but this method is unreliable without human coders supporting the effect to ensure the cases coded are attributable, code the specific variables needed for our analysis, and avoid duplication. Such an effort would require a massive amount of funding, which is yet unavailable.

2. Our data is subjective (as is most data), but we set out to minimize this with overlapping coding efforts, full rechecks by the primary authors, and support from a collection of cyber scholars. This research is an example of a representative sample of incidents and disputes, and future coding efforts will seek to continue to flesh out these questions and provide more data as incidents occur. The outcomes of the disputes are defined by our criteria and reinforced by multiple coder reliability checks and advice from the cyber security research community explained in Appendix 1.

3. For a complete overview of the dataset, the codebook and data are available at drryanmaness. wix.com/irprof. We also include the rivals of Russia in post-Soviet space (Estonia, Lithuania, Georgia, and Ukraine). While these are not included in the Klein, Diehl, and Goertz (2006) dataset, they have since crossed the minimal empirical threshold of militarized interstate disputes to be considered rivals.

4. Given that some cyber operations target multiple entities simultaneously, we code each rival targeted separately. Furthermore, there are sometimes multiple initiators of cyber events, and each initiated state is given a separate dyadic variable that is coded.

5. Electronic manipulation, such as electromagnetic pulses and radar jamming, either damages or destroys circuitry through radio waves and/or directed energy and is not included.

6. Deterrent operations are possible but also very rare empirically, since displaying cyber capabilities is rare (Maness and Valeriano 2016).

7. Whether the inferred impact was the result of compounding dilemmas emerging from other actions is beyond the scope of the current research.

8. The null hypothesis is that cyber degradation produces concessions at the same rate as the other forms. The independent variable is the form of cyber coercion. The dependent variable is the observed rate of concession. One can reject the null if cyber degradation episodes produce concessions at a statistically significant different rate and the rate is higher than the other forms (i.e., espionage, disruption).

9. An interesting exception to this assumption is North Korea, where cyber operators often travel outside of the country to launch their intrusions. See Mon May (2017).

10. These numbers are normalized into z-scores in order to have comparable observations across the six variables and allow us to construct a unified cyber power index to be used as independent variables in several of the analyses that follow. All six normalized scores from the variable extracted from the World Bank are averaged into one overall power score. For the purposes of keeping all cyber power scores positive for each country year, we add five to the averaged z-score, which is the minimum whole number that gets all scores above zero for a positive power index. Therefore, our cyber power index ranges from two to eight, with two being the absolute lowest possible cyber power score, and eight being the maximum possible score.

11. The null hypothesis is such that when the initiator has higher cyber capacity, concession is more likely. The independent variable is the difference in cyber capacity between the initiator and target. The dependent variable is the observed rate of concession. The controls are other measures of power: GDP, military expenditure, and CINC scores. The dependent variable is binary and measures the presence or absence of concession. One can reject the null if cyber capacity does not produce concessions or the observed rate is equal to or less than other measures of power.

12. The null hypothesis is that past cyber incidents increase the projected rate of concessions. The independent variable is whether or not there were past cyber incidents. The dependent variable is the whether or not there was a concession. As these are categorical variables, past cyber incidents and concessions can be evaluated through a case control study examining the odds ratio and comparing the rate of concession to controls: regime type, economic power, military power, and cyber capacity. One can reject the null if past cyber incidents produce a higher odds ratio than the controls.

13. A chi-squared score measures the overall difference between the expected values and observed values of all categories in a nonparametric sample. The null hypothesis is rejected if the chi-squared score is significant at the 95-percent-confidence level or higher. Given that there are a limited number of cases under consideration, more advanced statistical analysis is not possible given issues under consideration.

14. 17% represents the lower threshold of the first standard deviation.

15. On the surface, the crisis involved the placement of a World War II–era statue. Yet, the larger strategic logic involved how Moscow viewed Estonia's treatment of ethnic Russians.

16. An alternative approach advocated by Byman and Waxman is to analyze coercion outcomes "as a marginal change in probability of behavior" (2000: 14).

17. Rigorous reliability checks were undertaken to investigate the reliability of our coding of the compellence variables. Experts from the professional military education (both students and instructors) system were recruited to help with the subjective coding of the two key variables of interest. Objective achievement and concessions could vary by individual; because there is no

objective measurement of such issues, getting reliable variable coding is paramount. We held multiple sessions where coding was done independently and then majority opinion decided on the variables' values. Intercoder reliability tests were then estimated to establish the success of our efforts in ensuring trust and verification of the coding effort. For the objective achievement dependent variable, we obtained a Fleiss' Kappa score of .646. Fleiss' Kappa tests are appropriate for intercoder reliability when there are three or more coders. This score can be interpreted as finding to what extent the observed amount of agreement among raters exceeds what would be expected if all raters made their ratings completely randomly. The score of .646 denotes substantial agreement, which is to be expected, as there were 15 different examiners involved in this effort. For the concessionary behavioral change dependent variable, we obtained a .589 Fleiss' Kappa score using the same number of coders, which is also within the substantial threshold. For the independent variables of compellence type, the three authors code these variables and then came to agreement on the final values, obtaining a substantial agreement with Fleiss' Kappa score of 759.

18. See also Lonegran (2016) and Jervis (2017).

19. See the study by Ward et al. (2012), for a comparable study using this dataset.

20. For an overview of the case, see Koerner (2016). Our coding of the OPM hack as a concession was contentious. Within the group of three primary authors and coders, two agreed that it was a concession and one disagreed. Among the sample of coding reviewers (a team of 15 members of the professional military education system was recruited to review the coding, many of them having engaged in or operated cyber systems for the military), 10 agreed that the case was a concession while 5 disagreed. The disagreement is based on the judgment that the United States made a concession. The coders that counted the event as positive did so because either the diplomatic agreement between China and the United States would not have occurred without the hack, so the instance of bringing the United States to the bargaining table was a concession or change of behavior. Coders in the negative generally agree that there was an agreement after the event, but it is unclear whether and unlikely that the United States conceded anything. It could be that this case demonstrates a concession or change of behavior in that members of the US military and intelligence community now must behave differently knowing that they have been potentially compromised.

21. On the concept of tit-for-tat in competitive interactions as a form of learning under uncertainty and seeking cooperative outcomes, see Axelrod (1984).

22. Similar to the cyber capacity model, the findings report the odds ratio for a case control study.

23. The distribution of responses is significant in the lower and upper time frames based on a log rank (chi-square 7.139***) and Tarone-Ware (chi-square 5.090**). * $p < .1$, ** $p < .05$, *** $p < .01$.

CHAPTER 4

1. For a more detailed description of cutoff and coverage procedures, see Ragin (2006).

2. As there are two espionage combinations in the 192 cases that produce concessions, this independent variable did not make the 80% consistency cutoff for minimal membership requirement. This is not to say that the absence of espionage will not produce a concession, only that its absence when combined with a degradation is a necessary condition for concessions. Espionage, therefore, is neither a necessary nor sufficient condition for producing concessions, but its use for achieving concessions is not out of the realm of possibility.

3. Nine cases, 30 instruments.

4. Reduced Boolean Addition Equation

Frequency cutoff: 1 **Consistency cutoff:** 1.00	
~**Past_Disrupt*****Past_Espionage***Diplo_Negative*Diplo_Positive*Econ_Negative* ~**Econ_Positive***~Mil_Positive Raw Coverage: 0.222222 Unique Coverage: 0.111111 Consistency: 1.00	
~**Past_Disrupt*****Past_Espionage***Diplo_Negative*Econ_Negative*~**Econ_Positive*** Mil_Negative*~Mil_Positive Raw Coverage: 0.222222 Unique Coverage: 0.111111 Consistency: 1.00	
~**Past_Disrupt*****Past_Espionage***Diplo_Negative*Diplo_Positive*Econ_Negative* ~**Econ_Positive***Mil_Negative Raw Coverage: 0.222222 Unique Coverage: 0.111111 Consistency: 1.00	
~**Past_Disrupt*****Past_Espionage***~Diplo_Negative*~Diplo_Positive*~Econ_Negative* ~**Econ_Positive***Mil_Negative*~Mil_Positive Raw Coverage: 0.111111 Unique Coverage: 0.111111 Consistency: 1.00	
~**Past_Disrupt*****Past_Espionage***Diplo_Negative*Diplo_Positive*~Econ_Negative* ~**Econ_Positive***~Mil_Negative*Mil_Positive Raw Coverage: 0.111111 Unique Coverage: 0.111111 Consistency: 1.00	
Solution coverage: 0.777778 **Solution consistency:** 1.00	

CHAPTER 5

1. Generals Vorobyov and Kiseljov (2013).

2. For the original exposition, see Gerasimov (2013). For an overview of key concepts, see Bartel (2015). For a critique that questions whether or not there is a Gerasimov doctrine, see McDermott (2016).

3. For an overview of the proliferation challenged posed at the end of the Cold War, see Weiner (2011).

4. http://www.zdnet.com/article/ukraine-calls-out-russian-involvement-in-petya/

5. Escalation dominance is a strategic concept that evolved in both Western and Russian circles during the late Cold War. According to a RAND study (Morgan et al. 2008: 15), escalation dominance refers to "a condition in which a combatant has the ability to escalate a conflict in ways that will be disadvantageous or costly to the adversary while the adversary cannot do the same in return, either because it has no escalation options or because the available options would not improve the adversary's situation results through." This posture relies on "discovering, and effectively exploiting, some asymmetric vulnerability in an opponent, thereby imposing some cost that the opponent cannot avoid and is not willing to bear" (Morgan et al. 2008: xv).

6. For an overview of the attacks, see Tikk, Kaska, and Vihul (2010) and Davis (2007).

7. See also Kaspersky Lab's Global Research and Analysis Team (2013).

CHAPTER 6

1. Wang Pufeng (1995: 37).

2. These 48 incidents can be further broken down into short-term espionage, which China uses in 59.70% (40 of 67).

3. An example of this trend is found in Wang Pufeng (1995).

4. Note that overall, Murawiec (2004) is skeptical of the PLA approach and assesses there is a high probability of overextension and misjudging the efficacy of the approach.

CHAPTER 7

1. The centrality of information and the concepts of information warfare that connect precision strike and cyber operations is a major theme in Kaplan (2016: 21–38).

2. For an overview of the RMA both in American and Soviet thought, see Adamsky (2010).

3. For an overview of these earlier ideas about offsetting and how they relate to contemporary third offset initiatives, see Brimley (2014).

4. It is important to note that Boyd's work, especially his contributions to maneuver warfare and the integration of complex systems theory into the US Marine Corps produced divergent doctrine between US military services. Where the US Air Force and the US Army went toward "information dominance," the US Marine Corps embraced a view of systemic uncertainty that required rapid updating via the OODA loop construct.

5. For a discussion of Warden and the use of airpower in Iraq, see Hallion (1992) and Powell and Persico (1995: 460).

6. See also Pape (1996) and Ross (1993).

7. Examples of this work include: Adams (1998), Schwartau (1996), Arquilla and Ronfeldt (1996), Boulanger (1998), Denning (1999), Libicki (1995), and Molander and Riddile (1996).

8. On battlefield dynamics in the 1990s, see Bunker (1998).

9. Though cyber espionage was absent, in all likelihood some form of network mapping and penetration occurred prior to the degradation event.

10. This finding does not factor in the preliminary network mapping and intrusions that likely enabled the cyber degradation. Though the table lists the absence of cyber espionage as a necessary condition, the larger QCA process dropped two incidents based on the 80% threshold.

11. "Finding the target" is the title of Kagan's (2007) book on US defense transformation. The phrase is associated with the third major innovation, the integration of information technology to enable precision strike after the Cold War and showcased in the Gulf War.

12. For examples, see Kello (2013), Gary McGraw (2013), and Peterson (2013).

13. For examples, see Lindsay (2013), Rid (2011), Liff (2012), Betz (2012), and Rid and Buchanan (2015).

14. The cost estimate is for the munitions alone and does not include the sunk costs of ships, software, or personnel.

References

ABC. 2014. "NATO Websites Targeted in Attack Claimed by Ukrainian Hacker Group Cyber Berkut." *ABC*, 3/16/2014, accessed 5/2/2017, http://www.abc.net.au/news/2014-03-16/nato-websites-targeted-in-attack-claimed-by-ukrainian-hackers/5324362

Ablon, Lillian, Martin C. Libicki, and Andrea A. Golay. 2014. *Markets for Cybercrime Tools and Stolen Data: Hacker's Bazaar* (Santa Monica: RAND).

Abrahms, Max. 2006. "Why Terrorism Does Not Work. *International Security*, 31 (2): 42–78.

Abrahms, Max. 2012. "The Political Effectiveness of Terrorism Revisited." *Comparative Political Studies*, 45 (3): 366–393.

Acemoglu, Daron, and James A. Robinson. 2000. "Why Did the West Extend the Franchise? Democracy, Inequality, and Growth in Historical Perspective." *Quarterly Journal of Economics*, 115 (4): 1167–1199.

Acemoglu, Daron, and James A. Robinson. 2001. "A Theory of Political Transitions." *American Economic Review*: 938–963.

Adams, James. 1998. *The Next World War: Computers Are the Weapons and the Front Line Is Everywhere* (New York: Simon and Schuster).

Adamsky, Dima. 2010. *The Culture of Military Innovation: The Impact of Cultural Factors on the Revolution in Military Affairs in Russia, the US, and Israel* (Palo Alto: Stanford University Press).

Afinogenov, Gregory. 2013. "Andrei Ershov and the Soviet Information Age." *Kritika: Explorations in Russian and Eurasian History*, 14 (3): 561–584.

Aid, Matthew. 2015. "Prometheus Embattled: A Post-9/11 Report Card on the National Security Agency." In Loch K. Johnson (ed.), *The Essentials of Strategic Intelligence* (New York: Praeger).

Alexeeva, Lyudmila. 2013. "Vladimir Putin's Goal Is to Destroy Russian Civil Society." *The Guardian*, 5/24/2013, accessed 4/28/2017, https://www.theguardian.com/commentisfree/2013/may/24/vladimir-putin-goal-russian-civil-society

Alger, J. I. 1996. "Introduction." In W. Schwartau (ed.), *Information Warfare. Cyberterrorism: Protecting Your Personnel Security in the Electronic Age* (New York: Thunder's Mouth Press).

Alker, Hayward R. 1966. "The Long Road to International Relations Theory: Problems of Statistical Nonadditivity." *World Politics*, 18 (4): 623–655.

Alperovtich, Dmitri. 2016. "Bears in the Midst: Intrusion into the Democratic National Committee." Crowdstrike, 6/15/2016, accessed 5/2/2017, https://www.crowdstrike.com/blog/bears-midst-intrusion-democratic-national-committee/

Anderson, Elizabeth E. 1998. "The Security Dilemma and Covert Action: The Truman Years." *International Journal of Intelligence and CounterIntelligence*, 11 (4): 403–427.

Anderson, Nate. 2007. "Massive DDoS Attacks Target Estonia; Russia Accused." *Arstechnica*, 5/14/2007, accessed 4/22/2017, https://arstechnica.com/security/2007/05/massive-ddos-attacks-target-estonia-russia-accused/

Angwin, Julia, Charlie Savage, Jeff Larson, Henrik Moltke, Lisa Poitras, and James Risen. 2015. "AT&T Helped U.S. Spy on Internet on a Vast Scale." *New York Times*, 8/15/2015, accessed 7/23/2017, https://www.nytimes.com/2015/08/16/us/politics/att-helped-nsa-spy-on-an-array-of-internet-traffic.html

Applebaum, Jacob, Judith Horchert, and Christian Stocker. 2013. "Catalog Advertises NSA Toolbox." *Spiegel Online*, 12/29/2013, accessed 7/24/2017, http://www.spiegel.de/international/world/catalog-reveals-nsa-has-back-doors-for-numerous-devices-a-940994.html

Arquilla, John, and David Rondfeldt. 1996. *The Advent of Netwar* (Santa Monica: RAND).

Art, Robert J. 1980. "To What Ends Military Power?" *International Security*, 4 (4): 3–35.

Art, Robert J., and Patrick M. Cronin (eds.). 2003. *The United States and Coercive Diplomacy* (Washington: US Institute of Peace Press).

Axelrod, Robert. 1984. *The Evolution of Cooperation* (New York: Basic Books).

Axelrod, Robert, and Rumen Iliev. 2014. "Timing of Cyber Conflict." *Proceedings of the National Academy of Sciences*, 111 (4): 1298–1303.

BAE Systems. 2014. "The Snake Campaign." February 2014, accessed 5/2/2017, http://www.baesystems.com/en/cybersecurity/feature/the-snake-campaign

Baldwin, David A. 1985. *Economic Statecraft* (Princeton, NJ: Princeton University Press).

Bamford, James. 2015. "What @Snowden Told Me About the NSA's Cyberweapons." *Foreign Policy*, 9/29/2015, accessed 12/2/2017, http://foreignpolicy.com/2015/09/29/what-snowden-told-me-about-the-nsa-offensive-capabilities/.

Bartel, Charles. 2016. "Getting Gerasimov Right." *Military Review*, January/February: 30–38.

Baraniuk, Chris. 2015. "Could Russian Submarines Cut off the Internet?" *BBC*, 10/26/2015, accessed 3/28/2017, http://www.bbc.com/news/technology-34639148

BBC News. 2013. "Secret Talks Set Stage for Iran Nuclear Deal." *BBC News*, 11/25/2013, accessed 9/20/2017, http://www.bbc.com/news/world-middle-east-25086236

BBC News. 2014. "North Korea Threatens War on U.S. over Kim Jong-un Movie." *BBC News*, 6/26/2014, accessed 7/1/2017, http://www.bbc.com/news/world-asia-28014069

BBC News. 2016. "Iran Nuclear Deal: Key Details." *BBC News*, 1/16/2016, accessed 5/26/2017, http://www.bbc.com/news/world-middle-east-33521655

BBC News. 2017. "WannaCry Ransomware Cyber-Attacks Slow but Fears Remain." *BBC*, 5/15/2017, accessed 7/3/2017, http://www.bbc.com/news/technology-39920141.

Beaufre, Andre. 1963. *An Introduction of Strategy* (London: Faber and Faber, 1965 R.H. Barry translation).

Bennett, Cory. 2014. "Hackers Breach the Warsaw Stock Exchange." *The Hill*, October 2014, accessed 5/2/2017, http://thehill.com/policy/cybersecurity/221806-hackers-breach-the-warsaw-stock-exchange

Bennett, Scott D. 1998. "Integrating and Testing Models of Rivalry." *American Journal of Political Science*, 42 (4): 1200–1232.

Bergen, Peter. 2001. *Holy War Inc.* (New York: Free Press).

Betz, David. 2012. "Cyberpower in Strategic Affairs: Neither Unthinkable nor Blessed." *Journal of Strategic Studies*, 35 (5): 689–711.

Betz, David. 2015. *Carnage and Connectivity: Landmarks in the Decline of Conventional Military Power* (New York: Oxford University Press).

Biasini, Nick. 2016. "Connecting the Dots Reveals Crimeware Shake-Up." *Talso*, 7/7/2016, accessed 5/1/2017, http://blog.talosintelligence.com/2016/07/lurk-crimeware-connections.html

Biddle, Stephen. 2004. *Military Power: Explaining Victory and Defeat on Modern Battle* (Princeton, NJ: Princeton University Press).

Bijian, Z. 2005. China's "peaceful rise" to great-power status. *Foreign Affairs*, 18–24.

Bing, Chris. 2017a. "What We Know and Don't Know about a Rash of Middle East Mystery Attacks." *Cyberscoop*, 6/5/2017, accessed 6/9/2017, https://www.cyberscoop.com/know-dont-know-rash-middle-east-mystery-hacks/

Bing, Chris. 2017b. "How China's Cyber Command Is Being Built to Supersede Its U.S. Military Counterpart." *Cyberscoop*, 6/22/2017, accessed 7/7/2017, https://www.cyberscoop.com/china-ssf-cyber-command-strategic-support-force-pla-nsa-dod/

Bing, Chris. 2017c. "For Now, Many Conversations about Global 'Cyber Norms' Start with Beijing." *Cyberscoop*, 6/26/2017, accessed 7/23/2017, https://www.cyberscoop.com/competition-u-s-beijing-guiding-world-defines-cyber-norms/

Blainey, Geoffrey. 1973. *Causes of War* (New York: Free Press).

Blainey, Geoffrey. 1988. *Causes of War* (Simon and Schuster).

Blaker, James R., and Robert A. Manning. 1997. "Understanding the Revolution in Military Affairs: A Guide to America's 21st Century Defense." In *Defense Working Paper No. 3* (Washington, DC: Progressive Policy Institute).

Blechman, Barry M., and Stephan S. Kaplan. 1978. "Force without War: US." In *Armed Forces as a Political Instrument* (Washington, DC: Brookings Institution).

Bloomfield, Adrian. 2017. "War of Words over Bronze Soldier." *Telegraph*, 2/5/2017, accessed 4/25/2017, http://www.telegraph.co.uk/news/worldnews/1541641/War-of-words-over-bronze-soldier.html

Borghard, Erica, and Shawn Lonergan. 2017. "The Logic of Coercion in Cyberspace." *Security Studies*, 26 (3): 452–481.

Boschee, E., J. Lautenschlager, S. O'Brien, S. Shellman, J. Starz, and M. Ward. 2015. ICEWS coded event data. *Harvard Dataverse*, 10.

Boulanger, A. 1998. "Catapults and Grappling Hooks: The Tools and Technology of Information Warfare." *IBM Systems Journal*, 37 (1): 106–114.

Bowlby, Chris. 2015. "Vladimir Putin's Formative German Years." *BBC Magazine*, 3/27/2015, accessed 5/30/2017, http://www.bbc.com/news/magazine-32066222

Braithwaite, A. and Lemke, D. 2011. "Unpacking Escalation." *Conflict Management and Peace Science*, 28(2): 111–123.

Brands, Hal. 2015. *What Good Is Grand Strategy? Power and Purpose in American Statecraft from Harry S. Truman to George W. Bush* (Ithaca: Cornell University Press).

Brantly, Aaron F. 2016. *The Decision to Attack: Military and Intelligence Cyber Decision-Making* (Athens, GA: University of Georgia Press).

Brecher, Michael. 1993. *Crises in World Politics* (Oxford: Pergamon Press).

Brecher, Michael, and Jonathan Wilkenfeld. 2000. *A Study of Crisis* (Ann Arbor: University of Michigan Press).

Brecher, Michael, Patrick James, and Jonathan Wilkenfeld. 2000. "Escalation and War in the Twentieth Century." In John Vasquez (ed.), *What Do We Know about War*, (New York: Rowman and Littlefield): 7–53.

Brecher, Michael, Jonathan Wilkenfeld, Kyle Beardsley, Patrick James, and David Quinn 2016. *International Crisis Behavior Data Codebook, Version 11.* http://sites.duke.edu/icbdata/data-collections/

Brenner, Joel. 2015. "Correspondence: Debating the Chinese Cyber Threat." *International Security*, 40 (1): 191–195.

Brimley, Shawn. 2014. "Offset Strategies and Warfighting Regimes." *War on the Rocks*, 10/15/2014, accessed 6/3/2017, https://warontherocks.com/2014/10/offset-strategies-warfighting-regimes/

Broad, William J., and David E. Sanger. 2017. "U.S. Strategy to Hobble North Korea Was Hidden in Plain Sight." *New York Times*, 3/4/2017, accessed 5/6/2017, https://www.nytimes.com/2017/03/04/world/asia/left-of-launch-missile-defense.html?rref=collection%2Fbyline%2Fdavid-e.-sanger&mtrref=www.nytimes.com

Bryant, William D. 2016. *Resiliency in Future Cyber Combat*. Montgomery, AL: Air Force Research Institute Maxwell AFB United States.

Buchanan, Ben. 2017. *The Legend of Sophistication in Cyber Operations*. Belfer Center: Harvard Kennedy School.

Buchanan, Ben. 2016. *The Cybersecurity Dilemma: Hacking, Trust and Fear between Nations* (London, UK: Hurst Pubications).

Bunker, Robert J. 1998. *Five-dimensional (Cyber) Warfighting: Can the Army after Next Be Defeated through Complex Concepts and Technologies?* (Carlisle Barracks: US Army War College, Strategic Studies Institute).

Bunker, Robert J. 2002. "Battlespace Dynamics, Information Warfare to Network, and Bond-Relationship Targeting." *Small Wars and Insurgencies*, 13 (2): 97–108.

Business Report Staff. 2012. "Clarke: China Has Already Hacked Every Major U.S. Company." *Business Report*, 3/28/2012, accessed 6/6/2017, https://www.businessreport.com/article/clarke-china-has-already-hacked-every-major-u-s-company

Byman, Daniel, and Matthew Waxman. 2000. "Kosovo and the Great Air Power Debate." *International Security*, 24 (4): 5–38.

Byman, Daniel, and Matthew Waxman. 2002. *The Dynamics of Coercion* (New York, NY: Cambridge University Press).

Byman, Daniel L. 2006. "Do Targeted Killings Work?" *Foreign Affairs*, 85 (2): 17–30.

Byman, Daniel L., and Mathew C. Waxman. 2000. "Kosovo and the Great Air Power Debate" *International Security*, 24 (4): 5–38.

Cable, James. 1981. "The Useful Art of International Relations." *International Affairs (Royal Institute of International Affairs 1944–)*, 57 (2): 301–314.

Cable, James. 2016. *Gunboat Diplomacy, 1919–79: Political Applications of Limited Naval Force* (New York: Springer).

Calamur, Krishnadev. 2017. "Putin Says 'Patriotic Hackers' May Have Targeted US Election." *The Atlantic*, 6/1/2017, accessed 8/2/2017, https://www.theatlantic.com/news/archive/2017/06/putin-russia-us-election/528825/

Campbell, Brian. 2001. "Diplomacy in the Roman World (c. 500 BC–AD 235)." *Diplomacy and Statecraft*, 12 (1): 1–22.

Carson, Austin. 2016. "Facing Off and Saving Face: Covert Intervention and Escalation Management in the Korean War." *International Organization*, 70 (1): 103–131.

Carson, Austin. 2017. "Obama Used Covert Retaliation to Russian Election Meddling." *Washington Post: The Monkey Cage*, 6/29/2017, accessed 7/7/2017, https://www.washingtonpost.com/news/monkey-cage/wp/2017/06/29/obama-used-covert-retaliation-in-response-to-russian-election-meddling-heres-why/?utm_term=.2efd5d247c1c

Carson, A., and K. Yarhi-Milo. 2017. "Covert Communication: The Intelligibility and Credibility of Signaling in Secret." *Security Studies*, 26 (1): 124–156.

Carr, Jeffrey. 2013. "RBN Connection to Kaspersky's Red October Espionage Network." *Digital Dao*, 1/2013, accessed 5/2/2017, http://jeffreycarr.blogspot.com/2013/01/rbn-connection-to-kasperskys-red.html

Carr, Jeffrey. 2015. "Cyber Berkut and Anonymous Ukraine: Coopted Hacktivists and Accidental Comedians." *Digital Dao*, 3/15/2015, accessed 5/2/2017, http://jeffreycarr.blogspot.com/2014/03/cyber-berkut-and-anonymous-ukraine-co.html.

Castex, Rauol. 1937. *Strategic Theories* (Annapolis: Naval Institute Press, 2017 Eugenia Kiesling 2017 translation).

Castle, Stephen. 2013. "Report of U.S. Spying Angers European Allies." *New York Times*, 6/30/2013, accessed 6/3/2017, http://www.nytimes.com/2013/07/01/world/europe/europeans-angered-by-report-of-us-spying.html

Chairman of the Joint Chiefs of Staff. 2017. JP 3-0, Operations (Arlington: U.S. Department of the Defense), I–13.

Chalfant, Morgan. 2017. "Lawmakers Fear U.S. Has Fallen behind in Cyber Warfare." *The Hill*, 3/5/2017, accessed 5/5/2017, http://thehill.com/policy/cybersecurity/322313-lawmakers-fear-us-has-fallen-behind-in-cyber-warfare

Chan, Steve. 2003. "Explaining War Termination: A Boolean Analysis of Causes." *Journal of Peace Research*, 40 (1): 49–66.

Cheng, Dean. 2016. *Cyber Dragon, Inside China's Information Warfare and Cyber Operations* (Santa Barbara: Praeger).

Chenoweth, Erica, and Maria Stephan. 2011. *Why Civil Resistance Works: The Strategic Logic of Nonviolent Conflict* (New York: Columbia University Press).

Chew, Jonathan. 2015. "Chinese Hackers Targeted United Airlines." *Fortune*, 6/29/2015, accessed 6/7/2017, http://fortune.com/2015/07/29/chinese-hackers-targeted-united-airlines/

Choucri, N. 2012. *Cyberpolitics in International Relations* (Cambridge: MIT Press).

Chun, Lin. 2014. "What Is China's Comparative Advantage?" *The Chinese Economy*, (36) 2: 3–20.

Clark, Colin. 2016. "'It Sucks to Be ISIL': U.S. Deploys 'Cyber Bombs,' Says DipSecDef." *Breaking Defense*, 4/12/2016, http://breakingdefense.com/2016/04/it-sucks-to-be-isil-us-deploys-cyber-bombs-says-depsecdef/

Clark, Wesley, and Peter L. Levin. 2009. "Securing the Information Highway: How to Enhance the United States Electronic Defenses." *Foreign Affairs*, 88 (6): 2–10.

Clarke, Richard A., and Robert K. Knake. 2010. *Cyber War: The Next Threat to National Security and What to Do About It* (New York: Harper Collins).

Clayton, Mark. 2014. "Ukraine Election Narrowly Avoided 'Wanton Destruction' from Hackers." *Christian Science Monitor*, 6/17/2014, accessed 5/2/2017, http://www.csmonitor.com/World/Passcode/2014/0617/Ukraine-election-narrowly-avoided-wanton-destruction-from-hackers-video

Colaresi, Michael. 2001. "Shocks to the System: Great Power Rivalries and the Leadership Long Cycle." *Journal of Conflict Resolution*, 45 (5): 569–593.

Colaresi, Michael P., and William R. Thompson. 2002. "Hot Spots or Hot Hands? Serial Crisis Behavior, Escalating Risks, and Rivalry." *Journal of Politics*, 64 (4): 1175–1198.

Collins, Ben, Kevin Poulson, and Spencer Ackerman. 2017. "Russia's Facebook Fake News Could Have Reached 70 Million Americans." *Daily Beast*, 9/8/2017, accessed 10/1/2017, http://www.thedailybeast.com/russias-facebook-fake-news-could-have-reached-70-million-americans?source=twitter&via=mobile

Constantin, Lucian. 2015a. "Fanny Superworm Uses Decoys and Cloaking Techniques, and Probably Spawned Stuxnet." *PCWorld*, 2/17/2015, accessed 7/25/2017, http://www.pcworld.com/article/2885192/fanny-superworm-likely-the-precursor-to-stuxnet.html

Constantin, Lucian. 2015b. "Source Code Reveals Link between NSA and Reign Cyberespionage Malware." *PCWorld*, 1/27/2015, accessed 7/7/2017, http://www.pcworld.com/article/2876112/link-between-nsa-and-regin-cyberespionage-malware-becomes-clearer.html

Constantin, Lucian. 2015c. "The NSA Not Only Creates, but Also Hijacks, Malware with Quantambot." *ComputerWorld*, 1/19/2015, accessed 5/6/2017, http://www.computerworld.com/article/2871687/the-nsa-not-only-creates-but-also-hijacks-malware-with-quantumbot.html

Cooney, Michael. 2008. "Taskforce Seizes $76 Million in Counterfeit Cisco Network Hardware." *Network World*, 2/29/2008, accessed 5/26/2017, http://www.networkworld.com/article/2237296/security/taskforce-seizes--76-million-in-counterfeit-cisco-network-hardware.html

Craig, Anthony, and Brandon Valeriano. 2016. "Reacting to Cyber Threats: Protection and Security in the Digital Age." *Global Security and Intelligence Studies*, 1 (2): 4.

Creemer, Rogier. 2016. "National Cyberspace Security Strategy." *China Copyright and Media*, 12/27/2016, accessed 3/4/2017, https://chinacopyrightandmedia.wordpress.com/2016/12/27/national-cyberspace-security-strategy/

Cronin, Blaise, and Holly Crawford. 1999. "Information Warfare: Its Application in Military and Civilian Contexts." *Information Society*, 15 (4): 257–263.

CrowdStrike. 2015. "2015 Global Threat Report." Accessed 7/7/2017, https://go.crowdstrike.com/rs/281-OBQ-266/images/15GlobalThreatReport.pdf

CrowdStrike. 2017. "Use of Fancy Bear Android Malware in Tracking of Ukrainian Field Artillery Units." 3/23/2017, accessed 5/2/017, https://www.crowdstrike.com/resources/reports/idc-vendor-profile-crowdstrike-2/

Cyber Defense. 2015. "Reign and Qwerty Keylogger Are Linked with Five Eyes Intelligence." *Cyber Defense Magazine*, 1/30/2015, accessed 7/9/2017, http://www.cyberdefensemagazine.com/regin-and-qwerty-keylogger-are-linked-with-five-eyes-intelligence/

Danchev, Dancho. 2008. "300 Lithuanian Sites Hacked by Russian Hackers." *ZDNet*, 7/2/2008, accessed 4/27/2017, http://www.zdnet.com/article/300-lithuanian-sites-hacked-by-russian-hackers/

David, Steven. 2002. "Fatal Choices: Israel's Policy of Targeted Killing." *Mideast Security and Policy Studies* 51 (September): 1–25.

Davis, Joshua. 2007. "Hackers Take Down the Most Wired Country in Europe" *Wired*, 8/21/2007, accessed 4/27/2017, http://archive.wired.com/politics/security/magazine/15-09/ff_estonia?currentPage=all

Davis, Paul K. 2001. *Effects Based Operations: A Grand Challenge for the Analytical Community* (Santa Monica: RAND Corporation).

De Carbonnel, Alissa. 2013. "Hackers for Hire: Ex-Soviet Tech Geeks Play Outsized Role in Global Cyber Crime." *NBCNews.com/Technology*, 8/22/2013, accessed 2/3/2017, http://www.nbcnews.com/technology/hackers-hire-ex-soviet-tech-geeks-play-outsized-role-global-6C10981346

Demchak, Chris. 2011. *Wars of Disruption and Resilience* (Athens: University of Georgia Press).

Demchak, Chris C., and Peter Dombrowski. 2011. "Rise of a Cybered Westphalian Age." Strategic Studies Quarterly, 5 (1): 31–62.

De Mesquita, Bruce B., Morrow, James D. Morrow, and Ethan R. Zorick. 1997. "Capabilities, Perception, and Escalation." *American Political Science Review*, 91 (1): 15–27.

Denning, Dorothy E. 1999. *Information Warfare and Security* (Reading: Addison-Wesley).

Department of Defense. 2003. "Report of the Defense Science Board Task Force on Discriminate Use of Force," 7/2003, accessed 7/3/2017, http://www.acq.osd.mil/dsb/reports/2000s/ADA429181.pdf

Department of Defense. 2012. "Joint Operational Access Concept." 1/17/2012, accessed 7/7/2017, https://www.defense.gov/Portals/1/Documents/pubs/JOAC_Jan%202012_Signed.pdf

Department of Defense. 2013. *Air-Sea Battle: Service Collaboration to Address Anti-Access & Area Denial Challenges* (Alexandria: Air-Sea Battle Office).

Department of Defense. 2017. "Annual Report to Congress: Military and Security Developments Involving the People's Republic of China." Accessed 7/25/2017, https://www.defense.gov/Portals/1/Documents/pubs/2017_China_Military_Power_Report.PDF?source=GovDelivery&utm_content=bufferfa84f&utm_medium=social&utm_source=twitter.com&utm_campaign=buffer

Department of Defense Comptroller. 2014. *Program Acquisition Cost by Weapon System* (Arlington: Department of Defense): 5–14.

Department of Justice. 2014. "U.S. Charges Five Chinese Military Hackers for Cyber Espionage against U.S. Corporations and a Labor Organization for Commercial Advantage." 5/19/2014, accessed 5/23/2017, https://www.justice.gov/opa/pr/us-charges-five-chinese-military-hackers-cyber-espionage-against-us-corporations-and-labor

Der Spiegel. 2014. "Targeting Huawei: NSA Spied on Chinese Government and Networking Firm." *Spiegel Online*, 3/22/2014, accessed 5/23/2017, http://www.spiegel.de/international/world/nsa-spied-on-chinese-government-and-networking-firm-huawei-a-960199.html

Diamond, Larry. 2010. "Liberation Technology." *Journal of Democracy*, 21 (3): 69–83.

Farwell, James P., and Rafal Rohozinski. 2011. "Stuxnet and the Future of Cyber War." *Survival*, 53 (1): 23–40.

Diehl Paul F., and Gary Goertz. 2001. *War and Peace in International Rivalry* (Ann Arbor: University of Michigan Press).

Douhet, Giulio. 1921. *The Command of the Air* (Maxwell: Center for Air Force History, 1941; Dino Ferrari trans., publication date 1983).

Downes, Alexander B., and Todd S. Sechser. 2012. "The Illusion of Democratic Credibility." *International Organization*, 66 (3): 457–489.

Drass, Kriss A., and Charles C. Ragin. 1992. *Qualitative Comparative Analysis 3.0.* (Evanston, IL: Institute for Policy Research, Northwestern University).

Dui Hua. 2010. "Tiananmen Sanctions: 20 Years and Counting." *Dui Hua*, 1/29/2010, accessed 5/23/2017, http://duihua.org/wp/?p=2662

Durden, Tyler. 2015. "Hacked E-mails Expose George Soros as Ukraine Puppet-Master." *Zero Hedge*, 6/2/2015, accessed 5/2/2017, http://www.zerohedge.com/news/2015-06-01/hacked-emails-expose-george-soros-ukraine-puppet-master

Earle, Earle M. 1943. *Makers of Modern Strategy: Military Thought from Machiavelli to Hitler.* (Princeton: Princeton University Press).

Economist, The. 2007. "A Walk on the Dark Side." *The Economist*, 8/31/2007, accessed 3/26/2017, http://www.economist.com/node/9723768

Emerson, John B. 2015. "Exposing Russian Disinformation." *Atlantic Council*, 6/29/2015, accessed 6/2/2017, http://www.atlanticcouncil.org/blogs/ukrainealert/exposing-russian-disinformation

Engel, Richard, and Aggelos Petropoulos. 2016. "Who Are the Russian-Backed Hackers Attacking the U.S. Political System?" *NBC News*, 9/18/2016, accessed 5/2/2017, http://www.nbcnews.com/tech/internet/who-are-russian-backed-hackers-attacking-u-s-political-system-n649966

Erkman, Keith. 2014. *Winning the Peace through Cost Imposition* (Washington: Brookings Institute Press).

Espiner, Tom. 2007. "Estonia's CTO Speaks Out on Cyberattacks" *ZDNet*, 10/24/2007, accessed 4/26/2017, http://www.zdnet.com/article/estonias-cto-speaks-out-on-cyberattacks/;

European Community. 2009. "eGovernment in Estonia: Factsheets." Accessed 4/25/2017, http://ec.europa.eu/idabc/servlets/Docd7a7.pdf?id=32608

Falliere, Nicholas, Liam O Murchu, and Eric Chen. 2011. "W32.Stuxnet Dossier." *Symantec*, 2/2011, accessed 7/5/2017, https://www.symantec.com/content/en/us/enterprise/media/security_response/whitepapers/w32_stuxnet_dossier.pdf

Farrell, Henry. 2017. "Cyber Criminals Have Just Mounted a Massive World Wide Attack. Here's How NSA Secrets Helped Them." *Washington Post*, 5/12/2017, accessed 7/3/2017, https://www.washingtonpost.com/news/monkey-cage/wp/2017/05/12/cyber-criminals-have-just-mounted-a-massive-worldwide-attack-heres-how-nsa-secrets-helped-them/?utm_term=.bf81ee4c22e0

Farwell, James P., and Rafal Rohozinski. 2011. "Stuxnet and the Future of Cyber War." *Survival*, 53 (1): 23–40.

Farwell, James P., and Rafal Rohozinski. 2012. "The New Reality of Cyber War." *Survival*, 54 (4): 107–120.

Fearon, James. 1992. "Threats to Use Force: Costly Signals and Bargaining in International Crises." Dissertation. (Berkley: University of California Berkeley).

Fearon, James D. 1994. "Domestic Political Audiences and the Escalation of International Disputes." *American Political Science Review*, 88 (3): 577–592.

Fearon, James D. 1995. "Rationalist Expectations for War." *International Organization*, 49 (3): 379–414.

Fearon, James D. 1997. "Signaling Foreign Policy Interests Tying Hands versus Sinking Costs." *Journal of Conflict Resolution*, 41 (1): 68–90.

Feaver, Peter. 1998. "Blowback: Information Warfare and the Dynamics of Coercion." *Security Studies*, 7 (4): 88–120.

Fidler, David P. 2017. "U.S. Cyber Diplomacy Requires More Than an Office." *Council on Foreign Relations*, 7/26/2017, accessed 7/29/2017, https://www.cfr.org/blog-post/ keeping-cyber-coordinators-office-state-will-not-improve-us-cyber-diplomacy

Fife, Robert, and Steven Chase. 2017. "Canada and China Strike a Corporate Hacking Deal." *Globe and Mail*, 6/25/2017, accessed 7/4/2017, https://beta.theglobeandmail.com/news/politics/ china-agrees-to-stop-conducting-state-sponsored-cyberattacks-targeting-canadian-private-sector/article35459914/?ref=https://www.theglobeandmail.com&service=mobile&utm_content=buffercod6c&utm_medium=social&utm_source=twitter.com&utm_campaign=buffer

Finn, Peter. 2007. "Cyber Assault on Estonia Typify a New Baltic Tactic." *Washington Post*, 5/18/ 2007, accessed 4/25/2017, http://www.washingtonpost.com/wp-dyn/content/article/2007/ 05/18/AR2007051802122.html

FireEye iSIGHT Intelligence. 2016. "Red Line Drawn: China Recalculates Its Use of Cyber Espionage." *FireEye*, 6/20/2016, accessed 5/23/2017, https://www.fireeye.com/blog/threat-research/2016/06/red-line-drawn-china-espionage.html

FireEye Special Report. 2015. "HAMMERTOSS: Stealthy Tactics Define Russian Cyber Threat Group." *FireEye*, accessed 5/1/2017, https://www2.fireeye.com/rs/848-DID-242/images/rpt-apt29-hammertoss.pdf

Flynn, George. 2012. "Lt. Gen. Flynn's Media Briefing on the Joint Operational Access Concept (Joac)." Media interview (Washington, DC: Joint Chiefs of Staff).

Fox-Brewster, Thomas. 2016. "Shadow Brokers Give NSA Halloween Surprise with Leak of Hacked Servers." *Forbes*, 10/31/2016, accessed 7/2/2017, https://www.forbes.com/ sites/thomasbrewster/2016/10/31/shadow-brokers-halloween-nsa-leak-hacked-domains/ #7744b1043f43

Foxman, Simone. 2013. "Recent Cyberattacks Could Be Part of a Chinese Military Strategy Started Nearly 20 Years Ago." *Quartz*, 3/14/2013, accessed 5/22/2017, https://qz.com/62434/ recent-cyberattacks-could-be-part-of-a-chinese-military-strategy-started-nearly-20-years-ago/

Frankel, Matt. 2010. "The ABCs of HVT: Key Lessons from High Value Targeting Campaigns against Insurgents and Terrorists." *Studies in Conflict and Terrorism*, 34 (1): 17–30.

Fravel, M. Trevor. 2010. "International Relations Theory and China's Rise: Assessing China's Potential for Territorial Expansion." *International Studies Review*, 12 (4): 505–532.

Freedman, L. 2015. *Strategy: A history*. (Oxford: Oxford University Press).

Fried, Ina. 2008. "Report: Russia Passes China to Become Malware Leader." *CNET News*, 2/2/ 2008, accessed 5/6/2017, http://news.cnet.com/8301-13860_3-9875663-56.html

Frizell, Sam. 2014. "White House Computer Networks Hacked." *Time*, 10/29/2014, accessed 5/ 2/2017, http://time.com/3545542/white-house-hackers-breached/

Gallagher, Sean. 2015. "Seven Years of Malware Linked to Russian State-Backed Cyber Espionage." *Arstechnica*, 9/17/2015, accessed 5/2/2017, https://arstechnica.com/security/2015/09/seven-years-of-malware-linked-to-russian-state-backed-cyberespionage/

Gallagher, Sean. 2014. "Photos of an NSA 'Upgrade' Factory Show Cisco Router Getting Implant." *Arstechnica*, 5/14/2014, accessed 7/23/2017, https://arstechnica.com/tech-policy/2014/05/photos-of-an-nsa-upgrade-factory-show-cisco-router-getting-implant/

Gallagher, Sean. 2015. "NSA Secretly Hijacked Existing Malware to Spy on North Korea, Others." *Arstechnica*, 1/18/2015, accessed 7/2/2017, https://arstechnica.com/information-technology/2015/01/nsa-secretly-hijacked-existing-malware-to-spy-on-n-korea-others/

Gartzke, Erik. 2013. "The Myth of Cyberwar: Bringing War on the Internet Back Down to Earth." *International Security*, 38 (2): 41–73.

Gartzke, Erik. 2014. "Making Sense of Cyberwar." *Policy Brief, Belfer Center for Science and International Affairs,* (Cambridge, MA: Harvard Kennedy School), January: 41–73.

Gartzke, Erik, and Jon R. Lindsay. 2015. "Weaving Tangled Webs: Offense, Defense, and Deception in Cyberspace." *Security Studies*, 24 (2): 316–348.

Gartzke, Erik, and Jon R. Lindsay. 2017a. "Coercion through the Cyberspace: The Stability-Instability Paradox Revisited." In Kelly Greenhill and Peter Krause (eds.), *The Power to Hurt in the Modern World* (New York, NY: Oxford University Press).

Gartzke, Erik, and Jon R. Lindsay. 2017b. "Thermonuclear Cyberwar." *Journal of Cybersecurity*, 3 (1): 37–48.

Geller, Daniel S. 1990. "Nuclear Weapons, Deterrence, and Crisis Escalation." *Journal of Conflict Resolution*, 34 (2): 291–310.

Geller, Daniel S. 1993. "Power Differentials and War in Rival Dyads." *International Studies Quarterly*, 37 (2): 173–193.

Geller, Daniel S. 2000. "Material Capabilities: Power and International Conflict." In John A. Vasquez (ed)., *What Do We Know about War?* (New York: Rowman and Littlefield): 259–277.

Gellman, Barton, and Jerry Markon. 2013. "Edward Snowden Says Motive behind Leaks Was to Expose 'Surveillance State'." *Washington Post*, 6/10/2013, accessed 7/4/2017, https://www.washingtonpost.com/politics/edward-snowden-says-motive-behind-leaks-was-to-expose-surveillance-state/2013/06/09/aa3f0804-d13b-11e2-a73e-826d299ff459_story.html?utm_term=.6f41f0818c1d

Gellman, Barton, and Ellen Nakashima. 2013. "U.S. Spy Agencies Mounted 231 Offensive Cyber Operations in 2011." *Washington Post*, 8/30/2013, accessed 7/7/2017, https://www.washingtonpost.com/world/national-security/us-spy-agencies-mounted-231-offensive-cyber-operations-in-2011-documents-show/2013/08/30/d090a6ae-119e-11e3-b4cb-fd7ce041d814_story.html?utm_term=.e8aebc43ecob

George, Alexander L. 1991. *Forceful Persuasion: Coercive Diplomacy as an Alternative to War* (Washington: US Institute of Peace Press).

George, Alexander L. 2009. "Coercive Diplomacy." In Robert Art and Kenneth Waltz (eds.), *The Use of Force* (New York: Rowman and Littlefield).

George, Alexander L., and Richard Smoke. 1974. *Deterrence in American Foreign Policy: Theory and Practice* (New York: Columbia University Press).

George, A. L., Hall, D. K. and Simons, W. F. 1971. *The Limits of Coercive Diplomacy: Laos, Cuba, Vietnam.* (New York: Little Brown).

George, Alexander, and William F. Simons. 1994. *The Limits of Coercive Diplomacy* (Boulder: Westview Press).

Gerasimov, Valery. 2013. "The Value of Scientific Prediction." *Military-Industrial Kurier*, 6/7/2013, accessed 4/25/2017, https://inmoscowsshadows.wordpress.com/2014/07/06/the-gerasimov-doctrine-and-russian-non-linear-war/

Gertler, Jeremiah. 2014. *F-35 Joint Strike Fighter (JSF) Program* (Washington: Congressional Research Services).

Giles, Kier. 2015a. "Putin's Troll Factories." *Chatham House*, 71 (4), accessed 5/2/2017, https://www.chathamhouse.org/publication/twt/putins-troll-factories

Giles, Kier. 2015b. "Russia and Its Neighbours: Old Attitudes, New Capabilities." In Kenneth Geers (ed.), *Cyber War in Perspective: Russian Aggression against Ukraine* (Tallinn: NATO Cooperative Cyber Defence Center of Excellence): 19–28.

Gilli, Andrea, and Mauro Gilli. 2017. "American Military-Technological Superiority in the Age of Cyber Espionage, Globalization and of the Rise of China." Manuscript under review.

Glantz, David M. 1988. *Surprise and Maskirovka in Contemporary* War (Leavenworth: Soviet Army Studies Office).

Glantz, David M. 2016. "A Deception Primer for the Fledging Red Army." *War on the Rocks*, 5/20/2016, accessed 5/1/2017, https://warontherocks.com/2016/05/a-deception-primer-for-the-fledgling-red-army/

Glass, Andrew. 2011. "House Sanctions Post-Tiananmen China, June 29, 1989." *Politico*, 6/28/2011, accessed 5/23/2017, http://www.politico.com/story/2011/06/house-sanctions-post-tiananmen-china-june-29-1989-057928

Glaser, Charles L., and Chairn Kaufmann. 1998. "What Is the Offense-Defense Balance and How Can We Measure It?" *International Security*, 22 (4): 44–82.

Glenny, Misha. 2009. *McMafia: Through the Global Criminal Underworld* (New York: Vintage Books).

Gochman, Charles S., and Russell J. Leng. 1983. "Realpolitik and the Road to War: An Analysis of Attributes and Behavior." *International Studies Quarterly*, 27 (1): 97–120.

Goddard, Stacie E. 2009. *Indivisible Territory and the Politics of Legitimacy: Jerusalem and Northern Ireland* (New York, NY: Cambridge University Press).

Goertz, Gary, and Paul E. Diehl. 1993. "Enduring Rivalries: Theoretical Constructs and Empirical Patterns." *International Studies Quarterly*, 37 (2): 147–172.

Goertz, Gary, and Paul E. Diehl. 1995. "The Initiation and Termination of Enduring Rivalries: The Impact of Political Shocks." *American Journal of Political Science*, 39 (1): 30–53.

Goldgeier, James, and Philip Tetlock. 2001. "Psychology and International Relations." *Annual Review of Political Science*, 4 (1): 67–92.

Gomez, Miguel Alberto N. 2016. "Arming Cyberspace: The Militarization of a Virtual Domain." *Global Security and Intelligence Studies*, 1 (2): 5.

Goodin, Dan. 2017. "Found: Crash Override Malware That Triggered Ukrainian Power Outage." *Arstechnica*, 6/12/2017, accessed 7/7/2017, https://arstechnica.com/security/2017/06/crash-override-malware-may-sabotage-electric-grids-but-its-no-stuxnet/

Goodin, Dan. 2015. "How 'Omnipotent' Hackers Tied to NSA Hid for 14 years—And Were Found at Last." *Arstechnica*, 2/16/2015, accessed 7/24/2017, https://arstechnica.com/information-technology/2015/02/how-omnipotent-hackers-tied-to-the-nsa-hid-for-14-years-and-were-found-at-last/.

Goodman, Will. 2010. "Cyber Deterrence." *Strategic Studies*. 102.

Graff, Garret M. 2017. "Inside the Hunt for Russia's Most Notorious Hacker." *Wired*, 3/21/2017, accessed 5/2/2017, https://www.wired.com/2017/03/russian-hacker-spy-botnet/.

Gray, Colin. 2011. *The Strategy Bridge: A Theory of Practice*. (New York: Oxford University Press).

Gray, Ian. 2016. "Hacking the Elections" *Flashpoint*, 11/7/2016, accessed 5/1/2017, https://www.flashpoint-intel.com/blog/cybercrime/hacking-the-elections/.

GReAT. 2013. "Red October Diplomatic Cyber Attacks Investigation." *Secure List*, 1/14/2013, accessed 5/3/2017, https://securelist.com/analysis/publications/36740/red-october-diplomatic-cyber-attacks-investigation/

GReAT. 2015a. "Equation: The Death Star of Malware Galaxy." *SecureList*, 2/16/2015, accessed 7/9/2017, https://securelist.com/equation-the-death-star-of-malware-galaxy/68750/

GReAT. 2015b. "A Fanny Equation: 'I Am Your Father, Stuxnet.'" *SecureList*, 2/17/2015b, accessed 7/23/2017, https://securelist.com/blog/research/68787/a-fanny-equation-i-am-your-father-stuxnet/

Green, D. P., P. M. Aronow, and M. C. McGrath. 2013. "Field Experiments and the Study of Voter Turnout." *Journal of Elections, Public Opinion and Parties*, 23: 27–48.

Greenberg, Andy. 2017a. "How an Entire Nation Became Russia' Test Lab for Cyberwar." *Wired*, 6/20/2017, accessed 7/2/2017, https://www.wired.com/story/russian-hackers-attack-ukraine/

Greenberg, Andy. 2017b. "Russia Hacked 'Older' Republican Emails, FBI Director Says." *Wired*, 1/10/2017, accessed 7/4/2017, https://www.wired.com/2017/01/russia-hacked-older-republican-emails-fbi-director-says/

Greenwald, Glenn, Ewen MacAskill, and Laura Poitras. 2013. "Edward Snowden: The Whistleblower behind the NSA Surveillance Revelations." *The Guardian*, 6/11/2013, accessed 7/6/2017, https://www.theguardian.com/world/2013/jun/09/edward-snowden-nsa-whistleblower-surveillance

Gross, Michael L., Daphna Canetti, and Dana R. Vashdi. 2017. "Cyberterrorism: Its Effects on Psychological Well-Being, Public Confidence and Political Attitudes." *Journal of Cybersecurity* 3 (1): 49–58.

Guangqian, Peng, and Yao Youzhi (eds.). 2001. *Science of Strategy* (Beijing: Department of Strategic Research, Military Science Press).

Guangqian, Peng, and Yao Youzhi (eds.). 2005. *The Science of Military Strategy* (Beijing: Military Science Publishing House).

Haarmo, Eeva. 2017. "Interview: F-Secure's Mikko Hypponen on the Nordics, Russia, and the Internet of Insecure Things." *Computer Weekly*, 4/6/2017, accessed 5/17/2017, http://www.computerweekly.com/news/450416368/Interview-F-Secures-Mikko-Hyppoenen-on-the-Nordics-Russia-and-the-internet-of-insecure-things

Hackett, Robert. 2015. "Did Monkey Video Help Russian Hackers Access President Obama's E-mail?" *Fortune*, 4/27/2015, accessed 5/2/2017: http://fortune.com/2015/04/27/president-obama-email-hackers/

Hacquebord, Feike. 2015a. "Operation Pawn Storm Ramps Up Its Activities, Targets NATO, White House." *Trend Micro*, 8/16/2015, accessed 6/6/2017, http://blog.trendmicro.com/trendlabs-security-intelligence/operation-pawn-storm-ramps-up-its-activities-targets-nato-white-house/

Hacquebord, Feike. 2015b. "Pawn Storm's Domestic Spying Campaign Revealed; Ukraine and US Top Global Targets." *Trend Micro*, 8/18/2015, accessed 7/1/2017, http://blog.

trendmicro.com/trendlabs-security-intelligence/pawn-storms-domestic-spying-campaign-revealed-ukraine-and-us-top-global-targets/

Hallion, Richard. 1992. *Storm over Iraq: Airpower and the Gulf War* (Washington, DC: Smithsonian Institution Press).

Hamilton, David. 2008. "Lithuanian Sites Hacked by Russians." *Whir*, 7/7/2008, accessed 4/29/2017, http://www.thewhir.com/web-hosting-news/lithuanian-sites-hacked-by-russians

Hannas, William C., James Mulvenon, and Anna Puglisi. 2013. *Chinese Industrial Espionage: Technology Acquisition and Military Modernization* (New York: Routledge).

Haun, Phil. 2015. *Coercion, Survival, and War: Why Weak States Resist the United States* (Pal Alto: Stanford University Press).

Healey, Jason and Karl Grindal (ed.). 2013. *A Fierce Domain: Conflict in Cyberspace, 1986 to 2012.* (New York, NY: Cyber Conflict Studies Association).

Healey, Jason. 2016. "Winning and Losing in Cyberspace." *2016 8th Annual Conference on Cyber Conflict* (Tallinn, Estonia).

Healy, Patrick, David E. Sanger, and Maggie Haberman. "Donald Trump Find Improbable Ally in Wikileaks." *New York Times*, 10/12/2016, accessed 5/5/2017, https://www.nytimes.com/2016/10/13/us/politics/wikileaks-hillary-clinton-emails.html?mcubz=3

Helm, Toby, Daniel Boffey, and Nick Hopkins. "Snowden Spy Row Grows as US Is Accused of Hacking China." *The Guardian*, 6/22/2013, accessed 5/22/2017, https://www.theguardian.com/world/2013/jun/22/edward-snowden-us-china

Hendrix, Cullen. 2017. "The Streetlight Effect in Climate Change Research on Africa." *Global Environmental Change*, 43: 137–147.

Hensel, Paul R. 2001. "Contentious Issues and World Politics: The Management of Territorial Claims in the Americas, 1816–1992." *International Studies Quarterly*, 45 (1): 81–109.

Heuser, B. 2010. *The evolution of strategy: thinking war from antiquity to the present.* (Cambridge: Cambridge University Press).

Hjort, N. L., and G. Claeskens. 2006. "Focused Information Criteria and Model Averaging for the Cox Hazard Regression Model." *Journal of the American Statistical Association*, 101 (476): 1449–1464.

Hogg, David. 2002. "Rapid Decisive Operations: The Search for the Holy Grail of Joint Warfighting." In Williamson Murray (ed.), *Transformation Concepts for National Security in the 21st Century* (Carlisle: Strategic Studies Institute).

Holden, Dan. 2013. "Estonia, Six Years Later." *Arbor Networks*, 5/16/2013, accessed 4/25/2017, https://www.arbornetworks.com/blog/asert/estonia-six-years-later/

Holsti, Ole R. 1972. *Crisis Escalation War* (McGill-Queen's Press-MQUP).

Holsti, Ole R. 1989. "Crisis Decision Making." In Philip Tetlock, Jo Husbands, Robert Jervis, Paul Stern, and Charles Tilly (eds.), *Behavior, Society, and Nuclear War* (New York: International Atomic Energy Agency's International Nulcear Information System).

Horowitz, Michael, and Dan Reiter. 2001. "When Does Aerial Bombing Work? Quantitative Empirical Tests, 1917–1999." *Journal of Conflict Resolution*, 45 (2): 147–173.

Horowitz, Michael. 2010. *The Diffusion of Military Power: Causes and Consequences for International Politics* (Princeton: Princeton University Press).

Houqing, W., and Z. Xingye. 2000. *Zhanyi Xue* (The science of campaigns). (Beijing: National Defense University).

House of Representatives, Committee on Armed Services. 2014. *Rebalancing to the Asia-Pacific Region: Examining Its Implementation.* 1/23/2014, accessed 7/24/2017, https://armedservices.house.gov/legislation/hearings/rebalancing-asia-pacific-region-examining-its-implementation

Howard, Rick. 2009. "The Russian Business Network: Rise and Fall of a Criminal ISP." In *Cyber Fraud: Tactics, Techniques, and Procedures* (Boca Raton: Auerbach Publications).

Hudson, John. 2012. "Here's How the Stuxnet Virus Could Be Used against the U.S." *The Atlantic,* 6/1/2012, accessed 5/6/2017, https://www.theatlantic.com/technology/archive/2012/06/heres-how-stuxnet-virus-could-be-used-against-us/327389/

Hufbauer, Gary C., Jeffrey J. Schott, and Kimberly A. Elliott. 1990. *Economic Sanctions Reconsidered: History and Current Policy* (Vol. 1). (Washington: Peterson Institute).

Hulcoop, Adam, John Scott-Railton, Peter Tanchak, Matt Brooks, and Ron Deibert. 2017. "Tainted Leaks: Disinformation and Phishing with a Russian Nexus." *Citizen Labs*, May, accessed 7/20/2017, https://citizenlab.ca/2017/05/tainted-leaks-disinformation-phish/

Hultquist, John. 2016. "Sandworm Team and the Ukrainian Power Authority Attacks." *FireEye*, 1/7/2016, accessed 5/1/2017, https://www.fireeye.com/blog/threat-research/2016/01/ukraine-and-sandworm-team.html

Huth, Paul, and Bruce Russett. 1990. "Testing Deterrence Theory: Rigor Makes a Difference." *World Politics*, 42 (4): 466–501.

Huth, Paul, Christopher Gelpi, and D. Scott Bennett. 1993. "The Escalation of Great Power Militarized Disputes: Testing Rational Deterrence Theory and Structural Realism." *American Political Science Review,* 87 (3): 609–623.

InfoSec Institute. 2015. "Snowden's New Revelations on Dominance in Cyberspace." *InfoSec Institute*, 2/3/2015, accessed 5/6/2017, http://resources.infosecinstitute.com/snowdens-new-revelations-dominance-cyberspace/#gref

Inkster, Nigel. 2015. "The Chinese Intelligence Agencies: Evolution and Empowerment in the Digital Age." In Jon R. Lindsay, Tai Ming Cheung, and Derek S. Reveron (eds.), *China and Cybersecurity: Espionage, Strategy, and Politics in the Digital Domain* (New York, NY: Oxford University Press): 29–50.

Inkster, Nigel. 2016. "Information Warfare and the US Presidential Election." *Survival*, 58 (5): 23–32.

Ivanov, Igor S. 1998. "Letter dated 23 September 1998 from the Minster for Foreign Affairs of the Russian federation addressed to the Secretary-General." Accessed 12/2/2017, https://disarmament-library.un.org/UNODA/Library.nsf/1c90cfa42bbb0d6985257631004ff541/663e6453bdaa2e228525765000550277/$FILE/A-C1-53-3_russia.pdf.

Ivanov, S. P. 1974. *Nachal'tkvv peiood vovrv* (The initial period of war) (Moscow: Vovenizdat).

Jacobs, Andrew. 2014. "After Reports on NSA, China Urges End to Spying." *New York Times*, 3/24/2014, accessed 4/24/2017, https://www.nytimes.com/2014/03/25/world/asia/after-reports-on-nsa-china-urges-halt-to-cyberspying.html

Jain, Khyati. 2015. "NeoKylin: China's Linux OS That Seriously Looks Like Windows XP." *Hacker News*, 9/24/2015, accessed 7/7/2017, http://thehackernews.com/2015/09/neokylin-china-linux-os.html

Jaitner, Margarita Levin. 2015. "Russian Information Warfare: Lessons from Ukraine." In Kenneth Geers (ed.), *Cyber War in Perspective: Russian Aggression against Ukraine* (Tallinn: NATO Cooperative Cyber Defence Center of Excellence): 87–98.

Jensen, Benjamin. 2016. *Forging the Sword: Doctrinal Change in the U.S. Army* (Pal Alto: Stanford University Press).

Jensen, Benjamin. 2017. "The Role of Ideas in Defense Planning: Revisiting the Revolution in Military Affairs." *Defense Studies*, forthcoming.

Jensen, Benjamin, and Eric Shibuya. 2015. "The Military Rebalance as Retcon." In Hugo Meijer (ed.), *Origins and Evolution of the US Rebalance toward Asia Diplomatic, Military, and Economic Dimensions* (New York: Palgrave Macmillan).

Jervis, Robert. 1976. *Perception and Misperception in World Politics* (Princeton: Princeton University Press).

Jervis, Robert. 1979. "Deterrence Theory Revisited." *World Politics*, 31 (2): 289–324.

Jervis, Robert. 2017. "Some Thoughts on Deterrence in the Cyber Era." *Journal of Information Warfare*, forthcoming.

Johnson, Reuben F. 2017. "Experts: The U.S. Has Fallen Dangerously behind Russia in Cyber Warfare Capabilities." *Business Insider*, 6/26/2017, accessed 7/23/2017, http://www.businessinsider.com/us-behind-russia-cyber-warfare-2016-7.

Johnston, Alastair I. 1998. *Cultural Realism: Strategic Culture and Grand Strategy in Chinese History* (Princeton: Princeton University Press).

Johnston, Patrick B. 2012. "The Effectiveness of Leadership Decapitation in Combating Insurgencies," Policy Brief. *Quarterly Journal: International Security*. Belfer Center for Science and International Affairs, Harvard Kennedy School, June 2012.

Joint Chiefs of Staff. 2014. *JP 3–13, Information Operations* (Arlington: Department of Defense).

Jones, Sam. "Russian Government behind Cyber Attacks Says Security Group." *Financial Times*, 10/28/2017, accessed 5/1/2017, https://www.ft.com/content/93108ba0-5ebe-11e4-a807-00144feabdc0.

Jones, Daniel M., Stuart A. Bremer, and J. David Singer. 1996. "Militarized Interstate Disputes, 1816–1992: Rationale, Coding Rules, and Empirical Patterns." *Conflict Management and Peace Science*, 15 (2): 163–215.

Jordan, Jenna. 2009. "When Heads Roll: Assessing the Effectiveness of Leadership Decapitation." *Security Studies*, 18 (4): 719–755.

Kagan, Frederick. 2007. *Finding the Target: The Transformation of American Military Policy* (New York: Encounter Books).

Kan, Michael. 2016. "Suspected Russian Hackers Target U.S. Think Tanks after Election." *IT World*, 11/10/2016, accessed 4/27/2017, http://www.itworld.com/article/3140706/security/suspected-russian-hackers-target-us-think-tanks-after-election.html

Kaplan, Fred. 2016. *Dark Territory: The Secret History of Cyber War* (New York: Simon and Schuster).

Kash, Wyatt. 2008. "Lessons from the Cyberattacks on Estonia." *GCN*, 6/13/2008, accessed 5/1/2017: https://gcn.com/Articles/2008/06/13/Lauri-Almann--Lessons-from-the-cyberattacks-on-Estonia.aspx?Page=1

Kaspersky Labs. 2017. "The Epic Turla (snake/Uroburos) Attacks." Accessed 5/2/2017, https://usa.kaspersky.com/resource-center/threats/epic-turla-snake-malware-attacks

Kaspersky Lab's Global Research and Analysis Team. 2013. "The 'Red October' Campaign—An Advanced Cyber Espionage Network Targeting Diplomatic and Government Agencies." *Secure List*, 1/14/2013, accessed 5/1/2017: https://securelist.com/blog/incidents/57647/the-red-october-campaign/

Kaspersky Labs. 2014. "The Reign Platform: Nation-State Ownage of GSM Networks." *Kaspersky Labs*, 11/24/2014, accessed 5/4/2017, https://securelist.com/files/2014/11/Kaspersky_Lab_whitepaper_Regin_platform_eng.pdf

Kaspersky Labs. 2015. "Equation Group: Questions and Answers." *Kaspersky Labs*, 2/2015, accessed 7/5/2017, https://cdn.securelist.com/files/2015/02/Equation_group_questions_and_answers.pdf

Kaspersky Lab Global Research and Analysis Team. 2014. "Energetic Bear—Crouching Yeti." *Secure List*, 7/2014, accessed 5/4/2017, https://securelist.com/files/2014/07/EB-YetiJuly2014-Public.pdf.

Kaufmann, Chaim. 2004. "Threat Inflation and the Failure of the Marketplace of Ideas: The Selling of the Iraq War." *Quarterly Journal: International Security*, 29 (1): 5–48.

Keeney, Kevin. 2017. "Cyber Threats Facing America: An Overview of the Cybersecurity Threat Landscape." Testimony before U.S. Senate Homeland Security and Governmental Affairs Committee. accessed 5/10/2017, http://www.hsgac.senate.gov/download/testimony-keeney-2017-05-10.

Kello, Lucas. 2013. "The Meaning of the Cyber Revolution: Perils in Theory and Statecraft." *International Security*, 38 (2): 7–40.

Kennan, George F. 1948. "Review of Current Trends U.S. Foreign Policy." *Report by the Policy Planning Staff*, 24.

Keohane, Robert O., and Joseph S. Nye. 1977. *Power and Interdependence* (Boston: Little Brown).

Khanna, Parag. 2016. *Connectography: Mapping the Future of Global Civilization* (New York: Random House).

Klimburg, Alexander. 2017. *The Darkening Web: The War for Cyberspace* (New York: Penguin).

Kilovaty, Ido. 2017. "Violence in Cyberspace: Are Disruptive Cyberspace Operations Legal under International Humanitarian Law?" *Just Security*, 3/3/2017, accessed 3/10/2017, https://www.justsecurity.org/38291/violence-cyberspace-disruptive-cyberspace-operations-legal-international-humanitarian-law/

King, Gary, Jennifer Pan, and Margaret E. Roberts. 2013. "How Censorship in China Allows Government Criticism but Silences Collective Expression." *American Political Science Review*, 107 (2): 326–343.

Kinsella, David, and Bruce Russett. 2002. "Conflict Emergence and Escalation in Interactive International Dyads." *Journal of Politics*, 64 (4): 1045–1068.

Kirkpatrick, David, and Sheera Frenkel. "Hacking in Qatar Highlights a Shift towards Espionage-for-Hire." *New York Times*, 6/8/2017, accessed 6/9/2017, https://www.nytimes.com/2017/06/08/world/middleeast/qatar-cyberattack-espionage-for-hire.html?smid=tw-share&_r=0

Kir'yan, M. M. 1976. *Vnezapnost'* "[Surprise], *Sovetskaya x" ennraya entsiklopedi ya* [Soviet military encyclopedia] (Moscow: Voynizdat).

Klein, James P., Gary Goertz, and Paul F, Diehl. 2006. "The New Rivalry Dataset: Procedures and Patterns." *Journal of Peace Research* 43 (3): 331–348.

Knake, Robert K. 2017. "To Prevent Another Equifax Breach, Treat Data Leaks Like Oil Spills." *Council on Foreign Relations*, 9/8/2017, accessed 9/9/2017, https://www.cfr.org/blog/prevent-another-equifax-breach-treat-data-leaks-oil-spills?utm_content=buffer55d3e&utm_medium=social&utm_source=twitter.com&utm_campaign=buffer

Knopf, Jeffrey W. 2002. "Varieties of Assurance." *Journal of Strategic Studies*, 35 (3): 375–399.

Koenig-Archibugi, Mathias. 2004. "Explaining Government Preferences for Institutional Change in EU Foreign and Security Policy." *International Organization*, 58 (1): 137–174.

Koerner, Brandon I. 2016. "Inside the Cyberattack That Shocked the U.S. Government." *Wired*, 10/23/2016, accessed 5/26/2017, https://www.wired.com/2016/10/inside-cyberattack-shocked-us-government/

Kogan, Rami. 2015. "Bedep Trojan Malware Spread by the Angler Exploit Kit Gets Political." *Trustwave*, 4/29/2015, accessed 6/7/2017, https://www.trustwave.com/Resources/SpiderLabs-Blog/Bedep-trojan-malware-spread-by-the-Angler-exploit-kit-gets-political/

Koppel, Ted. 2015. *Lights Out: A Cyberattack, a Nation Unprepared, Surviving the Aftermath* (New York: Broadway Books).

Koschev, Konstantin. 2007. "An Insult to Our War Dead." *The Guardian*, 3/5/2007, accessed 4/25/2017, https://www.theguardian.com/commentisfree/2007/mar/06/comment.secondworldwar

Kostyuk, Nadia. 2015. "Ukraine: A Cyber Safe Haven?" In Kenneth Geers (ed.), *Cyber War in Perspective: Russian Aggression against Ukraine* (Tallinn: NATO Cooperative Cyber Defence Center of Excellence): 113–122.

Kovacs, Eduard. 2014. "Three NATO Website Disrupted by Ukrainian Hackers of Cyber Berkut." *Softpedia*, 3/17/2014, accessed 5/2/2017, http://news.softpedia.com/news/Three-NATO-Websites-Disrupted-by-Ukrainian-Hackers-of-Cyber-Berkut-432419.shtml

Koval, Nikolay. 2015. "Revolution Hacking." In Kenneth Geers (ed.), *Cyber War in Perspective: Russian Aggression against Ukraine* (Tallinn: NATO Cooperative Cyber Defence Center of Excellence): 55–65.

Krebs, Brian. 2007. "Shadowy Russian Firm Seen as Conduit for Cybercrime." *Washington Post*, 10/13/2007, accessed 3/26/2017, http://www.washingtonpost.com/wp-dyn/content/article/2007/10/12/AR2007101202461.html

Krebs, Brian. 2014. "Operation Tovar Targets GameOver Zeus Botnot, CryptoLocker Scourge." *Krebs on Security*, 6/2014, accessed 5/2/2017, https://krebsonsecurity.com/2014/06/operation-tovar-targets-gameover-zeus-botnet-cryptolocker-scourge/

Krepenvich, Andrew, and Barry Watts. 2015. *The Last Warrior: Andrew Marshall and the Shaping of Modern American Defense Strategy* (New York: Basic Books).

Kroenig, Matthew. 2012. "Time to Attack Iran: Why a Strike Is the Least Bad Option." *Foreign Affairs*, 91: 76–86.

Kshetri, Nir. 2013. "Cybercrime and Cyber-security Issues Associated with China: Some Economic and Institutional Considerations." *Electronic Commerce Research*, 13 (1): 41–69.

Kuzmenko, Oleksiy. 2017. "Cyber Firm Rewrites Part of Disputed Russian Hacking Report." *VOA News*, 3/24/2017, accessed 5/5/2017, https://www.voanews.com/a/cyber-firm-rewrites-part-disputed-russian-hacking-report/3781411.html

Kydd, Andrew H., and Barbara F. Walter. 2002. "Sabotaging the Peace: The Politics of Extremist Violence." *International Organization*, 56 (2): p263–296.

Kydd, Andrew H., and Barbara F. Walter. 2006. "The Strategies of Terrorism." *International Security*, 31 (1): 49–80.

Landler, Mark, and John Markoff. 2007. "Digital Fears Emerge after Data Siege in Estonia." *New York Times*, 5/29/2007, accessed 4/27/2017, http://www.nytimes.com/2007/05/29/technology/29estonia.html

Lawson, Sean. 2013. *Nonlinear Science and Warfare* (New York: Routledge).

Lawson, Sean, and Michael K. Middleton. 2016. "Cyber Pearl Harbor: Analogy, Fear, and the Framing of Cyber Security Threats in the United States, 1991–2016." Presented at *Legal and Policy Dimensions of Cybersecurity*, George Washington University, Washington, DC, September 27–29, 2016, https://www.seanlawson.net/2017/02/cyber-pearl-harbor-25-year-retrospective/lawsonmiddleton-cyberpearlharboressay/.

Lebow, Richard N. 1981. *Between War and Peace: The Nature of International Crisis* (Baltimore: Johns Hopkins Press).

Lebow, Richard N. 1984. "Windows of Opportunity: Do States Jump through Them?" *International Security*, 9 (1): 147–186.

Lebow, Richard N. 2007. *Coercion, Cooperation, and Ethics in International Relations.* (Oxford: Taylor & Francis).

Lee, Dave. 2012. "Flame: Massive Cyber-Attack Discovered, Researchers Say." *BBC News*, 5/28/2012, accessed 7/7/2017, http://www.bbc.com/news/technology-18238326

Lee, Timothy B. 2013. "Here's Everything We Know about PRISM to Date." *Washington Post*, 6/12/2013, accessed 6/7/2017, https://www.washingtonpost.com/news/wonk/wp/2013/06/12/heres-everything-we-know-about-prism-to-date/?utm_term=.d287818d5cfa

Legum, Judd. 2017. "Trump Mentioned Wikileaks 164 times in Last Month of Election, Now Claims It Did Not Impact One Voter." *Think Progress*, 1/8/2017, accessed 7/9/2017, https://thinkprogress.org/trump-mentioned-wikileaks-164-times-in-last-month-of-election-now-claims-it-didnt-impact-one-40aa62ea5002/.

Leng, Russell J. 1983. "When Will They Ever Learn? Coercive Bargaining in Recurrent Crises." *Journal of Conflict Resolution*, 27 (3): 379–419.

Leng, Russell J. 1993. "Reciprocating Influence Strategies in Interstate Crisis Bargaining." *Journal of Conflict Resolution*, 37 (1): 3–41.

Leng, Russell J. 2004. "Escalation: Competing Perspectives and Empirical Evidence." *International Studies Review*, 6 (4): 51–64.

Levy, Jack S. 1988. "When Do Deterrent Threats Work?" *British Journal of Political Science*, 18 (4): 485–512.

Levy, Jack. 2008. "Deterrence and Coercive Diplomacy: The Contributions of Alexander George" *Political Psychology*, 29 (4): 537–552.

Lewis, James Andrew. 2015. "Compelling Opponents to Our Will: The Role of Cyber Warfare in Ukraine." In Kenneth Geers (ed.), *Cyber War in Perspective: Russian Aggression against Ukraine* (Tallinn: NATO Cooperative Cyber Defence Center of Excellence): 39–48.

Lewis, Randall A., and Justin M. Rao. 2013. "On the Near Impossibility of Measuring the Returns to Advertising." Unpublished paper, Google, Inc. and Microsoft Research. http://justinmrao.com/lewis_rao_nearimpossibility.pdf.

Liang, Qiao, and Wang Xiangsui. 1999. *Unrestricted Warfare: China's Master Plan to Destroy America* (New York: Echo Point Books).

Liang, Qiao, and Wang Xiangsui. 2002. *Unrestricted Warfare: China's Master Plan to Destroy America* (New York: Pan American Publishers).

Libicki, Martin. 1995. *What Is Information Warfare?* (Washington, DC: National Defense University Press).

Libicki, Martin. 2007. *Conquest in Cyberspace: National Security and Information Warfare* (Cambridge: Cambridge University Press).

Libicki, Martin. 2009. *Cyberdeterrence and Cyberwar* (Santa Monica: RAND).

Libicki, Martin. 2012. *Crisis and Escalation in Cyberspace* (Santa Monica: Rand Corporation).

Libicki, Martin. 2016. *Information Technology Standards: Quest for the Common Byte.* (Amsterdam: Elsevier).

Lieber, Kier, and Daryl Press. 2013. *Coercive Nuclear Campaigns in the 21st Century: Understanding Adversary Incentives and Options for Nuclear Escalation* (Monterey: PASCC, Report Number 2013–001).

Lieberthal, Kenneth, and Peter W. Singer. 2016. *Cybersecurity and U.S.-China Relations,* (Washington: Brookings Institute Press).

Liff, Adam P. 2012. "Cyberwar: A New Absolute Weapon? The Proliferation of Cyberwarfare Capabilities and Interstate War." *Journal of Strategic Studies*, 35 (3): 401–428.

Lin, Herbert. 2012. "Operational Considerations in Cyber Attack and Cyber Exploitation." In Derek Reveron (ed.), *Cyberspace and National Security: Threats, Opportunity and Power in a Virtual World* (Washington, DC: Georgetown University Press): 37–57.

Lindsay, Jon R. 2013. "Stuxnet and the Limits of Cyber Warfare." *Security Studies*, 22 (3): 365–404.

Lindsay, Jon R. 2015a. "Tipping the Scales: The Attribution Problem and the Feasibility of Deterrence against Cyberattack." *Journal of Cybersecurity* 1 (1): 53–67.

Lindsay, Jon R. 2015b. "The Impact of China on Cybersecurity: Fiction and Friction." *International Security* 39 (3): 7–47.

Lindsay, Jon R. 2015c. "Introduction: China and Cybersecurity: Controversy and Context." In Jon R. Lindsay, Tai Ming Cheung, and Derek S. Reveron (eds.), 2015. *China and Cybersecurity: Espionage, Strategy, and Politics in the Digital Domain* (Oxford: Oxford University Press): 1–28.

Lindsay, Jon R. 2017. "Cyber Espionage." In P. Cornish (ed.), *The Oxford Handbook of Cyber Security* (New York: Oxford University Press).

Lindsay, Jon R., and Tai Ming Cheung. 2015. "From Exploitation to Innovation: Acquisition, Absorption, and Application." In Jon R. Lindsay, Tai Ming Cheung, and Derek S. Reveron (eds.), *China and Cybersecurity: Espionage, Strategy, and Politics in the Digital Domain* (New York: Oxford University Press): 51–86.

Lindsay Jon R., and Erik Gartzke. 2016. "Coercion through Cyberspace: The Stability-Instability Paradox Revisited." In Kelly Greenhill and Peter Krause (eds.), *The Power to Hurt: Coercion in the Modern World* (New York, NY: Oxford University Press).

Lipton, Eric, David E. Sanger, and Scott Shane. 2016. "The Perfect Weapon: How Russian Cyberpower Invaded the U.S." *New York Times*, 12/13/2016, accessed 7/7/2017, https://www.nytimes.com/2016/12/13/us/politics/russia-hack-election-dnc.html?_r=0

Livingston, Steven, and Gregor Walter-Drop (eds). 2014. *Bits and Atoms: Information and Communication Technology in Areas of Limited Statehood* (New York: Oxford University Press).

Lobell, Steven E., Norrin M. Ripsman, and Jeffrey W. Taliaferro (eds.). 2009. *Neoclassical Realism, the State, and Foreign Policy* (New York: Cambridge University Press).

LoBianco, Tom. 2017. "Angry Lawmakers Want More from Facebook, Mull Next Move." *CNN*, 9/7/2017, accessed 9/8/2017, http://www.cnn.com/2017/09/07/politics/facebSook-congressional-investigation-russia/index.html

Lonergan, Shawn. 2016. "Cooperation under the Cybersecurity Dilemma." In Hugh Liebert, Thomas Sherlock, and Cole Pinheiro (eds.), *Confronting Inequality: Wealth, Rights, and Power* (New York: Sloan).

Luhn, Alec. 2015. "Russia Bans 'Undesirable' International Organisations ahead of 2016 Elections." *The Guardian*, 5/19/2015, accessed 8/9/2017, https://www.theguardian.com/world/2015/may/19/russia-bans-undesirable-international-organisations-2016-elections.

Lu-YueYang, Maggie. 2012. "Australia Blocks Huawei from Broadband Tender." *Reuters*, 3/26/2012, accessed 5/23/2017, http://www.reuters.com/article/us-australia-huawei-nbn-idUSBRE82P0GA20120326

Lynn, William J. 2010. "Defending a New Domain: The Pentagon's Cyberstrategy." *Foreign Affairs*, 89 (5): 97–108.

Lynn-Jones, Sean M. 1995. "Offense-Defense Theory and Its Critics." *Security Studies*, 4 (4): 660–691.

Maat, Eelco van der. 2011. "Sleeping Hegemons: Third Party Intervention Following Territory Integrity Transgressions." *Journal of Peace Research*, 48 (2): 201–215.

Machiavelli, N., P. Bondanella, and M. Viroli. 2008. *The Prince*. (Oxford: Oxford University Press).

MacKinnon, Rebecca. 2011. "China's Networked Authoritarianism." *Journal of Democracy* 22(2): 32–46.

Mahnken, Thomas. 2003. *U.S. Intelligence and Foreign Military Innovation, 1918–1941* (Ithaca: Cornell University Press).

Mahnken, Thomas. 2014. *Cost-Imposing Strategies: A Brief Primer* (Washington: CNAS).

Mandiant Report. 2014. "APT1: Exposing One of China's Cyber Espionage Units." *FireEye*, accessed 5/22/2017, https://www.fireeye.com/content/dam/fireeye-www/services/pdfs/mandiant-apt1-report.pdf.

Maness, Ryan C., and Brandon Valeriano. 2015. *Russia's Coercive Diplomacy: Energy, Cyber and Maritime Policy as New Sources of Power* (London: Palgrave Macmillan).

Maness, Ryan C., and Brandon Valeriano. 2016. "The Impact of Cyber Conflict on International Interactions." *Armed Forces and Society*, 42 (2): 301–323.

Maness, Ryan C., Brandon Valeriano, and Benjamin Jensen. 2017. *Coding Manual for v1.1 of the Dyadic Cyber Incident and Dispute Dataset, 2000–2014*. Unpublished manuscript. Available at: drryanmaness.wix.com/irprof

Marshall, Monty G., Keith Jaggers, and Ted Robert Gurr. 2011. *Polity IV Project: Dataset Users' Manual*. Arlington: Polity IV Project.

Martin, Rachel. 2016. "In Fight against ISIS, U.S. Adds Cyber Tools." *NPR*, 2/28/2016, accessed 7/23/2017, http://www.npr.org/2016/02/28/468446138/in-fight-against-isis-u-s-adds-cyber-tools

Masters, Sam. 2014. "Ukraine Crisis: Telephone Networks Are First Casualty of Conflict." *The Independent*, 3/25/2014, accessed 5/2/2107, http://www.independent.co.uk/news/world/europe/ukraine-crisis-telephone-networks-are-first-casualty-of-conflict-9171771.html

Maurer, Tim. 2015. "Cyber Proxies and the Crisis in Ukraine." In Kenneth Geers (ed.), *Cyber War in Perspective: Russian Aggression against Ukraine* (Tallinn: NATO Cooperative Cyber Defence Center of Excellence): 79–86.

May, Mon. 2017. "North Korea's Unit 180, the Cyber Warfare Cell That Worries the West." *Reuters*, 5/22/2017, accessed 5/23/2017: http://www.reuters.com/article/us-cyber-northkorea-exclusive-idUSKCN18H020

Mazanec, Brian M. 2015. *The Evolution of Cyber War: International Norms for Emerging-technology Weapons* (Lincoln: University of Nebraska Press).

Mazzetti, Mark, Adam Goldman, Michael S. Schmidt, and Matt Apuzzo. "Killing CIA Informants, China Crippled U.S. Spying Operations." *New York Times*, 5/20/2017, accessed 5/24/2017, https://www.nytimes.com/2017/05/20/world/asia/china-cia-spies-espionage. html

McAfee Labs. 2008. "One Internet, Many Worlds." *Sage*, 2 (1), February 2008, accessed 2/3/2017, http://www.mcafee.com/us/resources/reports/rp-mcafee-labs-sage-2008.pdf

McDermott, N. 2016. "Does Russia Have a Gerasimov Doctrine?" *Parameters*, 46 (1): 97–105.

McDonald, Geoff, Liam O Murchu, Stephen Doherty, Eric Chen. "Stuxnet 0.5: The Missing Link." *Symantec*, 2/26/2013, accessed 6/2/2017, http://www.symantec.com/content/en/us/ enterprise/media/security_response/whitepapers/stuxnet_0_5_the_missing_link.pdf

McGraw, Gary. 2013. "Cyber War Is Inevitable (Unless We Build Security In)." *Journal of Strategic Studies*, 36 (1): 109–119.

McQuaid, James. 2008. "The RBN Operatives Who Attacked Georgia." *Secure Home Network*, 8/18/ 2008, accessed 3/4/2017, www.securehomenetwork.blogspot.com/2008/08/rbn-operatives- who-attacked-georgia.html

Mearsheimer, John J. 1985. "Prospects for Conventional Deterrence in Europe." *Bulletin of the Atomic Scientists*, 41 (7): 158–162.

Mearsheimer, John J. 2001. *The Tragedy of Great Power Politics* (W.W. Norton & Company).

Meijer, Hugo (ed.). 2015. *Origins and Evolution of the US Rebalance toward Asia: Diplomatic, Military, and Economic Dimensions* (New York: Palgrave Macmillan).

Meijer, Hugo, and Benjamin Jensen. 2018. "The Strategist Dilemma." *European Journal of International Security*, forthcoming.

Menn, Joseph. "Russian Researchers Expose Breakthrough U.S. Spying Program." *Reuters*, 2/16/2015a, accessed 7/16/2017, http://www.reuters.com/article/us-usa-cyberspying- idUSKBN0LK1QV20150216

Menn, Joseph. "Exclusive: U.S. Tried Stuxnet-Style Campaign against North Korea but Failed—Sources." *Reuters*, 5/29/2015b, accessed 6/2/2017, http://www.reuters.com/article/ us-usa-northkorea-stuxnet-idUSKBN0OE2DM20150529

Metzl, Lothar. 1974. "Reflections on the Soviet Secret Police and Intelligence Services." *Orbis*, 18 (3): 917–930.

Miller, Steven Lee. 2007. "Youth Group Created by Kremlin Serve Putin's Cause." *New York Times*, 7/8/2007, accessed 4/25/2017, http://www.nytimes.com/2007/07/08/world/europe/ 08moscow.html

Miller, Chuck. 2009. "Russia Confirms Involvement with Estonia DDoS Attacks." *SC Magazine*, 3/12/2009, accessed 4/23/2017, https://www.scmagazine.com/russia-confirms-involvement- with-estonia-ddos-attacks/article/555577/

Miller, Greg, Ellen Nakashima, and Adam Entous. 2017. "Obama's Secret Struggle to Punish Russia for Putin's Election Assault." *Washington Post*, 6/23/2017, accessed 7/2/2017, https:// www.washingtonpost.com/graphics/2017/world/national-security/obama-putin-election- hacking/?utm_term=.244e43fa7389

Missiou-Ladi, Anna. 1987. "Coercive Diplomacy in Greek Interstate Relations." *Classical Quarterly*, 37 (2): 336–345.

Modelski, George. 1964. "Kautilya: Foreign Policy and International System in the Ancient Hindu World." *American Political Science Review*, 58 (3): 549–560.

Molander, R. C., and A. S. Riddile. 1996. *Strategic Information Warfare: A New Face of War* (Santa Monica: RAND).

Moore, Daniel, and Thomas Rid. 2016. "Cryptopolitik and the Darknet." *Survival* 58 (1): 7–38.

Morgan, Forrest E., Karl P. Mueller, Evan S. Medeiros, Kevin L. Pollpeter, and Roger Cliff. 2008. *Dangerous Thresholds: Managing Escalation in the 21st Century* (Santa Monica: RAND Corporation).

Morgan, T. Clifton, Navin Bapat, and Yoshi Kobayashi. 2014. "The Threat and Imposition of Sanctions: Updating the TIES Dataset." *Conflict Management and Peace Science*, 31 (5): 541–558.

Morgenthau, Hans. 1948. *Politics AMONG Nations: The Struggle for Power and Peace.* (New York: Alfred Kopf).

MSS Global Threat Response. 2014. "Emerging Threat: Dragonfly/Energetic Bear—APT Group" *Symantec*, 6/30/2014, accessed 5/2/2017, https://www.symantec.com/connect/blogs/emerging-threat-dragonfly-energetic-bear-apt-group

Mullen, Jethro. 2017. "China Is No Longer the Biggest Foreign Holder of U.S. Debt." *CNN Money*, 12/16/2017, http://money.cnn.com/2016/12/16/investing/china-japan-us-debt-treasuries/index.html

Mulvenon, James. 1999. "The PLA and Information Warfare." In James Mulvenon and Richard H. Yang (eds.), *The People's Liberation Army in the Information Age*, (Santa Monica: RAND).

Murawiec, Laurent. 2004. *Vulnerabilities in the Chinese Way of War* (Washington, DC: Hudson Institute).

Murray, W. R. and A. R. Millett (eds.). 1998. *Military Innovation in the Interwar Period.* (Cambridge: Cambridge University Press).

Myers, Adam. 2016. "Danger Close: Fancy Bear Tracking of Ukrainian Field Artillery Units." *CrowdStrike*, 12/22/2016, accessed 5/26/2017, https://www.crowdstrike.com/blog/danger-close-fancy-bear-tracking-ukrainian-field-artillery-units/

Nakashima, Ellen. 2011. "Cyber Intruder Sparks Response Debate." *Washington Post*, 12/8/2011, accessed 7/3/2017, https://www.washingtonpost.com/national/national-security/cyber-intruder-sparks-response-debate/2011/12/06/gIQAxLuFgO_story.html?utm_term=.4c8ecaf94501

Nakashima, Ellen. 2016. "Russian Government Hackers Penetrated DNC, Stole Opposition Research on Trump." *Washington Post*, 6/14/2016, accessed 4/30/2017, https://www.washingtonpost.com/world/national-security/russian-government-hackers-penetrated-dnc-stole-opposition-research-on-trump/2016/06/14/cf006cb4-316e-11e6-8ff7-7b6c1998b7a0_story.html?utm_term=.7e2cdfe278eb.

Nakashima, Ellen. 2017. "U.S. Officials Say Russian Government Hackers Have Penetrated Energy and Nuclear Company Business Networks." *Washington Post*, 7/8/2017, accessed 7/9/2017, https://www.washingtonpost.com/world/national-security/us-officials-say-russian-government-hackers-have-penetrated-energy-and-nuclear-company-business-networks/2017/07/08/bbfde9a2-638b-11e7-8adc-fea80e32bf47_story.html?utm_term=.17811b2d39c6.

Nakashima Ellen, and Missy Ryan. 2016. "U.S. Military's Digital War against the Islamic State Is off to a Slow Start." *Washington Post*, 7/15/2016, accessed 7/13/2017, https://www.washingtonpost.com/world/national-security/us-militarys-digital-war-against-the-islamic-state-is-off-to-a-slow-start/2016/07/15/76a3fe82-3da3-11e6-a66f-aa6c1883b6b1_story.html?postshare=1271468837044977&tid=ss_tw&utm_term=.03c749a21ff3.

Nazario, Jose. 2008. "Radio Free Europe DDoS." *Arbor Networks*, 4/29/2008, accessed 4/29/2017, https://www.arbornetworks.com/blog/asert/radio-free-europe-ddos/

Neuman, Craig, and Michael Poznansky. 2016. "Swaggering in Cyberspace: Busting the Conventional Wisdom in Cyber Coercion." *War on the Rocks*, 6/28/2016, accessed 4/5/2017, https://warontherocks.com/2016/06/swaggering-in-cyberspace-busting-the-conventional-wisdom-on-cyber-coercion/

New York Times. "Slides Describe Mission Involving Huawei." *New York Times*, 3/23/2014, accessed 7/23/2017, https://www.nytimes.com/interactive/2014/03/23/world/asia/23nsa-docs.html

Nielsen, Thomas E. 2015. *#Weaponization of Social Media @ Characteristics of Contemporary Conflict* (Copenhagen: Royal Danish Defense College).

Norton. 2017. "Cybercrime Rings: Gameover Zeus." *Norton*, accessed 5/2/2017, https://us.norton.com/internetsecurity-malware-cybercrime-rings-gameover-zeus.html

Null, Christopher. 2015. "The Soviet Legacy behind Russian Hacking Prowess." *Wired*, 10/26/2015, accessed 3/26/2017, https://www.ca.com/us/rewrite/articles/security/the-soviet-legacy-behind-russias-hacking-prowess.html

Nye, Joseph S. 2004. *Soft Power: The Means to Success in World Politics* (Washington: Public Affairs).

Nye, Joseph S. 2017. "Deterrence and Dissuasion in Cyberspace." *International Security*, 41 (3): 44–71.

Office of the Director of National Intelligence. 2017. "Background to 'Assessing Russian Activities and Intentions in Recent US Elections': The Analytic Process and Cyber Incident Attribution." 1/6/2017, accessed 3/2/2017, https://www.dni.gov/files/documents/ICA_2017_01.pdf

Organski, A. F. K., and Jacek Kugler. 1980. *The War Ledger* (Chicago: University of Chicago Press).

Osinga, Frans. 2007. *Science, Strategy, and War: The Strategic Theory of John Boyd* (New York: Routledge).

Paganni, Pierluigi. 2015. "The CozyDuke, The Last Russian APT Group." *Security Affairs*, 4/23/2015, accessed 5/3/2017, http://securityaffairs.co/wordpress/36195/cyber-crime/cozyduke-russian-apt-group.html

Pakharenko, Glib. 2015. "Cyber Operations at Maidan: A First-Hand Account." In Kenneth Geers (ed.), *Cyber War in Perspective: Russian Aggression against Ukraine* (Tallinn: NATO Cooperative Cyber Defence Center of Excellence): 49–58.

Palmer, Glenn, Vito D'Orazio, Michael Kenwick, and Matthew Lane. 2015. "The MID4 Data Set: Procedures, Coding Rules, and Description." *Conflict Management and Peace Science*. 32 (2): 222–242.

Pape, Robert. 1996. *Bombing to Win* (Ithaca: Cornell University Press).

Pape, Robert. 1997. "Why Economic Sanctions Do Not Work." *International Security*, 22 (2): 90–136.

Pape, Robert. 2003. "The Strategic Logic of Suicide Terrorism." *American Political Science Review*, 97 (3): 343–361.

Pauli, Darren. 2015. "NSA We're in YOUR BOTNET." *The Register*, 1/19/2015, accessed 5/22/2017, https://www.theregister.co.uk/2015/01/19/nsa_steals_malware/

Perlroth, Nicole. 2013. "Hackers in China Attacked the Times for Last 4 Months." *New York Times*, 1/30/2013, accessed 5/23/2017, http://www.nytimes.com/2013/01/31/technology/chinese-hackers-infiltrate-new-york-times-computers.html

Perlroth, Nicole. 2017. "More Evidence Points to North Korea in Ransomware Attack." *New York Times*, 5/22/2017, accessed 7/6/2017, https://www.nytimes.com/2017/05/22/technology/north-korea-ransomware-attack.html

Peters, Sarah. 2015a. "MiniDuke, CosmicDuke APT Group Likely Sponsored by Russia." *Dark Reading*, 9/17/2015, accessed 5/12017, http://www.darkreading.com/analytics/miniduke-cosmicduke-apt-group-likely-sponsored-by-russia/d/d-id/1322230

Peters, Sarah. 2015b. "Chinese ISP: China Is Victim of Foreign State-Backed APT Group." *DarkReading*, 6/4/2015, accessed 7/8/2017, http://www.darkreading.com/vulnerabilities---threats/chinese-isp-says-its-victim-of-foreign-state-backed-apt-group/d/d-id/1320716?_mc=RSS_DR_EDT&linkId=14725478

Peterson, Dale. 2013. "Offensive Cyber Weapons: Construction, Development, and Employment." *Journal of Strategic Studies*, 36 (1): 120–124.

Peterson, Scott. 2014. "Covert War against Iran's Nuclear Scientists: A Widow Remembers." *Christian Science Monitor*, 7/17/2014, accessed 7/23/2017, https://www.csmonitor.com/World/Middle-East/2014/0717/Covert-war-against-Iran-s-nuclear-scientists-a-widow-remembers

Phillips, Brian J. 2015. "How Does Leadership Decapitation Affect Violence? The Case of Drug Trafficking Organizations in Mexico." *Journal of Politics* 77 (2): 324–336.

Polityuk, Pavel. 2016. "Ukraine Investigates Suspected Cyber-Attack on Kiev Power Grid." *Reuters*, 12/20/2016, accessed 5/1/2017, http://www.reuters.com/article/us-ukraine-crisis-cyber-attacks-idUSKBN1491ZF

Pollack, Kenneth Michael. 2002. *The Threatening Storm: The Case for Invading Iraq*. (New York: Random House).

Pollpeter, Keith. 2015. "Chinese Writings on Cyberwarfare and Coercion." In Jon R. Lindsay, Tai Ming Cheung, and Derek S. Reveron (eds.), *China and Cybersecurity: Espionage, Strategy, and Politics in the Digital Domain* (New York: Oxford University Press): 138–162.

Posen, Barry R. 1996. "Military Responses to Refugee Disasters." *International Security*, 21 (1): 72–111.

Powell, Colin, and Joseph Persico. 1995. *American Journey* (New York: Ballantine Books).

Powell, Robert. 1999. *In the Shadow of Power: States and Strategies in International Politics* (Princeton: Princeton University Press).

Powell, Robert. 2002. "Bargaining Theory and International Conflict." *Annual Review of Political Science*, 5 (1): 1–30.

Powell, Robert. 2004. "Bargaining and Learning While Fighting." *American Journal of Political Science*, 48 (2): 344–361.

Powell, Robert. 2006. "War as a Commitment Problem." *International Organization*, 60 (1): 169–203.

Poznansky, Michael and Perkoski, Evan, Rethinking Secrecy in Cyberspace (November 23, 2016). Available at SSRN: https://ssrn.com/abstract=2836087 or http://dx.doi.org/10.2139/ssrn.2836087.

Prasad, Eswar. 2009. "The Effect of the Crisis on the U.S.-China Economic Relationship." *Brookings*, 2/17/2009, accessed 7/24/2017, https://www.brookings.edu/testimonies/the-effect-of-the-crisis-on-the-u-s-china-economic-relationship/

Press, Darryl. 2005. *Calculating Credibility: How Leaders Assess Military Threats*. (Ithaca: Cornell University Press).

Price, Bryan. 2012. "Targeting Top Terrorists: How Leadership Decapitation Contributes to Counterterrorism." *International Security* 36 (4): 9–46.

Prince, Brian. 2015. "Operation Armageddon' Cyber Espionage Campaign Aimed at Ukraine." *Security Week*, 4/28/2015, accessed 5/12017, http://webcache.googleusercontent.

com/search?q=cache:tZzub9plLbQJ:www.securityweek.com/operation-armageddon-cyber-espionage-campaign-aimed-ukraine-lookingglass+&cd=1&hl=en&ct=clnk&gl=us

Prine, Carl. 2017. "The Unimaginable about Wars Is Being Imagined Again, Says Acclaimed Military Strategist Peter Singer." *San Diego Union-Tribune*, 5/3/2017, accessed 6/6/2017, http://www.sandiegouniontribune.com/military/sd-me-pw-singer-20170503-story.html?utm_content=bufferd3391&utm_medium=social&utm_source=facebook.com&utm_campaign=buffer.

Pufeng, Wang. 1995. *Xinxi zhanzheng yu junshi geming (Information Warfare and the Revolution in Military Affairs)* (Beijing: Junshi Kexueyuan).

Pytlak, Allison, and George E. Mitchell. 2016. "Power, Rivalry and Cyber Conflict." In Karsten Friis and Jens Ringsmore (eds.), *Conflict in Cyber Space: Theoretical, Strategic and Legal Perspectives* (London, UK: Routledge).

Radio Free Europe/Radio Liberty. 2008. "RFE/RL Websites Hit by Mass Cyberattack." *Radio Free Europe Radio Liberty*, 4/28/2008, accessed 4/29/2017: http://www.rferl.org/a/1109642.html

Radio Free Europe/Radio Liberty. 2009. "Behind the Estonia Cyberattacks." *Radio Free Europe, Radio Liberty*, 3/6/2009, accessed 5/1/2017, http://www.rferl.org/a/Behind_The_Estonia_Cyberattacks/1505613.html

Radio Free Europe/Radio Liberty. 2014. "Russian TV Announces Right Sector Leader Led Ukraine Polls." *Radio Free Europe Radio Liberty*, 5/26/2014, accessed 5/1/2017, http://www.rferl.org/a/russian-tv-announces-right-sector-leader-yarosh-led-ukraine-polls/25398882.html

Rafati, Mohammad. 2015. "OceanLouts Cyber Attack Steals China's Government Institutions Data." *Cyberwarzone*, 5/30/2015, accessed 7/9/2017, http://cyberwarzone.com/oceanlotus-cyber-attack-steal-chinas-government-institutions-data/

Ragin, Charles C. 2000. *Fuzzy Set Social Science* (Chicago: University of Chicago Press).

Ragin, Charles C. 2006. *User's Guide to Fuzzy-Set/Qualitative Comparative Analysis 2.0*. Tucson: Department of Sociology, University of Arizona.

Ragin, Charles C. 2014. *The Comparative Method* (Berkeley: University of California Press).

Ragin, Charles C., and Sean Davey. 2016. *Fuzzy-Set/Qualitative Comparative Analysis 3.0*. Irvine, California: Department of Sociology, University of California.

Raiu, Costin, and Igor Soumenkov. 2015. "Comparing the Reign Module 50251 and the 'Qwerty' Keylogger." *SecureList*, 1/27/2015, accessed 7/25/2017, https://securelist.com/blog/research/68525/comparing-the-regin-module-50251-and-the-qwerty-keylogger/.

Rashid, Fahmida Y. 2017. "Shadow Brokers Dump Contained Solaris Hacking Tools." *InfoWorld*, 4/12/2017, accessed 7/12/2017, http://www.infoworld.com/article/3189637/security/shadow-brokers-dump-contained-solaris-hacking-tools.html

Rasler, Karen, and William R. Thompson. 2001. "Rivalries and the Democratic Peace in the Major Power Subsystem." *Journal of Peace Research*, 38 (6): 659–683.

Rattray, G. J. 1999. *Strategic Warfare in Cyberspace* (Cambridge: MIT Press).

Reiter, Dan. 2003. "Exploring the Bargaining Model of War." *Perspectives on Politics*, 1 (1): 27–43.

Rid, Thomas. 2011. "Cyber War Will Not Take Place" *Journal of Strategic Studies* 35 (1): 5–32.

Rid, Thomas. 2013. "Cyber Sabotage Is Easy: So Why Aren't Hackers Crashing the Grid?" *Foreign Policy*, 7/23/2013, accessed 7/3/2017, http://foreignpolicy.com/2013/07/23/cyber-sabotage-is-easy/

Rid, Thomas. 2016. "How Russia Pulled Off the Biggest Election Hack in US History." *Esquire*, 10/20/2016, accessed 8/2/2017, http://www.esquire.com/news-politics/a49791/russian-dnc-emails-hacked/

Rid, Thomas, and Ben Buchanan. 2015. "Attributing Cyber Attacks." *Journal of Strategic Studies*, 38 (1): 4–37.

Rid, Thomas. 2017. "Disinformation: A Primer in Russian Active Measures and Influence Campaigns." *U.S. Senate Select Committee on Intelligence Hearing*, 3/30/2017, accessed 10/1/2017, https://www.intelligence.senate.gov/sites/default/files/documents/os-trid-033017.pdf

Romanosky, Sasha. 2016. "Examining the Costs and Causes of Cyber Incidents." *Journal of Cyber Security*, 2 (2): 121–135.

Ross, Bruce A. 1993. "The Case for Targeting Leadership in War." *Naval War College Review*, 46 (Winter 1993): 73–93.

Rosenbach, Marcel, Hilmar Schmundt, and Christian Stocker. "Experts Unmask 'Reign' Trojan as NSA Tool." *Spiegel Online*, 1/27/2015, accessed 7/4/2017, http://www.spiegel.de/international/world/regin-malware-unmasked-as-nsa-tool-after-spiegel-publishes-source-code-a-1015255.html

Rovner, Joshua, and Tyler Moore. 2017. "Does the Internet Need a Hegemon?" *Journal of Global Security Studies*, 2 (3): 184–203.

Rubin, Jeffrey Z., Dean G. Pruitt, and Sung Hee Kim. 1994. *Social Conflict: Escalation, Stalemate, and Settlement* (New York: McGraw-Hill).

Rumsfeld, Donald. 2006. *National Military Strategy for Cyberspace Operations*. 12/11/2006, accessed 2/2/2007, http://nsarchive.gwu.edu/NSAEBB/NSAEBB424/docs/Cyber-023.pdf

Saari, Sinnikukka. 2014. "Russia's Post-Orange Revolution Strategies to Increase Its Influence in Former Soviet Republics: Public Diplomacy." *Europe-Asia Studies*, 66 (1): 50–66.

Sanger, David E. 2012a. *Confront and Conceal: Obama's Secret Wars and Surprising Use of American Power* (New York: Crown Publishing).

Sanger, David E. 2012b. "Obama Order Sped Up Wave of Cyberattacks against Iran." *New York Times*, 6/1/2012, accessed 5/26/2017, http://www.nytimes.com/2012/06/01/world/middleeast/obama-ordered-wave-of-cyberattacks-against-iran.html

Sanger, David E. 2015. "U.S. Decides to Retaliate against China's Hacking" *New York Times*, 8/1/2015, accessed 7/31/2017, https://www.nytimes.com/2015/08/01/world/asia/us-decides-to-retaliate-against-chinas-hacking.html

Sanger, David E. 2016a. "US Cyberattacks Target ISIS in a New Line of Combat." *New York Times*, 4/24/2016, accessed 5/26/2017, https://www.nytimes.com/2016/04/25/us/politics/us-directs-cyberweapons-at-isis-for-first-time.html

Sanger, David E. 2016b. "'Shadow Brokers' Leak Raises Alarming Question: Was the NSA Hacked?" *New York Times*, 8/16/2016, accessed 7/8/2017, https://www.nytimes.com/2016/08/17/us/shadow-brokers-leak-raises-alarming-question-was-the-nsa-hacked.html?_r=1

Sanger, David E., and Nick Corasaniti. 2016. "DNC Says Russian Hackers Penetrated Its Files, Including Dossier on Donald Trump." *New York Times*, 6/14/2016, accessed 9/29/2017, https://www.nytimes.com/2016/06/15/us/politics/russian-hackers-dnc-trump.html?mcubz=3&_r=0

Sanger, David, and Steven Erlanger. 2014. "Suspicion Falls on Russia as Snake Cyberattacks Target Ukraine's Government." *New York Times*, 3/9/2014, accessed 5/2/2017, https://www.

nytimes.com/2014/03/09/world/europe/suspicion-falls-on-russia-as-snake-cyberattacks-target-ukraines-government.html?_r=0

Sanger, David E., and Nicole Perlroth. 2014. "NSA Breached Chinese Servers Seen as Security Threat." *New York Times*, 3/22/2014, accessed 7/3/2017, https://www.nytimes.com/2014/03/23/world/asia/nsa-breached-chinese-servers-seen-as-spy-peril.html?_r=0

Sanger, David E., and Charlie Savage. 2016. "US Says Russia Directed Hacks to Influence Elections." *New York Times*, 10/7/2016, accessed 9/27/2017, https://www.nytimes.com/2016/10/08/us/politics/us-formally-accuses-russia-of-stealing-dnc-emails.html?mcubz=3

Sanger, David E., and William J. Broad. 2017. "Trump Inherits a Secret Cyberwar against North Korean Missiles." *New York Times*, 3/4/2017, accessed 5/6/2017, https://www.nytimes.com/2017/03/04/world/asia/north-korea-missile-program-sabotage.html?rref=collection%2Fbyline%2Fdavid-e.-sanger&mtrref=www.nytimes.com

Sarkees, M. R. 2010. *The COW Typology of War: Defining and Categorizing Wars* (version 4 of the data). Note with version 4 of the Correlates of War Data.

Schelling, Thomas. 1960. *Strategy of Conflict* (Cambridge: Harvard University Press).

Schelling, Thomas. 1962. "The Role of Deterrence in Total Disarmament." *Foreign Affairs*, 40 (3): 392–406.

Schelling, Thomas. 1966. *Arms and Influence* (New Haven: Yale University Press).

Schmitt, Michael N. (ed.). 2017. *Tallinn Manual 2.0 on the International Law Applicable to Cyber Operations* (Cambridge: Cambridge University Press).

Schmitt, Michael N., and Jeffrey Biller. 2017. "The NotPetya Cyber Operation as a Case Study of International Law." *European Journal of International Law Talk*, 7/11/2017, accessed 7/20/2017, https://www.ejiltalk.org/the-notpetya-cyber-operation-as-a-case-study-of-international-law/

Schneier, Bruce. 2013. "Attacking Tor: How the NSA Targets Users' Online Anonymity." *The Guardian*, 10/4/2013, accessed 7/21/2017, http://www.theguardian.com/world/2013/oct/04/tor-attacks-nsa-users-online-anonymity

Schneier, Bruce. 2015. "The Equation Group's Sophisticated Hacking and Exploitation Tools." *Lawfare Blog*, 2/17/2015, accessed 7/26/2017, https://www.lawfareblog.com/equation-groups-sophisticated-hacking-and-exploitation-tools

Schrodt, Philip. 2012. "CAMEO: Conflict Mediation Event Observations Event and Actor Codebook." http://data.gdeltproject.org/documentation/CAMEO.Manual.1.1b3.pdf

Schultz, Kenneth A. 1998. "Domestic Opposition and Signaling in International Crises." *American Political Science Review*, 92 (4): 829–844.

Schultz Kenneth A. 2001. *Democracy and Coercive Diplomacy* (New York: Cambridge University Press).

Schultz, Kenneth A. 2012. "Why We Needed Audience Costs and What We Need Now." *Security Studies*, 21 (3): 369–375.

Schwartau, W. 1996. (ed). *Information Warfare. Cyberterrorism: Protecting Your Personnel Security in the Electronic Age* (New York: Thunder's Mouth Press).

Scott, James, and Drew Spaniel. 2016. *Know Your Enemies 2.0* (Washington: Institute for Critical Infrastructure Technology).

Sechser, Todd S. 2007. *Winning without a Fight: Power, Reputation, and Compellent Threats in International Crises* (Stanford: Stanford University Press).

Secsher, Todd S. 2010. "Goliath's Curse: Coercive Threats and Asymmetric Power" *International Organization*, 64 (4): 627–660.

Secsher, Todd. 2011. "Militarized Compellent Threats, 1918–2001" *Conflict Management and Peace Science*, 28 (4): 377–401.

Secsher, Todd S., and Matthew Fuhrmann. 2017. *Nuclear Weapons and Coercive Diplomacy* (New York, NY: Cambridge University Press).

Segal, Adam. 2015. "OceanLotus: China Hits Back with Its Own Cybersecurity Report." *Council of Foreign Relations*, 6/3/2015, accessed 7/5/2017, http://blogs.cfr.org/cyber/2015/06/03/oceanlotus-china-fights-back-with-its-own-cybersecurity-report/

Shane, Scott, David E. Sanger, and Andrew E. Kramer. "Russians Charged with Treason Worked in Office Linked to Election Hacking." *New York Times*, 1/27/2017, accessed 3/4/2017, https://www.nytimes.com/2017/01/27/world/europe/russia-hacking-us-election.html?rref=collection%2Fbyline%2Fdavid-e.-sanger

Shane, Scott, Matthew Rosenberg, and Andrew W. Lehren. 2017. "WikiLeaks Releases Trove of Alleged CIA Hacking Document." *New York Times*, 3/7/2017, accessed 5/25/2017, https://www.nytimes.com/2017/03/07/world/europe/wikileaks-cia-hacking.html

Sharp, Travis. 2017. "Theorizing Cyber Coercion: The 2014 North Korea Operation against Sony." *Journal of Strategic Studies*, April 12: 1–29.

Sheldon, Robert, and Joe McReynolds. 2015. "Civil-Military Integration and Cybersecurity: A Study of Chinese Information Warfare Militias." In Jon R. Lindsay, Tai Ming Cheung, and Derek S. Reveron (eds.), *China and Cybersecurity: Espionage, Strategy, and Politics in the Digital Domain* (New York: Oxford University Press): 188–224.

Shevchenko, Vitaly. 2014. "Ukraine Conflict: Hackers Take Sides in Virtual War." *BBC*, 12/20/2014, accessed 5/2/2017, http://www.bbc.com/news/world-europe-30453069

Shinal, John. 2017. "Russians Targeted Black Lives Matter and Other Hot-Button Issues in Facebook Ads." *CNBC*, 9/25/2017, accessed 10/1/2017, https://www.cnbc.com/2017/09/25/russian-facebook-ads-targeted-black-lives-matter-muslims-election.html

Shinkman, Paul D. 2016. "America Is Losing the Cyber War." *US News and World Report*, 9/29/2016, accessed 7/5/2017, https://www.usnews.com/news/articles/2016-09-29/cyber-wars-how-the-us-stacks-up-against-its-digital-adversaries.

Shultz, R., and R. Godson. 1984. *Dezinformatsiya: Active Measures in Soviet Strategy* (McLean, VA, Pergamon-Brassey's International Defense Publishers).

Silove, Nina. 2016. "The Pivot before the Pivot: U.S. Strategy to Preserve the Power Balance in Asia" *International Security*, 40 (4): 45–88.

Singer, J. David, Stuart Bremer, and John Stuckey. 1972. "Capability Distribution, Uncertainty, and Major Power War, 1820–1965." In Bruce Russett (ed.), *Peace, War, and Numbers* (Beverly Hills: Sage): 19–48.

Singer, J. D., and M. Small. 1994. *Correlates of War Project: International and Civil War Data, 1816–1992* (ICPSR 9905). Ann Arbor, MI: Inter-University Consortium for Political and Social Research.

Singer, Peter W., and August Cole. 2015. *Ghost Fleet* (New York: Houghton Mifflin Harcourt).

Slayton, Rebecca. 2017. "What Is the Cyber Offense-Defense Balance? Conceptions, Causes, and Assessment." *International Security*, 41 (3): 72–109.

Smith, Jack, IV. "Pro-Russian Hackers Expose U.S. Military Contractor Activity in Ukraine." *The Observer*, 3/2/2015, accessed 5/2/2017, http://observer.com/2015/03/pro-russian-hackers-expose-u-s-military-contractor-activity-in-ukraine/

Smoke, Richard. 1977. *Controlling Escalation* (Cambridge, MA: Harvard University Press).

Snegovaya, Maria. 2015. *Putin's Information in Ukraine: Soviet Origins of Russia's Hybrid Warfare* (Washington: Institute for the Study of War).

Snyder, Glenn H. 1984. "The Security Dilemma in Alliance Politics." *World Politics*, 36 (4): 461–495.

Snyder, Glenn H., and Paul Diesing. 1977. *Conflict among Nations* (Princeton: Princeton University Press).

Snyder, Jack. 1991. *Myths of Empire: Domestic Politics and International Ambition* (Ithaca: Cornell University Press).

Snyder, Jack. 2000. *From Voting to Violence: Democratization and Nationalist Conflict* (New York: W.W. Norton).

Snyder, Jack, and Erica Borghard. 2011. "The Cost of Empty Threats: A Penny, Not a Pound." *American Political Science Review*, 105 (3): 437–456.

Sputnik News. 2015. "CyberBerkut Group Claims Kiev in Talks on Supplying Missiles to Qatar." *Sputnik News*, 11/21/2015, accessed 5/5/2017, https://sputniknews.com/military/201511211030519375-cyberberkut-missiles-qatar/.

Stahl, Leslie. 2016. "The Great Brain Robbery." *CBS News*, 1/17/2016, accessed 7/5/2017, http://www.cbsnews.com/news/60-minutes-great-brain-robbery-china-cyber-espionage/.

Stevens, Tim. 2015. *Cyber Security and the Politics of Time* (Cambridge, UK: Cambridge University Press).

Stockholm International Peace Research Institute (SIPRI). 2017. *Military Expenditure Database.* Accessed 7/23/2017, https://www.sipri.org/databases/milex

Stokes, Mark A. 2015. "The Chinese People's Liberation Army Computer Network Operations Infrastructure." In Jon R. Lindsay, Tai Ming Cheung, and Derek S. Reveron (eds.), *China and Cybersecurity: Espionage, Strategy, and Politics in the Digital Domain* (New York, NY: Oxford University Press): 163–187.

Stone, Jeff. 2015. "Russian Cyber Berkut Hackers Linked ISIS to Ukrainian Weapons Negotiations with Qatar: Russian Media." *International Business Times*, 11/21/2015, accessed 5/2/2017, http://www.ibtimes.com/russian-cyberberkut-hackers-link-isis-ukrainian-weapons-negotiations-qatar-russian-2195165

Stone, Jeff. 2016. "Meet Fancy Bear and Cozy Bear, Russian Groups Blamed for DNC Hack." *Christian Science Monitor*, 6/15/2016, accessed 4/30/2017, http://www.csmonitor.com/World/Passcode/2016/0615/Meet-Fancy-Bear-and-Cozy-Bear-Russian-groups-blamed-for-DNC-hack

Sullivan, Sean. 2017. "At Senate Hearing, Most Republicans Avoid Crossing Trump on Russian Election Meddling." *Washington Post*, 1/5/2017, accessed 7/4/2017, http://www.washingtonpost.com/news/powerpost/wp/2017/01/05/at-senate-hearing-most-republicans-avoid-crossing-trump-on-russian-meddling-in-election/?utm_term=.417958193bc7

Swaine, Michael D. 2013. "Chinese Views on Cybersecurity in Foreign Relations." *China Leadership Monitor*, 10/13/2013, accessed 4/4/2017, http://carnegieendowment.org/email/South_Asia/img/CLM42MSnew.pdf

Swift, Art. 2016. "Americans' Trust in Mass Media Sinks to New Low." *Gallup News*, 9/14/2016, accessed 10/1/2017, http://news.gallup.com/poll/195542/americans-trust-mass-media-sinks-new-low.aspx

Symantec Corporation. 2014. "Dragonfly: Cyberespionage Attacks against Energy Suppliers." *Symantec Security Response*, 7/7/2014, accessed 5/2/2017, https://www.symantec.com/

content/en/us/enterprise/media/security_response/whitepapers/Dragonfly_Threat_Against_Western_Energy_Suppliers.pdf: 5.

Symantec Security Response. 2015. "Reign: Top-Tier Espionage Tool Enables Stealthy Surveillance." *Symantec*, 8/27//2015, accessed 7/8/2017, http://www.symantec.com/content/en/us/enterprise/media/security_response/whitepapers/regin-analysis.pdf

Syring, J. D. 2016. "Unclassified Statement before the Senate Armed Services Committee, Subcommittee on Strategic Forces." 4/13/2016, https://www.armed-services.senate.gov/imo/media/doc/Syring_04-13-16.pdf.

Tai, Zixue. 2016. "Networked Resistance: Digital Populism, Online Activism, and Mass Dissent in China." *Popular Communication*, 13 (2): 120–131.

Tanner, Murray Scott. 2007. *Chinese Economic Coercion against Taiwan: A Tricky Weapon to Use* (Santa Monica: RAND Corporation).

Taubman, Philip. 1982. "U.S. Reportedly Sending Million to Foster Moderates in Nicaragua." *New York Times*, 3/11/1982, accessed 7/24/2017, http://www.nytimes.com/1982/03/11/world/us-reportedly-sending-millions-to-foster-moderates-in-nicaragua.html

Teresi, Holly, and Melissa R. Michelson. 2015. "Wired to Mobilize: The Effect of Social Networking Messages on Voter Turnout." *Social Science Journal* 52 (2): 195–204.

Thayer, Bradley. 2000. "The Political Effects of Information Warfare: Why New Military Capabilities Cause Old Political Dangers." *Security Studies*, 10 (1): 43–85.

Thiem, Alrik. 2011. "Conditions of Intergovernmental Armaments Cooperation in Western Europe, 1996–2006." *European Political Science Review*, 3 (1): 1–33.

Thomas, Timothy. 1998. *Behind the Great Firewall of China: A Look at RMA/IW Theory from 1996–1998* (Leavenworth: Foreign Military Studies Office).

Thomas, Timothy. 1999. "Human Attack Networks." *Military Review*, September–October, accessed 1/30/2017, http://fmso.leavenworth.army.mil/documents/humannet/humannet.htm

Thomas, Timothy L. 2004. "Russia's Reflexive Control Theory and the Military." *Journal of Slavic Military Studies*, 17 (2): 237–256.

Thomas, Timothy. 2013. *China's Cyber Incursions: A Theoretical Look at When They See and Why They Do It Based on a Different Strategic Method of Thought* (Leavenworth: Foreign Military Studies Office).

Thompson, William R. 1995. "Principal Rivalries." *Journal of Conflict Resolution*, 39 (2): 195–223.

Thompson, William R. 2001. "Identifying Rivals and Rivalries in World Politics." *International Studies Quarterly*, 45 (4): 557–587.

Thompson, William R. 2003. "A Streetcar Named Sarajevo: Catalysts, Multiple Causation Chains, and Rivalry Structures." *International Studies Quarterly*, 47 (3): 453–474.

Threat Intelligence. 2014. "APT28: A Window into Russia's Cyber Espionage Operations." *FireEye*, 10/27/2014, accessed 5/2/2017, https://www.fireeye.com/blog/threat-research/2014/10/apt28-a-window-into-russias-cyber-espionage-operations.html.

Tikk, Eneken, Kadri Kaska, and Liis Vihul. 2010. *International Cyber Incidents: Legal Consideration* (Tallinn: Cooperative Cyber Defence Centre of Excellence), accessed 24 April 2017, https://ccdcoe.org/publications/books/legalconsiderations.pdf.

Timberg, Craig, and Barton Gellman. 2013. "NSA Paying U.S. Companies for Access to Communications Networks." *Washington Post*, 8/29/2013, accessed 5/23/2017, https://www.washingtonpost.com/world/national-security/nsa-paying-us-companies-for-

access-to-communications-networks/2013/08/29/5641a4b6-10c2-11e3-bdf6-e4fc677d94a1_
story.html?utm_term=.7620788f2fod.

Trachtenberg, Marc. 2012. "Audience Costs: An Historical Analysis." *Security Studies*, 21 (1): 3–42.

Trend Micro. 2015. "Hacktivist Group CyberBerkut behind Attacks on German Official Websites." *Trend Micro*, 1/20/2015, accessed 5/2/2017: http://blog.trendmicro.com/trendlabs-security-intelligence/hacktivist-group-cyberberkut-behind-attacks-on-german-official-websites/

Trend Micro. 2016. "Operation Pawn Storm: Fast Facts and the Latest Developments." *Trend Micro*, 1/16/2016, accessed 7/6/2017, https://www.trendmicro.com/vinfo/us/security/news/cyber-attacks/operation-pawn-storm-fast-facts

Tsai, Wen-Hsuan. 2016. "How 'Networked Authoritarianism' Was Operationalized in China: Methods and Procedures of Public Opinion Control." *Journal of Contemporary China*, 25 (101): 731–744.

Tse-tung, Mao. 1967. "On Protracted War." *Selected Works of Mao Tse-tung*, Vol. II, (Beijing: Foreign Languages Press): 113–194.

Tucker, Patrick. 2016. "The Same Culprits That Targeted US Election Boards Might Have Also Targeted Ukraine" *Defense One*, 9/3/2016, accessed 5/1/2017, http://www.defenseone.com/threats/2016/09/same-culprits-targeted-us-election-boards-might-have-also-targeted-ukraine/131277/

US Air Force. 1998. *AFDD 2–5, Information Operations* (Arlington: Secretary of the Air Force).

US Army. 2003. *FM 3–13, Information Operations: Doctrine, Tactics, Techniques, and Procedures* (Arlington: Headquarters, Department of the Army).

Valeriano, Brandon. 2013. *Becoming Rivals: The Process of Interstate Rivalry Development*. (London: Routledge).

Valeriano, Brandon, Sean Lawson, and Heather Roff. 2016. "Dropping the Cyber Bomb? Spectacular Claims and Unremarkable Effects." *Council on Foreign Relations*, 5/24/2016, accessed 7/4/2017, http://blogs.cfr.org/cyber/2016/05/24/dropping-the-cyber-bomb-spectacular-claims-and-unremarkable-effects/

Valeriano, Brandon, and Ryan C. Maness. 2012. "Persistent Enemies and Cyber Security: The Future of Rivalry in an Age of Information Warfare." In Derek Reveron (ed.), *Cyberspace and National Security: Threats, Opportunity and Power in a Virtual World* (Washington D.C.: Georgetown University Press): 139–158.

Valeriano, Brandon, and Ryan C. Maness. 2014. "The Dynamics of Cyber Conflict between Rival Antagonists, 2001–2011." *Journal of Peace Research*, 51 (3): 347–360.

Valeriano, Brandon, and Ryan C. Maness. 2015. *Cyber War versus Cyber Realities: Cyber Conflict in the International System* (New York: Oxford University Press).

Valeriano, Brandon, and Ryan C. Maness. 2016. "International Political Theory and Cyber Security." In Robyn Eckersley and Chris Brown (eds.), *The Oxford Handbook of International Political Theory* (London, UK: Oxford University Press) forthcoming.

Valeriano, Brandon, Ryan C. Maness, and Benjamin Jensen. 2017a. "Five Things We Can Learn from the Russian Hacking Scandal." *Washington Post: The Monkey Cage*, 1/9/2017, accessed 6/6/1017, https://www.washingtonpost.com/news/monkey-cage/wp/2017/01/09/5-things-we-can-learn-from-the-russian-hacking-scandal/?utm_term=.88a86da7b25c.

Valeriano, Brandon, Ryan C. Maness, and Benjamin Jensen. 2017b. "Cyberwarfare Has Taken a New Turn: Yes, It's Time to Worry." *Washington Post: The Monkey Cage*, 7/13/2017, accessed 7/15/2017, https://www.washingtonpost.com/news/monkey-cage/wp/

2017/07/13/cyber-warfare-has-taken-a-new-turn-yes-its-time-to-worry/?utm_term=.
ccbd9e98fd24#comments

Van Evera, Stephen. 1998. "Offense, Defense, and the Causes of War." *International Security*, 22 (4): 5–43.

Van Tol, J., M. Gunzinger, A. Krepinevich, and J. Thomas. (2010). *AirSea Battle: A Point-of-Departure Operational Concept* (Washington DC: Center for Strategic and Budgetary Assessments).

Vasconcelos, H. 2005. "Tacit Collusion, Cost Asymmetries, and Mergers." *RAND Journal of Economics*, 36 (1): 39–62.

Vasquez, John A. 1993. *The War Puzzle* (New York, NY: Cambridge University Press).

Vasquez, John A. 1996. "Distinguishing Rivals That Go to War from Those That Do Not: A Quantitative Comparative Case Study of the Two Paths to War." *International Studies Quarterly*, 40 (4): 531–558.

Vasquez, John A., and Brandon Valeriano. 2010. "Classification of Interstate Wars." *Journal of Politics*, 72 (2): 292–309.

VK. "Cyber Berkut Cracked Kiev Billboards." *vk.com*, 10/24/2014, accessed 5/3/2017, https://vk.com/wall-67432779_14678

Vorobyov, I., and V. Kiseljov. 2013. "Russian Military Theory: Past and Present." *Military Thought*, (3). https://scholar.google.com/scholar?hl=en&as_sdt=0%2C5&q=Vorobyov%2C+I.%2C+and+V.+Kiseljov.+2013.+%E2%80%9CRussian+Military+Theory%3A+Past+and+Presen t.%E2%80%9D+&btnG=.

Waddell, Kaveh. 2016. "Why Didn't Obama Reveal Intel about Russia's Influence on the Election?" *The Atlantic*, 12/11/2016, accessed 3/1/2017, https://www.theatlantic.com/tech-nology/archive/2016/12/why-didnt-obama-reveal-intel-about-russias-influence-on-the-election/510242/

Wagner, Harrison. 2007. *War and the State: The Theory of International Politics* (Ann Arbor: University of Michigan Press).

Wagstyl, Stephan. 2015. "Ukraine Separatists Claim Cyber-Attack on German Government Sites." *Financial Times*, 1/7/2015, accessed 5/2/2017, https://www.ft.com/content/08270324-9678-11e4-a40b-00144feabdc0+&cd=1&hl=en&ct=clnk&gl=us

Waltz, Kenneth N. 2000. "Structural Realism after the Cold War." *International Security*, 25 (1): 5–41.

Ward, M. D., N. W. Metternich, C. Carrington, C. Dorff, M. Gallop, F. M. Hollenbach, A. Schultz, and S. Weschle. 2012. "Geographical Models of Crises: Evidence from ICEWS." *Advances in Design for Cross-Cultural Activities*, 429.

Warden, John A., III. 1992. "Employing Air Power in the Twenty-first Century." In Richard Schultz and Robert Pfaltzgraff Jr. (eds.), *The Future of Air Power in the Aftermath of the Gulf War* (Maxwell Air Force Base: Air University Press).

Warren, Peter. 2007. "Hunt for Russia's Web Criminals." *The Guardian*, 11/15/2007, accessed 3/26/2017, https://www.theguardian.com/technology/2007/nov/15/news.crime

Waterman, Shaun. 2016. "Russia Seeks to Discredit, Not Hack Election Results." *Cyberscoop*, 11/7/2016, accessed 5/2/2017, https://www.cyberscoop.com/russia-hacking-2016-election-flashpoint/

Waterman, Shaun. 2017. "Government Not 'Sitting on Hundreds of Zero Days,' Former NSA Official Says." *fedscoop*, 5/22/2017, accessed 5/26/2017, https://www.fedscoop.

com/government-not-sitting-hundreds-zero-days-former-nsa-official-says/?utm_content=buffer9566c&utm_medium=social&utm_source=twitter.com&utm_campaign=buffer

Watkins, Ali. 2017. "Obama Team Was Warned in 2014 about Russian Interference." *POLITICO*, 8/14/2017, accessed 9/2/2017, http://www.politico.com/story/2017/08/14/obama-russia-election-interference-241547

Watson, Adam. 1992. *The Evolution of International Society* (New York: Routledge).

Watts, Barry D. 2007. *Six Decades of Guided Munitions and Battle Networks: Progress and Prospects* (Washington, DC: Center for Strategic and Budgetary Assessments).

Weaver, Nicholas. 2013. "Our Government Has Weaponized the Internet. Here's How They Did It." *Wired*, 11/13/2013, accessed 7/23/2017, https://www.wired.com/2013/11/this-is-how-the-internet-backbone-has-been-turned-into-a-weapon/

Weedon, Jen. 2015. "Beyond Cyber War: Russia's Use of Strategic Cyber Espionage and Information Operations in Ukraine." In Kenneth Geers (ed.), *Cyber War in Perspective: Russian Aggression against Ukraine* (Tallinn: NATO Cooperative Cyber Defence Center of Excellence): 66–78.

Weeks, Jessica L. 2008. "Autocratic Audience Costs: Regime Type and Signaling Resolve." *International Organization*, 62 (1): 35–64.

Weiner, Sharon. 2011. *Our Own Worst Enemy? Institutional Interests and the Proliferation of Nuclear Weapons Expertise* (Cambridge: MIT Press).

Weiss, Gus W. 1996. "The Farewell Dossier: Duping the Soviets." *Studies in Intelligence*, 39 (5): 121–126.

Weland, James. 1994. "Misguided Intelligence: Japanese Military Intelligence Officers in the Manchurian Incident, September 1931." *Journal of Military History*, 58 (3): 445–460.

Whyte, Christopher. 2016. "Ending cyber Coercion: Computer Network Attack, Exploitation and the Case of North Korea." *Comparative Strategy*, 35(2): 93–102.

Winkler, Jonathan Reed. 2009. "Information Warfare in World War I." *Journal of Military History*, 73 (3): 845–867.

Wolford, Scott. 2014. "Showing Restraint, Signaling Resolve: Coalitions, Cooperation, and Crisis Bargaining." *American Journal of Political Science*, 58 (1): 144–156.

World Bank. 2017. "Work Bank Databank." Accessed 7/23/2017, http://data.worldbank.org/

Wright, Austin. 2015. "Price Tag for Syrian Rebels: $4 million Each." *Politico*, 7/8/2015, accessed 4/23/2017, http://www.politico.com/story/2015/07/price-for-syrian-rebels-4-million-each-119858

Wright, Quincy. 1942. *A Study of War.* (Chicago: University of Chicago Press).

Yglesias, Matthew. 2017. "What Really Happened in 2016, in 7 Charts." *Vox*, 9/18/2017, accessed 10/1/2017, https://www.vox.com/policy-and-politics/2017/9/18/16305486/what-really-happened-in-2016

Yuen, Derrick. 2014. *Deciphering Sun Tzu: How to Read the Art of War* (New York: Oxford University Press).

Zetter, Kim. 2012. "Meet 'Flame,' The Massive Spy Malware Infiltrating Iranian Computers." *Wired*, 5/28/2012, accessed 7/9/2017, https://www.wired.com/2012/05/flame/

Zetter, Kim. 2012. "Russian Sandworm Hack Has Been Spying on Foreign Governments for Years." *Wired*, 10/14/2012, accessed 4/29/2017, https://www.wired.com/2014/10/russian-sandworm-hack-isight/

Zetter, Kim. 2013. "UK Spy Agency Secretly Taps Over 200 Fiber-Optic Cables, Shares Data with the NSA." *Wired*, 6/21/2013, accessed 7/8/2017, https://www.wired.com/2013/06/gchq-tapped-200-cables/

Zetter, Kim. 2014. *Countdown to Zero Day: Stuxnet and the Launch of the World's First Digital Weapon* (New York: Crown).

Zetter, Kim. 2015a. "Suite of Sophisticated Nation-State Attack Tools Found with Connection to Stuxnet." *Wired*, 2/16/2015, accessed 7/10/2017, https://www.wired.com/2015/02/kapersky-discovers-equation-group/

Zetter, Kim. 2015b. "How the NSA's Firmware Hacking Works and Why It's So Unsettling." *Wired*, 2/22/2015, https://www.wired.com/2015/02/nsa-firmware-hacking/

Zetter, Kim. 2016. "Inside the Cunning, Unprecedented Hack of Ukraine's Power Grid." *Wired*, 3/3/2016, accessed 7/7/2017, https://www.wired.com/2016/03/inside-cunning-unprecedented-hack-ukraines-power-grid/

Index

Figures, notes, and tables are indicated by *f*, n, and *t* following page numbers.